T0237658

The Authoritative Guide on Harbor

The Authoritative Guide on Harbor

Haining Zhang • Yan Wang

The Authoritative Guide on Harbor

Management and Practice of Cloud Native Artifacts Such as Container Images and Helm Charts

Haining Zhang
Cloud Native Lab, OCTO
VMware China R&D
Beijing, China

Yan Wang
Modern Application Platform
VMware China R&D
Beijing, China

ISBN 978-981-19-2726-3 ISBN 978-981-19-2727-0 (eBook)
https://doi.org/10.1007/978-981-19-2727-0

Jointly published with Publishing House of Electronics Industry
The print edition is not for sale in China (Mainland). Customers from China (Mainland) please order the print book from: Publishing House of Electronics Industry

This Springer imprint is published by the registered company Springer Nature Singapore Pte Ltd.
The registered company address is: 152 Beach Road, #21-01/04 Gateway East, Singapore 189721, Singapore

"Harbor is the first CNCF project founded in China and also the first project in China to reach graduated status in CNCF. We're thrilled to see its community thriving globally and key enterprises leveraging it successfully. Authored by its maintainers, The Authoritative Guide on Harbor *is the first book about Harbor. It provides key insights into the architecture, mechanics, configuration, and case studies based on the latest Harbor v2.0. This book is geared towards cloud native architects, DevOps engineers, developers, and end users of Harbor. I hope you will enjoy reading it."*

—*Priyanka Sharma,* CNCF's General Manager

"It's been amazing to watch the progress of Harbor since its inception in 2014. It's been equally inspiring to see the energy and passion of the team behind Harbor. What started as a small side project in VMware's China R&D office is now a graduated CNCF project, with tens of thousands of businesses leveraging Harbor's powerful role-based access control, image replication, vulnerability scanning, and notary. And so this book, The Authoritative Guide on Harbor, *is timely. It's the first book about Harbor, authored by the maintainers and contributors. You get insights into the architecture, configuration, and customization of Harbor. Hats off to the entire Harbor team for writing this book!"*

—*Kit Colbert,* CTO of VMware

For my parents, my brother John who brought me into the world of computer science. And for my wife Judy who always cares for me and backs me up.—Haining Henry Zhang

For my Dad, I love you and miss you very much. And for Sally, for your love, company and support.—Yan Wang

For my son, who brings me a lot of joy during the book writing.—Wenkai Yin

For Katherine, my love, always gives me great support! For Eddie, my cute boy, who brings me happiness and makes me relax in my busy schedule.—Steven Zou

Abstract: *In the cloud native ecosystem, the management and distribution of container images and other cloud native artifacts is a crucial part. This is the first book which provides a comprehensive explanation of Harbor, an open-source trusted cloud native registry. It is authored by the maintainers and contributors of Harbor. The content covers Harbor's architecture, principles, functions, deployment and configuration, operation and maintenance, customized development, and API.*

The intended audience of the book include developers and contributors of Harbor, cloud native software development engineers, test engineers, operational staffs, IT architects and IT technical managers, and college students in computer science or related disciplines. This book is an ideal reference for Harbor users and developers.

Foreword

The proliferation of open-source technologies has progressed significantly following the widespread adoption of LAMP (Linux, Apache, MySQL, and PHP). In nowadays cloud computing era, developers are increasingly utilizing open-source cloud native management tools and platforms like Docker and Kubernetes. As a result, China has emerged as a critical contributor to the Cloud Native Computing Foundation (CNCF).

Against this backdrop, cloud native technology became the most actively engaged and contributed technology in the Chinese open-source community. VMware has been involved since its outset, and open sourced internal projects like Cloud Foundry to the cloud native community in 2011. VMware also pioneered the cloud native community in China and has been actively supporting community activities. In 2016, for example, VMware launched the Cloud Native Forum, and in 2018, it promoted the international cloud native conference KubeCon + CloudNativeCon in China.

Harbor is an open-source enterprise-grade registry server, that stores, signs, and scans the cloud native artifacts, and its wide adoption demonstrates VMware's influence in the cloud native open-source field. Harbor was originally an internal project of the Cloud Native Lab at VMware China R&D Center, initiated by Henry Zhang, one of the authors of this book, myself, and others in 2014, and was first promoted to the Chinese open-source community since early 2016. After being open sourced, Harbor swiftly proved the pervasiveness of cloud native infrastructure software and garnered usage by domestic users including major Internet companies, large enterprises, and startups.

Harbor's impact has steadily spread from China to the rest of the world, gaining unanimous recognition from global cloud native community. Harbor became the first CNCF project originated from China and was the first donation to CNCF by VMware in July 2018. It has received over 15,000 stars on GitHub and attracted more than 200 code contributors from 80+ businesses globally, including Anchore, NetEase Cloud, Caicloud Technology, Tencent Cloud, and OVHcloud, and has over 30,000 monthly downloads as of September 2021.

At the same time, Project Harbor established several community-led working groups, such as the Remote Replication Working Group, P2P Distribution Working Group, and Image Scanning Working Group. They formulate and develop roadmap for each specific feature of Harbor. The community's participation has greatly enriched and improved the functionality of Harbor.

Based on the success of Project Harbor, VMware China joined hands with innovation departments of leading companies in various industries, startups, universities, and research institutions to launch the VMware Innovation Network (VIN), to build an open, diverse, and symbiotic ecosystem covering cloud native, edge computing, machine learning, cloud networking, cloud data analytics, and other technology areas.

In June 2020, Harbor became the first graduated CNCF project originated from China and the 11th worldwide; other graduated projects include Kubernetes, Prometheus, and Helm. This book is one of the most authoritative publications on cloud native technology in China, and its release arrived at just the right time. Authors are the original developers and hardcore community maintainers of Project Harbor, including Henry Zhang, Steven Zou, Steven Ren, Daniel Jiang, Wenkai Yin, Yan Wang, Mingming Pei, etc. Readers will get a comprehensive understanding of cloud native technologies, particularly the principles, features, and practical approaches of managing cloud native artifacts like container images.

"If you want to go fast, go alone. If you want to go far, go together." I believe this book will bring readers new beginnings and gains, and I hope more users and developers will join the cloud native community and innovate together!

Alan Ren
General Manager, VMware China R&D Center, Beijing, China
Co-founder of Project Harbor, Beijing, China

Preface

Why We Wrote This Book

After its release in 2013, Docker achieved the unprecedented success and became one of the most popular development tools in history. In addition to Docker's simplicity and ease of use, the container image technology is its core, including the innovative image format and the registry service for image distribution. Docker's famous slogan "Build, Ship and Run" summarizes the essence of the application development. The slogan implies that the application life cycle management is image centric. It can be seen that image is a key technology for containerized applications, and a series of management tasks surrounding images become one of the top priorities in the actual operation and maintenance.

When we first came into contact with Docker, we were shocked by its smooth user experience and the excellent container solutions. We deeply felt that this would be a game changer in application development. After doing some research, we found that container images are the lifeblood of Docker. However, there were not many good image management tools at that time. At technical conferences, many users complained about the difficulties in container image management.

Therefore, to tackle the pain points of image management, we led a team in VMware R&D China to develop a container image management software. We were dogfooding the software inside the company and achieved some good results. This software became the prototype of Harbor.

Harbor was open sourced in 2016 and its popularity far exceeded our expectations. Harbor met the key points of container management and won the favor of a large number of users in China. The number of developers contributing to the Harbor open-source project was increasing day by day.

In 2018, VMware donated Harbor to the Cloud Native Computing Foundation (CNCF). Harbor and the global cloud native community have cooperated more closely ever since. In 2020, CNCF announced Harbor was a graduation project, which was also the first graduated CNCF project originated in China.

Currently, thousands of users have deployed Harbor in production for the management of container images and Helm Charts. The maintainers of Harbor have received a considerable number of problems encountered by users. The main reasons for these problems are twofold. First, users do not have a thorough understanding of the installation and configuration of Harbor. Second, the documentation is incomplete or missing. Users urgently need a reference book as a guide to use Harbor. At this time, Guoxia Zhang, the editor of the Publishing House of Electronics Industry, invited us to write a technical book on Harbor. We accepted the invitation and authored this book to fully introduce all aspects of the Harbor and bring greater value to users.

This book was originally published in Chinese in 2020. It has been revised based on readers' feedback and translated into English for global audience.

Highlights of This Book

This book comprehensively introduces Harbor, an open-source trusted cloud native registry project hosted by CNCF. It covers the content of Harbor architecture, principles, configuration, customized development, and governance. It is authored by the maintainers and contributors of the Harbor open-source project, including the developers who built the Harbor prototype.

Some content of this book is published for the first time, including Harbor's architecture, the support of OCI artifacts, the design considerations of a highly available registry, the image scanning policy, and the access control of artifacts. This book is an ideal reference for Harbor users and developers.

Intended Audience

- Software development engineers, test engineers, and operational staff in the cloud native space
- Users, developers, and contributors of the Harbor open-source project
- IT architects and IT technical managers
- University students in computer science of related disciplines

How This Book Is Organized

There are 9 chapters in this book. They are organized as follows.

Chapter 1 introduces the background of cloud native applications, the principles and specifications of artifact management, the role of artifact registry, and the overall architecture of Harbor.

Chapter 2 details the installation and deployment of Harbor, including the key points of high-availability deployment, and also includes the basic operations of Harbor.

Chapter 3 explains the principles of Harbor's access control, as well as related configuration methods.

Chapter 4 analyzes the security policies that can be used in Harbor, including trusted content distribution and vulnerability scanning mechanisms.

Chapter 5 explains the principle of artifact remote replication for images and Helm Charts, as well as the integration with other registry services.

Chapter 6 details Harbor's advanced management functions, including resource quotas, garbage collection, immutable artifacts, retention policies, and Webhooks.

Chapter 7 explains the life cycle management of Harbor, including steps for backup, recovery, and upgrade.

Chapter 8 sorts out the use of Harbor's API and gives a programming example.

Chapter 9 introduces the governance principles, security release process, and participation methods of the Harbor open-source community.

We recommend that readers use this book like this:

- Readers who are not familiar with the cloud native field, especially container technology, can read the basic knowledge in Chap. 1 first.
- Readers who are new to Harbor can directly start with Chap. 2 to quickly understand the deployment of Harbor and the basic operations.
- Readers who have some experience with Harbor can read through the content of Chaps. 3–8 as needed.
- Developers who are customizing the Harbor open-source project can focus on reading Chap. 9.

Beijing, China

Haining Zhang
Yan Wang

About The Authors and Translators[1]

Henry Zhang is the Technical Director at VMware China R&D. He leads innovation projects in the areas of cloud native, AI/ML and edge. He is a long-time open-source community evangelist and contributor. Henry is the founder and maintainer of CNCF's Harbor open-source project and a maintainer of open-source project FATE/KubeFATE, a federated learning framework hosted by Linux Foundation. Henry is the editor-in-chief of the "Harbor Authoritative Guide" and one of the key authors of the "Blockchain Technical Guide."

Yan Wang is a Staff Engineer working at VMWare as one of the core maintainers of CNCF project Harbor and the maintainer of CNCF project Distribution. Yan focuses on technical research and innovation in the cloud native field.

Wenkai Yin works at VMware as a Senior Software Engineer, focusing on cloud native and container projects. He has been a contributor of Harbor since its inception. Wenkai is the maintainer of Harbor and a contributor of the open-source project Velero.

Steven Zou is a Staff Engineer of VMware China R&D center. He is leading several innovative projects to help users run businesses with cloud native technologies on multiple clouds. Meanwhile, he is maintainer and architect of the CNCF graduated OSS project Harbor and assists the user community to run Harbor well. Steven holds PMP certifications and files many worldwide patents. He is also an active speaker and sharing sessions in many global technical conferences like KubeCon and VMworld. At present, Steven is living in Beijing China together with his wife Katherine and 7-year-old son Eddie.

Besides the above people, other authors with contribution to the content of this book include:
Qian Deng, Member of Technical Staff, VMware

[1] This book is written by the maintainers and contributors of the Harbor.

Weiwei He, Sr. Member of Technical Staff, VMware
Mingming Pei, Cloud Native Architect, NetEase
Steven Ren, Engineering Director, VMware
Daniel Jiang, Staff Engineer, VMware
Ziming Zhang, Sr. Member of Technical Staff, VMware
Fanjian Kong, Senior Engineer, Tencent
People who contributed to the translation and the review:
Zhenkai Tu, Support Escalation Engineer, Microsoft
Jiaolin Yang, Engineering Manager, VMware

Acknowledgments

This book is truly the collective effort of the community. All the authors, translators, and reviewers generously gave of their time, expertise, and energy by contributing content to the book. Thanks to their effort and dedication, this book covers a broad range of topics and addresses many common problems from the users.

We are thankful to Guoxia Zhang, the editor of the Publishing House of Electronics Industry, who inspired us to write this book and helped us publish the book in English. Our gratefulness also goes to Alan Ren, the general manager of VMware China R&D and the co-initiator of Project Harbor. He has been supporting and promoting the development of Harbor since its inception. We offer our deepest thanks to Kit Colbert, CTO of VMware, who brought Harbor into VMware's cloud native products and made Harbor a world-renowned open-source project.

We want to express our appreciations to Alex Xu, Cameron Wang, Cynthia Song, and Spenser Wang for their long-time evangelization of the Harbor community, as well as their assistance in publishing this book. We thank our partners for adopting Harbor in production and for providing valuable feedback: E Chen, Xin Liu, Yang Qiu, Xin Zhang, Li Fang, Vivian Zhang, and Hua Zhang.

Contents

Chapter 1
Artifact Management in the Cloud Native Environment

The development history of computer technology can be attributed to the history of the continuous pursuit and improvement of computing efficiency by human. Efficiency is reflected in two aspects: a shorter time to complete computing and fewer resources to complete computing. Since the birth of general-purpose computers, the architecture of computers includes two parts: hardware and software. A computing task is executed by unchangeable general-purpose hardware and changeable software. Hardware and software are two main lines of development that complement and promote each other.

Since the beginning of the 21st century, the popularity of the Internet, especially the birth of the mobile Internet, has brought explosive growth of users and the demand for around-the-clock access service. Applications often need to respond to service requests growing at a high speed and require the capability of processing massive data. It is difficult for the traditional hardware and software architecture to adapt to the user needs that change dynamically. In this background, the cloud computing service emerges. Cloud computing allows users to access the shared computing resource pool (computing, networks, storage and applications) on demand over the network. For users, resources can be provisioned and released quickly without much management cost. Cloud computing service providers provide centralized management, operation and maintenance for the computing resource pool to provide users with a delivery method to balance cost and efficiency.

After more than 10 years of development, cloud computing has become a ubiquitous public service facility like tap water and power. Modern application software architecture is also transforming towards the client/cloud (C/C) mode. The characteristics of cloud services, such as elasticity, fault tolerance and ease of management, reduce the iterative cycle of development, testing, deployment, operation and maintenance to respond to the changing user needs. The architecture of modern applications must be transformed towards cloud, that is, the architecture must be designed with the thinking and concepts of the cloud era, to give full play to the potential of cloud as much as possible. This leads to the cloud native architecture.

H. Zhang, Y. Wang, *The Authoritative Guide on Harbor*,
https://doi.org/10.1007/978-981-19-2727-0_1

The term cloud native does not refer to a specific technology but instead is a collection of ideas and technologies, including virtualization, container, microservice, continuous integration and delivery (CI/CD) and DevOps. Among these technologies, the container technology has become the most important fundamental technology in the cloud native field. It has derived a huge ecosystem. Most of other related technologies center around container. For example, Kubernetes is responsible for the container orchestration platform, microservices are implemented relying on containers and DevOps uses containers throughout the process.

The essence of a container is to encapsulate the operating environment of applications, including the executable code, configuration files and dependent software packages. The static files generated after an application is encapsulated is called an image. A large number of container-related operations are based on container images. Therefore, the management of container images becomes one of the important aspects in cloud native applications.

This chapter first describes the principles of cloud native technologies and the container technology. It then introduces the specifications of cloud native artifacts such as container image and explains the key role of container registry in container management. Finally, it briefly introduces the functions and architecture of Harbor.

1.1 Overview of Cloud Native Application

The concept of "cloud native" was first proposed by Matt Stine from Pivotal, a company. He first proposed the concept of cloud native in 2013. In the book *Migrating to Cloud-Native Application Architectures* published in 2015, he defined some characteristics of the cloud native application architecture, including the 12-factor app, microservices and API-based collaboration.

Cloud Native Computing Foundation (CNCF) defined cloud native V1.0 in 2019: Cloud native technologies empower organizations to build and run scalable applications in modern, dynamic environments such as public, private, and hybrid clouds. Containers, service meshes, microservices, immutable infrastructure, and declarative APIs exemplify this approach.

Although the cloud native definitions given by different organizations are different, all the definitions reflect the following key points: application development, deployment, operation and maintenance in the cloud. The entire lifecycle of these applications stays in the cloud. Therefore, these applications are usually called "cloud native applications". Cloud native technologies are the cornerstone of modern applications. The emergence of cloud native applications helps enterprises with their digital transformation. As mentioned above, the rise of cloud native applications is driven by the new needs of users and the mainstream computing infrastructure.

Cloud native introduces many new concepts and ways of thinking and affects the implementation technologies adopted by applications. To sum up, the main technologies used in cloud native applications are virtualization, container, microservice architecture and service mesh. The development process adopts continuous integration and delivery and the philosophy of integrated management of development and operations.

1.2 Introduction to the Container Technology

This section introduces the background and basic principles of the container technology. Sections 1.3–1.5 explain the structure and management model of container images in detail.

1.2.1 Development Background of the Container Technology

In recent years, the container technology has swept the world rapidly, subverting the application development, delivery and operational model. It has been widely used in the fields such as cloud computing and Internet. In fact, the container technology appeared about 20 years ago. It, however, was not widely used until 2013 after Docker was launched. This is caused by both accidental and inevitable factors due to the general industry environment. The following sections review the background and development process of container.

When electronic computers emerged for the first time, due to the high hardware cost, people tried to find a way to share computing resources among multiple users in order to improve resource utilization and reduce costs. In the 1960s, the host virtualization technology based on hardware appeared. A physical machine can be divided into several smaller machines. The hardware of these smaller machines is not shared with each other and each machine can have its own instance of operating system (OS) installed. In the late 1990s, the hardware virtualization technology of x86 architecture gradually arose, which can isolate multiple OS instances on the same physical machine, thereby bringing many advantages. At present, the vast majority of data centers adopt the hardware virtualization technology.

Although hardware virtualization provides the capability of separating resources, isolating applications by using virtual machine (VM) is inefficient because an OS instance needs to be installed in each VM and applications need to be deployed in each OS instance. Therefore, people explored a lighter solution—OS virtualization, which makes application-oriented management more convenient.

OS virtualization means that an OS creates a virtual system environment so that an applications cannot perceive the existence of other applications as if it is occupying all system resources alone, so as to achieve the purpose of application isolation. In this model, VMs are not needed. Because applications share the same OS instance, OS virtualization saves more resources and provides better performance than VMs. OS virtualization is also called container in many systems. The term container is also used to refer to OS virtualization below.

OS virtualization appeared in around 2000 when FreeBSD 4.0 launched Jail. Jail enhances and improves the chroot environment used for file system isolation. In 2004, Sun Microsystems launched Containers for Solaris 10, including zones and resource management. In 2007, Control Groups (cgroups for short) entered the Linux kernel, which can limit and isolate the resources (including CPU, memory, I/O and network) used by a group of processes.

In 2013, Docker, a company, released the Docker open source project, which provides a series of simple tool chains to manipulate containers. It is not exaggerating to say that Docker took the lead in igniting the flame of the container technology, opening the curtain of cloud native application revolution and promoting the rapid development of the container ecosystem. By 2020, Docker Hub recorded 130 billion image downloads accumulatively and users created about 6 million container repositories. As it can be seen from the data, users are switching from the traditional paradigm to the container-based paradigm of application lifecycle management at an amazing speed.

In 2015, the Open Container Initiative (OCI) was established as a Linux Foundation project, aiming to promote the open source community to develop container Image and Runtime Specifications so that container solutions of different vendors can be interoperable with each other. CNCF was also established in the same year, aiming to promote application of the container technology in the cloud native field and lower the threshold for users to develop cloud native applications. Its founding members included multiple companies and organizations such as Google, Red Hat, Docker and VMware.

In the early days after CNCF was established, it had only one open source project, namely Kubernetes which became famous later. Kubernetes is an orchestration tool for container applications. It was first developed by Google and was later donated to CNCF as a seeding project. As Kubernetes is a vendor neutral open source project, it attracts wide participation and support from community users and developers. By 2018, Kubernetes became the de facto standard in the field of container orchestration and became the first graduated project of CNCF. In August 2020, the number of open source projects under CNCF increased to 63, including projects such as Harbor originally created in China.

It can be seen from the development history that the container technology did not attract wide attention from people in the early period after it emerged. This was mainly because the open cloud computing environment did not emerge or became mainstream at that time. After 2010, as the cloud services such as IaaS, PaaS and SaaS gradually become mature, users attach more importance to the efficiency of application development, deployment, operation and maintenance in the cloud and rediscover the value of container, which finally contribute to the popularity of the container technology.

1.2.2 *Basic Principles of Container*

This section takes a Linux container as an example to explain the implementation principles of container. The container mainly includes namespace and control groups (cgroups).

1.2.2.1 Namespace

Namespace is a method used by the Linux OS kernel to isolate resources. It makes different processes have different system views. System views are the system environments processes can perceive, for example, host name, file system, network protocol stack and other users and processes. When namespaces are applied, a process can have an independent system environment and it cannot feel the existence of other processes. Therefore, processes are isolated from each other. At present, Linux has six types of namespace which can be nested.

- Mount: Mount namespace isolates the mount points of the file system. Processes in different "mount" namespace can see different file systems.
- Network: Network namespace isolates system resources in the aspect of process network, including network devices, IPv4 and IPv6 protocol stacks, routing tables and firewalls.
- IPC: IPC (Interprocess Communication) namespace isolates processes from SysV style inter-process communication
- PID: PID (Process ID) namespace provides independent process IDs in different namespace. Processes in different namespace may have the same process IDs. Of course, the global (default namespace) process IDs in the OS are unique.
- UTS: UTS (Unix Time Sharing) namespace provides system identifiers to processes. Each UTS namespace may have a different host name and NIS domain name.
- User: User namespace allows processes to have user IDs and group IDs that are different from global user IDs and group IDs.

Namespace provides a method for isolating processes in the same OS instance with hardly any additional system overhead. Therefore, it is a lightweight isolation method. The procedure of starting and running a process in a namespace is almost the same as that outside the namespace.

1.2.2.2 cgroups

Namespace implements the function of process isolation. However, because processes in each namespace are still sharing system resources such as CPU, disk I/O and memory. When a process occupies some resources for a long time, the processes in other namespace will be affected. This is called the phenomenon of "noisy neighbors". Therefore, namespace does not fully achieve the purpose of process isolation. To overcome this shortcoming, the Linux kernel provides the cgroups function.

Linux divides processes into cgroups and sets resource usage rules and restrictions for each group of processes. When resource competition occurs, the system allocates resources among cgroups based on the proportion predefined for each group. The resources for which cgroups can set rules include CPU, memory, disk I/O and network. In this way, some processes cannot preempt resources of other processes indefinitely.

Linux sets the visible and available resources of a process through namespace and stipulates the resource usage of a process through cgroups, so that a virtual environment (namely container) for isolating processes is created.

1.2.3 Container Runtime

Linux provides two system functions: namespace and cgroups, which are the foundation of container. However, to run a process in a container, the user also needs to have a convenient software development kit (SDK) or commands to call the system functions of Linux so as to create a container. Container runtime is a tool for running and managing containerized processes.

Container runtime is classified into low-level runtime and high-level runtime, which provide different functions. Low-level runtime is responsible for running a container. It can run the processes of a container in a given container file system. High-level runtime prepares the necessary operating environment for a container. For example, it downloads and decompresses container images, converts the images into the file system needed by containers and creates a network for containers. Finally, it calls a low-level runtime to launch a container. Figure 1.1 shows the relationship of some major container runtimes.

1.2.3.1 OCI Runtime Specification

Established in 2015, the OCI is a cooperative project under the Linux Foundation. It develops open industrial standards for OS virtualization (especially Linux containers) by means of open governance. It mainly includes the specifications of container image format and container runtime. Its founding members include companies such as Docker, Amazon, CoreOS, Google and VMware. In the early period after the OCI was established, Docker donated the container image format, the draft of container runtime and the corresponding implementation code. The libcontainer project that originally belonged to Docker was donated to the OCI and became an independent container runtime project, namely runC.

The OCI Runtime Specification defines the standards of container configuration, execution environment and lifecycle of a container. The mainstream container

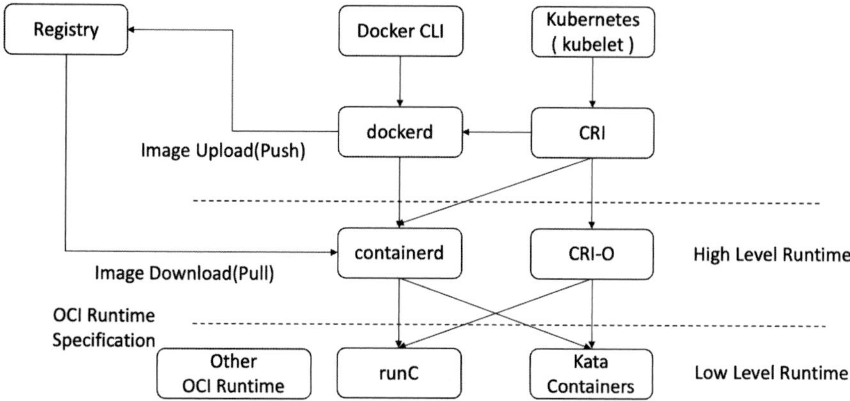

Fig. 1.1 The relationship of major container runtimes

runtimes follow the OCI Runtime Specification, so that the portability and interoperability of container are improved.

Before a container is started, the required files with a certain layout must be stored in the file system. The OCI Runtime Specification defines the standard of a container's filesystem bundle. In the implementation of OCI runtime, high-level runtime usually downloads OCI images and decompresses the OCI images into an OCI runtime filesystem bundle. Then OCI runtime reads configuration information and launches processes in the container.

Based on the definition of filesystem bundle, the OCI Runtime Specification establishes the standards of container runtime and lifecycle management. A lifecycle defines the entire process of a container from creation to deletion and includes three commands: **create**, **start** and **delete**.

1.2.3.2 runC

runC is a reference implementation of the OCI Runtime Specification and the most commonly used container runtime. It is used by many other projects such as containerd and CRI-O. runC is also a low-level container runtime. Developers can manage the lifecycle of containers through runC to avoid troublesome OS calls. According to the OCI Runtime Specification, runC does not include the container image management functionalities. It assumes that the files of a container have been extracted from images and stored in the file system. A container created by runC can be connected to other containers or network nodes only after the network is manually configured. Therefore, the network can be set up through the event hook defined by the OCI before the container is started.

Because the functionalities provided by runC are relatively simple, a higher-level container runtime is required for the generation of a complex runtime environment.

For this reason, runC often becomes the underlying building blocks of other high-level container runtimes.

1.2.3.3 containerd

When the OCI was established, Docker, the company, split its Docker project into the low-level runtime (runC) and the high-level runtime. In 2017, Docker put the functions of the high-level container runtime into the containerd project and donated it to CNCF.

containerd has become the high-level container runtime used by multiple projects. It provides image management functions such as container image download and decompression. When running a container, containerd first decompresses images into a filesystem bundle according to the OCI Runtime Specification and then calls runC to run the container. Through containerd API, other applications can interact with containerd. **ctr** is the command line tool of containerd. It is similar to the **docker** command. As a container runtime, however, containerd focuses on only the behavior of running containers. Therefore, it does not include functions such as image building and image uploading to the registry.

1.2.3.4 Docker

Docker engine is one of the earliest popular and the most widely used container runtime. It is a container management tool. Figure 1.2 shows its components. Docker client (CLI tool) calls APIs of the container engine Docker Daemon (dockerd) to complete container management tasks.

Docker engine is a single application when it was released. All functions were integrated in an executable file. Later, Docker engine was split based on functions

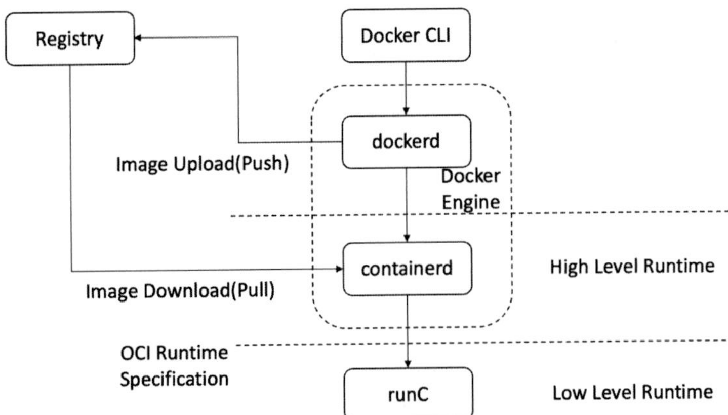

Fig. 1.2 The Docker engine container runtime

into runtimes of two different levels: runC and containerd, which were donated to the OCI and CNCF respectively. The above two sections respectively introduce the main features of runC and containerd. The remaining dockerd is the container runtime maintained by Docker, Inc.

dockerd provides functions for both developers and operators. For developers, it mainly provides image management functions. Generally, container images are built through Dockerfile. Dockerfile is a text file that defines the base images, required software packages and related applications encapsulated in a container image through a group of command keywords. After Dockerfile is defined, the **docker build** command can be used to build an image.

After the image of a container is built, the image is stored in the local repository. When an image needs to be shared with other nodes, the image can be uploaded to a registry so that other nodes can download it.

1.2.3.5 CRI and CRI-O

Kubernetes is a mainstream container orchestration platform nowadays. In order to adapt to the requirements of different scenarios, Kubernetes must have the capability to use different container runtimes. For this reason, Kubernetes adds a container runtime interface (CRI) in kubelet since version 1.5. The container runtime that needs to be plugged into Kubernetes must implement the CRI. Because kubelet is responsible for managing the workload of the local node, kubelet must have the capability to manage images and run containers. Therefore, only high-level container runtimes can implement the CRI. Figure 1.3 shows the relationship between the CRI and container runtimes.

An interface layer is required between the CRI and a container runtime, which is usually called a shim and is used to match corresponding container runtime.

Docker's container runtime is widely used. Its CRI shim is called dockershim, which is embedded in kubelet of Kubernetes and is developed and maintained by Kubernetes project team (Dockershim was deprecated in Kubernetes 1.20 in December 2020). Other runtime needs to provide external shims. containerd has a built-in CRI plugin since version 1.1 and no external shim is needed to forward requests. So it is more efficient. When installing the latest version of Docker,

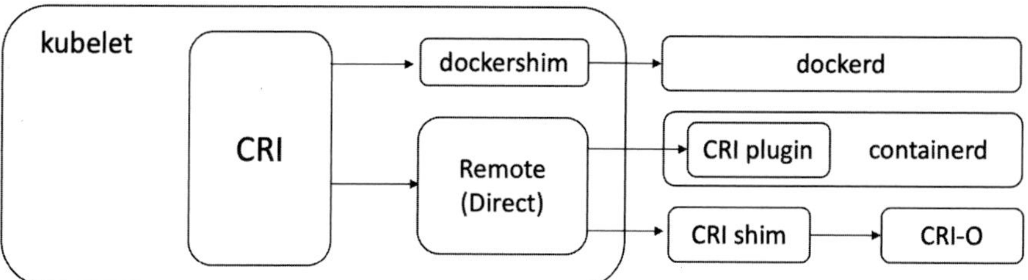

Fig. 1.3 The CRI and container runtimes

containerd is automatically installed. Therefore, in some systems, Docker and Kubernetes can use containerd to run containers at the same time. However, the images of the two are separated by namespace and are mutually independent, that is, the images cannot be shared.

CRI-O is designed to run containers in production systems. It provides a simple command line tool for testing but cannot manage containers. CRI-O supports the OCI container image format and can download images from a container registry. CRI-O supports two low-level container runtimes: runC and Kata Containers.

1.3 Structure of Container Images

A container features immutability and portability. It packages the executable files, dependent files and OS files of an application into images, so that the runtime environment of the application becomes immutable. Meanwhile, the images of the container can reproduce the same runtime environment in other systems. These features bring great convenience to operation, maintenance and application release, which is attributed to the images that encapsulate applications.

Considering the importance of container images, this section introduces the structure and mechanism of container images and then explains details of the OCI Image Specification by taking a Docker image as an example. The OCI Image Specification is supported and used by many cloud native projects and is even used in other fields. You can first get to know how a Docker image is implemented and then understand the OCI Image Specification on this basis.

1.3.1 Development of Container Images

In 2013, Docker released an image management tool and image format that encapsulate applications. This is a significant advantage of Docker's solution over previous ones. It is also the main reason that Docker won out and was widely spread rapidly. It can be said that container images reflected the core value of Docker.

In 2014, Docker summarized and defined its image format as Docker Image Specification v1. In 2016, Docker developed the Image Specification v2 and implemented it in Docker 1.10.

The OCI released OCI Image Specification 1.0 in July 2017. Because Docker Image Specification v2 has become a de facto standard, the OCI Image Specification is essentially based on Docker Image Specification v2. Therefore, the two are compatible or similar in most cases. For example, the image index in Docker Image Specification is equivalent to the manifest index in OCI Image Specification.

1.3.2 Structure of Docker Images

Docker container images mainly include the root file system (rootfs) on which applications depend. The rootfs stores information by layer. It usually stores OS files at the base layer and then overlays new layers on top of the base layer. Finally, it combines these layers to form a complete image. When a container is started through an image, all layers in the image are converted into a real-only file system in the container. Meanwhile, the container adds a read/write layer for applications to read or write files during runtime. The layer structure can be implemented via a union file system (UnionFS).

A Docker image can be generated using the **docker commit** command. This method applies to experimental images. When a user performs various operations in a container and reaches a desired state, the user uses the **docker commit** command to solidify the state of the container into an image. This method requires the user to manually enter the command. Therefore, it is not suitable to use in an automated pipeline. Generally, an image is built through the **docker build** command according to Dockerfile. Dockerfile describes all content and configuration information contained in the image, such as the start command. The following shows a simple example of Dockerfile:

```
FROM ubuntu:20.04
RUN apt update && apt install -y python
RUN apt install -y python-numpy
ADD myApp.py /opt/
```

In this example, the base image of the container is the OS Ubuntu 20.04. Then the Python software package and Python library NumPy are installed in turn and finally the application myApp is added. After the image is built, four layers exist, as shown in Fig. 1.4.

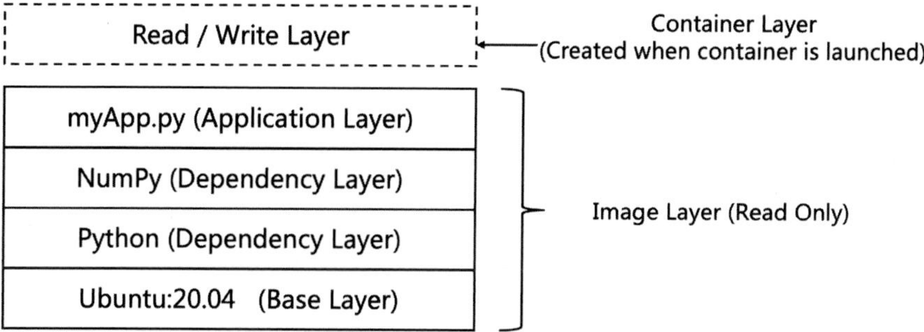

Fig. 1.4 Layered file system of a container

The image layer shown in Fig. 1.4 is loaded to the container as a read-only file system when the container is created. In addition, the container runtime creates a read/write layer for each container instance and overlays the layer as the top layer of the file system so that applications can read and write files. The immutability of a container is achieved through the (read-only) image layers of images. In addition, no matter images are started in whatever environment, the same image layers always exist, thereby achieving the portability of applications.

Docker manages images by layer, which brings in the following benefits:

1. It is convenient to share the base layers and the dependent software layers (including OS files and software packages, for example). Different images can share the same base layer or software layers, and only one copy of each layer needs to be saved on one machine. This greatly reduces the file storage space.
2. When an image is built, the built layers are saved in the cache. When the image is rebuilt, if a layer remains unchanged, the building time can be shortened by reusing the content of the cache.
3. Because in most cases only the top layer (application layer) is changed when the image of an application is updated, layering can reduce the distribution time of the same image.
4. Layering makes it more convenient to track the changes of images. Because each layer is associated with the build command, layering can better manage the change history of images.

The file system layering mechanism of Docker containers is implemented through the UnionFS. It also implements the read/write feature of container files while ensuring the read-only feature of images.

1.3.3 OCI Image Specification

The OCI Image Specification is based on Docker Image Specification v2. It defines the scenarios in which the registry stores and distributes images and is closely related to the OCI Distribution Specification (see Sect. 1.4.2) being developed. Before creating a container, an OCI runtime downloads and decompresses the container image into a filesystem bundle that meets the Runtime Specification, converts the configuration of the image into a runtime configuration and then starts the container.

An image defined by the OCI specification includes four parts: Image Index, Manifest, Configuration and Layers. Manifest is a description file in the JSON format and lists the configuration and layers of the image. Configuration is a description file in the JSON format and describes parameters for running an image. Layers are the content of an image, that is, files contained in the image, which are generally in the binary data file format (Blob). One image may have one or more layers. The image index is not mandatory. If the image index exists, it indicates a group of related images supporting platforms of different architecture. The four

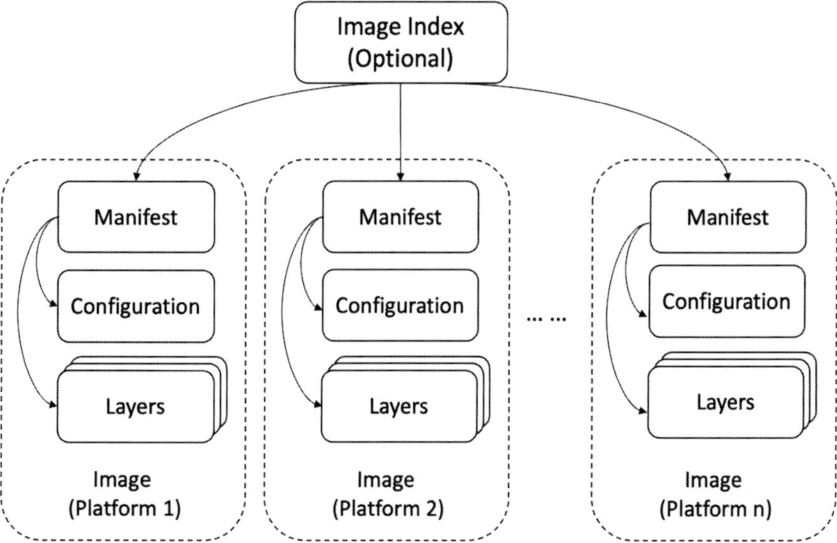

Fig. 1.5 Structure of an OCI image

parts of an image are mutually referenced through digest. Figure 1.5 shows the relationship between the four parts of an image.

The following explain the structures and functions of the four parts in detail.

1.3.3.1 Image Index

The image index is an optional part in an image. An image may not contain the image index. If an image does contain an image index, the image index is mainly to identify images for different type of platforms and represent a group of images that have the same name and are associated with each other. The difference is only in the supported architecture (for example, i386 and arm64v8, Linux and Windows). The advantage of image index is that the commands for using images on different platforms do not need to be modified. For example, the same **docker** command can be used on the Windows with amd64 architecture and the Linux with ARM architecture to run the Nginx service.

```
$ docker run -d nginx
```

The user does not need to specify the OS and platform and can fully rely on the client to obtain the correct version of the images. The image index of the OCI is also widely used by tools such as CNAB to manage distributed applications unrelated to cloud platforms.

The following shows an example of image index:

```
{
 "schemaVersion": 2,
 "manifests": [
  {
   "mediaType": "application/vnd.oci.image.manifest.v1+json",
   "size": 8342,
   "digest": "sha256:d81ae89b30523f5152fe646c1f9d178e5d10f28d0
   0b70294fca965b7b96aa3db",
   "platform": {
    "architecture": "arm64v8",
    "os": "linux"
   }
  },
  {
   "mediaType": "application/vnd.oci.image.manifest.v1+json",
   "size": 6439,
           "digest":  "sha256:2ef4e3904905353a0c4544913bc0caa
   48d95b746ef1f2fe9b7c85b3badff987e",
   "platform": {
    "architecture": "amd64",
    "os": "linux"
   }
  }
 ],
 "annotations": {
  "io.harbor.key1": "value1",
  "io.harbor.key2": "value2"
 }
}
```

After a client obtains the above image index, the client parses the image index and finds that the image index points to images of two different platform architectures. In this case, the client can pull corresponding images according to the platform where it runs. For example, a client on the Linux amd64 platform pulls the second image because the platform.architecture attribute of the image is amd64 and the platform.os attribute of the image is Linux.

The mediaType and digest attributes in the index file are important concepts in the OCI Image Specification. The following explains these two attributes in detail:

1. The mediaType is the media attribute that describes files contained in an image. When a client downloads images from services such as a registry, the client can obtain the mediaType of downloaded files from the HTTP header attribute Content-Type so that it can determine how to process the downloaded files. For example, the image index and manifest both are files in the JSON format and the difference between them is the mediaType. Table 1.1 describes the mediaType defined by the OCI Image Specification. It can be seen from the example above that the mediaType of manifest is application/vnd.oci.image.manifest.v1+json and the mediaType of the image index is application/vnd.oci.image.index.v1+json.

Table 1.1 mediaType defined by OCI Image Specification

mediaType	Meaning
application/vnd.oci.descriptor.v1+json	Content descriptor
application/vnd.oci.layout.header.v1+json	OCI layout description
application/vnd.oci.image.index.v1+json	Image index
application/vnd.oci.image.manifest.v1+json	Manifest
application/vnd.oci.image.config.v1+json	Image configuration
application/vnd.oci.image.layer.v1.tar	Layer in the tar format
application/vnd.oci.image.layer.v1.tar+gzip	Layer in the tar format, compressed by gzip
application/vnd.oci.image.layer.v1.tar+zstd	Layer in the tar format, compressed by zstd
application/vnd.oci.image.layer.nondistributable.v1.tar	Non-distribution layer in the tar format
application/vnd.oci.image.layer.nondistributable.v1.tar+gzip	Non-distribution layer in the tar format, compressed by gzip
application/vnd.oci.image.layer.nondistributable.v1.tar+zstd	Non-distribution layer in the tar format, compressed by zstd

2. The digest attribute is the digest in the sense of cryptography and serves as the identifier of image content to implement addressable content. Most content of images in the OCI Image Specification, such as a file, is identified and referenced through digest.

   The generation of digest is implemented through a specific hash algorithm based on the binary byte data of the file content. The hash algorithm must guarantee that bytes are collision resistant so that it can generate unique identifiers. As long as the hash algorithm is appropriate, the hash values of different files will hardly be duplicated. Therefore, it can be approximately considered that the digest of each file is unique. This uniqueness enables the digest to be used as the identifier for content addressing. Furthermore, if the digest is transmitted in a secure way, the receiver can recalculate the digest to ensure that content is not modified during transmission, thereby eliminating the content from insecure sources. The OCI Image Specification also requires validating the received content by using the digest value.

   The digest value is a string composed of two parts: algorithm and code. The algorithm specifies the hash function and algorithm identifier, and the code contains the encoding result of the hash function. The specific format is "<algorithm identifier>:<coding result>".

   At present, the OCI Image Specification recognizes two hash algorithms, namely SHA-256 and SHA-512. Table 1.2 lists the algorithm identifiers of the two algorithms.

The digest value of two manifests in the above index respectively correspond to two manifest files, namely blobs/sha256/d81ae89b30523f5152fe646c1f9d178e5d10f28d00b70294fca965b7b96aa3db and blobs/sha256/2ef4e3904905353a0c4544913bc0caa48d95b746ef1f2fe9b7c85b3badff987e.

Table 1.2 Algorithm identifiers of hash algorithms

Algorithm identifier	Algorithm name	Example of digest
sha256	SHA-256	sha256:d81ae89b30523f5152fe646c1f9d178e5d10f28d00b70294fca965b7b96aa3db
sha512	SHA-512	sha512:d4ca54922bb802bec9f740a9cb38fd401b09eab3c0135318192b0a75f2...

1.3.3.2 Manifest

A manifest is a file that describes the configuration and content of an image. The analysis of an image generally starts with the manifest. The manifest provides the following functions:

1. supporting the image model with addressable content. In the model, hash processing can be carried out for image configuration to generate an image and its unique identifier;
2. _containing multiple architecture images through image index and obtaining the image version of a specific platform by referencing the manifest;
3. supporting conversion into the OCI Runtime Specification to run a container.

The manifest includes information about configuration and layers. The following shows an example of a manifest:

```
{
 "schemaVersion": 2,
 "config": {
  "mediaType": "application/vnd.oci.image.config.v1+json",
  "size": 6883,
  "digest": "sha256:
b5b2b2c507a0944348e0303114d8d93aaaa081732b86451d9bce1f432a
537bc7"
 },
 "layers": [
  {
   "mediaType": "application/vnd.oci.image.layer.v1.tar+gzip",
   "size": 168654,
   "digest":   "sha256:58394f6dcfb05cb167a5c24953eba57f28f2f9d
09af107ee8f08c4ac89b1adf5"
  },
  {
   "mediaType": "application/vnd.oci.image.layer.v1.tar+gzip",
   "size": 645724,
   "digest":   "sha256:6d94e421cd3c3a4604a545cdc12745355bca5b5
28f4da2eb4a4c6ba9c1905b15"
  },
  {
   "mediaType": "application/vnd.oci.image.layer.v1.tar+gzip",
   "size": 53709,
   "digest": "sha256:419d1af06b5f7636b4ac3da7f12184802ad867736
ec4b8955958665577945c89"
  }
 ],
 "annotations": {
  "io.harbor.example.key1": "value1",
  "io.harbor.example.key2": "value2"
 }
}
```

The meanings of some attributes above are as follows:

- **config**: information about the image configuration file. The value **application/vnd.oci.image.config.v1+json** of mediaType indicates the mediaType of image configuration. **size** indicates the size of the image configuration file. **digest** indicates the hash digest of the image configuration file.
- **layers**: layer array. The above example includes three layers, which indicate layers of the container rootfs. When a container is running, the container overlays layers in order. Layer 1 is at the bottom (see Fig. 1.4). **mediaType** indicates the type of media and its value **application/vnd.oci.image.layer.v1.tar+gzip** indicates the file is a layer. **size** indicates the size of the layer. **digest** indicates the digest of the layer.
- **annotations**: additional information in the form of key value pair (optional).

1.3.3.3 Image Configuration

Image configuration mainly describes the rootfs of a container, execution parameters used by container runtime and some image metadata.

The configuration defines the composition of the image file system. The image file system is composed of several image layers. Except for the base image, the file systems of other layers record the changeset of the parent layer, including files to be added, changed or deleted.

Through the differences of layer-based file, union file system (for example, AUFS) or file system snapshot, the changeset of a file system can be used to aggregate a series of image layers so that all layers seem like a complete file system after overlaying.

The following shows an example of an image configuration:

```
{
  "created": "2020-06-28T12:28:58.058435234Z",
  "author": "Henry Zhang <hz@example.com>",
  "architecture": "amd64",
  "os": "linux",
  "config": {
    "ExposedPorts": {
      "8888/tcp": {}
    },
    "Env": [
     "PATH=/usr/local/sbin:/usr/local/bin:/usr/sbin:/usr/bin:/
sbin:/bin",
      "FOO=harbor_registry",
    ],
    "Entrypoint": [
      "/bin/myApp "
```

(continued)

```
      ],
      "Cmd": [
        "-f",
        "/etc/harbor.cfg"
      ],
      "Volumes": {
        "/var/job-result-data": {},
      },
      "Labels": {
        "io.goharbor.git.url": "https://github.com/goharbor/
harbor.git",
      }
    },
    "rootfs": {
     "diff_ids": [
     "sha256:e928294e148a1d2ec2a8b664fb66bbd1c6f988f4874bb0add23
a778f753c65ef",
     "sha256:ea198a02b6cddfaf10acec6ef5f70bf18fe33007016e948b04a
ed3b82103a36b"
     ],
     "type": "layers"
    },
    "history": [
     {
      "created": "2020-05-28T12:28:56.189203784Z",
      "created_by": "/bin/bash -c #(nop)
ADD file:4fb4eef1ea3bc1e842b69636f9df5256c49c537281fe3f282c65f
b853e563ab3 in /"
     },
     {
      "created": "2020-05-28T12:28:57.789430183Z",
      "created_by": "/bin/bash -c #(nop) CMD [\"bash\"]",
      "empty_layer": true
     }
    ]
}
```

The meanings of main attributes in the above example are as follows. For specific description, refer to OCI specifications.

- **created**: image creation time (optional).
- **author**: image author (optional).
- **architecture**: CPU architecture supported by the image.
- **os**: OS of images.
- **config**: some parameters for running the image, including service port, environment variable, entry point command, command parameters, data volumes, user and working directory (optional).

- **rootfs**: root file system of the image. It consists of the changeset of a series of layers.
- **history**: historical information about each layer of the image (optional).

1.3.3.4 Layer

It can be seen from the manifest and configuration information that the rootfs of images is composed of multiple layers through overlay. Each layer must be packed into a tar file when it is distributed. The compression or non-compression mode can be selected and the compression tool can be gzip or zstd. The advantage of packing the content of each layer into a file is that the file digest can be generated to facilitate validation and content addressing. In the manifest and configuration information, the mediaType must be declared according to whether the tar file is compressed and the compression tool in use, so that the image client can identify the file type and process the file accordingly.

The mediaType of several layers in Table 1.1 is non-distributable. This indicates that the layers cannot be publicly distributed due to legal or other reasons and must be obtained from the distributor.

1.4 Image Management and Distribution

Image management and distribution are basic functions of container application, including local image management, image distribution of registry and the interface between clients and the registry. Because Docker is the container management software that is widely used and provides full functions at present, this section first introduces the distribution mechanism of Docker images and then explains the OCI Distribution Specification on this basis.

1.4.1 Docker Image Management and Distribution

Docker implements a relatively complete workflow of image management and distribution, which includes the operations of pushing, pulling and deleting images. Table 1.3 describes the specific functions.

Docker images are distributed through the interaction between Docker Registry, Docker client and Docker Daemon. As shown in Fig. 1.6, Docker Daemon listens to client requests and manages resources such as local images, containers, networks and storage volumes; Docker client is a tool used by most users to interact with the Docker toolset. You can pull images from the configured registry service by executing the **docker pull** command; when you execute the **docker push** command, images can be pushed to the registry service from the local storage. Docker registry

Table 1.3 Image management operations of Docker

Image management operation	Function
Pull	Downloads images from the registry to a local machine through Docker client.
Push	Uploads local images to the registry through Docker client.
Delete	Deletes images from local storage (through Docket client) or deletes images from the registry (by calling the interface of the registry).

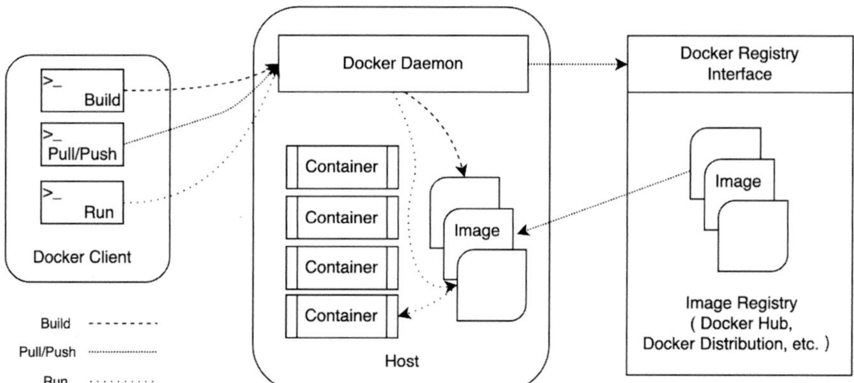

Fig. 1.6 Docker's image management and distribution

service is the registry for storing images. By default, Docker uses Docker Hub as the public service. Docker can also use software such as Docker Distribution[1] to provide the registry service locally.

Docker Distribution is the first tool that implements the functionalities of packaging, releasing, storing and distributing images and plays the role of Docker Registry. Docker Distribution provides support for several storage drivers, including memory, local file system, Amazon S3, Microsoft Azure block storage, OpenStack Swift, Alibaba Cloud OSS and Google cloud storage. The registry storage module defines a standard programming interface, through which users can implement new storage drivers as needed.

Docker Distribution implements most of the OCI Distribution Specification and is compatible with the specification to a large extent. Harbor uses Docker Distribution as the backend image storage. In versions earlier than Harbor 2.0, most of the image-related functions are provided by Docker Distribution. Since Harbor 2.0, the metadata of container images or OCI artifacts is maintained by Harbor. Docker Distribution is only used as the storage of OCI artifacts.

[1] Docker Inc. donated the open source project Docker Distribution to CNCF on Feb 4, 2021. It has been renamed as Distribution under the GitHub repo: https://github.com/distribution/distribution

1.4.2 OCI Distribution Specification

The OCI is also developing the Distribution Specification, which defines the interaction interface of image operations between clients and the registry based on the OCI Image Specification. The philosophy of the OCI is to first practice in the industry and then summarize practices into the technical specification. Therefore, although the Distribution Specification is not officially issued[2], the registry based on Docker Distribution has been used in many practical environments and Docker Registry HTTP API V2 used by Docker Distribution has become the de facto standard.

The OCI Distribution Specification is developed based on the standard container image distribution process of Docker Registry HTTP API V2. The OCI Distribution Specification defines the protocol for interaction between the registry service and registry clients, which mainly includes the URI format for namespace, registry service that can pull and push the V2 manifest, push process that supports resumable transmission.

1.4.3 OCI Artifact

It can be seen from Fig. 1.5 that the structural feature of OCI Image Specification is as follows: an optional image index points to multiple manifests, each manifest points to a configuration and several layers. If an image does not contain an image index, the image may contain only one manifest and the manifest points to one configuration and several layers. Whether or not an image contains an image index, the definition of image structure does not involve the content contained in the layers. In other words, data of any kind, for example, artifacts such as Helm Chart and CNAB, can be packed into a layer using the structures (manifest and index) defined by the OCI Image Specification, so as to become the "images" that meet OCI specifications. The images can be pushed to a registry that supports the OCI Distribution Specification or downloaded from the registry like pulling images.

To differentiate from OCI images, any content can be referred to as OCI artifacts (Artifacts for short) as long as it follows the definitions of OCI manifest and index. Artifacts can be pushed and pulled through the OCI Distribution Specification. In the OCI Distribution Specification, several tags can also be marked on an artifact's manifest or index to attach information such as version, so as to facilitate subsequent access and use, as shown in Fig. 1.7. If an artifact does not contain an index, a tag can be marked on the manifest; if an artifact uses an index, the tag can be marked on the index and the tag on the manifest is optional. If an artifact is not marked with any tag, the artifact can only be accessed through the manifest or the digest of the index.

[2]This book was originally published in Nov 2020. In May 2021, OCI announced the Distribution Specification v1.0.

From the perspective of composition structure, OCI image is only a "special case" of OCI artifacts. Readers can deepen their understanding by comparing Fig. 1.7 with Fig. 1.5.

One of the advantages of encapsulating data of various types into OCI artifacts is that the storage, permission, replication and distribution capabilities of the data can be achieved by means of existing registry services (such as Harbor 2.0) which support the OCI Distribution Specification, without the need to establish or develop different registry services for each specific type of data, so that developers can focus on innovation of new artifacts types.

If developers hope to define a new artifact type, developers can define the structures such as configuration, manifest and index by following the Artifact Author Guidance (https://github.com/opencontainers/artifacts) from the OCI. After developers define a new artifact type, appropriate client software can be used to pack, push and pull data so that the new artifact type can interact with the registry service complying with the OCI Distribution Specification.

Because OCI artifacts bring convenience in management, operation and maintenance, developers have created a variety of OCI artifacts, including Helm Chart, CNAB and Singularity. In order to meet the needs of cloud native users, Harbor 2.0 makes great adjustment and improvement to its architecture, so that users can access and manage artifacts which comply with OCI specifications in Harbor. All container image management functions in Harbor, for example, access control, pushing and pulling images, query in user interface and remote replication, can be extended to OCI artifacts when applicable. This greatly facilitates users' management of cloud native artifacts.

1.5 Registry

The registry is an important hub for container images to be distributed and shared between different environments and is one of the indispensable components in the container application platform. This section details the role of registry, types of registry service and features of Harbor Registry.

1.5.1 Role of Registry

Container images are generally built by developers through commands such as **docker build** or are created occasionally through the **docker commit** command. No matter which method is used, images that are generated are saved in the local image cache of the development machine for local development and testing.

On the other hand, an important role of container images is that container images, as a portable application packaging format, run encapsulated applications in different environments without distinction. Therefore, locally generated images sometimes

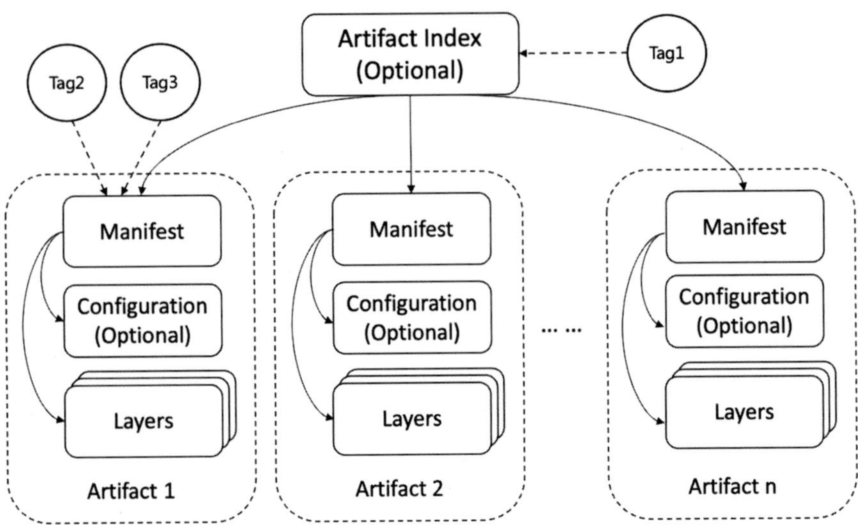

Fig. 1.7 Structure of an OCI artifact

need to be sent to other environments such as other developers' machines, servers in the data center or cloud computing nodes. In this circumstance, an effective method is needed to transmit images between different environments. A key component in image transmission and distribution is the registry of images.

Figure 1.8 illustrates the state transition of images in the lifecycle of the container on a single (local) computer. For developers, images can also be pushed to a registry or downloaded from a registry.

If the push and pull operations shown in Fig. 1.8 are performed in different computing environments, image transmission across environments can be accomplished. In addition, the images obtained in different environments are the same and can be run without distinction, as shown in Fig. 1.9.

In the actual environment, there are a few image builders (such as developers) and the vast majority of users or machine clusters are image consumers. This model is usually called image distribution. It enables members of a development team to share application images or enables operation and maintenance personnel to publish images to a cluster of the production machines through image distribution, as shown in Fig. 1.10.

It can be seen from the above distribution model that the registry is a key component which connects both container image producers and consumers and is also the fundamental reason why almost all container-based platforms cannot work without a registry. Because of the importance of the registry and its key role in application distribution, the registry is suitable for image management, such as access control, remote replication and vulnerability scanning. Registry software such as Harbor adds in these rich management capabilities in addition to the basic functionalities of image distribution, thus winning the favor of users.

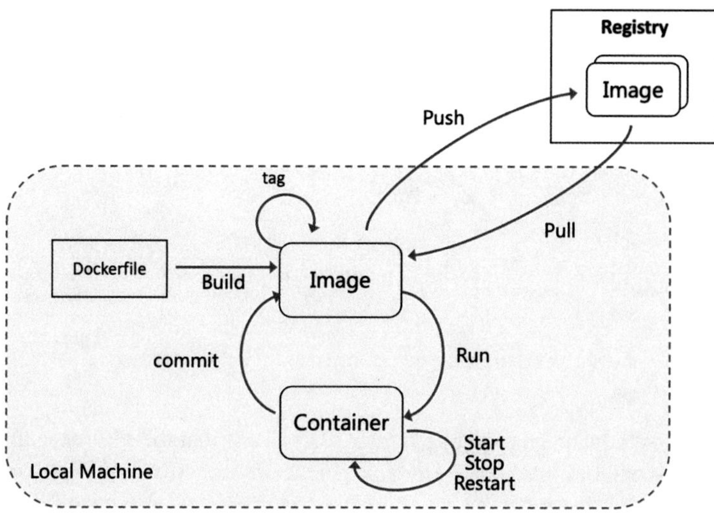

Fig. 1.8 State transition of a container image

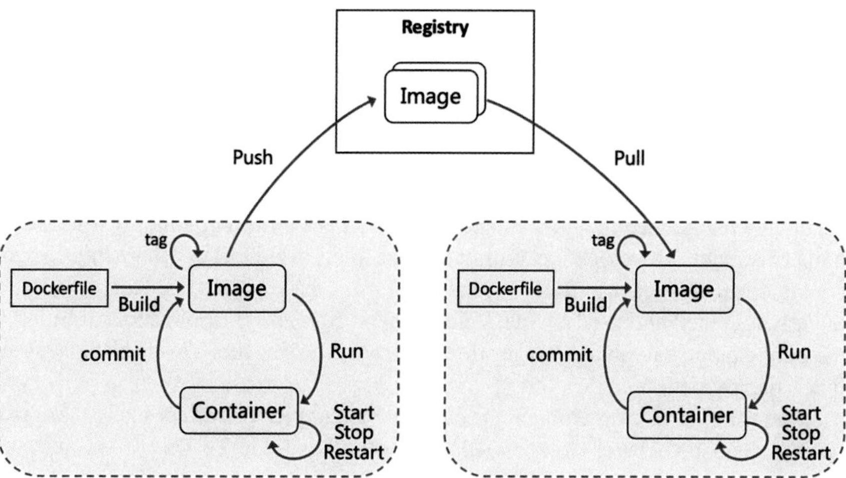

Fig. 1.9 Image registry in the distribution of container images

1.5.2 Public Registry Services

In terms of the user access model, registry services are divided into public registry services and private registry services. Public registry services are generally deployed in public cloud. Public registry services can be accessed through the Internet. Private registry services are usually deployed in the internal network of an organization and serve only users of the organization.

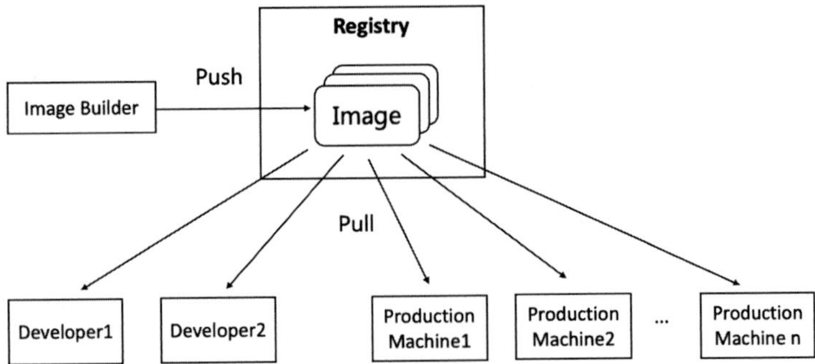

Fig. 1.10 Container images distribution across different environments

The biggest advantage of public registry services is that the services can be used conveniently without installation or deployment. Users between different organizations can share or distribute images. Public registry services also have the disadvantage: Because images are stored in the cloud, private data in images may be disclosed. Therefore, many enterprises and governments that have security requirements often do not allow images to be stored in the public registry. In addition, when public registry services are used, images need to be downloaded from the public network. It may take a long time to transmit images. In the scenarios in which images are frequently used, for example, image building and pull during application development and testing, the efficiency is low. Therefore, public registry services do not fit the scenarios in which images are frequently used.

At present, the most famous public registry service is Docker Hub. The service is set up and maintained by the company Docker. It is the most commonly used public registry service. Developers can directly and freely use Docker Hub using Docker container management toolset. This is one of the reasons why Docker tool can be quickly accepted and used by many developers. Nowadays, applications running in the public cloud can obtain images directly from Docker Hub. This is also a way for quick deployment.

In addition to Docker Hub, major public cloud service providers such as Amazon AWS, Microsoft Azure, Google GCE, Alibaba Cloud and Tencent Cloud all have their own registry services. The registry services provided by these cloud service providers can meet the image usage requirements of their own cloud native users and accelerate the access efficiency of cloud native applications. Moreover, the registry services can also provide public users with the image access capability, which facilitates image distribution and transmission. For example, users can push internal images to a public registry.

1.5.3 Private Registry Services

Private registry services can overcome the shortcomings of public registry services: Images are stored in the internal storage of organizations, which can not only ensure the security of images but also improve the image access efficiency. Meanwhile, management operations such as image access control and vulnerability scanning can be performed in private registry services. Therefore, private registry is usually the preferred solution in large and medium-sized organizations. The main disadvantage of private registry services is that organizations need to bear the cost of purchasing software and hardware and a team is required to operate the service.

The easiest way to set up registry services in a private environment is to pull images from Docker Hub and deploy the Docker Registry. Docker Registry stores and distributes Docker and OCI images and is intended for developers and small environments. Docker Registry features simple structure and fast deployment. It is applicable to image sharing between small development teams or application image distribution in small-scale production environments. Docker Registry's open source code is available at: https://github.com/distribution/distribution.

In larger organizations, due to the large number of users, applications and complex management requirements, Docker Registry can hardly meet the requirements. Therefore, more comprehensive image management solutions are needed. Open source projects such as Harbor can be selected as appropriate solutions according to their needs.

Private registry can also be established in the public cloud, that is, users deploy their registry services in the public cloud to provide image services for users' applications in the cloud. This deployment model has obvious advantages: applications can obtain images from a nearby registry service and the privacy of images can be maintained to a certain extent.

As hybrid cloud becomes more and more commonly used in enterprises, users often run applications in both private and public cloud. This involves the synchronization and publishing images in two registry services (local and in the cloud). In terms of efficiency and management, deploying a registry service in both the private cloud and the public cloud enables images to be downloaded as close as possible to the registry service. The application images developed in the private environment are replicated to the production environment of the public cloud through image synchronization between the two registries to achieve image consistency and application publishing.

1.5.4 Harbor Registry

Harbor Registry (also known as Project Harbor) was originally created by the Cloud Native Lab of VMware China R&D and it was open source in March 2016. Based on Docker Registry, Harbor adds in some important functions such as access control, image signature, vulnerability scanning and remote replication, which are highly needed by enterprise users. Harbor also provides a graphical management. After the project was open source, Harbor Registry rapidly became popular among the Chinese developer community and used as the mainstream container registry by Chinese cloud native users.

In July 2018, VMware donated Harbor to CNCF, making it an open source project jointly maintained by the community and the first CNCF project originated from China. After joining CNCF, Harbor is integrated into the global cloud native community. Many partners, users and developers have contributed to Harbor. Thousands of users deploy Harbor in production. The monthly downloads of Harbor exceed more than 30,000 times. In June 2020, Harbor became the first CNCF graduated project originated from China.

Harbor is designed to meet the requirements of enterprise security compliance and aims to provide secure and trusted management of cloud native artifacts. Harbor provides functions of four categories: multi-user control (role-based access control and project isolation), image management policy (storage quota, artifact retention, vulnerability scanning, provenance signature, immutable artifact and garbage collection), security and compliance (identity authentication, scanning and CVE exception rules) and interoperability (Webhook, remote content replication, pluggable scanner, REST API and robot account).

Harbor is a completely open source software. It also uses many other open source projects such as PostgreSQL, Redis and Docker Distribution, reflecting the idea of "from the community and to the community". After several years of development, based on the feedback and contributions provided by community users and developers, Harbor can provide rich and complete functions and can be connected to and integrated with different systems.

Harbor can use mainstream file systems and object storage, support the authentication of LDAP/AD and OIDC, provide an interface for external pluggable image scanners, synchronize images with major public or private registry services and support clients of multiple cloud native tools such as Docker/Notary, kubelet, Helm and ORAS OCI.

The content of this book is based on Harbor 2.0. Harbor 2.0 is a version that includes many improved features. The most important one is that it supports artifacts which comply with the OCI Image Specification and OCI Distribution Specification, so that Harbor can store not only container images but also cloud native artifacts such as Helm Chart and CNAB. Access control and remote replication policies can be set for these types of artifacts just like container images. In addition, these artifacts are displayed in a unified way on the user interface, which greatly facilitates users and extends the management scope of Harbor. Therefore, Harbor has evolved into a universal cloud native artifact registry from an image registry.

As its functions become increasingly comprehensive, Harbor is used in more and more scenarios, which are summarized as follows:

1. Continuous integration and continuous delivery (CI/CD). One of the earliest usage scenarios of containers is CI/CD. After the source code of an application

is compiled and tested through the automation pipeline, container images are built and stored in Harbor. The images are then published to the production or other environments. In this process, Harbor plays the role in connecting the development and production.

2. Unifying image sources within an organization. Organizations usually have certain requirements and rules of the sources and security of images. If internal users download any images from public sources and run them inside enterprises, security risks such as viruses and system vulnerabilities may be introduced. For this reason, organizations often set up internal standard image sources to store verified or tested images for their users. Using Harbor can be a good choice for this purpose. Access control can be set for images and images are isolated by project team. Furthermore, images can be scanned regularly. When any security vulnerability is found, users are not allowed to download images and patches can be applied in time. The administrator can also create digital signature to provide the provenance of images.
3. Cross-environment image transmission. An important feature of container images is its immutability, that is, images encapsulate the operating environment of applications and can reproduce the environment without distinction in other systems. This feature allows container images to be moveable and can be transferred in different environments. Harbor's remote content replication provides the container synchronization capability. Harbor can perform image synchronization no matter it is between different data centers, or between public cloud and private cloud. In addition, Harbor provides the retry function in the case of error, greatly improving the efficiency of operation and maintenance.
4. Artifact backup. The backup of artifacts such as container images is a use case that derives from cross-environment image transmission. It is used to replicate artifacts such as images to other systems and retain one or more copies. When necessary, these copies can be replicated back to the original Harbor instance so as to achieve the purpose of artifact recovery.
5. Local access to artifacts. The local access to artifacts is also a use case derived from cross-environment image transmission. Harbor can replicate artifacts such as images to several remote locations at the same time, for example, from the data center in San Francisco to the data centers in Seattle, New York and Austin. In this way, users in different geographical locations can obtain artifact data from the nearest location and the download time is shortened.
6. Data storage. After Harbor 2.0 supports OCI specifications, more applications can store non-image data into Harbor, such as model data and training data of artificial intelligence (AI). After the data is stored in Harbor, the biggest advantage is that functions such as content replication and access control can be automatically applied, without the need to develop similar functions again.

1.6 Introduction to Harbor Components

This section briefly introduces the architecture, components and typical processing flow of Harbor.

1.6.1 Overall Architecture

In early versions of Harbor, Harbor mainly focuses on management of Docker images. It allows users to push and pull images at the same time through URIs and to browse and manage images by using the graphical interface. As for the push and pull functions, Docker's open source Distribution project is widely used. It supports different types of storage and is mature and stable. Therefore, Harbor chooses Distribution to handle requests from clients to pull and push images and provides management functions by adding other components around Distribution. On the one hand, this reduces the workload of development; on the other hand, since Distribution is basically the de facto standard of registry, it ensures the stability of the image push and pull functions. Later, with the iteration of the project, Harbor gradually reduces its dependency on Distribution. However, Distribution is still a bridge between Harbor and user storage in terms of the image read/write and access functions.

Figure 1.11 shows the architecture of Harbor 2.0, which is divided into the Proxy Layer, Functionality Layer and Data Layer from top to bottom.

The function of the Proxy Layer is simple. It can be considered as the gateway of Harbor and is essentially an Nginx reverse proxy. It is responsible for receiving requests from different types of clients, including browsers, user scripts, Docker and other artifact command line tools such as Helm and ORAS, and forwarding the requests to different backend services for processing according to the request type

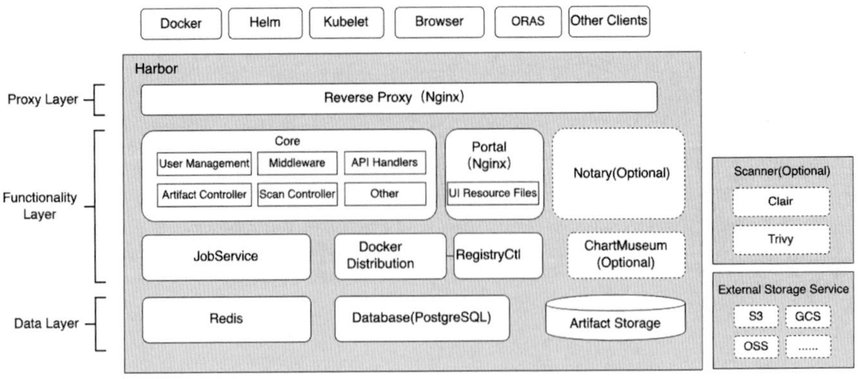

Fig. 1.11 Architecture of Harbor 2.0

and URI. The Proxy Layer ensures that all functions of Harbor are exposed through a single hostname.

The Functionality Layer is a group of HTTP services, which provide the core functions of Harbor, including core functional components Core, Portal, JobService, Docker Distribution and RegistryCtl, as well as optional components Notary, ChartMuseum and the image scanners. In actual deployment, except for the Notary component that includes the server and signer containers, each of other components is composed of one container. These components are designed as stateless components for horizontal scaling through multiple instances.

The Data Layer includes the PostgreSQL relational database, Redis cache service and storage services (file system or object storage) provided by users. These services are shared by functional components of the Functionality Layer and are used to store application data in different scenarios. Because functional components are stateless, when planning high-availability deployment of Harbor, users only need to ensure that application data is consistent and will not be lost.

Components can be divided into two categories: core components and optional components, which are introduced in the following two sections.

1.6.2 Core Components

Core components are mandatory components when Harbor is installed and are necessary for the main functions of Harbor. Core components include core functional components and data storage components. Core functional components include reverse proxy Nginx, Portal, Core, RegistryCtl, Docker Distribution and JobService. Data storage components include the database (PostgreSQL), cache (Redis) and artifact storage. Reverse proxy Nginx is explained in the previous section. The following introduces other components in turn with the actual usage scenarios.

1.6.2.1 Core Functional Components

- Portal: Portal is a frontend application based on Angular. The container corresponding to the component is "portal". The Nginx server inside the container serves the static resources. When a user accesses the user interface of Harbor through a browser, the Nginx reverse proxy of the Proxy Layer forwards the request to the Nginx service in the portal container, so that the browser can obtain the static resources, such as JavaScript files and icons, to render the frontend interface.
- Core: Core is a core component in Harbor. It encapsulates most service logic of Harbor. Based on the Beego framework, the component provides middleware and RESTful API Handlers to process API requests from the user interface and other clients. After an HTTP request arrives at the Core process, the request is first

preprocessed by a group of middleware corresponding to the requested URL, and operations such as security check and context generation are performed. Later, API Handlers parse the data object of the request and calls the internal service logic module. The internal service logic of Harbor is exposed by interfaces of different controllers. For example, a specific controller is assigned to handle each of the following tasks: adding, deleting, modifying, and querying an artifact or project. Some functions such as image signature query or artifact scanning need to call the interfaces of other components. This part of work is also done by the controllers. The Core component is also responsible for connecting the internal database or external identity authentication services (such as LDAP) to verify the credentials entered by users. In addition, push and pull artifact requests sent by the command line tool also arrive at the component. After the middleware checks permissions and deducts quota, the middleware forwards the requests to the Docker Distribution component, which reads from or writes to the storage.

- Docker Distribution: Docker Distribution is a registry maintained by the Docker Inc.. It implements image push and pull functions. Harbor implements functions of read/write and access of artifacts through Docker Distribution.
- RegistryCtl: RegistryCtl is the control component of Docker Distribution. It shares configuration with Docker Distribution and provides a RESTful API to trigger garbage collection.
- JobService: JobService is a component of scheduling asynchronous tasks. It is responsible for running time-consuming functions in Harbor, such as artifact replication, scanning and garbage collection. These functions run in the form of backend asynchronous tasks. JobService provides management of task scheduling.

Taking the scenario in which a user pushes images as an example (the authentication process is omitted to focus on the principles), the following explains how the Nginx, Core and Docker Distribution components process client requests, as shown in Fig. 1.12.

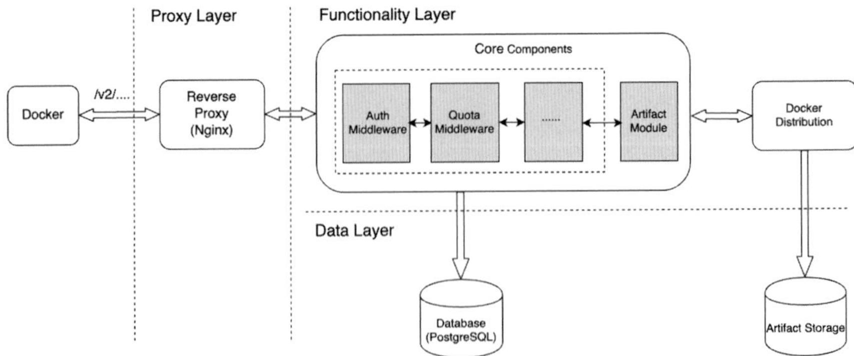

Fig. 1.12 Process flow of Harbor for handling a push request of a container image

First, the Docker client sends HTTP requests to Harbor to call APIs of "POST / v2/<name>/blobs/uploads" and "PATCH /v2/<name>/blobs/uploads/<session_id>" to upload the data layer of images. The request is then forwarded to the Core component by Nginx. The middleware of the Core component performs various checkings, for example, querying the database to check whether the requests have the permission, and the target project quota are exhausted. After the request passes all the checkings, the request is sent to Docker Distribution, which writes data to the storage. After data is successfully written, a response goes through the middleware of the Core component again, which then updates the usage of project quota in the database and returns a successful message to the client.

After all data layers of an image are uploaded successfully, the Docker client sends a request to Harbor and calls the API "PUT /v2/<name>/manifests/<reference>" to upload the image manifest, which is a data object in the JSON format. After the request is preprocessed by the Core component, the request is forwarded to Docker Distribution. After Docker Distribution writes and stores data successfully, the middleware of the Core component calls the metadata processor in the artifact functional module for images, inserts records into the database according to the content of the JSON object and saves the metadata of the image.

After the upload is done, the push request is completed. The content of the image is written into Docker Distribution and its metadata is written into the database by the Core component for subsequent queries.

The above-mentioned image uploading and processing also apply to other artifacts that are compatible with the OCI format, including Helm Chart, CNAB and image index. In addition to images, Harbor 2.0 provides different artifact metadata processors for the image index, Helm Chart and CNAB to extract their own unique metadata. For artifacts of other types, for example, local files packed by ORAS, the default artifact metadata processor extracts basic information such as type and size.

1.6.2.2 Data Storage Components

The above core components are only responsible for processing the service logic and user requests and all run in the form of stateless services. The storage and persistence of service data and artifacts are processed through data storage components.

The data storage components of Harbor are divided into three parts:

- Database (PostgreSQL): Application data of Harbor, for example, project information, membership of the projects, management policy and configuration information, is saved in the relational database. Metadata of artifacts, for example, type, size and tag, is also saved in the database. In addition, some optional components such as Notary and Clair (image scanner), which are responsible for managing image signature, share the database service with the core components of Harbor in default installation mode. During installation, external database services can also be configured, and databases can be created for corresponding components. Harbor initializes the database table schema during

a startup. In addition, it should be noted that, at present, Harbor only supports PostgreSQL as the backend relational database and is not fully compatible with other databases such as MySQL.
- Cache service (Redis): The cache service stores data of relatively short lifecycle, for example, state information shared by multiple instances during horizontal scaling. In addition, due to the considerations on the aspects such as performance, a small amount of persistent data of the JobService component is also stored in Redis. A few databases in Redis are used by different components. Database 0 corresponds to the Core component. It stores user session information and temporary information such as read-only data and the upload status of artifact data layers; database 1 is used by Docker Distribution to store data layer information to accelerate APIs calls; database 2 is provided to JobService. It is used to store task information and implement a function like a queue. Multiple instances of JobService can schedule tasks and update their status based on database 2. Optional components such as ChartMuseum and image scanning software Clair and Trivy also use Redis as the default cache to store temporary data. Similar to database services, you can also configure Harbor during installation to use external Redis services.
- Artifact storage: It stores the content of artifacts and is the final destination for storing data of pushed artifacts such as images and Helm Chart. In default installation mode, Harbor writes artifacts to the local file system. You can also modify the configuration and use third-party storage services such as Amazon's Simple Storage Service (S3), Google Cloud Storage (GCS) or Alibaba Cloud object storage service (OSS) as the backend storage to save artifacts. As mentioned previously, Harbor reads and writes the content of artifacts through Docker Distribution. Therefore, Harbor adapts to various storage services by means of different drivers in Docker Distribution.

By default, the persistent service components installed are not of high availability. During the deployment of highly available Harbor, you need to set up data services of high availability and direct Harbor to use these services. For more details, see Chap. 2.

1.6.3 Optional Components

Core components implement basic artifact management functions. In addition to that, Harbor integrates third-party open source software to provide functions such as image signature and vulnerability scanning. This part of functional services are called optional components. During the installation of Harbor, you can choose whether to install these components as needed. To reduce the deployment complexity, the installer configures these optional components to make them share services such as database and Redis with the core components of Harbor.

Harbor has the following optional components:

- Notary: It provides image signature management based on TUF. After you choose to install Notary during the installation process of Harbor, the notary-server and notary-signer components will be deployed. The notary-server component is responsible for handling the requests for managing signatures from clients, and the notary-signer component is responsible for signing the signed metadata again to improve the security. In the default installation, the two components share the same database with the Core component of Harbor. After Docker Content Trust is enabled, the Docker client sends the signature to port 4443 of Harbor services after it pushes images. When the Nginx component of Harbor receives the request from port 4443, the Nginx component forwards the request to notary-server. When a user sends an API request for querying images, the Core component sends a request to notary-server to query whether images are signed and return the result to the user.
- Scanner: Harbor 2.0 supports installing Clair or Trivy as the image scanner within Harbor. The scanners are automatically registered with Harbor during installation. Although their working mechanisms are different, Harbor has two corresponding adapters which implement the same RESTful API based on the adapter specification. During image scanning, the JobService component calls the API of an adapter to scan images and obtains a vulnerability report and stores the report in the database.
- ChartMuseum: It provides an API to manage Helm Chart that is not within the scope of OCI specifications. After the ChartMuseum component is installed, when the user uses the **helm** command to push a chart to or pull a chart from Harbor, the Core component of Harbor receives the request, validates the request and then forwards the request to ChartMuseum so that it can read and write the chart file. As Helm Chart compatible with OCI specifications becomes more widely adopted by the community, Helm Chart can be stored and managed in Harbor as OCI artifact and no longer depends on ChartMuseum. Therefore, Harbor may consider to deprecate the support of ChartMuseum in future releases.

The above sections introduce the architecture and components of Harbor. How these components interact with each other and work together in different scenarios will be introduced in detail in the following chapters.

Chapter 2
Installation and Configuration

Harbor provides a variety of installation methods, including online installation, offline installation, source code installation and installation based on Helm Chart.

- Online installation: Harbor is installed through the online installation package. During the installation, the prebuilt official component images of Harbor must be obtained from Docker Hub.
- Offline installation: Harbor is installed through the offline installation package. The required component images of Harbor are loaded from the offline installation package.
- Source code installation: Harbor is installed through compiling the source code.
- Installation based on Helm Chart: Harbor is installed to the Kubernetes cluster through Helm Chart.

This chapter details the installation methods of Harbor based on the environment of Ubuntu 18.04.

2.1 Installing Harbor in the Stand-alone Environment

In the stand-alone environment, you can install Harbor via the online, offline or source code installation method. Before Harbor is installed, make sure that the machine where Harbor will be installed meets the hardware and software requirements listed in Table 2.1 and Table 2.2, respectively.

2.1.1 Basic Configuration

From version 1.8.0 on, Harbor changes the format of the configuration file to harbor.yml from harbor.cfg to provide better readability and scalability. In addition, Harbor

H. Zhang, Y. Wang, *The Authoritative Guide on Harbor*,
https://doi.org/10.1007/978-981-19-2727-0_2

Table 2.1 Post-Installation requirement of hardware

Hardware	Minimum Configuration	Recommended Configuration
CPU	2 CPUs	4 CPUs
Memory	4 GB	8 GB
Hard disk	40 GB	160 GB

Table 2.2 Post-Installation requirement of software

Software	Version	Description
Docker Engine	17.06.0-Ce or later	See its official installation document.
Docker Compose	1.18.0 or later	See its official installation document.
OpenSSL	The latest version is recommended.	The software generates certificates and private keys required during installation.

provides centralized management of installation and configuration and reduces the dependence on the user's base environment by a container called prepare. It should be noted that if Harbor is installed based on harbor.cfg (for versions earlier than 1.8.0), Python v2.7 must be preinstalled in the environment.

This chapter explains the details of configuration based on Harbor 2.0. After decompressing the online or offline installation packages of Harbor, the **harbor.yml.tmpl** file can be found from the packages. It is the template of the configuration file of Harbor. You can copy the **harbor.yml.tmpl** file, rename it **harbor.yml** and use it as the configuration file for installation. Note: Each time after the **harbor.yml** configuration file is modified, run the prepare script and restart Harbor so that the configuration can take effect.

The following section introduces the specifics of the **harbor.yml.tmpl** file.

2.1.1.1 hostname

This item configures the network access address of the Harbor service. **hostname** can be set to the IP address or the fully qualified domain name (FQDN) of the host in the current installation environment. Do not to set **hostname** to **127.0.0.1** or **localhost**. Otherwise, Harbor cannot be accessed by external clients except for the local machine.

2.1.1.2 HTTP and HTTPS

This entry is used to configure the network access protocol of Harbor. The default value is **HTTPS**. Note: If you choose to install the Notary component, you must set HTTPS as the network access protocol of Harbor. If HTTPS is in use, you must provide the SSL/TLS certificate and configure the location of the certificate and private key files for the **certificate** and **private_key** options.

- **port**: the port number. The default value is **443**.
- **certificate**: the local path of the SSL/TLS certificate file.
- **private_key**: the local path of the private key file.

If HTTP is used, you must comment out the section of HTTPS in the configuration file:

```
# https:
#  # https port for harbor, default is 443
#  port: 443
#  # The path of cert and key files for nginx
#  certificate: /your/certificate/path
#  private_key: /your/private/key/path
```

2.1.1.3 internal_tls

This entry is to configure TLS communication between modules of Harbor. By default, the communication between components (harbor-core, harbor-jobservice, proxy, harbor-portal, registry, registryctl, trivy_adapter, clair_adapter and chartmuseum) is based on HTTP. To ensure security, however, It is recommended to enable TLS communication in the production environment. To enable TLS communication, the related section can be uncommented in the configuration file:

```
internal_tls:
  # set enabled to true means internal tls is enabled
  enabled: true
  # put your cert and key files on dir
  dir: /etc/harbor/tls/internal
```

The item **enabled** indicates whether TLS is enabled; **dir** indicates the local path of the certificates and private keys of the components.

Harbor provides an automated certificate generation tool. The command is as follows:

```
$ docker run -v /:/hostfs goharbor/prepare:v2.0.0 gencert -p /
path/to/internal/tls/cert
```

In the above command, the option **-p** specifies the local directory for saving certificates. It is recommended that the directory should be the same as **dir** in the configuration file. If they are different, you need to manually copy the generated files to the directory specified by **dir**.

By default, the automated certificate generation tool generates certificate authority(CA) and the certificates of components based on the CA.

To use your own CA to generate certificates of components, you can name your own CA and private keys as **harbor_internal_ca.crt** and **harbor_internal_ca.key**, and put them in the directory specified by **dir**. Next, execute the above command to generate the certificates and private keys of components.

If you do not use the automated certificate generation tool, you need to provide your own CA and private keys, name them as **harbor_internal_ca.crt** and **harbor_internal_ca.key** and put them in the directory specified by **dir**. The directory must also contains the certificates and private keys of all components. Note: The certificates of all components must be issued by your own CA. The file names of certificates and the common name (CN) attributes of certificates must be specified according to Table 2.3.

2.1.1.4 harbor_admin_password

This item sets the initial password of Harbor's administrator. The default value is **Harbor12345**. It is recommended to modify this password before installing Harbor. The password is only valid for the first launch of Harbor. After the first launch, the password in the configuration file will be no longer used. To change the administrator's password, log in to Harbor's management console and update the password.

2.1.1.5 database

This item configures the built-in database of Harbor.

- **password**: the password of the database administrator. The default value is **root123**. The password is used by the administrator to log in to the database. It is recommended to modify the this password before installing Harbor.
- **max_idle_conns**: the maximum number of idle connections between Harbor components and the database.
- **max_open_conns**: the maximum number of connections between Harbor components and the database. When this parameter is set to an integer less than 0, the number of connections is unlimited.

2.1.1.6 data_volume

This item is used to configure the local data storage of Harbor. The default location is the **/data** directory, which stores artifact files, database data and cache data.

Table 2.3 TLS self-signed certificate configuration details

Name	Description	CN
harbor_internal_ca.key	Private key of CA	Not required
harbor_internal_ca.crt	Certificate of CA	Not required
core.key	Private key of the Core component	Not required
core.crt	Certificate of the Core component	core
jobservice.key	Private key of the JobService component	Not required
jobservice.crt	Certificate of the JobService component	jobservice
proxy.key	Private key of the Proxy component	Not required
proxy.crt	Certificate of the Proxy component	proxy
portal.key	Private key of the Portal component	Not required
portal.crt	Certificate of the Portal component	portal
registry.key	Private key of the Registry component	Not required
registry.crt	Certificate of the Registry component	registry
registryctl.key	Private key of the Registryctl component	Not required
registryctl.crt	Certificate of the Registryctl component	registryctl
notary_server.key	Private key of the Notary Server component	Not required
notary_server.crt	Certificate of the Notary Server component	notary-server
notary_signer.key	Private key of the Notary Signer component	Not required
notary_signer.crt	Certificate of the Notary Signer component	notary-signer
trivy_adapter.key	Private key of the Trivy Adapter component	Not required
trivy_apapter.crt	Certificate of the Trivy Adapter component	trivy-adapter
clair.key	Private key of the Clair component	Not required
clair.crt	Certificate of the Clair component	clair
clair_adpater.key	Private key of the Clair Adapter component	Not required
clair_adatper.crt	Certificate of the Clair Adapter component	clair-adatper
chartmuseum.key	Private key of the ChartMuseum component	Not required
chartmuseum.crt	Certificate of the ChartMuseum component	chartmuseum

2.1.1.7 storage_service

This item is used to configure external storage. By default, Harbor uses local storage. To use external storage in Harbor, uncomment this section and provide values as follows.

- **ca_bundle**: specifies the path for storing CA. Harbor injects files in the path into the trust stores of all containers except for the log, database, redis and notary containers.
- The types of external storage include **filesystem**, **azure**, **gcs**, **s3**, **swift** and **oss**. The default value is **filesystem**.

When configuring the external storage, you need to specify one of the storage types, as listed in Table 2.4. If multiple storage types were specified, an error occurs during the startup of Harbor.

Table 2.4 Storage configuration details

Storage Type	Description
filesystem	Local storage is used. **Maxthreads** indicates the maximum number of concurrent file block operations allowed by the storage. The default value is **100** and the value cannot be smaller than **25**.
azure	Microsoft Azure storage is used. For details of the configuration, see the following file: **github.com/docker/docker.github.io/blob/master/registry/storage-drivers/azure.md**.
gcs	Google cloud storage is used. For details of the configuration, see the example below.
s3	Amazon S3 and storage compatible with S3 are used. For details of the configuration, see the following file: **github.com/docker/docker.github.io/blob/master/registry/storage-drivers/s3.md**.
swift	Openstack Swift object storage is used. For details of the configuration, see the following file: **github.com/docker/docker.github.io/blob/master/registry/storage-drivers/swift.md**.
oss	Aliyun OSS object storage is used. For details of the configuration, see the following file: **github.com/docker/docker.github.io/tree/master/registry/storage-drivers/oss.md**.

An example of using Google cloud storage is as follows:

```
storage_service:
  gcs:
   bucket: example
    keyfile:: /harbor/gcs/gcs_keyfile
   rootdirectory: harbor/example
   chunksize: 524880
```

Table 2.5 lists the attributes in the example.

2.1.1.8 clair

This item is used to configure the image scanning tool Clair. **Updaters_interval** indicates the interval (in hours) for Clair to retrieve the common vulnerabilities and exposures(CVE) data. When this parameter is set to **0**, the data retrieval is disabled. To ensure that vulnerability data can be updated in time, the data retrieval should be enabled.

Table 2.5 Google cloud storage configuration details

Attribute	Mandatory	Description
bucket	Yes	Name of the bucket used for Google cloud storage. It must be created in advance.
keyfile	No	The key file of a service account for Google cloud storage. It is in the JSON format.
rootdirectory	No	The root directory for storing artifact files. It must be created in advance.
chunksize	No (The default value is **524880**.)	It is used to specify the chunk size for uploading large files. The value must be a multiple of 256 × 1014.

2.1.1.9 trivy

This item is used to configure the image scanning tool Trivy.

- **ignore_unfixed**: The flag to determine whether unfixable vulnerabilities are ignored. The default value is **false**. If this parameter is **true**, only fixable vulnerabilities are listed in vulnerability scanning results.
- **skip_update**: The flag to enable or disable Trivy database downloading from GitHub. The default value is false. If the flag is enabled you have to download the trivy data archive manually, and then mount them in the path **/home/scanner/.cache/trivy/db**. You might want to enable this flag in a testing or CI/CD environment to avoid GitHub rate limiting issues.
- **insecure**: The flag to skip verifying the registry certificate. The default value is **false**. If the flag is enabled, Trivy does not check the certificate of the Core component when it pulls images.
- **github_token**: The access token used by Trivy to download data from data sources of GitHub. Anonymous downloads from GitHub are subject to the limit of 60 requests per hour. Generally, this limitation cannot satisfy the need of a production environment. If, for any reason, it's not enough, you could increase the rate limit to 5000 requests per hour by specifying the Github access token). It is recommended to configure this item in a production environment. For details on how to generate a GitHub token, see the following official documents: **help.github.com/en/github/authenticating-to-github/creating-a-personal-access-token-for-the-command-line**.

2.1.1.10 jobservice

This item is used to configure the JobService component. **Max_job_workers** indicates the maximum number of job execution units. The default value is **10**.

2.1.1.11 notification

This item is used to configure event notification. **Webhook_job_max_retry** indicates the maximum number of retries for a failuare of event notification. The default value is **10**.

2.1.1.12 chart

This item is used to configure the ChartMuseum component. **Absolute_url** indicates whether or not the URL in **index.yaml** of the chart obtained by the client is an absolute path. When this item is not configured, the ChartMuseum component returns a relative path.

2.1.1.13 log

This item is used to configure logs.

- **level**: The log level. Supported log levels include Debug, Error, Warning and Info. The default value is **Info**.
- **local**: The local log configuration.
  - **rotate_count**: the maximum number of rotations before a log file is deleted. When this item is **0**, the rotation is disabled. The default value is **50**.
  - **rotate_size**: the rotation size of a log file. When the size of a log file exceeds the this value, the log file will be rotated. The default value is **200 MB**.
  - **location**: local path for storing log files.
- **external_endpoint**: the external syslog configuration. To enable the configuration, uncomment this section.
  - **protocol**: the protocol of the external log transmission. UDP and TCP are supported. The default value is **TCP**.
  - **host**: the hostname or the IP address of the external log service.
  - **port**: the port number of the external log service.

2.1.1.14 external_database

This item is used to configure the external database. To enable the configuration, remove the comment. Moreover, you must manually create an empty database for Harbor. For details, see the section of high-availability solution of Harbor. Note: Harbor 2.0.0 supports only the PostgreSQL database.

- **harbor**: the database configuration of Harbor.
  - **host**: the hostname or the IP address of the database.
  - **port**: the port number of the database.
  - **db_name**: the database name.
  - **username**: the user name of the database administrator.
  - **password**: the password of the database administrator.
  - **ssl_mode**: the security mode.
  - **max_idle_conns**: the maximum number of idle connections between Harbor components and the database.
  - **max_open_conns**: the maximum number of connections between Harbor components and the database. When this item is an integer less than 0, the number of connections is unlimited.
- **clair**: database configuration of Clair.
  - **host**: the hostname or IP address of the database.
  - **port**: the port number of the database.
  - **db_name**: the database name.
  - **username**: the user name of the database administrator.
  - **password**: the password of the database administrator.
  - **ssl_mode**: the security mode.
- **notarysigner**: database configuration of Notary Signer.
  - **host**: the hostname or IP address of the database.
  - **port**: the port number of the database.
  - **db_name**: the database name.
  - **username**: the user name of the database administrator.
  - **password**: the password of the database administrator.
  - **ssl_mode**: the security mode.
- **notaryserver**: database configuration of Notary Server.
  - **host**: the hostname or IP address of the database.
  - **port**: the port number of the database.
  - **db_name**: the database name.
  - **username**: the user name of the database administrator.
  - **password**: the password of the database administrator.
  - **ssl_mode**: the security mode.

2.1.1.15 external_redis

This item is used to configure the external Redis service. To enable the configuration, remove the comment. Note: The data index cannot be set to 0 because it is exclusively used by the Core component of Harbor.

- **host**: the hostname or IP address of the external Redis.
- **port**: the port number of the external Redis.

- **password**: the access password of the external Redis.
- **registry_db_index**: the data index value of the Registry component.
- **jobservice_db_index**: the data index value of the JobService component.
- **chartmuseum_db_index**: the data index value of the ChartMuseum component.
- **clair_db_index**: the data index value of the Clair component.
- **trivy_db_index**: the data index value of the Trivy component.
- **idle_timeout_seconds**: the timeout interval of idle connections. When this item is set to **0**, idle connections will not be closed.

2.1.1.16 uaa

This item is used to configure UAA. **Ca_file** indicates the path where self-signed certificates of the UAA server are stored.

2.1.1.17 proxy

This item is used to configure the reverse proxy. When Harbor runs in an Intranet environment, a reverse proxy can be used to access the Internet (i.e., the external network). Note: The proxy configuration does not affect the communication between Harbor components.

- **proxy**: the network proxy service address. Where, **http_proxy** indicates the network service address of an HTTP proxy and **https_proxy** indicates the network service address of an HTTPS proxy.
- **no_proxy**: the domain name that does not need to go through the network proxy service. Harbor components automatically add in their own no_proxy rules. Therefore, users only configure their own services. For example, when Harbor needs to replicate artifacts from another registry service in the same Intranet environment, it does not need the proxy service. The hostname or IP address of this internal registry service can be added to this item.
- **components**: By default, the proxy service configuration is applied for the Core, JobService, Clair and Trivy components. To disable the proxy service of a component, remove the component from the list. Note: For the artifact replication to make use of the proxy service, the Core and JobService components must be included in the list.

2.1.2 Offline Installation

First of all, obtain the offline installation package of Harbor. You can download the offline installation package from the official release website of Harbor: **github.com/goharbor/harbor/releases**, as shown in Fig. 2.1. Note: RC releases or pre-releases

▾ Assets 7

harbor-offline-installer-v2.0.0.tgz	478 MB
harbor-offline-installer-v2.0.0.tgz.asc	819 Bytes
harbor-online-installer-v2.0.0.tgz	9.12 KB
harbor-online-installer-v2.0.0.tgz.asc	819 Bytes
md5sum	286 Bytes
Source code (zip)	
Source code (tar.gz)	

Fig. 2.1 Github release assets download page of Harbor installer

are not suitable for production environment. They are used only in the test environment.

The release page of Harbor provides the offline and online installation files.

- **harbor-offline-installer-v2.0.0.tgz**: the offline installation package. It contains all image files and configuration files prebuilt by Harbor.
- **harbor-offline-installer-v2.0.0.tgz.asc**: the signature file of the offline installation package. Through this file, you can validate whether the offline installation package is officially signed and verified.
- **md5sum**: the file contains the md5 values of the above two files. Through this value, you can validate the downloaded files.

Next, pick a version, download and decompress the offline installation package:

```
$ curl https://github.com/goharbor/harbor/releases/download/
v2.0.0/harbor-offline-installer-v2.0.0.tgz
$ tar -zvxf ./harbor-offline-installer-v2.0.0.tgz
```

After the offline installation package is decompressed, the following files are in the **harbor** folder.

- **LICENSE**: the license file.
- **common.sh**: the tool script used by the installation script.
- **harbor.v2.0.0.tar.gz**: the compressed image file of functional components.
- **harbor.yml.tmpl**: the template for the configuration file. After this file is configured, remove the suffix "tmpl" from the file name or copy it to a new file **harbor.yml**.
- **install.sh**: the installation script.
- **prepare**: the preparation script. It injects the configuration specified in **harbor.yml** into the actual configuration files of each component.

Finally, complete the configuration by following Sect. 2.1.1 and run the installation script **install.sh** to start the installation. The flow of the installation script is roughly as follows:

1. Environment check. Mainly to check the versions of Docker and docker-compose on the local machine.
2. Offline image files are loaded into Docker local image repository.
3. The configuration files and the **docker-compose.yml** file are generated.
4. Containers of all Harbor components are launched through docker-compose.

The installation script supports the optional Harbor components. Except core components, other functional components can be specified through parameters. When the following parameters are used, corresponding components are installed. Otherwise, the components are not installed.

- **--with-notary**: Install the image signature component Notary, which includes Notary Server and Notary Signer. If Notary is installed, the network protocol of Harbor must be set to HTTPS.
- **--with-clair**: Install the image scanning component Clair.
- **--with-trivy**: Install the image scanning component Trivy.
- **--with-chartmuseum**: Install the chart file management component ChartMuseum.

After the installation is complete, log in to Harbor admin console or push an image via Docker client to determine whether the components have been successfully installed. For more details, see Sect. 2.5.

2.1.3 Online Installation

Different from the offline installation, the online installation requires the host to install Harbor with network connection to Docker Hub. This is because the prebuilt Harbor images need to be pulled from Docker Hub during the installation.

First of all, obtain the online installation package of Harbor. You can obtain the online installation package from the official release website of Harbor: **github.com/goharbor/harbor/releases**, as shown in Fig. 2.2. Note: RC releases or pre-releases are not suitable for production environment. They are used only in the test environment.

The release page of Harbor provides the online installation file.

- **harbor-online-installer-v2.0.0.tgz**: the online installation package. It contains the prest installation script, configuration file template and license file.
- **harbor-online-installer-v2.0.0.tgz.asc**: the signature file of the offline installation package. Through this file, you can validate whether the offline installation package is officially signed and verified.
- **md5sum**: the file contains the md5 values of the above two files. Through this value, you can validate the downloaded files.
- Next, select a version, download and decompress the online installation package:

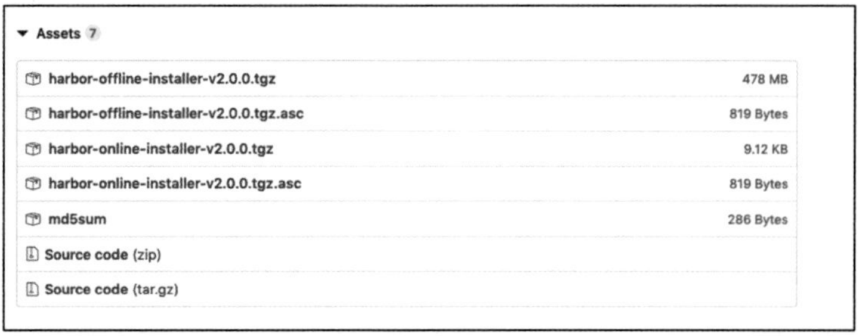

Assets 7	
harbor-offline-installer-v2.0.0.tgz	478 MB
harbor-offline-installer-v2.0.0.tgz.asc	819 Bytes
harbor-online-installer-v2.0.0.tgz	9.12 KB
harbor-online-installer-v2.0.0.tgz.asc	819 Bytes
md5sum	286 Bytes
Source code (zip)	
Source code (tar.gz)	

Fig. 2.2 Github release assets download page of Harbor installer

```
$ curl https://github.com/goharbor/harbor/releases/download/
v2.0.0/harbor-online-installer-v2.0.0.tgz
$ tar -zvxf ./harbor-online-installer-v2.0.0.tgz
```

After the online installation package is decompressed, you can see the following files:

- **LICENSE**: the license file.
- **common.sh**: the tool script for the installation script.
- **harbor.yml.tmpl**: the template for configuration files.
- **install.sh**: the installation script.
- **prepare**: the preparation script. It injects the configuration specified in **harbor.yml** into the actual configuration files of each component.

Run the installation command. For details, see Sect. 2.1.2.

2.1.4 Source Code Installation

Harbor's source code written in Go programming language can be compiled and built into containers for the installation. In most cases, users do not need to build from the source code in order to install Harbor. However, developers who want to customize or extend Harbor's functions find it necessary to understand the source code and the build process. This section explains the installation process based on the source code of Harbor 2.0.0.

Before the installation, make sure Docker and docker-compose are installed locally and the host can connect to the Internet.

The source code compilation and installation process of Harbor is roughly as follows:

1. The source code is downloaded.
2. The configuration file of the source code is modified.
3. The **make** command is executed.

First download the source code. Execute the following command to obtain the source code of Harbor 2.0.0:

```
$ git clone -b v2.0.0 https://github.com/goharbor/harbor.git
```

Then modify the configuration file of the source code by referring to Sect. 2.1.2.

Next, run the **make** command in the root directory of the source code. The **make** command includes the following subcommands. This section explains how to install Harbor based on Go source code.

- **compile**: Compiles the source code of Harbor components through the Go image to generate binary files.
- **build**: Builds images of all components based on the binary files. Dockerfiles of all functional components are in the **./make/photon** folder. For details about the build process of each component, refer to the Dockerfiles.
- **prepare**: Generates configuration of each component based on **harbor.yml** .
- **install**: The source code installation command. It includes the **compile**, **build** and **prepare** commands and starts all functional components through docker-compose.
- **package_online**: Generates the online installation package of Harbor.
- **package_offline**: Generates the offline installation package of Harbor.

The overall execution process of the **make install** command is as follows: First compile the source code into binaries through a Go compiling image, which include the components such as Core, Registryctl and JobService; then build component images with the binaries and base images of the components; then parse the configuration file and generate the **docker-compose** file based on the template; finally, start Harbor through the command **docker-compose**.

Parameters in the **make install** command are as follows:

- **CLAIRFLAG**: The default value is **false**. When this flag is enabled, an image of Clair is built so that image scanning can be enabled after Harbor is started.
- **TRIVYFLAG**: The default value is **false**. When this flag is enabled, an image of Trivy is built so that image scanning can be enabled after Harbor is started.
- **NOTARYFLAG**: The default value is **false**. When this flag is enabled, images of Notary Signer and Notary Server are built so that Notary can be enabled after Harbor is started. Here, the network protocol of **harbor.yaml** must be set to HTTPS.
- **CHARTFLAG**: The default value is **false**. When this flag is enabled, an image of ChartMuseum is built so that the ChartMuseum can be enabled after Harbor is started.

- **NPM_REGISTRY**: The default value is the official registry address of NPM. If the official registry of NPM cannot be accessed when the image of Harbor portal is built, or the user has specific requirements, the registry address can be specified through this parameter.
- **VERSIONTAG**: The default value is **dev**. This parameter specifies the tag name of each component image.
- **PKGVERSIONTAG**: The default value is **dev**. This parameter specifies the version of the online or offline installation package.

The **make build** command builds images of components according to the Dockerfile of each components. For example, the Dockerfile of the Core component is stored in the **./make/photon/core** directory. The location of other component is similar. The build process is as follows:

1. Build the base image of Harbor. To ensure that the same code can always create the same image, a fixed base image is used. For details on how to build the base image, see the **Dockerfile.base** file in the same directory.

```
ARG harbor_base_image_version
FROM goharbor/harbor-core-base:${harbor_base_image_version}
```

2. Copy the compiled binary file and the corresponding script, and set the permission and the entrypoint of the image.

```
HEALTHCHECK CMD curl --fail -s http://127.0.0.1:8080/api/v2.0/
ping || curl -k --fail -s https://127.0.0.1:8443/api/v2.0/ping
|| exit 1
COPY ./make/photon/common/install_cert.sh /harbor/
COPY ./make/photon/core/entrypoint.sh /harbor/
COPY ./make/photon/core/harbor_core /harbor/
COPY ./src/core/views /harbor/views
COPY ./make/migrations /harbor/migrations
RUN chown -R harbor:harbor /etc/pki/tls/certs \
  && chown harbor:harbor /harbor/entrypoint.sh && chmod u+x /
harbor/entrypoint.sh \
  && chown harbor:harbor /harbor/install_cert.sh && chmod u+x /
harbor/install_cert.sh \
  && chown harbor:harbor /harbor/harbor_core && chmod u+x /
harbor/harbor_core
WORKDIR /harbor/
USER harbor
ENTRYPOINT ["/harbor/entrypoint.sh"]
COPY make/photon/prepare/versions /harbor/
```

Note: Among all Harbor components, except the Log component that uses the root user, other components use non-root users.

```
CONTAINER ID        IMAGE                                   COMMAND                  CREATED          STATUS                    PORTS
                                  NAMES
ef08c03e76c0        goharbor/nginx-photon:v2.0.0            "nginx -g 'daemon of…"   2 minutes ago    Up 2 minutes (healthy)    0.0.0.0:4443->4443/tcp, 0.0.0.0:8
0->8080/tcp, 0.0.0.0:443->8443/tcp   nginx
fb99fd0a6394        goharbor/harbor-jobservice:v2.0.0       "/harbor/entrypoint.…"   2 minutes ago    Up 2 minutes (healthy)
                                  harbor-jobservice
e689c1a70e90        goharbor/clair-adapter-photon:v2.0.0    "/home/clair-adapter…"   3 minutes ago    Up 2 minutes (healthy)    8080/tcp
                                  clair-adapter
7323a9c871aa        goharbor/harbor-core:v2.0.0             "/harbor/entrypoint.…"   3 minutes ago    Up 2 minutes (healthy)
                                  harbor-core
d20a6bed488e        goharbor/notary-server-photon:v2.0.0    "/bin/sh -c 'migrate…"   3 minutes ago    Up 3 minutes
                                  notary-server
4b182e094d25        goharbor/notary-signer-photon:v2.0.0    "/bin/sh -c 'migrate…"   3 minutes ago    Up 3 minutes
                                  notary-signer
c7ad5275c450        goharbor/clair-photon:v2.0.0            "./docker-entrypoint…"   3 minutes ago    Up 3 minutes (healthy)    6060-6061/tcp
                                  clair
a007a342ea6c        goharbor/harbor-portal:v2.0.0           "nginx -g 'daemon of…"   3 minutes ago    Up 3 minutes (healthy)    8080/tcp
                                  harbor-portal
8cd5cd27d904        goharbor/registry-photon:v2.0.0         "/home/harbor/entryp…"   3 minutes ago    Up 3 minutes (healthy)    5000/tcp
                                  registry
a21752846526        goharbor/harbor-registryctl:v2.0.0      "/home/harbor/start.…"   3 minutes ago    Up 3 minutes (healthy)
                                  registryctl
c50a4cbf3814        goharbor/chartmuseum-photon:v2.0.0      "./docker-entrypoint…"   3 minutes ago    Up 3 minutes (healthy)    9999/tcp
                                  chartmuseum
330ba681758d        goharbor/redis-photon:v2.0.0            "redis-server /etc/r…"   3 minutes ago    Up 3 minutes (healthy)    6379/tcp
                                  redis
73894d4a2b0b        goharbor/harbor-db:v2.0.0               "/docker-entrypoint.…"   3 minutes ago    Up 3 minutes (healthy)    5432/tcp
                                  harbor-db
602ad13955c3        goharbor/harbor-log:v2.0.0              "/bin/sh -c /usr/loc…"   3 minutes ago    Up 3 minutes (healthy)    127.0.0.1:1514->10514/tcp
                                  harbor-log
```

Fig. 2.3 The running status of the containers built from the source code

Table 2.6 Post-Installation requirement of Harbor helm chart

Software	Version	Description
Kubernetes	Version 1.10 or later	See the official installation document.
Helm	Version 2.8.0 or later	See the official installation document.

3. After the **make install** command is successfully executed, Harbor is installed properly. Execute the **docker ps** command to check the status of each component, as shown in Fig. 2.3.

2.2 Installing Harbor Through Helm Chart

Section 2.1 describes how to install Harbor in the stand-alone environment. When running Harbor in a multi-node environment or in the production, you may need to deploy Harbor in a Kubernetes cluster. For this purpose, Harbor provides Helm Chart to help users deploy Harbor on Kubernetes.

This section describes how to deploy Harbor to a Kubernetes cluster by using Helm Chart.

Before Harbor is installed on Kubernetes based on Helm Chart, the hosts where Harbor will be installed must meet the requirements listed in Table 2.6.

2.2.1 Obtaining Helm Chart

Before the installation, execute the following command to add the Helm Chart repository:

```
$ helm repo add harbor https://helm.goharbor.io
```

The official releases of the Harbor Helm Chart can be found in the directory of **github.com/goharbor/harbor-helm/releases**, as shown in Fig. 2.4. Note: it is not recommended to directly download the release from GitHub. Rather, the release should be downloaded via Helm.

2.2.2 Configuring Helm Chart

This section explains in detail how to configure Helm Chart. The configuration introduced below can be specified through the **--set** command during installation or specified through the **values.yaml** file.

If you hope to complete installation by modifying minimal Helm Chart settings, you can focus on the following three configuration items.

2.2.2.1 Configuring the Service Exposure Mode

Harbor Helm-Chart supports four service exposure modes including Ingress, ClusterIP, NodePort and LoadBalancer. If Harbor is used within a Kubernetes cluster, the ClusterIP mode can be configured. If Harbor is to service requests external to the Kubernetes cluster, Ingress, NodePort or LoadBalancer can be selected.

The access exposure mode can be specified by the value of **expose.type**.

- **Ingress**: The Kubernetes cluster must install the Ingress controller. Note: If TLS is not enabled, the port number must be added to the command when images are being pushed or pulled. For the specific reason, see the following page: github.com/goharbor/harbor/issues/5291.

Fig. 2.4 Github release assets download page of Harbor helm chart

- **ClusterIP**: The Harbor service is exposed on an internal IP address in the cluster. This mode supports the scenario where Harbor is used within the same Kubernetes cluster.
- **NodePort**: The Harbor service is exposed on the IP address of each node and the same static port. When a request is coming from outside the cluster, a NodePort service can be accessed by requesting NodeIP:NodePort.
- **LoadBalancer**: The load balancer of a cloud service provider can be used to expose the Harbor service.

2.2.2.2 Configuring an External Address

The external address refers to the IP address or the hostname used by clients to access Harbor. It is also displayed on the Harbor management page for the **docker** and **helm** commands. During the interaction between Harbor and a Docker client or a Helm client, the external address is used in the address of the token service.

The external address can be specified by the value of **externalURL** in the format of "protocol://domain[:port]". The domain portion of the format may differ depending on the access mode.

- **Ingress**: When the access mode is Ingress, the domain should be the same as the value of **expose.ingress.hosts.core**.
- **ClusterIP**: When the access mode is ClusterIP, the domain should be the same as the value of **expose.clusterIP.name**.
- **NodePort**: When the access mode is NodePort, the domain should be set to the IP address and the port number of a Kubernetes, e.g. node_IP_address:port number.
- **LoadBalancer**: When the access mode is LoadBalancer, the domain should the same as the public domain name of the user. In addition, a CNAME record of the DNS should be added to correctly resolve the public domain name to the cloud service provider's load balancer.

If Harbor is deployed behind a load balancer or a reverse proxy, the external address must be set to the access address of the load balancer or the reverse proxy.

2.2.2.3 Configuring Data Persistence

Harbor Helm Chart supports the following storage modes:

- **Disable**: Disables the persistent data. In this mode, the data is ephemeral and does not survive the termination of a pod. It is not recommended that persistent data be disabled in a production environment.
- **Persistent Volume Claim**: During the deployment of Harbor on a Kubernetes cluster, a default StorageClass is required, which is used to dynamically provision the storage for PersistentVolumeClaims that do not have a storage class. If a non-default StorageClass needs to be used, specify the value of storageClass in

the configuration of the corresponding component. If an existing persistent volume needs to be used, specify the value of existingClaim under the configuration of the corresponding component.
- **External Storage**: External storage can store only images and Chart files. Supported external storage types include azure, gsc, s3, swift and oss.

The following tables describe the detailed configuration of each item.

- Table 2.7 shows the configuration of the service exposure mode.
- Table 2.8 describes the configuration of TLS.
- Table 2.9 describes the configuration of storage.
- Table 2.10 describes the general configuration.
- Table 2.11 describes the configuration of the Nginx component. Note: If the access mode is Ingress, the Nginx component does not need to be configured.
- Table 2.12 describes the configuration of the Portal component.
- Table 2.13 describes the configuration of the Core component.
- Table 2.14 describes the configuration of the JobService component.
- Table 2.15 lists the configuration of the Registry component.
- Table 2.16 describes the configuration of the ChartMuseum component.
- Table 2.17 describes the configuration of the Clair component.
- Table 2.18 describes the configuration of the Trivy component.
- Table 2.19 describes the configuration of the Notary component.
- Table 2.20 describes the configuration of the database.
- Table 2.21 describes the configuration of the Redis component.

2.2.3 *Installing Helm Chart*

After configuring the Chart, install Harbor Helm Chart by the following command, in which **my-release** is the deployment name.

- Helm 2:

```
$ helm install --name my-release harbor/harbor
```

- Helm 3:

```
$ helm install my-release harbor/harbor
```

Table 2.7 The configuration of service exposure mode in detail

Parameter	Description	Default Value
expose.type	Helm-Chart supports the following service exposure modes: **ingress**, **clusterIP**, **nodePort** and **loadBalancer**.	ingress
expose.tls.enable	Whether TLS is enabled.	true (enabled)
expose.ingress.controller	Ingress controller type. The current version supports the following values: **default**, **gce** and **ncp**.	default
expose.tls.secretName	Secret name of the user's own TLS certificate.	
expose.tls.notarySecretName	By default, the Notary service uses the same certificate and private key as specified by **expose.tls.secretName**. To use other certificate and private key, this item must be configured. Note: This item is valid only when **expose.type** is **ingress**.	
expose.tls.commonName	This item is used to generate a certificate. When **expose.type** is set to **clusterIP** or **nodePort** and the value of **expose.tls.secretName** is null, this item is mandatory.	
expose.ingress.hosts.core	Host name of the Harbor Core service in the Ingress rule.	core.harbor.domain
expose.ingress.hosts.notary	Host name of the Harbor Notary service in the Ingress rule.	notary.harbor.domain
expose.ingress.annotations	Annotations used by Ingress.	
expose.clusterIP.name	Name of the ClusterIP service.	harbor
expose.clusterIP.ports.httpPort	In ClusterIP mode, the port listened on by Harbor's HTTP service.	80
expose.clusterIP.ports.httpsPort	In ClusterIP mode, the port listened on by Harbor's HTTPS service.	443
expose.clusterIP.ports.notaryPort	In ClusterIP mode, the port listened on by Harbor's Notary service.	4443
expose.nodePort.name	Name of the NodePort service.	harbor
expose.nodePort.ports.http.port	In NodePoart mode, the service port listened on by Harbor when using the HTTP protocol.	80
expose.nodePort.ports.http.nodePort	In NodePoart mode, the node port listened on by Harbor when using the HTTP protocol.	30002
expose.nodePort.ports.https.port	In NodePoart mode, the service port listened on by Harbor when using the HTTPS protocol.	443
expose.nodePort.ports.https.nodePort	In NodePoart mode, the node port listened on by Harbor when using the HTTPS protocol.	30003
expose.nodePort.ports.notary.port	In NodePoart mode, the notary service port listened on by Harbor when using the HTTPS protocol. This item is valid only when **notary.enabled** is set to **true**.	4443
expose.nodePort.ports.notary.nodePort	In NodePoart mode, the notary node port listened on by Harbor when using the HTTPS protocol.	30004

(continued)

Table 2.7 (continued)

Parameter	Description	Default Value
expose.loadBalancer.name	Name of the LoadBalancer service.	harbor
expose.loadBalancer.IP	IP address of the LoadBalancer service. The configuration of this item is valid only when LoadBalancer supports IP address assignment.	""
expose.loadBalancer.ports.httpPort	In LoadBalancer mode, the service port listened on by Harbor when using the HTTP protocol.	80
expose.loadBalancer.ports.httpsPort	In LoadBalancer mode, the service port listened on by Harbor when using the HTTPS protocol.	30002
expose.loadBalancer.ports.notaryPort	In LoadBalancer mode, the notary service port listened on by Harbor when using the HTTPS protocol. This item is valid only when **notary.enabled** is set to **true**.	4443
expose.loadBalancer.annotations	Annotations used by LoadBalancer.	{}
expose.loadBalancer.sourceRanges	Range of the source IP addresses assigned to LoadBalancer.	[]

To uninstall Harbor Helm Chart by using the following command, in which **my-release** is the deployment name.

- Helm 2:

```
$ helm delete --purge my-release
```

- Helm 3:

```
$ helm uninstall my-release
```

2.3 High-availability Solution

As Harbor is increasingly deployed in the production environment, the high availability of Harbor has become a hot spot for users. In some large and medium-sized enterprises, if only a single-instance Harbor service is established, the pipeline from the development to the delivery may be forced to stop once a failure of Harbor occurs. Therefore, a single-instance Harbor can hardly satisfy the high availability requirements of enterprises.

Table 2.8 The configuration of TLS in detail

Parameter	Description	Default Value
internalTLS.enabled	TLS communication between components is enabled, including chartMuseum, clair, core, jobservice, portal, registry and trivy.	false
internalTLS.certSource	Method for generating a certificate when TLS is enabled. Available methods include **auto**, **manual** and **secret**.	auto
internalTLS.trustCa	The certificate authority (CA) is valid only when **certSource** is **manual**. The certificates of all internal components must be issued by the CA.	
internalTLS.core.secretName	Secret name of the Core component. This item is valid only when **certSource** is **secret**. The secret must include the following three items (the explanations of the three items are the same for subsequent configuration items): • **ca.crt**: the trusted CA. The certificates of all internal components must be issued by this CA. • **tls.crt**: the content of a TLS certificate file. • **tls.key**: the content of a TLS private key file.	
internalTLS.core.crt	Content of a TLS certificate file of the Core component. This item is valid only when **certSource** is set to **manual**.	
internalTLS.core.key	Content of a TLS private key file of the Core component. This item is valid only when **certSource** is set to **manual**.	
internalTLS.jobservice.secretName	Secret name of the JobService component. This item is valid only when **certSource** is set to **secret**. The secret must include the following three items: **ca.crt**, **tls.crt** and **tls.key**.	
internalTLS.jobservice.crt	Content of a TLS certificate file of the JobService component. This item is valid only when **certSource** is set to **manual**.	
internalTLS.jobservice.key	Content of a TLS private key file of the JobService component. This item is valid only when **certSource** is set to **manual**.	
internalTLS.registry.secretName	Secret name of the Registry component. This item is valid only when **certSource** is set to **secret**. The secret must include the following three items: **ca.crt**, **tls.crt** and **tls.key**.	
internalTLS.registry.crt	Content of a TLS certificate file of the Registry component. This item is valid only when **certSource** is set to **manual**.	
internalTLS.registry.key	Content of a TLS private key file of the Registry component. This item is valid only when **certSource** is set to **manual**.	
internalTLS.portal.secretName	Secret name of the Portal component. This item is valid only when **certSource** is set to **secret**. The secret must include the following three items: **ca.crt**, **tls.crt** and **tls.key**.	
internalTLS.portal.crt	Content of a TLS certificate file of the Portal component. This item is valid only when **certSource** is set to **manual**.	

(continued)

Table 2.8 (continued)

Parameter	Description	Default Value
internalTLS.portal.key	Content of a TLS private key file of the Portal component. This item is valid only when **certSource** is set to **manual**.	
internalTLS. chartmuseum. secretName	Secret name of the ChartMuseum component. This item is valid only when **certSource** is set to **secret**. The secret must include the following three items: **ca.crt**, **tls.crt** and **tls.key**.	
internalTLS. chartmuseum.crt	Content of a TLS certificate file of the ChartMuseum component. This item is valid only when **certSource** is set to **manual**.	
internalTLS. chartmuseum.key	Content of a TLS private key file of the ChartMuseum component. This item is valid only when **certSource** is set to **manual**.	
internalTLS.clair. secretName	Secret name of the Clair component. This item is valid only when **certSource** is set to **secret**. The secret must include the following three items: **ca.crt**, **tls.crt** and **tls.key**.	
internalTLS.clair.crt	Content of a TLS certificate file of the Clair component. This item is valid only when **certSource** is set to **manual**.	
internalTLS.clair.key	Content of a TLS private key file of the Clair component. This item is valid only when **certSource** is set to **manual**.	
internalTLS.trivy. secretName	Secret name of the Trivy component. This item is valid only when **certSource** is set to **secret**. The secret must include the following three items: **ca.crt**, **tls.crt** and **tls.key**.	
internalTLS.trivy.crt	Content of a TLS certificate file of the Trivy component. This item is valid only when **certSource** is set to **manual**.	
internalTLS.trivy.key	Content of a TLS private key file of the Trivy component. This item is valid only when **certSource** is set to **manual**.	

This section discusses the high-availability solutions based on different installation packages of Harbor, aiming to remove the single point of failure to achieve the high availability of the system. The high-availability solution based on Harbor Helm Chart is an officially validated solution and the solutions based on multiple Kubernetes clusters and the offline installation package are for reference.

2.3.1 High-availability Solution Based on Harbor Helm Chart

The Kubernetes platform has the self-healing capability. When a container crashes or does not respond, the container can be automatically restarted. When necessary, the container can be rescheduled to a normal node from the failed node. This solution deploys Harbor Helm Chart to a Kubernetes cluster through Helm to ensure that each

Table 2.9 The configuration of Storage in detail

Parameter	Description	Default Value
persistence.enabled	Whether data persistence is enabled.	true
persistence.resourcePolicy	This item must be set to **keep** to prevent persistent volumes from being removed when the Helm delete operation is performed.	keep
persistence. persistentVolumeClaim.registry.existingClaim	If the Registry component uses an existing persistent volume, make sure that the persistent volume has been successfully created before binding. In addition, if the persistent volume is shared with other components, please specify the item **persistence.persistentVolumeClaim.registry.subPath**.	
persistence. persistentVolumeClaim.registry.storageClass	Specifies the storageClass when a volume is allocated to the Registry component. If no storageClass is specified, the default value is used here. If the dynamic allocation must be disabled, the value can be set to "-".	
persistence. persistentVolumeClaim.registry.subPath	Subpath used by the persistent volume of the Registry component.	
persistence. persistentVolumeClaim.registry.accessMode	Access mode used by the persistent volume of the Registry component.	
persistence. persistentVolumeClaim.registry.size	Size of the persistent volume of the Registry component.	
persistence. persistentVolumeClaim. chartmuseum.existingClaim	If the ChartMuseum component uses an existing persistent volume, make sure that the persistent volume has been successfully created before binding. In addition, if the persistent volume is shared with other components, specify the item: **persistence.persistentVolumeClaim.registry. subPath**.	
persistence. persistentVolumeClaim. chartmuseum.storageClass	Specifies the storageClass when a volume is allocated to the ChartMuseum component. If no storageClass is specified, the default value is used here. If the dynamic allocation must be disabled, the value can be set to "-".	
persistence. persistentVolumeClaim. chartmuseum.subPath	Subpath used by the persistent volume of the ChartMuseum component.	
persistence. persistentVolumeClaim. chartmuseum.accessMode	Access mode used by the persistent volume of the ChartMuseum component.	
persistence. persistentVolumeClaim. chartmuseum.size	Size of the persistent volume of the ChartMuseum component.	

(continued)

Table 2.9 (continued)

Parameter	Description	Default Value
persistence. persistentVolumeClaim. jobservice.existingClaim	If the JobService component uses an existing persistent volume, make sure that the persistent volume has been successfully created before binding. In addition, if the persistent volume is shared with other components, specify the configuration item **persistence. persistentVolumeClaim.registry.subPath**.	
persistence. persistentVolumeClaim. jobservice.storageClass	Specifies the storageClass when a volume is allocated to the JobService component. If no storageClass is specified, the default value is used here. If the dynamic allocation must be disabled, the value can be set to "-".	
persistence. persistentVolumeClaim. jobservice.subPath	Subpath used by the persistent volume of the JobService component.	
persistence. persistentVolumeClaim. jobservice.accessMode	Access mode used by the persistent volume of the JobService component.	
persistence. persistentVolumeClaim. jobservice.size	Size of the persistent volume of the JobService component.	
persistence. persistentVolumeClaim.database.storageClass		
persistence. persistentVolumeClaim.database.storageClass	Specifies the storageClass when a volume is allocated to the Database component. If no storageClass is specified, the default value is used here. If the dynamic allocation must be disabled, the value can be set to "-".	
persistence. persistentVolumeClaim.database.subPath	Subpath used by the persistent volume of the database.	
persistence. persistentVolumeClaim.database.accessMode	Access mode used by the persistent volume of the database.	
persistence. persistentVolumeClaim.database.size	Size of the persistent volume of the database.	
persistence. persistentVolumeClaim.redis. storageClass	Specifies the storageClass when a volume is allocated to the Redis component. If no storageClass is specified, the default value is used here. If the dynamic allocation must be disabled, the value can be set to "-".	

(continued)

Table 2.9 (continued)

Parameter	Description	Default Value
persistence. persistentVolumeClaim.redis. subPath	Subpath used by the persistent volume of the Redis component.	
persistence. persistentVolumeClaim.redis. accessMode	Access mode used by the persistent volume of the Redis component.	
persistence. persistentVolumeClaim.redis. size	Size of the persistent volume of the Redis component.	
persistence.imageChartStorage. disableredirect	Whether storage redirection is disabled. If the storage service does not support redirection, for example, minio and s3, this item must be **true**. For the configuration of redirection, see official documents of Docker Distribution.	false
persistence.imageChartStorage. caBundleSecretName	If the storage service uses a certificate, configure this item. The secret must include the key value of **ca.crt**. This key value will be injected into the trust stores of the Registry and ChartMuseum components.	
persistence.imageChartStorage. type	Artifact storage type, including **filesystem**, **azure**, **gcs**, **s3**, **swift** and **oss**. If the Registry and ChartMuseum components need to use persistent volumes, this item must be set to **filesystem**. For the configuration of other storage types, see official documents of Docker Distribution.	filesystem

Harbor component has multiple replicas running in the Kubernetes cluster. When a Harbor container becomes unavailable, the Harbor service can still be used properly.

2.3.1.1 Basic Requirements for the Installation of Harbor

Before Harbor is installed, make sure that the basic requirements listed in Table 2.22 are met.

2.3.1.2 High-availability Architecture

Most components of Harbor are stateless to achieve high availability in a Kubernetes cluster. The status of stateful components is stored in shared storage instead of memory. In this way, the Harbor service on a Kubernetes cluster only needs to

Table 2.10 The general configuration in detail

Parameter	Description	Default Value
externalURL	External address of the Harbor Core component.	https://core.harbor.domain
uaaSecretName	When the self-signed external UAA authentication service is used, set this item to the secret name of Kubernetes. The secret must include a **key:ca.crt**, which include the content of the self-signed certificate.	
imagePullPolicy	Image pull policy: **IfNotPresent** or **Always**.	IfNotPresent
imagePullSecrets	Name of imagePullSecrets used when an image is being pulled.	
updateStragety.type	Policy for updating persistent volumes of the JobService, Registry and ChartMuseum components, including **RollingUpdat**e and **Recreate**. When persistent volumes do not support RWM, this item must be set to **Recreate**.	RollingUpdate
logLevel	Log level: **debug**, **info**, **warning**, **error** and **fatal**.	info
harborAdminPassword	Initial password of the Harbor administrator. It is recommended to log in to Harbor and change the initial password after deploying Harbor.	Harbor12345
secretkey	This item is the key used to encrypt the password of the Registry component. The value is a string of 16 characters. When the user uses the remote replication function, the password must be entered for the creation of a Registry endpoint. This item is used to encrypt the password. It is recommended to modify this item to a non-default value.	not-a-secure-key
proxy.httpProxy	Address of the HTTP proxy server.	
proxy.httpsProxy	Address of the HTTPS proxy server.	
proxy.noProxy	Domains or IP addresses that do not need to go through the proxy server.	127.0.0.1, localhost, .local and .internal
proxy.components	List of components served by the proxy server.	core, jobservice and clair

configure the number of replicas of components to achieve high availability based on the Kubernetes platform.

- The Kubernetes platform ensures all components of Harbor to maintain the expected number of replicas through the reconciliation loop, so as to achieve the high availability of services.
- The PostgreSQL and Redis clusters implement the high availability and consistency of data and the shared sessions of the frontend.
- The shared data storage provides the consistency of artifact data.

Table 2.11 The configuration of the Nginx component in detail

Parameter	Description	Default Value
nginx.image.repository	Repository of Nginx images.	goharbor/nginx-photon
nginx.image.tag	Tag of the Nginx image.	v2.0.0
nginx.replicas	Number of Pod replicas of the Nginx component.	1
nginx.resources	Resources allocated to the Pod.	Undefined
nginx.nodeSelector	Node label during the Pod allocation.	{}
nginx.tolerations	Node tolerations during the Pod allocation.	[]
nginx.affinity	Affinities of the Nginx node/Pod.	{}
nginx.podAnnotations	Annotations of the Nginx Pod.	{}

Table 2.12 The configuration of the Portal component in detail

Parameter	Description	Default Value
portal.image.repository	Repository of Portal images.	goharbor/harbor-portal
portal.image.tag	Tag of the Portal image.	v2.0.0
portal.replicas	Number of Pod replicas of the Portal component.	1
portal.resources	Resources allocated to the Pod.	Undefined
portal.nodeSelector	Node label during the Pod allocation.	{}
portal.tolerations	Node tolerations during the Pod allocation.	[]
portal.affinity	Affinities of the Portal node/Pod.	{}
portal.podAnnotations	Annotations of the Portal Pod.	{}

As for the storage layer, it is recommended that users store the application data in highly available PostgreSQL and Redis clusters and save images or Chart files in a persistent storage or a highly available object storage, as shown in Fig. 2.5.

2.3.1.3 Configuring Harbor Helm Chart

Download the Harbor Helm Chart by the following command:

```
$ helm repo add harbor https://helm.goharbor.io
$ helm fetch harbor/harbor --untar
```

Edit the **values.yaml** configuration file to meet the requirements of high availability. For details of the configuration, see Sect. 2.2.3.

Table 2.13 The configuration of the Harbor-Core component in detail

Parameter	Description	Default Value
core.image.repository	Repository of Core image.	goharbor/harbor-core
core.image.tag	Tag of the Core image.	v2.0.0
core.replicas	Number of Pod replicas of Core component.	1
core.livenessProbe.initialDelaySeconds	Seconds the system has to wait before the ready detector is initialized after a Core container is started.	**300**. The minimum value is **0**.
core.resources	Resources allocated to the Pod.	Undefined
core.nodeSelector	Node label during the Pod allocation.	{}
core.tolerations	Node tolerations during the Pod allocation.	[]
core.affinity	Affinities of the Core node/Pod.	{}
core.podAnnotations	Annotations of the Core Pod.	{}
core.secrect	Secret used when the Core component communicates with other components. If this item is not configured, Helm generates a random string. The secret must be a string of 16 characters.	
core.secretName	When the self-signed TLS certificate and private key is needed to encrypt or decrypt the bear token of the Registry component and the JWT token of the robot account, this item is set to the secret name of Kubernetes. The secret must include the following keys: • **tls.crt**: TLS certificate. • **tls.key**: TLS private key. If this item is omitted, Harbor uses the default certificate and private key.	
core.xsrfKey	XSRF key. This configuration item is used by Harbor to prevent cross-site attacks and generate the key of the CSRF token. The key must be a string of 32 characters. If this item is omitted, Harbor automatically generates a random string.	

- **Ingress rule:** Configure **expose.ingress.hosts.core and expose.ingress.hosts.notary**.
- **External URL:** Set externalURL to a URL used by an external client to access Harbor.
- **External PostgreSQL:** Set the configuration item **database.type** to **external** and fill in database information to the configuration item **database.external**. Four empty databases must be created in the external PostgreSQL as registry, clair, notaryserver and notarysinger for the Core, Clair, Notary Server and Notary Signer components, respectively. Then configure the external database of each of the components. When Harbor is started, tables in the corresponding databases are automatically provisioned.
- Storage: During the deployment of a Kubernetes cluster, a default StorageClass is needed to provide a persistent volume for storing artifacts, Charts and job logs.

Table 2.14 The configuration of the Jobservice component in detail

Parameter	Description	Default Value
jobservice.image.repository	Repository of JobService image.	goharbor/harbor-jobservice
jobservice.image.tag	Tag of the JobService image.	v2.0.0
jobservice.replicas	Number of Pod replicas of the JobService component.	1
jobservice.maxJobWorkers	Maximum number of execution units of the JobService component.	10
jobservice.jobLogger	Logger of the JobService component: **file**, **database** or **stdout**.	file
jobservice.resources	Resources allocated to the Pod.	Undefined
jobservice.nodeSelector	Node label during the Pod allocation.	{}
jobservice.tolerations	Node tolerations during the Pod allocation.	[]
jobservice.affinity	Affinities of the JobService node or Pod.	{}
jobservice.podAnnotations	Annotations of the JobService Pod.	{}
jobservice.secrect	Secret used when the JobService component communicates with other components. If this item is not configured, Helm generates a random string. The secret must be a string of 16 characters.	

- To specify the StorageClass, configure **persistence.persistentVolumeClaim.registry.storageClass**, **persistence.persistentVolumeClaim.chartmuseum.storageClass** and **persistence.persistentVolumeClaim.jobservice.storageClass**.
- To use a StorageClass, regardless the default or the custom StorageClass, set the configuration items of **persistence.persistentVolumeClaim.registry.accessMode**, **persistence.persistentVolumeClaim.chartmuseum.accessMode** and **persistence.persistentVolumeClaim.jobservice.accessMode** to **ReadWriteMany** and ensure that the persistent volume is shared among nodes.
- To use an existing PersistentVolumeClaims to store data, set the configuration items of **persistence.persistentVolumeClaim.registry.existingClaim**, **persistence.persistentVolumeClaim.chartmuseum.existingClaim** and **persistence.persistentVolumeClaim.jobservice.existingClaim**.
- If no PersistentVolumeClaims can be shared among nodes, use the external object storage to store artifacts and Charts and use a database to store the job logs. Set the value of **persistence.imageChartStorage.type** to the

Table 2.15 The configuration of the Registry component in detail

Parameter	Description	Default Value
registry.registry.image.repository	Repository of Registry image.	goharbor/registry-photon
registry.registry.image.tag	Tag of the Registry image.	v2.0.0
registry.registry.resources	Resources allocated to the Pod.	Undefined
registry.controller.image.repository	Repository of Registry Controller image.	goharbor/harbor-registryctl
registry.controller.image.tag	Tag of the Registry Controller image.	dev
registry.controller.resources	Resources allocated to the Registry Controller.	Undefined
registry.replicas	Number of Pod replicas of the Registry component.	1
registry.nodeSelector	Node label during the Pod allocation.	{}
registry.tolerations	Node tolerations during the Pod allocation.	[]
registry.affinity	Affinities of the Registry node or Pod.	{}
registry.middleware	Middleware can be used to support the CDN between the backend storage and the receiver of the docker pull command. For the specific configuration of middleware, see official documents of DokerDistribution.	{}
registry.podAnnotations	Annotations of the Registry Pod.	{}
registry.secrect	Secret used when the Registry component communicates with other components. If this item is not configured, Helm generates a random string. The secret must be a string of 16 characters. For details, see official documents of Docker Distribution.	
registry.credentials.username	User name used to access Registry when the Registry component is set to the htpasswd authentication mode. For details, see official documents of Docker Distribution.	harbor_registry_user

(continued)

Table 2.15 (continued)

Parameter	Description	Default Value
registry.creden-tials.password	Password used to access Registry when the Registry component is set to the htpasswd authentication mode. For details, see official documents of Docker Distribution.	harbor_registry_password
registry.creden-tials.htpasswd	Content of the htpasswd file generated based on the user name and password items above. Because Helm does not support bcrypt in the template file, to update the value of this item, use the following command to generate the value: htpasswd -nbBC10 $username $password For details, see official documents of Docker Distribution.	harbor_registry_user:$2y$10$9L4Tc0DJbFFMB6RdSCunrOpTHdwhid4ktBJmLD00bYgqkkGOvll3m

Table 2.16 The configuration of the Chartmuseum component in detail

Parameter	Description	Default Value
chartmuseum.enabled	Whether the ChartMuseum component is enabled.	true
chartmuseum.absoluteUrl	The flag to determine whether the ChartMuseum component should return the absolute path. The default value is **false**. The ChartMuseum component returns a relative path.	false
chartmuseum.image.repository	Repository of ChartMuseum image.	goharbor/chartmuseum-photon
chartmuseum.image.tag	Tag of the ChartMuseum image.	v2.0.0
chartmuseum.replicas	Number of Pod replicas of the ChartMuseum component.	1
chartmuseum.resources	Resources allocated to the Pod.	Undefined
chartmuseum.nodeSelector	Node label during the Pod allocation.	{}
chartmuseum.tolerations	Node tolerations during the Pod allocation.	[]
chartmuseum.affinity	Affinities of the ChartMuseum node or Pod.	{}
chartmuseum.podAnnotations	Annotations of the ChartMuseum Pod.	{}

Table 2.17 The configuration of the Clair component in detail

Parameter	Description	Default Value
clair.enabled	The flag to determine whether the Clair component is enabled.	true
clair.clair.image.repository	Repository of Clair image.	goharbor/clair-photon
clair.clair.image.tag	Tag of the Clair image.	v2.0.0
clair.clair.resources	Resources allocated to the Pod.	Undefined
clair.adapter.image.repository	Repository of Clair adapter image.	goharbor/clair-adapter-photon
clair.adapter.image.tag	Tag of the Clair adapter image.	dev
clair.adapter.resources	Resources allocated to the Pod.	Undefined
clair.replicas	Number of Pod replicas of the Clair component.	1
clair.updatersInterval	Interval for Clair updater to retrieve the vulnerability data. Its unit is hour. If the data retrieval needs to be disabled, set this item to **0**.	
clair.nodeSelector	Node label during the Pod allocation.	{}
clair.tolerations	Node tolerations during the Pod allocation.	[]
clair.affinity	Affinities of the Clair node or Pod.	{}
clair.podAnnotations	Annotations of the Clair Pod.	{}

corresponding storage type and set the value of **jobservice.jobLogger** to **database**.

- **Replica:** Set **portal.replicas**, **core.replicas**, **jobservice.replicas**, **registry.replicas**, **chartmuseum.replicas**, **clair.replicas**, **trivy.replicas**, **notary.server.replicas** and **notary.signer.replicas** to values greater than or equal to 2 so that each component of Harbor can have multiple replicas.

2.3.1.4 Installing Harbor Helm Chart

After configuring the Helm Chart, install Harbor Helm Chart by using the following command, in which **my-release** is the deployment name.

- Helm2:

```
$ helm install --name my-release harbor/harbor
```

Table 2.18 The configuration of the Trivy component in detail

Parameter	Description	Default Value
trivy.enabled	The flag to determine whether the Trivy component is enabled.	true
trivy.image.repository	Repository of Trivy adapter image.	goharbor/trivy-adapter-photon
trivy.image.tag	Tag of the Trivy adapter image.	v2.0.0
trivy.resources	Resources allocated to the Pod.	Undefined
trivy.replicas	Number of Pod replicas of the Trivy component.	1
trivy.debugMode	The flag to determine whether the Trivy debug mode is enabled.	false
trivy.vulnType	Filtered list of vulnerabilities of the specified type (s). The delimiter is a comma. Available values are as follows: • **os**: Vulnerabilities of software packages in the operating system are displayed. • **library**: Vulnerabilities in the dependency packages of programming languages such as Ruby, Python, PHP, Node.js and Rust are displayed.	os,library
trivy.sererity	Filtered list of vulnerabilities of the specified severity level(s). The delimiter is a comma. Available values are as follows: • **UNKNOWN**: unknown level. • **LOW**: low level. • **MEDIUM**: medium level. • **HIGH**: high level. • **CRITICAL**: critical level.	UNKNOWN, LOW, MEDIUM, HIGH, CRITICAL
trivy.ignoreUnfixed	The flag to determine whether only fixable vulnerabilities are displayed.	false
trivy.skipUpdate	The flag to determine whether the function of downloading vulnerability data from GitHub by the Trivy component is disabled.	false
trivy.githubToken	Token used by the Trivy component to download vulnerability data from GitHub. It is recommended to configure this item in the production environment. This is because GitHub limits the request frequency of unauthenticated users to 60 requests per hour by default. The limit of the request frequency of authenticated users is 5000 requests per hours.	

- Helm3:

```
$ helm install my-release harbor/harbor
```

Table 2.19 The configuration of the Notary component in detail

Parameter	Description	Default Value
notary.server.image.repository	Repository of Notary Server image.	goharbor/notary-server-photon
notary.server.image.tag	Tag of the Notary Server image.	v2.0.0
notary.server.replicas	Number of Pod replicas of the Notary Server.	1
notary.server.resources	Resources allocated to the Pod.	Undefined
notary.signer.image.repository	Repository of Notary Signer image.	goharbor/notary-signer-photon
notary.signer.image.tag	Tag of the Notary Signer image.	dev
notary.signer.replicas	Number of Pod replicas of the Notary Signer.	1
notary.signer.resources	Resources allocated to the containers.	Undefined
notary.nodeSelector	Node label during the Pod allocation.	{}
notary.tolerations	Node tolerations during the Pod allocation.	[]
notary.affinity	Affinities of the Notary node or Pod.	{}
notary.podAnnotations	Annotations of the Notary Pod.	{}
notary.secretName	If the user needs to encrypt or decrypt Notary communication by their own TLS certificate and private key, this item is set to the secret name of Kubernetes. The secret must include the following keys: • **tls.crt**: TLS certificate. • **tls.key**: TLS private key. If this item is omitted, Harbor uses the default certificate and private key.	

After the installation is completed, run the **kubectl get pod** command to view the status of the Pods, as shown in Fig. 2.6.

2.3.2 *High-availability Solution for Multiple Kubernetes Clusters*

Section 2.3.1 introduces the solution for a highly available environment of Harbor in a Kubernetes cluster by using Harbor Helm Chart. However, the overall availability of the services is still affected by the availability of the Kubernetes cluster on which

Table 2.20 The configuration of the Database component in detail

Parameter	Description	Default Value
database.type	Indicates whether an internal or external database is used. When an external database is used, this item is set to **external**.	internal
database.internal.image.repository	Repository of internal database image.	goharbor/harbor-db
database.internal.image.tag	Tag of an internal database image.	v2.0.0
database.internal.initContainerImage.repository	Repository of the initialization image. The image is used to set the permission of the database directory. The default value can be used if there is no special requirement.	busybox
database.internal.initContainerImage.tag	Tag of the initialization image.	latest
database.internal.password	Password for the internal database image. It is recommended to modify this item.	changeit
database.internal.resources	Resources allocated to the container.	Undefined
database.internal.nodeSelector	Node label during the Pod allocation.	{}
database.internal.tolerations	Node tolerations during the Pod allocation.	[]
database.internal.affinity	Affinities of the Database node or Pod.	{}
database.external.host	Hostname or IP address of an external database.	192.168.0.1
database.external.port	Port of an external database.	5432
database.external.username	User name for an external database.	user
database.external.password	Password for an external database.	password
database.external.coreDatabase	Core database name of an external database.	registry
database.external.clairDatabase	Clair database name of an external database.	clair
database.external.notaryServerDatabase	Notary Server database name of an external database.	notaryserver
database.external.nignerServerDatabase	Notary Signer database name of an external database.	notarysigner
database.external.sslmode	Connection mode of an external database. • require • verify-full • verify-ca • disable	disable
database.maxIdleConns	Maximum number of idle connections of the database.	50
database.maxOpenConns	Maximum number of connections between Harbor components and the database.	100
database.podAnnotations	Annotations of the database Pod.	{}

Table 2.21 The configuration of the Redis component in detail

Parameter	Description	Default Value
redis.type	Indicates whether internal or external Redis is used. When external Redis is used, this item is set to **external**.	internal
redis.internal.image.repository	Repository of internal Redis images.	goharbor/redis-photon
redis.internal.image.tag	Tag of an internal Redis image.	v2.0.0
redis.internal.resources	Resources allocated to the Pod.	Undefined
redis.internal.nodeSelector	Node label during the Pod allocation.	{}
redis.internal.tolerations	Node tolerations during the Pod allocation.	[]
redis.internal.affinity	Affinities of the Redis node or Pod.	{}
redis.external.host	Hostname or IP address of external Redis.	192.168.0.2
redis.external.port	Port of external Redis.	6739
redis.external.password	Password for external Redis.	password
redis.external.coreDatabaseIndex	Core component database index number of external Redis. Note: Do not modify the value of this item here because database 0 is exclusive to the Core component.	0
redis.external.jobserviceDatabaseIndex	JobService component database index number of external Redis.	1
redis.external.registryDatabaseIndex	Registry component database index number of external Redis.	2
redis.external.chartmuseumDatabaseIndex	ChartMuseum component database index number of external Redis.	3
redis.external.clairAdapterIndex	Clair component database index number of external Redis.	4
redis.podAnnotations	Annotations of the Redis Pod.	{}

the services run. If the cluster crashes, the services will become unavailable. Some production environments may have higher requirements for availability. Therefore, the high-availability solution for multiple Kubernetes clusters deployed in multiple data centers is of particular importance. This section provides a reference solution for building a highly available environment of Harbor on multiple Kubernetes clusters across data centers.

2.3.2.1 Installing Harbor

Install Harbor in different Kubernetes clusters in each data center in turn by referring to Sect. 2.3.1. Note: During all the installation processes, ensure that the values of **core.secretName** and **core.xsrfKey** in the configuration item **values.yml** are the

Table 2.22 Post-Installation requirement of Harbor HA

Software	Version	Description
Kubernetes	1.10 or later versions	See its official installation document.
Helm	2.8.0 or later versions	See its official installation document.
Highly available Ingress Controller	The user can select an Ingress Controller supported by the Kubernetes community.	Harbor Helm Chart does not include the software. The users need to prepare the software on their own. If Internal TLS is enabled, the Nginx Ingress Controller officially maintained by Kubernetes must be used because Internal TLS needs intonation and only the Nginx Ingress Controller can identify and load the intonation of Internal TLS.
Highly available PostgreSQL cluster	PostgreSQL V9.6.14 or later.	Harbor Helm Chart does not include the software.
Highly available Redis cluster	The user can select the Redis service.	Harbor Helm Chart does not include the software.
Shared persistent storage or external storage	The user can select the external storage service.	Harbor Helm Chart does not include the software.

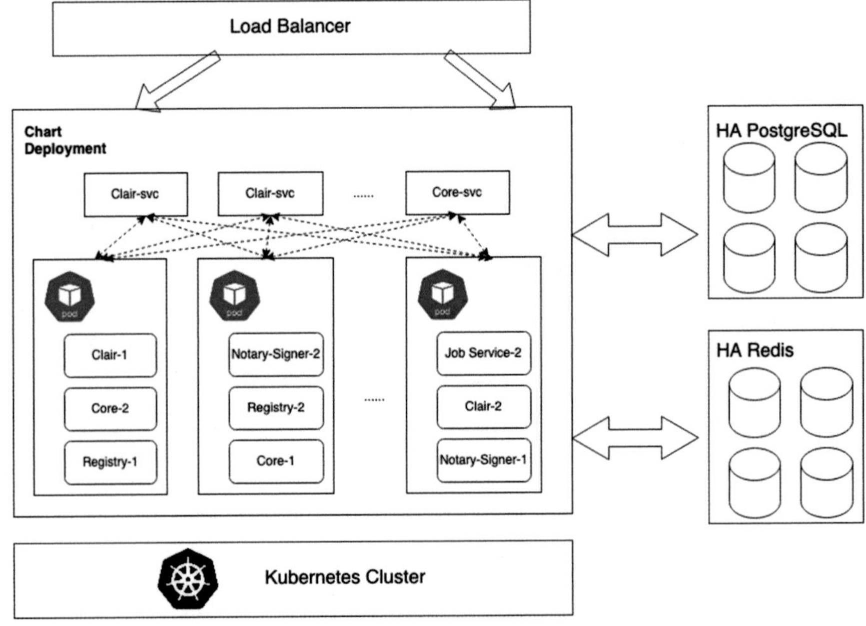

Fig. 2.5 The architecture of Harbor HA based on helm chart

```
NAME                                             READY   STATUS    RESTARTS   AGE
my-release-harbor-chartmuseum-58d59cd6cb-nwgwq   1/1     Running   0          99s
my-release-harbor-clair-f94f97ff7-h75hx          2/2     Running   2          99s
my-release-harbor-core-5598fcf87c-q7wt2          1/1     Running   0          99s
my-release-harbor-database-0                     1/1     Running   0          99s
my-release-harbor-jobservice-59666cc874-fgm4l    1/1     Running   0          99s
my-release-harbor-notary-server-7c4f78f9fc-r9rv5 1/1     Running   1          99s
my-release-harbor-notary-signer-6fccf95557-7gdhq 1/1     Running   1          99s
my-release-harbor-portal-79fcc8df86-nw8mv        1/1     Running   0          99s
my-release-harbor-redis-0                        1/1     Running   0          99s
my-release-harbor-registry-6657d5bf96-vlqg6      2/2     Running   0          99s
my-release-harbor-trivy-0                        1/1     Running   0          99s
```

Fig. 2.6 The running status of the containers installed from the helm chart

same. Other configuration items can be configured according to requirements of different data centers.

For the specific reason why the values of **core.secretName** and **core.xsrfKey** must be the same, refer to Sect. 2.3.3 about the files or configuration that must be shared among multiple Harbor instances.

2.3.2.2 Highly Available Architecture of Multiple Kubernetes clusters

Let's assume the user has two data centers. After Harbor is installed on the Kubernetes clusters of the two data centers, a high-availability solution in active-standby mode can be set up. Harbor in one of the data centers provides service and Harbor in the other data center is in the standby state. When Harbor in the active state fails, Harbor in the standby state can be activated to take over the workload. This ensures that the Harbor service can be restored to the accessible state within a short period of time.

Outside the Kubernetes cluster of one data center, the Local Traffic Manager (LTM) is used for the load balancing of the services. On top of the load balancing services of the two data centers, the Global Traffic Manager (GTM) is used to provide global traffic routing. The GTM monitors the service states of the data centers through the states reported by the LTM. When the GTM finds that the data center in the active state fails, the GTM directs all network traffic to the data center in the standby state, as shown in Fig. 2.7.

We can see from Fig. 2.7 that Harbor instances in the two data centers respectively has the independent storage of the data and content. The remote replication is configured between the two data centers to synchronize the artifact data (such as images). The data storage of the two Kubernetes clusters ensures the consistency of artifact data by remote replication. To keep data consistency of PostgreSQL and Redis between the two data centers, the user needs to set up their own data backup solution.

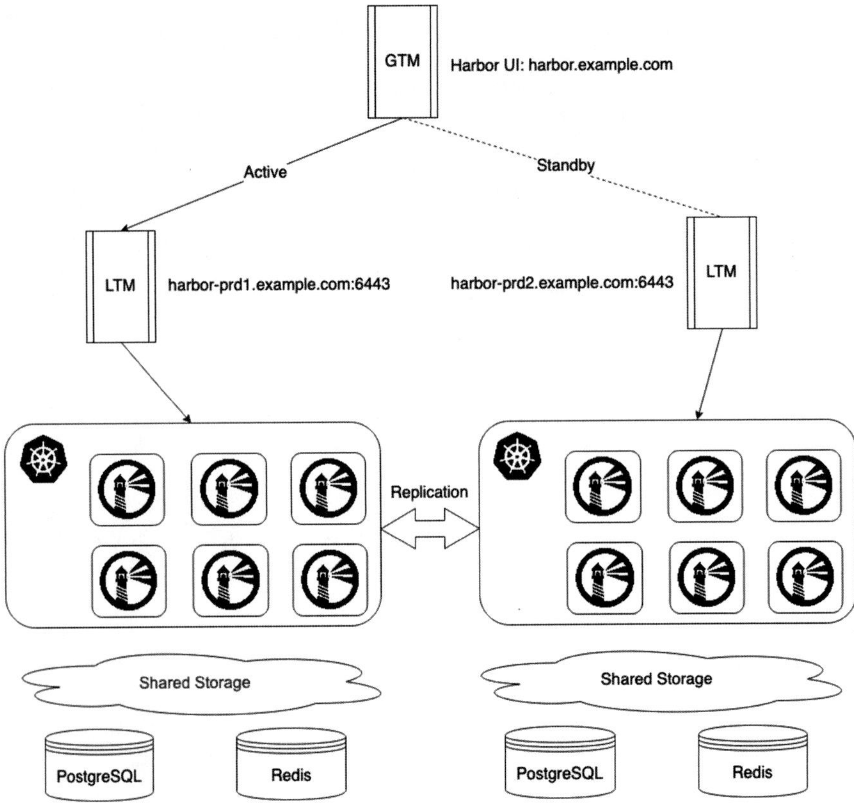

Fig. 2.7 The architecture of Harbor HA based on multiple Kubernetes clusters

This solution adopts the active-standby mode of Harbor. Due to the use of the remote replication of artifacts, some propagation delay may exist during the data synchronization. In practice, we need to pay attention to its impact on the application. The users that do not have high requirements of real-time performance may utilize this solution to build a high-availability registry service for multiple Kubernetes clusters across data centers.

2.3.3 High-availability Solution Based on the Offline Installation Package

The high-availability architecture set up based on Kubernetes clusters is Harbor's official solution. However, users may be unable to deploy independent Kubernetes clusters due to some reasons and prefer to create a high-availability solution based on the offline installation package of Harbor.

Users are encouraged to leverage Kubernetes clusters to achieve high availability because the Harbor Helm Chart is maintained by the Harbor team and the community is provided with technical support. Due to differences in user environments, the high-availability solution based on the offline installation package requires users to explore and solve problems in their respective environments. Meanwhile, because Harbor does not officially come up with a high-availability solution based on the offline installation package, technical support is not available to the community.

Setting up a high-availability system based on the offline installation package is a complex task. Users need to have relevant technical knowledge of high availability and in-depth understanding of the architecture and configuration of Harbor. The two conventional approaches introduced in this section are only for conceptual reference. Users are advised to first read the content of this chapter to well understand the installation and deployment of Harbor before they start to implement the high-availability solution by taking into the considerations of the actual environment.

The following two solutions use a load balancer as the gateway. The setup and configuration of the load balancer for multiple Harbor instances are beyond the scope of this section.

Solution 1: High-availability solution based on shared service

The basic idea of this solution is to share PostgreSQL, Redis and storage between multiple Harbor instances and to load balance multiple servers of the Harbor service, as shown in Fig. 2.8.

2.3.3.1 The Setup of the Load Balancer

During the installation of each Harbor instance, the **external_url** in the configuration file of Harbor must point to the domain name or the IP address of the load balancer. After the load balancer is specified by the **external_url**, Harbor no longer uses **hostname** in the configuration file as the access address. Clients (such as Docker and browser) access the API of Harbor services through the address of the load balancer (specified by **external_url**). If **external_url** is not set, clients still access the API of backend services through the address specified by **hostname**. This may lead to the failure of accessing the Harbor service.

When Harbor instances have their own (self-signed) certificates for HTTPS, the load balancer must be configured to trust the certificate of each Harbor instance. Meanwhile, the certificate of the load balancer must be placed in each Harbor instance. The certificate should be placed in the **ca_download** subfolder under the path specified by the **data_volume** item in the **harbor.yml** configuration file. The folder must be manually created. In this way, the certificate downloaded by the user from any Harbor instance's management console is the certificate of the load balancer, as shown in Fig. 2.9.

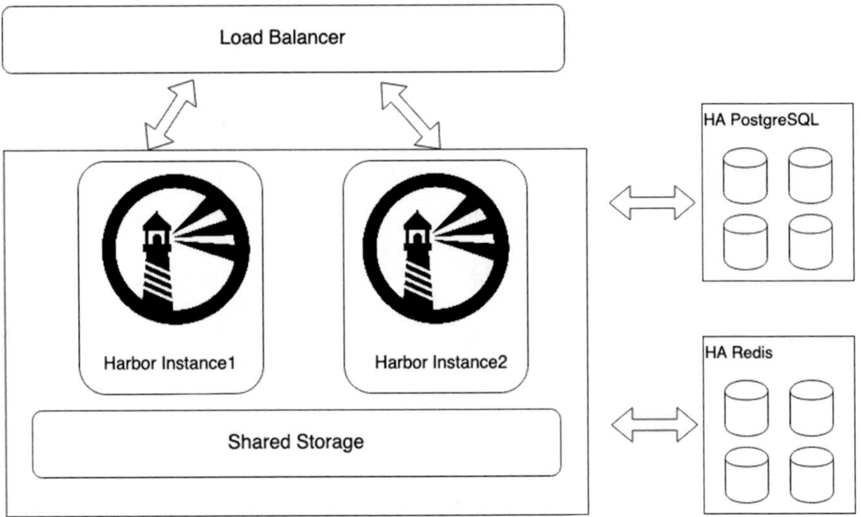

Fig. 2.8 The architecture of Harbor HA based on shared storage

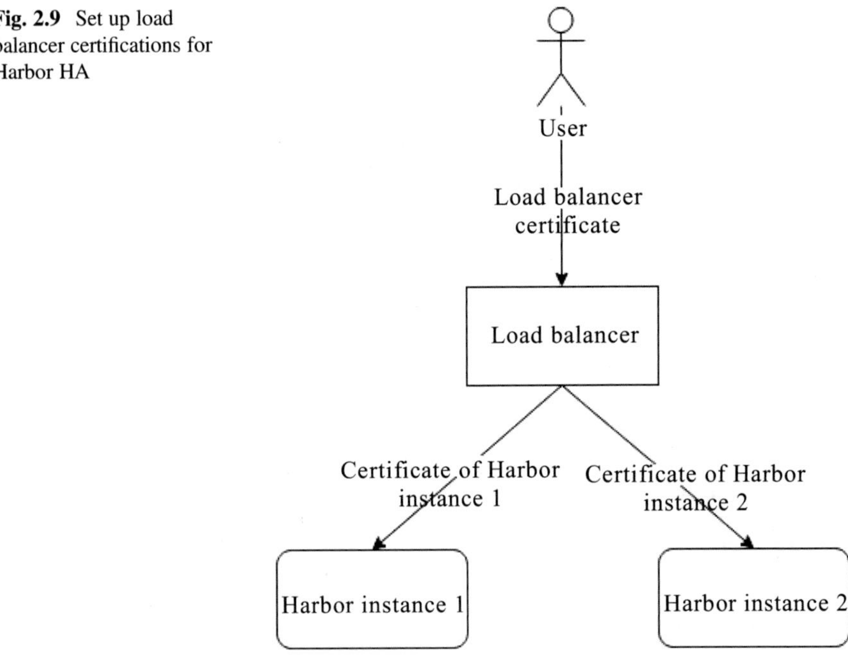

Fig. 2.9 Set up load balancer certifications for Harbor HA

2.3.3.2 The Configuration of External Database

The user needs to create a PostgreSQL shared instance or cluster, and configure each Harbor instance with the database information. Note: The external PostgreSQL must create in advance four empty databases of registry, clair, notary_server and notary_singer, respectively, for the Core, Clair, Notary Server and Notary Signer components of Harbor. The created databases must be configured as the external database of the corresponding components. When Harbor is started, database tables of the corresponding databases are automatically created.

2.3.3.3 The Configuration of External Redis

The user needs to create a Redis shared instance or cluster and configure it into the external Redis configuration item of each Harbor instance.

2.3.3.4 The Configuration of External Storage

The user needs to provide local or cloud shared storage, and configure it into the external storage configuration item of each Harbor instance.

2.3.3.5 Files or Configuration that Must Be Shared Among Multiple Harbor Instances

To achieve high availability of Harbor, the following files among multiple instances must be the same. Because these files are generated during the installation of each Harbor instance, they must be manually copied to each instance to ensure the consistency.

private_key.pem and root.crt files

In the client authentication flow (see Chap. 3), Harbor provides a certificate file and a private key file for Docker Distribution to create and check the bearer token in the request. In the multi-instance solution of Harbor, the bearer token created by any instance must be recognized and validated by other instances. For this reason, all Harbor instances must use the same **private_key.pem** and **root.crt** files.

If the two files are different among multiple Harbor instances, depending on which instance the load balancer forwards the request to, the authentication to Harbor may fail or succeed randomly. If the request is forwarded to the instance which created the bearer token, it can be validated by that instance. Otherwise, the bearer token in the request cannot be parsed and recognized by the instance, which results in an authentication failure. Because the **private_key.pem** file is also used to check the JWT token of the robot account, if this file is not the same across multiple instances, a random success or failure also occurs for the robot account due to the same reason above.

The **private_key.pem** file is in the **secret/core** subdirectory specified by **data_volume** in the **harbor.yml** configuration file. The **root.crt** file is in the **secret/registry** subdirectory specified by **data_volume** in the **harbor.yml** configuration file.

csrf_key

To prevent Cross-Site Request Forgery (CSRF), Harbor enables the validation of the CSRF token. Harbor generates a random number as the CSRF token and attaches it in the cookie. When a user submits a request, the client extracts the random number from the cookie and submits it as the CSRF token. If the value of **csrf_key** is null or invalid, Harbor rejects the access request. When there are multiple Harbor instances in service, the CSRF token created by any instance must be successfully validated by any other instance. As a result, the private key of the CSRF token should be the same on each instance.

The configuration of CSRF token is stored in the **common/config/core/env** file in the installation directory of Harbor. The user needs to manually copy the CSRF private key of one Harbor instance to other instances so that the key can be same on all instances.

Note: When the user manually modifies the above file or configuration, the user must restart Harbor instances to let the configuration take effect. In addition, if the prepare script in the installation package of Harbor is run later, the above manual copy process must be repeated. This is due to the fact that the script creates a random string and rewrites the CSRF token key in the configuration, overwriting the manually modified configuration.

Solution 2: Highly available solution based on replication policy

The basic idea of this solution is that multiple Harbor instances replicate artifacts between each other to keep the artifacts consistent so that a unified Harbor service can be provided through a load balancer, as shown in Fig. 2.10.

The configuration of the load balancer, resources that must be shared among multiple Harbor instances and the configuration method are the same as those of solution 1.

Solution 2 differs from solution 1 in that external PostgreSQL, Redis and storage do not need to be specified during the installation of Harbor instances. Each instance uses its own independent storage. The multiple instances of Harbor maintain the consistency of artifact data through the remote replication between each other. As for the data consistency of PostgreSQL and Redis, users need to synchronize the data by themselves. The multi-instance solution based on replication provides lower real-time performance than the solution that shares storage. However, its setup is simpler. The user only needs to use the PostgreSQL and Redis provided in the offline installation package of Harbor.

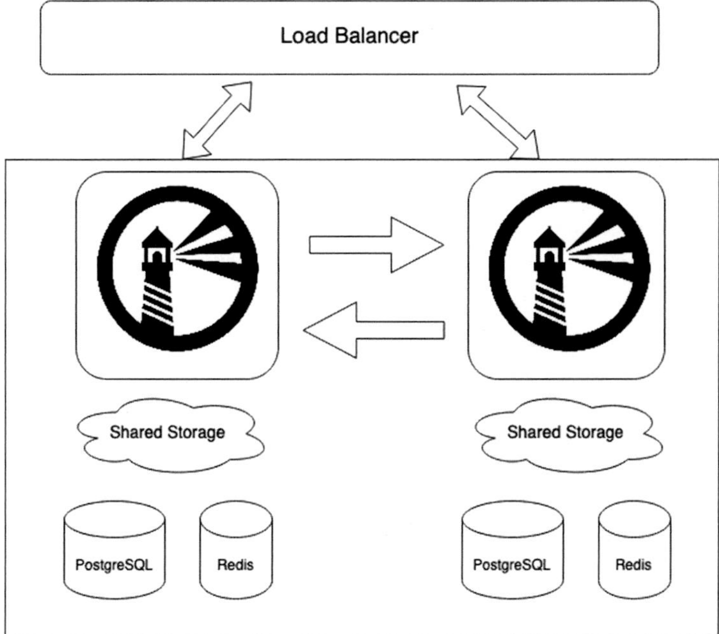

Fig. 2.10 The architecture of Harbor HA based on replication

2.4 Configuring the Storage System

By default, the Harbor system uses the local file system to store persistent data. Because the local file system has limited capacity and performance and is not highly reliable, other storage service be considered to improve the performance and reliability. Harbor supports Amazon Simple Storage Service (S3), Azure Blob Storage, Google Cloud Storage, Object Storage Service (OSS) of Alibaba Cloud, Cloud Object Storage (COS) of Tencent Cloud and Swift provided by OpenStack.

This section details how to configure Harbor to make use of persistent storage besides local file system, such as Amazon S3, Network File System (NFS) and OSS of Alibaba Cloud.

2.4.1 Amazon S3

Due to the popularity of Amazon S3, many storage projects are compatible with S3 interface protocol in the open source community, for example, Ceph RADOS Gateway and MinIO. This section describes how to configure Harbor to make it work with Amazon S3 or MinIO to store artifact data. The configuration of Amazon S3 is mostly the similar for other compatible storage services.

2.4.1.1 Creating an S3 Storage Bucket

Before configuring Harbor, create a bucket on the S3 service. To improve the service availability, stability and access rate, the user should try to select the S3 service that is geographically closer to Harbor instances. For example, S3 service that is in the same Availability Zone (AZ) as the Harbor instances or S3 compatible service that is in the same data center as Harbor instances. As shown in Fig. 2.11, the bucket created in MinIO adopts the default read/write policy.

First create an S3 storage bucket. Then set the read/write policy for the storage bucket to prevent the S3 storage bucket from unauthorized access (which may cause data leakage). As shown in Fig. 2.11, generally, the permission of the S3 storage bucket created in MinIO is with private access(read/write). Here, make sure that the permission of the storage bucket is not set to public access (read/write). Finally, obtain the Access Key and Secret Key from the Amazon console. The Access Key and Secret Key of MinIO are set when the MinIO service is deployed.

2.4.1.2 Configuring harbor.yml

Previous sections describe how to configure the external storage through **harbor.yml**. The following describes how to configure Harbor to work with Amazon S3 storage:

```
storage_service:
 s3:
  accesskey: awsaccesskey
  secretkey: awssecretkey
  region: us-west-1
  regionendpoint: http://myobjects.local
  bucket: bucketname
  encrypt: true
  keyid: mykeyid
  secure: true
  v4auth: true
  chunksize: 5242880
```

(continued)

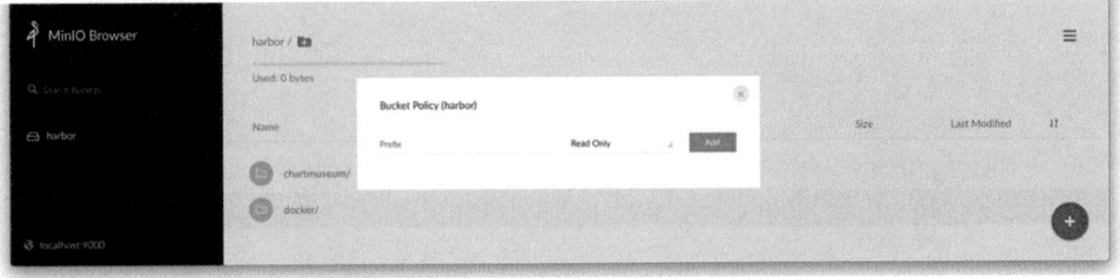

Fig. 2.11 The Minio settings page

Table 2.23 Amazon S3 storage configuration in detail

Attribute	Mandatory	Description
accesskey	No	Access Key of Amazon S3
secretkey	No	Secret Key of Amazon S3
region	Yes	Region where Amazon S3 storage bucket is located
regionendpoint	No	Endpoint of S3 compatible storage service
bucket	Yes	Name of S3 storage bucket
encrypt	No	Whether to encrypt the stored images. The value is a Boolean type and the default value is **false**.
keyid	No	Key ID of KMS. The value is valid only when **encrypt** is **true**. The default value is **none**.
secure	No	Whether HTTPS is used. The value is a Boolean type and the default value is **true**.
v4auth	No	Whether the Version 4 for AWS identity authentication is used. The default value is **true**.
chunksize	No	The S3 API requires the size of a multipart upload chuck to be at least 5 MB. The value must be greater than or equal to $5 \times 1024 \times 1024$.
rootdirectory	No	Prefix used in all S3 keys.

```
multipartcopychunksize: 33554432
multipartcopymaxconcurrency: 100
multipartcopythresholdsize: 33554432
rootdirectory: /s3/object/name/prefix
```

Table 2.23 lists the parameter attributes.

2.4.2 NFS

Harbor can use NFS as the backend storage. The NFS file storage can be the NFS service created in the organization or the file storage service provided by a public cloud that is compatible with the NFS protocol.

Before installing or configuring Harbor to use the NFS, check the environment and make sure that:

- The NFS server has been correctly configured and has a fixed IP address.
- The correct NFS client has been installed on the hosts of Harbor instances.
- Harbor hosts are connected with the NFS server via network.

Directly mount the NFS service to the hosts of Harbor instances so that Harbor can consume the NFS as the backend persistent storage.

2.4.2.1 Configuring the NFS on Each Node

Before mounting the NFS, make sure that nfs-utils or nfs-common is installed on each node.

- CentOS: Execute the **sudo yum install nfs-utils** command to install nfs-utils.
- Debian or Ubuntu: Execute the **sudo apt install nfs-common** command to install nfs-common.

After installing the NFS client, execute the command **mkdir /mnt/harbor/** to create the mount directory and then run the command **sudo mount -t nfs -o vers=4.0 <IP address of NFS server>:/ <mount directory>** to mount the NFS directory.

Note: The autofs tool can be used for automatic mounting.

2.4.2.2 Configuring Harbor

To configure NFS in Harbor, set the value of the **data_volume** to **<mount directory>** in the **harbor.yml** configuration file, (e.g. **/mnt/harbor/** mentioned previously) and then install Harbor.

2.4.3 OSS of Alibaba Cloud

When the OSS of Alibaba Cloud is used as backend storage of Harbor, its configuration flow is similar to that of Amazon S3 service.

2.4.3.1 Creating an OSS storage bucket

Before configuring Harbor, create a bucket on Alibaba Cloud OSS console. To improve the service availability, stability and access rate, select Alibaba Cloud OSS that is geographically closer to Harbor instances to create a bucket.

2.4.3.2 Configuring harbor.yml

Section 2.2.1 already describes how to configure the external storage. The following introduces how to configure Harbor to use OSS storage.

Table 2.24 Alibaba Cloud OSS configuration in detail

Attribute	Mandatory	Description
accesskeyid	Yes	Access key ID of the OSS
accesskeysecret	Yes	Access key of the OSS
region	Yes	Region where the data center of the OSS is located
endpoint	No	Endpoint of OSS external service
internal	No	Hostname or IP address for internal communication within Alibaba Cloud in the same region
bucket	Yes	Name of OSS storage bucket
encrypt	No	Whether data is encrypted on the server. The default value is **false**.
secure	No	Whether data transmission is based on SSL. The default value is **true**.
chunksize	No	Size of a multipart upload chunck. The default value is **10 MB** and the minimum value is **5 MB**.
rootdirectory	No	Root directory used to store all registry files.

```
storage_service:
 oss:
  accesskeyid: accesskeyid
  accesskeysecret: accesskeysecret
  region: OSS region name
  endpoint: optional endpoints
  internal: optional internal endpoint
  bucket: OSS bucket
  encrypt: optional enable server-side encryption
  encryptionkeyid: optional KMS key id for encryption
  secure: optional ssl setting
  chunksize: optional size valye
  rootdirectory: optional root directory
```

Table 2.24 lists the parameter attributes.

2.5 First Experience of Harbor

After Harbor is installed, it can be accessed through various clients such as browser, Docker client, kubelet, Notary, Helm and ORAS. This section walks through the functions of Harbor's graphical admin console (also known as management console, web management console, management portal) and introduces the way for image operation in the Docker and Kubernetes environment, respectively.

2.5.1 Admin Console

When we install Harbor, we set the hostname of Harbor service in the **harbor.yml** configuration file. After you enter **https://hostname** in the address bar of the browser, you can see the login page of Harbor. Initially, there is only one admin account in the newly installed Harbor instance and the password is the value of **harbor_admin_password** specified in the **harbor.yml** configuration file. For security reasons, it is recommended to modify the default value of **harbor_admin_password** before the installation or change the password of the admin account immediately after the first login (after the first launch of Harbor, the password in the configuration file is no longer valid).

After you enter the user name and password on the login page and successfully log in to Harbor, you can see the admin console interface, as shown in Fig. 2.12.

As shown in Fig. 2.12, Harbor's admin console is composed of three parts: the navigation bar in the upper part, the vertical menu bar on the left and the management page area on the right.

On the left side of the navigation bar are the Harbor icon and the global search box; on the right side of the navigation bar are the language switching menu and the user profile management menu. In the vertical menu bar, the main menus from top to bottom are **Projects**, **Logs**, **Administration**, **Theme Switching** and **API Explorer**. The management page area varies as the function is switched. Through the language switching menu, we can switch the interface language of the admin console to English, Simplified Chinese, Spanish, French, Brazilian Portuguese and Turkish.

Through the global search box, we can look up in a fuzzy way by the project name, repository and artifacts such as Helm Charts. As shown in Fig. 2.13, entering

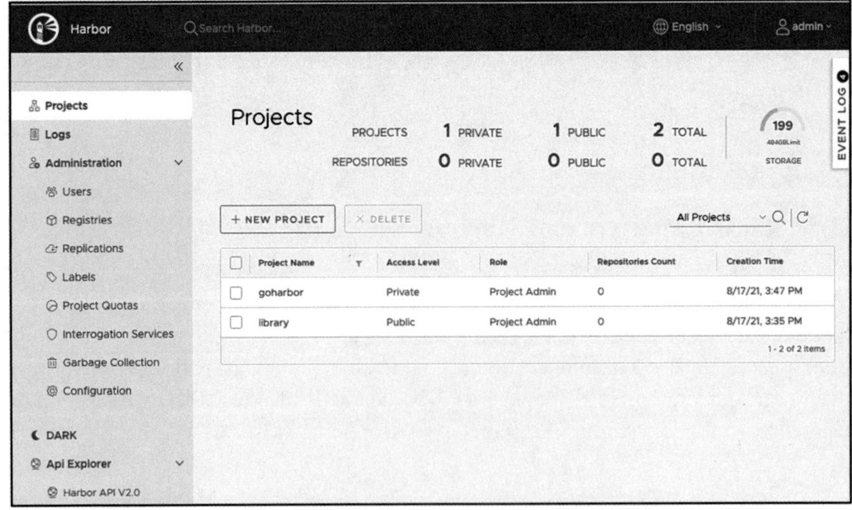

Fig. 2.12 Administrator home page

Harbor Q library English admin

< Back

Projects

Project Name	Access Level	Repositories Count	Creation Time
library	Public	1	8/31/21, 12:42 AM

1 - 1 of 1 items

Repositories

Name	Artifacts	Pulls
library/hello-world	1	0

1 - 1 of 1 items

Charts

Name	Version	Status	Maintainers	Created Time
library/harbor	1.7.1	Active	Wenkai Yin and 3 others	Aug 21, 2021

1 - 1 of 1 items

Fig. 2.13 Global search page

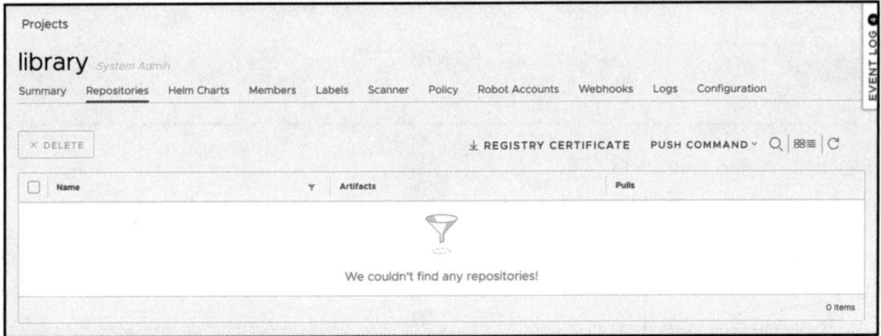

Fig. 2.14 Project detail page

the search keyword **library** in the global search box to get the result of projects, repositories and Helm Charts whose names contain the keyword "library".

2.5.1.1 Projects

Click on **Projects** in the vertical menu bar. You can see the project management page in the management page area. On the project management page, you can create a project or batch delete projects. Click on the hyperlink of a project name (for example, **library**), the right pane is switched to the management page of the project, as shown in Fig. 2.14. The **Summary** tab shows summary information such as the number of repositories, the number of Helm Charts, the project quota and the project members.

System administrators and project administrators have the access and management privileges for all tabs of the project, while other users have different management and access privileges depending on to their roles.

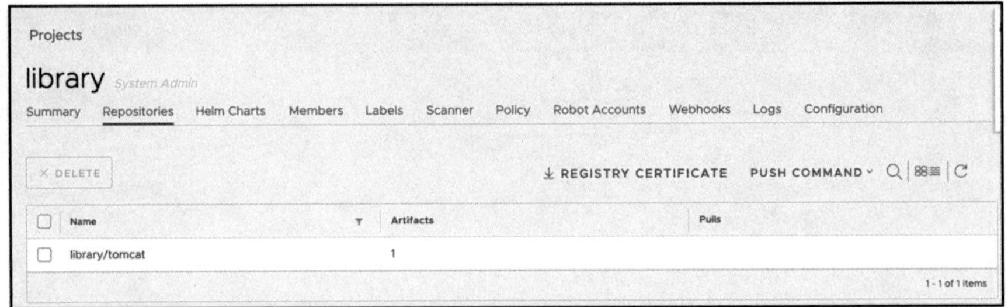

Fig. 2.15 Project repository page

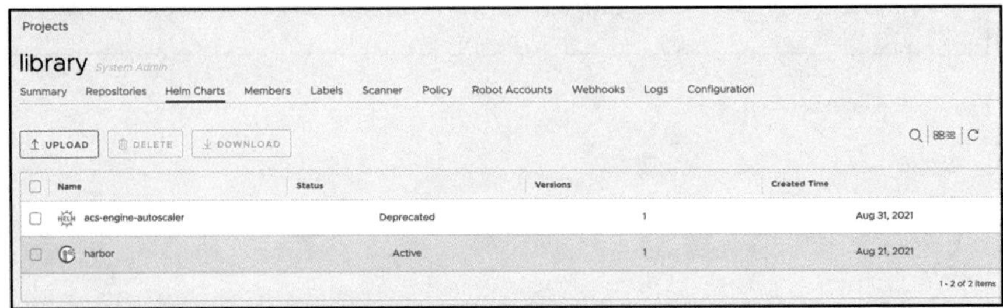

Fig. 2.16 Project helm chart page

- Maintainer role: Maintainers can access these tabs: **Summary**, **Repositories**, **Helm Charts**, **Members** (no management privileges), **Labels**, **Scanner** (no management privileges), **Policy**, **Robot Accounts**(no management privileges), **Webhooks**, **Logs** and **Configuration** (no management privileges).
- Developer role: Developers can access these tabs: **Summary**, **Repositories**, **Helm Charts**, **Members** (no management privileges), **Labels**, **Scanner** (no management privileges), **Robot Accounts**(no management privileges), **Logs** and **Configuration** (no management privileges).
- Guest role: Guests can access the same tabs as developers but have no management privileges.
- Limited Guest role: Limited Guests have no management privileges and can access only these tabs: **Summary**, **Repositories**, **Helm Charts**, **Scanner** and **Configuration** .

Click on the **Repositories** tab to switch to the list of repositories, as shown in Fig. 2.15. On this page, you can view the repository list, filter repositories or delete one or more repositories. Click on **Push Command** link to obtain the push commands for different artifacts such as Docker images, Helm Charts and CNAB.

If the ChartMuseum service is enabled, you can see the **Helm Charts** tab on the project management page. Click on the **Helm Charts** tab to show the Helm Charts management page, as shown in Fig. 2.16. On this page, you can view the chart list, upload, download and filter charts and delete one or more charts.

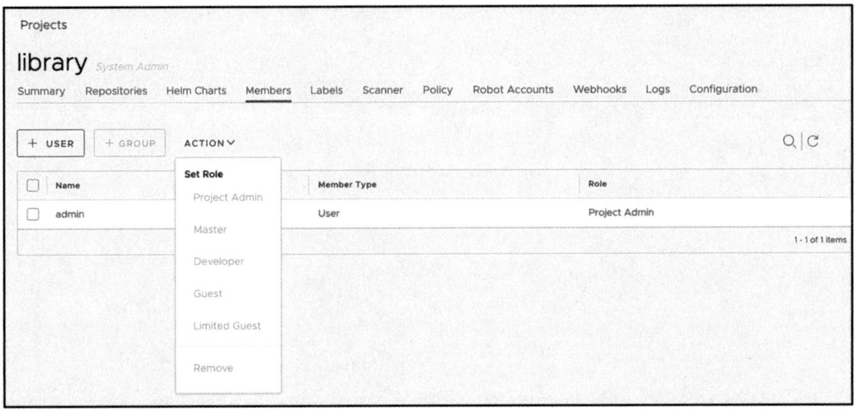

Fig. 2.17 Project member page

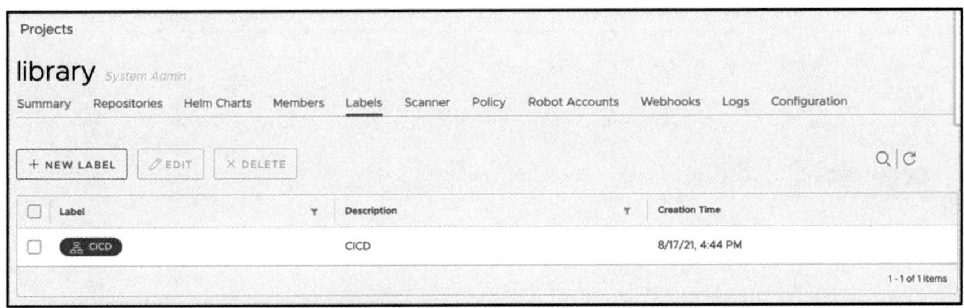

Fig. 2.18 Project label management page

Click on the **Members** tab to reach the project member management page, as shown in Fig. 2.17. On this page, you can view the list of project members, add existing users to the project and give or remove corresponding roles, search for and filter project members and perform management operations.

Click on the **Label** tab to get to the project label management page, as shown in Fig. 2.18. On this page, you can create, edit, delete and filter labels. The labels here belong to the project only.

If the Clair or Trivy vulnerability scanning service is enabled, you can see the **Scanner** tab on the project management page. Click on the **Scanner** tab for the scanner management page, as shown in Fig. 2.19. This page shows information about the vulnerability scanner such as name, endpoint, adapter, vendor and version. The administrator can select the default vulnerability scanner.

Click on the **Policy** tab to display the policy management page, as shown in Fig. 2.20. Under the interface of tag retention, project administrators and project maintainers can view, add, disable, enable and delete the tag retention policy, or run or dry run the tag retention operation manually. Click on the **Immutable Tag** label to manage rules of immutable tag. Up to 15 rules can be associated with each project.

Projects
library System Admin
Summary Repositories Helm Charts Members Labels Scanner Policy Robot Accounts Webhooks Logs Configuration
Name Clair Healthy
Endpoint http://clair-adapter:8080
Adapter Clair
Vendor CoreOS
Version 2.x
SELECT SCANNER

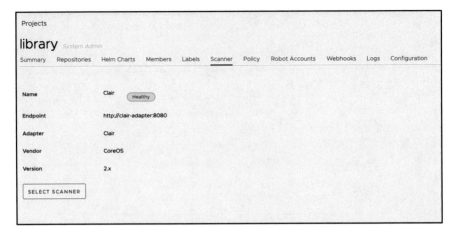

Fig. 2.19 Project scanner page

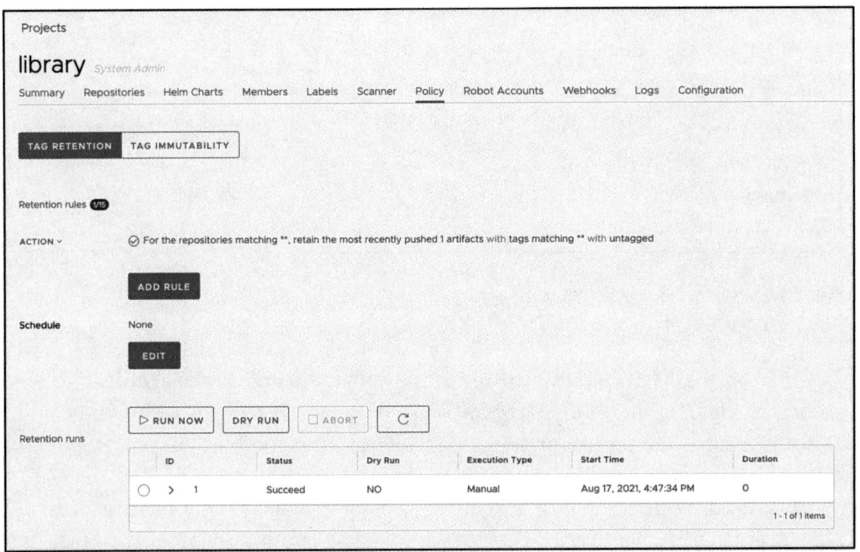

Fig. 2.20 Project policy management page

Click on the **Robot Accounts** tab to bring up the robot account management page, as shown in Fig. 2.21. On this page, the project administrator can add, delete, disable and filter robot accounts, and manage one or more robot accounts.

Click on the **Webhooks** tab to bring out the Webhooks management page, as shown in Fig. 2.22. On this page, project administrators and project maintainers can create, disable, edit, delete and filter Webhooks, and perform management operations on one or more Webhooks.

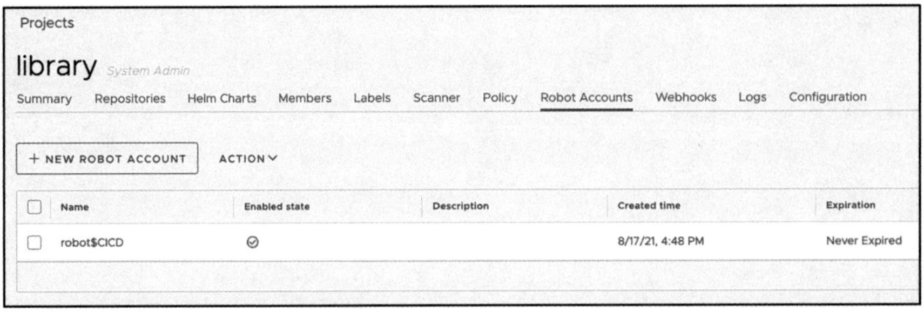

Fig. 2.21 Project robot management page

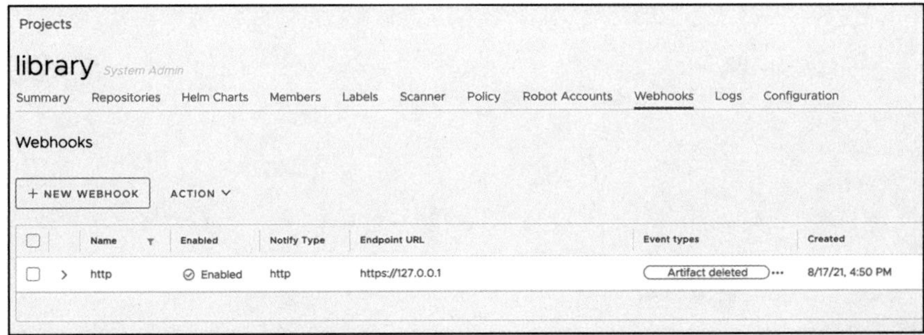

Fig. 2.22 Project webhook management page

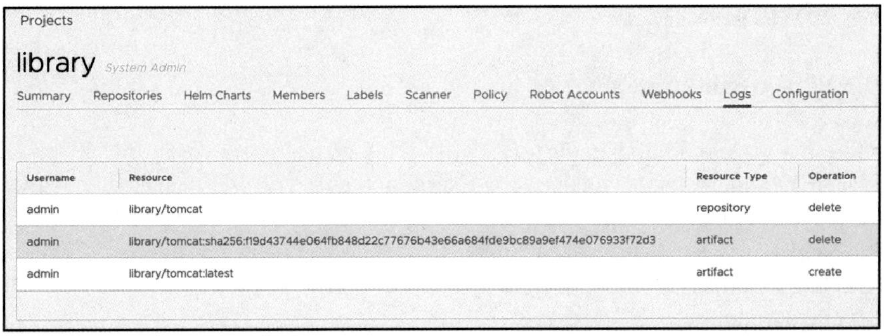

Fig. 2.23 Project logs page

Click on the **Log** tab to get to the log management page, as shown in Fig. 2.23. On this page, you can simply search for logs based on keyword or click on **Advanced** to apply more filters on the search for logs.

Click on the **Configuration** tab to view the project configuration management page, as shown in Fig. 2.24. On this page, the project administrator can configure whether the project registry is public to everyone and set options such as **Deployment security**, **Vulnerability scanning** and **CVE whitelist**.

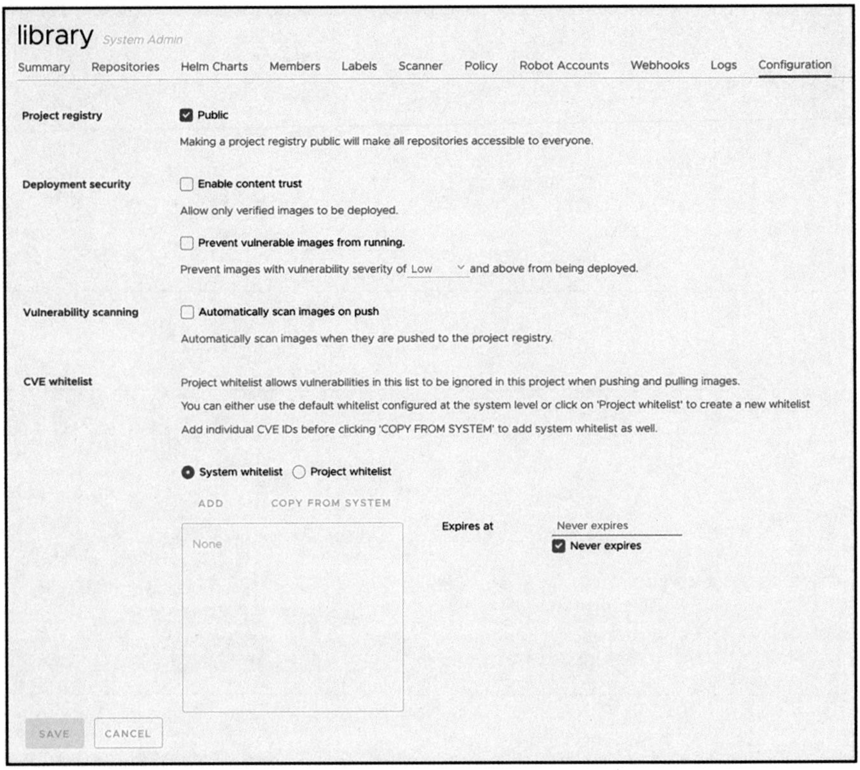

Fig. 2.24 Project configuration page

2.5.1.2 Administration

Only the system administrator role can see this menu, as shown in Fig. 2.25. The system administrator can click on the **Users** submenu. The user management page is displayed in the right pane. The system administrator can also access submenus such as **Registries**, **Replications**), **Labels**, **Project Quotas**, **Interrogation Services**, **Garbage Collection** and **Configuration** to complete the management of system-level configuration.

2.5.1.3 Theme switching

After you click on the **Dark/Light** menu in the lower left menu bar, the admin console can be switched between the dark theme or the light theme, as shown in Fig. 2.26.

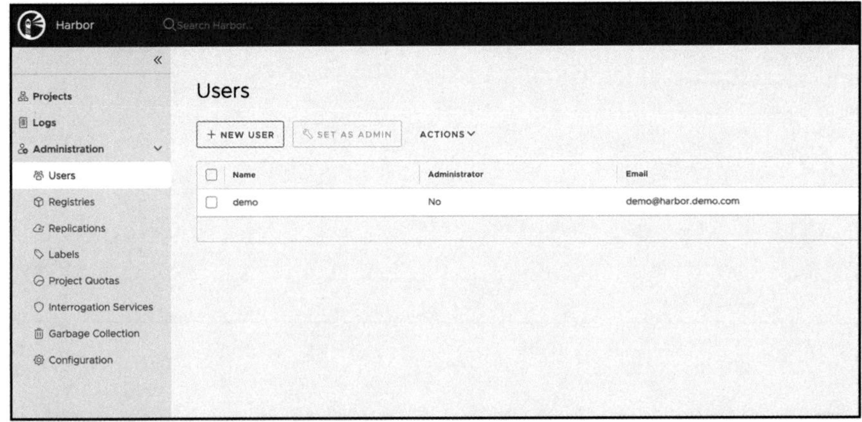

Fig. 2.25 Administrator management page

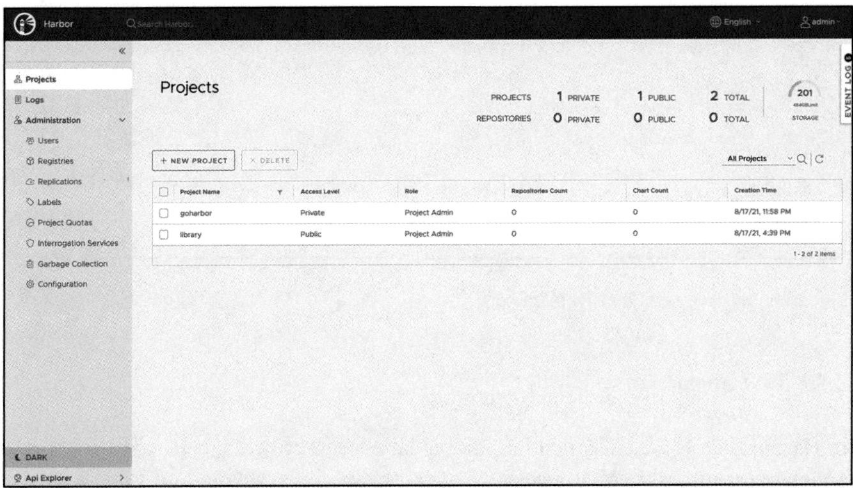

Fig. 2.26 Theme switching page

2.5.1.4 API Explorer

As shown in Fig. 2.27, click the **Harbor API v2.0** menu under the **API Explorer** menu. A new browser window pops up to display the **Harbor API Swagger** document. On the **Harbor API Swagger** document page, you can view the API path of Harbor, request parameters and response parameters or create an API request for a API test.

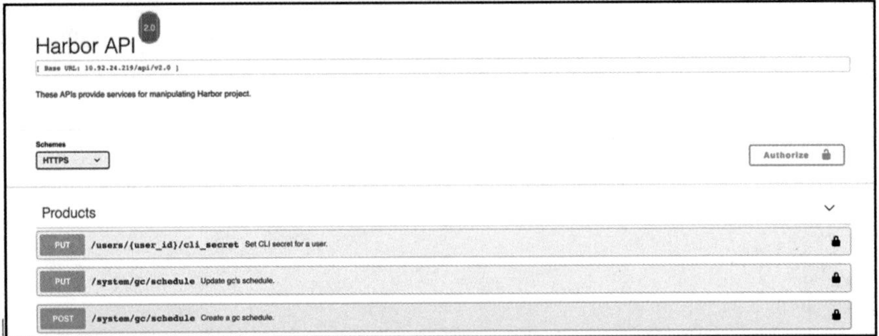

Fig. 2.27 API explorer page

Fig. 2.28 System label management page

2.5.1.5 Labels

In Harbor, labels are classified into global labels and project labels. They are used to annotate resources. Global labels are managed by the system administrator and can be used for resources in the entire Harbor system. Global labels can be added to any project. Project labels are managed by the project administrator and can be added to only resources of the project.

The system administrator can choose **Administration** > **Labels** to view, create, update and delete global labels, as shown in Fig. 2.28.

The project administrator and system administrator can access the **Labels** tab of a specific project to view, create, update and delete project labels, as shown in Fig. 2.29.

Created labels can be used to put annotation on artifacts such as images. A user with the system administrator, project administrator or project developer role can enter the artifact list by clicking on the **Project** > **{Project name}** > **Repositories** > **{Repository name}** in the repository list (e.g., **library/alpine** registry shown in Fig. 2.30) and select a specific artifact. Then the user chooses **Action** > **Add**

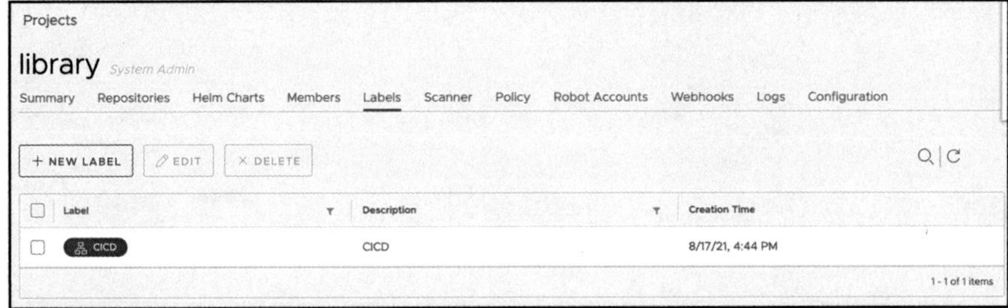

Fig. 2.29 Project label management page

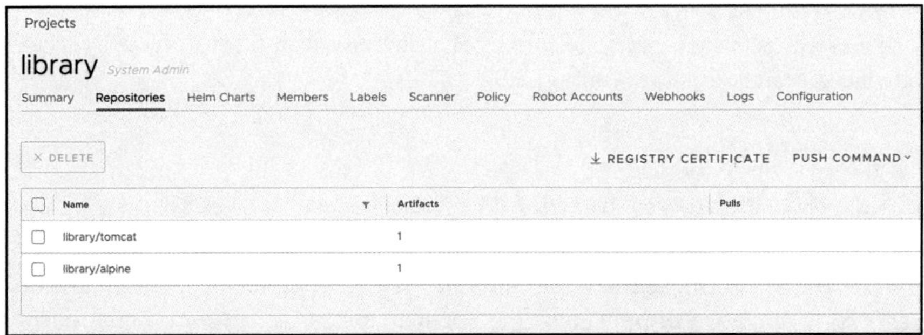

Fig. 2.30 Project repository page

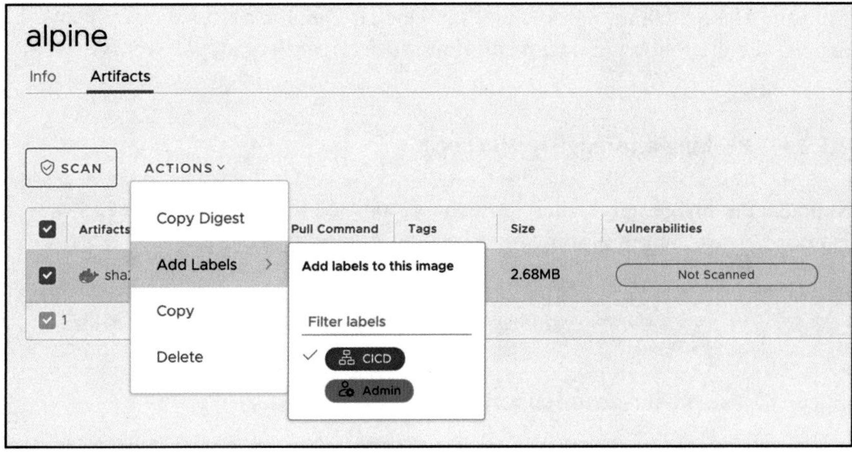

Fig. 2.31 Add label dialog box

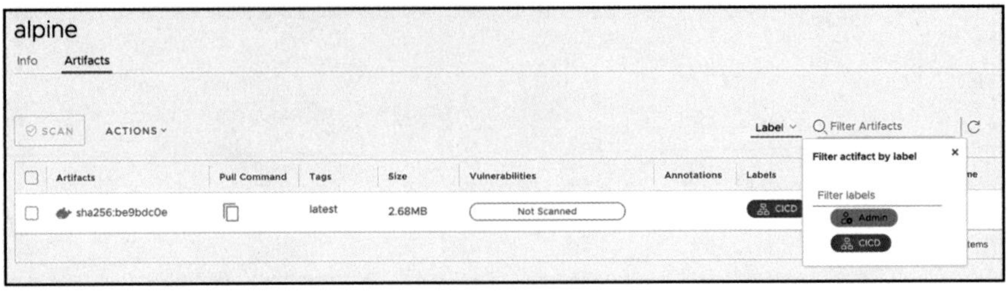

Fig. 2.32 Filter artifact by label page

Labels and click on the label name to add the label to a specific image or artifact (Fig. 2.31).

After artifacts such as images are labeled, the user can filter artifacts by label in advanced search, as shown in Fig. 2.32.

2.5.2 *Using Harbor in Docker*

To use Harbor in Docker, first log in to the Harbor. Assume the address of Harbor registry is **harbor.example.com**, the login command is **docker login harbor.example.com**. Enter the user name and password to log in to the registry. Note: If Harbor is using HTTP, configure the list of insecure-registries of the Docker client. If Harbor adopts a self-signed certificate in HTTPS, the certificate can be downloaded from the Harbor admin console and the Docker client can trust the certificate. For details, see the following document: **docs.docker.com/registry/insecure**.

2.5.2.1 Pushing an Image to Harbor

Suppose the image nginx:latest needs to be pushed to the project named "web" in Harbor registry, run the following command to modify the tag of the image:

```
$ docker tag nginx:latest harbor.example.com/web/nginx:latest
```

Next, push the image to Harbor:

```
$ docker push harbor.example.com/web/nginx:latest
```

2.5.2.2 Pulling an Image from Harbor

On the node which needs the web/nginx:latest image, first run the **docker login** command to log in to Harbor and then execute the following command to pull the image:

```
$ docker pull harbor.example.com/web/nginx:latest
```

2.5.3 *Using Harbor in Kubernetes*

For the reasons of security and confidentiality, most users choose to keep images of business applications private in Harbor. To set up private images in Harbor on a Kubernetes cluster, configure the Kubernetes cluster.

2.5.3.1 imagePullPolicy

In the yaml file to declare a Kubernetes Pod, two attributes are used to control the image download behavior, namely imagePullPolicy and imagePullSecret, which respectively specify the image pulling policy and the credential for accessing the registry.

The imagePullPolicy attribute determines the policy for kubelet to pull images. When this attribute is missing, the default value is **IfNotPresent** and kubelet pulls images only when the images are not cached on the node. This method brings in potential security risks in a multi-tenant environment. If the Pod of user A pulls an image and user B on the same node also starts a pod using the same image, because the image already exists, user B may be able to use the image without permission. In short, in a multi-tenant environment, kubelet must pull an image every time. In this case, you may refer to the following methods:

1. Set the imagePullPolicy attribute to **Always** (or the attribute exists and its value is null). In this way, kubelet always pulls images no matter whether the images exist locally.
2. Enable the AlwaysPullImages plug-in in the admission controller. This is a global setting which does not require setting the imagePullPolicy attribute to **Always** in the yaml file of each Pod. It forces the pulling of images every time when a Pod is created.
3. Delete the imagePullPolicy attribute. No tag is used for images or the tag is latest. In this way, kubelet is forced to always download images. Note: In the production environment, you should not use the latest tag for images because the latest image is often updated and it is difficult to track the version of the images actually in use.

When Kubernetes pulls private images from a registry, credentials such as user name and password must be provided to obtain authorization. The administrator can configure the authentication between kubelet nodes and the registry service. After the authentication is configured, all Pods can access the registry service.

If Kubernetes uses Docker container runtime, the user can save the credentials for accessing the registry service in the **$HOME/.dockercfg** or **$HOME/.docker/config.json** file after logging in to the Harbor registry by the **docker login** command. If you copy the files to the corresponding directory on the worker node of Kubernetes, kubelet reads related credentials to pull images. In the Kubernetes environment, especially in clusters supporting the automatic scaling, it is necessary to ensure that each worker node is configured with these credentials.

2.5.3.2 imagePullSecrets attribute

Compared with the above method that uses Docker credentials, another method is to use Kubernetes' Secret to save credentials of registries. You can access the registry service by specifying the name of the Secret in the imagePullSecrets attribute of the Pod configuration file. You can first create a docker-registry Secret. The command is as follows:

```
$ kubectl create secret docker-registry myregistrykey \
--docker-server=HARBOR_REGISTRY_SERVER --docker-
username=HARBOR_USER \
--docker-password=HARBOR_PASSWORD --namespace default
```

The uppercase variables in the above command must be replaced with the address, the user name and the password of the Harbor service respectively. The Secret in Kubernetes is bound to a namespace, and its default namespace is **default**. If the Pod belongs to other namespace, you need to substitute the **default** namespace in the above command with the desired namespace. Each namespace that needs to pull images should be configured with the Secret.

To use the Secret, the yaml file of a Pod can be specified as follows:

```
apiVersion: v1
kind: Pod
metadata:
 name: app1
 namespace: harborapps
spec:
 containers:
  - name: app1
   image: goharbor/harborapps:v1
```

(continued)

```
    imagePullPolicy: Always
  imagePullSecrets:
   - name: myregistrykey
```

If you want to avoid specifying imagePullSecrets during the deployment of each Pod, you can configure the default serviceaccount of the namespace to deploy a Pod. The command is as follows:

```
$ kubectl patch serviceaccount default --namespace
<your_namespace> \
 -p '{"imagePullSecrets": [{"name": "myregistrykey"}]}'
```

After the above configuration, images can be pulled from a Harbor registry for the deployment on a Kubernetes cluster.

2.6 FAQ

1. How to search for logs of Harbor?

   The default path of Harbor's log is **/var/log/harbor**. If the **log** option and the **location** field in the **local** log option in the **harbor.yml** configuration file are modified before Harbor is installed, the location of the log is the path specified by the **location** field. By default, Harbor output logs with the ".log" suffix.

2. After Harbor is installed using the offline installation package, Harbor is unavailable after the host is restarted. How to solve this problem?

   The offline installation package starts containers using the **docker-compose** command. If the host is restarted, Docker daemon restarts the containers that were running before the machine restarted. When the containers are not started using the docker-compose command, it will cause many errors. The solution to this problem is as follows: enter the installation directory of Harbor and run the **docker-compose down -v** and **docker-compose up -d** commands to restart Harbor. The above commands must be used after each restart. If you want to solve such a problem thoroughly, you may use the systemd service and control the lifecycle of Harbor through the **docker compose** command. For details, see Chap. 7.

3. After Harbor is successfully installed, Harbor cannot be accessed. How to solve this problem?

   First check the container status of each component to see whether any container is in the restarting status. Then view the log of the corresponding container for troubleshooting. If an external database is used but was misconfigured, the components cannot connect to the database. As a result, the Harbor service fails.

Chapter 3
Access Control

Access control is a basic function of data security in the Harbor. It defines which users can access resources in which projects. Through authentication and authorization, the access control policy ensures that users' identities are real and users have the corresponding permissions to access Harbor resources. In most production environments, access control is an issue of concern during operation and maintenance. This chapter explains the role-based access control (RBAC) mechanism of Harbor, including the principles of authentication and authorization, the configuration of authentication modes, the authorization of various roles and FAQs.

3.1 Overview

This section describes the main authentication and authorization modes, the resource isolation method and the typical flow of client authentication.

3.1.1 Authentication and Authorization

Authentication is used to determine the identity of a visitor. At present, Harbor supports authentication modes of local database, Lightweight Directory Access Protocol (LDAP) and OpenID Connect (OIDC). Authentication modes can be configured in **Administration** > **Configuration** > **Authentication**. In the authentication mode of local database, user information is stored in a local relational database. Harbor system administrator can manage various attributes of users. In the authentication modes of LDAP and OIDC, user information including passwords is stored in systems external to Harbor. After a user logs in, Harbor creates a corresponding user account in the local relational database. In addition, Harbor updates the account information of the user every time after the user logs in.

H. Zhang, Y. Wang, *The Authoritative Guide on Harbor*,
https://doi.org/10.1007/978-981-19-2727-0_3

Authorization determines the permissions of visitors. Currently, Harbor's permissions are based on the RBAC model.

3.1.2 Resource Isolation

Resources in the Harbor are divided into two categories: resources that can be accessed by only system administrators and resources that are managed based on project and are accessed by common users. The system administrator of Harbor can access resources of both categories.

The resources that can only be accessed by system administrators include users, registries, replications, tags, project quotas, interrogation service, garbage collection and system configuration management.

The resources that are managed based on project include project summary, artifact repositories, Helm Charts, project members, labels, scanners, artifact (tag) retention, immutable artifacts (tags), robot accounts, Webhook, audit logs and project configuration management.

When a user requests access to system resources, the security middleware of Harbor's Core component obtains the Security Context instance and then determines the authorization for resources according to the Security Context.

The security middleware supports nine security generators: secret, oidcCli, v2Token, idToken, authProxy, robot, basicAuth, session and unauthorized. These generators create Security Context instances according to a user's information. Table 3.1 lists the specific functions of the generators.

Based on the authentication mode, the above security generators can generator four types of Security Context instances. Each type of instances implements a method: Can(action type.Action, resource types.Resource) bool, which can be used to determine whether the user's access is permitted, so as to decide whether the user can continue with relevant operations.

Harbor implements four types of Security Context: local, robot, secret and v2token, which can be applied to different scenarios. Table 3.2 describes the Security Context.

Figure 3.1 shows the relationship between Security Generators and Security Context instances. The generators process user information in turn based on a certain sequence until a generator outputs the Security Context instance of a user.

3.1.3 Client Authentication

Clients that comply with the OCI Distribution Specification (for example, Docker client) must log in when they pull or push artifacts, and then users are authenticated during the request process. Harbor adopts the token authentication mode of Docker Distribution. The authentication flow of a Docker client is as follows:

Table 3.1 Functions of generators

Name	Description
secret	Generates secret Security Context instances according to the environment variables for other components of Harbor to access system resources.
oidcCli	Generates local Security Context instances in OIDC authentication mode according to the user name and the CLI password for OIDC users to access the system by using the CLI password.
v2Token	Generates v2token Security Context instances according to the bearer token of Docker Distribution for clients to access the system through the interface with "/v2" as the endpoint.
idToken	Generates local Security Context instances in OIDC authentication mode according to the bearer token (OIDC ID Token) in Authorization Header for OIDC users to access the system by using the OIDC ID token through the interface with "/api" as the endpoint.
authProxy	If the user name in Basic Authorization starts with "tokenreview$", generates local Security Context instances according to the user name and password by using the Kubernetes Webhook Token Authentication mode for users to access the system through the interface with "/v2" as the endpoint.
robot	If the user name in Basic Authorization starts with "robot$", generates robot Security Context instances according to the robot account corresponding to the user name and password for the robot account to access the system.
basicAuth	Generates local Security Context instances according to the Harbor user corresponding to the user name and password in Basic Authorization to access the system.
session	Generates local Security Context instances according to the user information saved in the session for users to access the system through the browser.
unauthorized	Access Harbor as an anonymous user.

Table 3.2 Security Context of Harbor

Name	Function	Remarks
local	Determines the permissions of project members based on RBAC.	Security generators such as oidcCli, idToken, authProxy, basicAuth, session and unauthorized return local Security Context instances according to the Harbor users corresponding to requests.
robot	Determines the permissions of the robot account.	The robot Security generator generates robot Security Context instances by using the robot account token.
secret	Determines the permissions of Harbor components to access system resources.	The secret Security generator returns secret Security Context and can access all resources under a project.
v2token	Determines the permissions of Docker Distribution bearer token.	The v2Token security generator returns v2token Security Context.

1. The Docker client attempts the pull or push operation through the Daemon.
2. If the pull or push operation requires authentication, Harbor returns a response code of 401, which carries the information about how to perform the authentication.

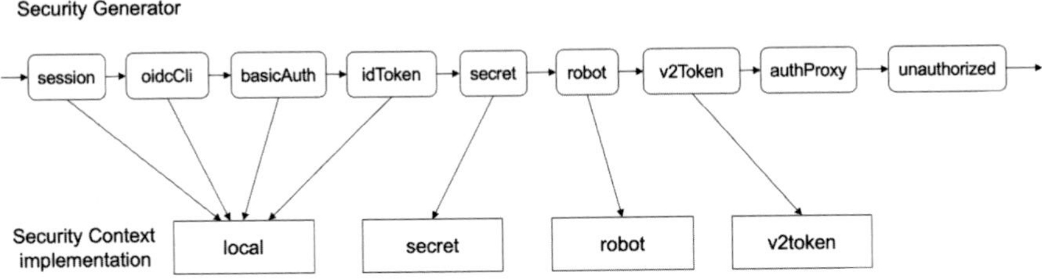

Fig. 3.1 The mapping of Security Context and Security Generator

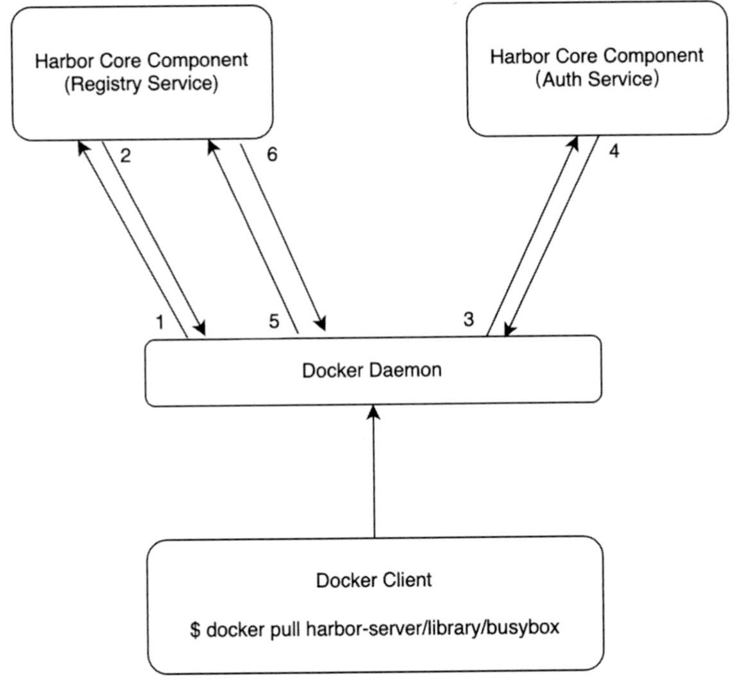

Fig. 3.2 The authentication flow of Docker client

3. The client requests a bearer token from the authentication service (in the Core component) of Harbor.
4. The authentication service of Harbor returns a bearer token containing the client's permissions.
5. The client embeds the bearer token into the HTTP request header and sends the previous request again.
6. Harbor verifies the bearer token provided by the client and responds to the request.

Figure 3.2 shows the above process. In Step 3, after Harbor receives a request for a bearer token from the client, Harbor checks whether the user logs in according to the security context generated by the security middleware, filters all pull and push operations in the scope of all requests according to the permissions of the user, generates a bearer token and returns it to the client.

3.2 User Authentication

To support multiple identity providers, Harbor offers three authentication modes: local database authentication, LDAP authentication and OIDC Provider authentication. This section explains the principles of different authentication modes and describes how to configure the LDAP and OIDC authentication modes by giving examples.

3.2.1 *Local Database Authentication*

By default, Harbor uses the local database authentication mode. In this authentication mode, user information is stored in the PostgreSQL database and users are allowed to self register accounts in Harbor.

On the **Administration** > **Users** page, the system administrator can create and delete a user, reset a user's password and set other users as system administrators, as shown in Fig. 3.3.

On the **Users** page, click **New User**. In the **New User** dialog box, enter the user name, email address, full name, password and confirmation password to create a user. As shown in Fig. 3.4, a user named jack is created.

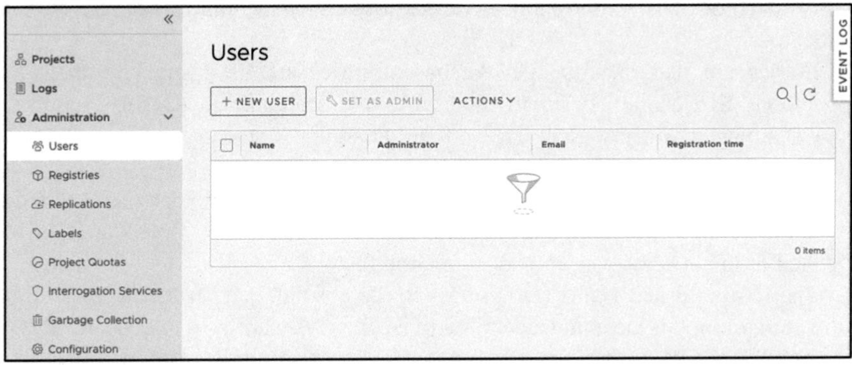

Fig. 3.3 Users page

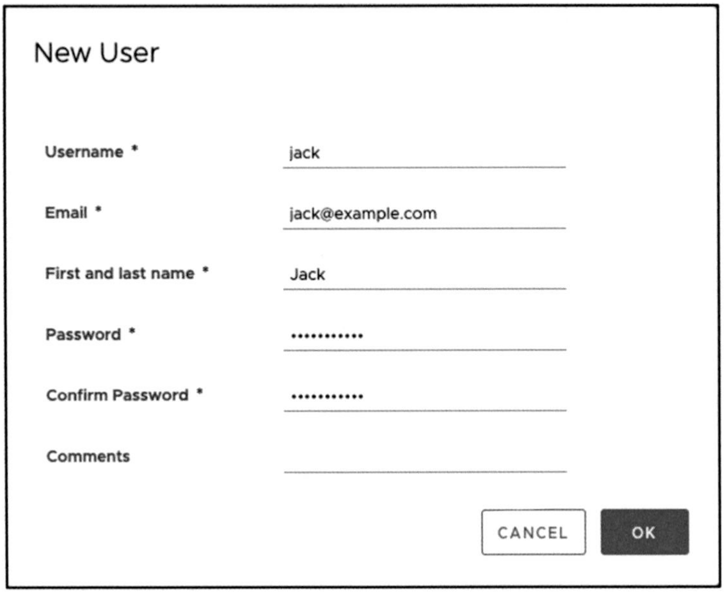

Fig. 3.4 New User dialog box

3.2.2 LDAP Authentication

Harbor can authenticate against an LDAP service, such as OpenLDAP and Active Directory (AD).

LDAP (Lightweight Directory Access Protocol) is a software protocol based on the X.500 standard. A directory is a database that is optimized for query, browse and search. In LDAP, data is organized in the form of a tree. The basic unit of a tree is an entry. Each entry is composed of several attributes. Some entries can also contain subentries.

Entries are like records in a database. Entries are the basic objects in the operations like adding, deleting, modifying and searching in LDAP. Figure 3.5 shows a typical directory tree. Each box in the figure is an entry and the root node is "dc=goharbor,dc=io".

The Domain Component (DC) is the domain part of an entry identifier. It divides a complete domain name into several parts, for example, the domain name "goharbor.io" is converted into "dc=goharbor,dc=io".

The Distinguished Name (DN) refers to the absolute path from the root of the directory tree and is the unique identifier of an entry. As shown in Fig. 3.5, the DN of the entry in the lower left corner is "cn=user1,ou=Users,dc=goharbor,dc=io".

The base Distinguished Name (base DN) generally refers to the root of a whole directory. The base DN in Fig. 3.5 is "dc=goharbor,dc=io".

Each entry may have a few attributes such as name, date of birth, address and telephone number. Each attribute has its name and corresponding value. An attribute

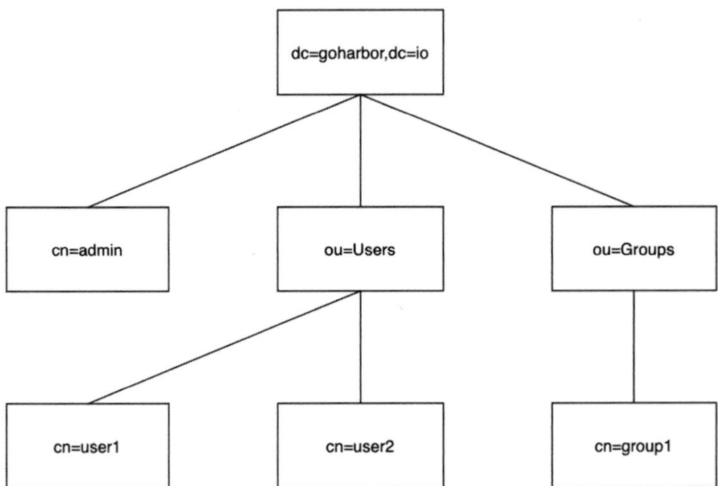

Fig. 3.5 An LDAP tree of entries

Table 3.3 Common attributes of the object class mailAccount

Attribute	Alias	Syntax	Description	Example
commonName	cn	Directory String	Name	jack
organizationalUnitName	ou	Directory String	Organization unit name	IT

may have one or more values. For example, a person has only a date of birth but may have multiple telephone numbers. Attributes must meet certain rules, which are generally defined through schema. For example, if an entry is not included in the mailAccount schema (i.e. not with the schema of "objectClass: mailAccount"), the mail attribute may not be specified for the entry. ObjectClass is an object containing a collection of attributes. LDAP has many built-in objects which are encapsulated into object classes. For example, the object class of person has attributes such as surname (sn), given name (cn) and password (userPassword). The object class of mailAccount has attributes such as mail. Table 3.3 lists some common attributes.

The following example describes how to make Harbor work with OpenLDAP in a Kubernetes environment.

1. Install Harbor using Helm 3.

   First add and update the Helm repository of Harbor.

```
$ helm repo add harbor https://helm.goharbor.io
$ helm repo update
```

   Then install Harbor (**192.168.1.2** indicates the IP address of the ingress controller of Kubernetes).

```
$ cat <<EOF | helm install harbor harbor/harbor --version=1.4.0 --
values=-
expose:
 type: ingress
 ingress:
  hosts:
   core: harbor.192.168.1.2.nip.io
   notary: notary.192.168.1.2.nip.io
externalURL: https://harbor.192.168.1.2.nip.io
EOF
```

2. Install OpenLDAP using Helm 3.
   Add a stable repository and update the Helm repository.

```
$ helm repo add stable https://kubernetes-charts.storage.
googleapis.com
$ helm repo update
```

   Install OpenLDAP and enable the Memberof module.

```
$ cat <<EOF | helm install openldap stable/openldap --
version=1.2.4 --values=-
env:
 LDAP_ORGANISATION: "Harbor Org."
 LDAP_DOMAIN: "goharbor.io"
 LDAP_BACKEND: "hdb"
 LDAP_TLS: "true"
 LDAP_TLS_ENFORCE: "false"
 LDAP_REMOVE_CONFIG_AFTER_SETUP: "true"
customLdifFiles:
 memberof_load_configure.ldif: |
  dn: cn=module{1},cn=config
  cn: module{1}
  objectClass: olcModuleList
  olcModuleLoad: memberof
  olcModulePath: /usr/lib/ldap

  dn: olcOverlay={0}memberof,olcDatabase={1}hdb,cn=config
  objectClass: olcConfig
  objectClass: olcMemberOf
  objectClass: olcOverlayConfig
  objectClass: top
  olcOverlay: memberof
  olcMemberOfDangling: ignore
  olcMemberOfRefInt: TRUE
```

(continued)

```
    olcMemberOfGroupOC:groupOfNames
    olcMemberOfMemberAD:member
    olcMemberOfMemberOfAD:memberOf
  refint1.ldif:|
    dn:cn=module{1},cn=config
    add:olcmoduleload
    olcmoduleload:refint
  refint2.ldif:|
    dn:olcOverlay={1}refint,olcDatabase={1}hdb,cn=config
    objectClass:olcConfig
    objectClass:olcOverlayConfig
    objectClass:olcRefintConfig
    objectClass:top
    olcOverlay:{1}refint
    olcRefintAttribute:memberof member manager owner
persistence:
  enabled:true
EOF
```

3. Prepare LDAP entries.
   Enter the OpenLDAP environment.

```
$ kubectl exec -i -t $(kubectl get pod -l "app=openldap" -o name)
-- bash
```

   Create the entries of Groups and Users OU.

```
$ ldapadd -H ldapi:/// -D "cn=admin,dc=goharbor,dc=io" -w
$LDAP_ADMIN_PASSWORD << EOF
dn:ou=Users,dc=goharbor,dc=io
objectClass:organizationalUnit
ou:Users

dn:ou=Groups,dc=goharbor,dc=io
objectClass:organizationalUnit
ou:Groups
EOF
```

   Create users kate and jack and set the user passwords to **Harbor12345**.

```
$ ldapadd -H ldapi:/// -D "cn=admin,dc=goharbor,dc=io" -w
$LDAP_ADMIN_PASSWORD << EOF
dn:cn=kate,ou=Users,dc=goharbor,dc=io
```

(continued)

```
  objectClass:person
  objectClass:mailAccount
  mail:kate@goharbor.io
  sn:kate
  userPassword:'slappasswd -s Harbor12345'

dn:cn=jack,ou=Users,dc=goharbor,dc=io
objectClass:person
objectClass:mailAccount
mail:jack@goharbor.io
sn:jack
userPassword:'slappasswd -s Harbor12345'
EOF
```

Create the groups of administrator and developer respectively and add the user kate into the administrator group and the users kate and jack into the developer group.

```
$ ldapadd -H ldapi:/// -D "cn=admin,dc=goharbor,dc=io" -w
$LDAP_ADMIN_PASSWORD << EOF
dn:cn=administrator,ou=Groups,dc=goharbor,dc=io
objectClass:groupOfUniqueNames
cn:administrator
uniqueMember:cn=kate,ou=Users,dc=goharbor,dc=io
EOF

$ ldapadd -H ldapi:/// -D "cn=admin,dc=goharbor,dc=io" -w
$LDAP_ADMIN_PASSWORD << EOF
dn:cn=developer,ou=Groups,dc=goharbor,dc=io
objectClass:groupOfUniqueNames
cn:developer
uniqueMember:cn=kate,ou=Users,dc=goharbor,dc=io
uniqueMember:cn=jack,ou=Users,dc=goharbor,dc=io
EOF
```

4. Log in to Harbor admin console as the system administrator, choose **Administration** > **Configuration** > **Authentication** and configure the LDAP authentication mode. For the main configuration items, see Table 3.4 and Fig. 3.6.
5. After the configuration is done, log in to the Harbor as user kate and jack respectively. The password is **Harbor12345**. The user kate accesses Harbor as system administrator while the user jack accesses as a normal user.

   Note: When using functions related to the LDAP group, make sure that the current LDAP software supports the memberof overlay function. For details on how to configure the function, see relevant documentation of the LDAP software. The method for determining whether this function has been enabled is as follows: If this function is enabled, when an entry is added to or deleted from a group, the

Table 3.4 The configuration items of LDAP authentication

Configuration Item	Value	Description
LDAP URL	ldap://openldap	URL of the LDAP server
LDAP search DN	cn=admin,dc=goharbor, dc=io	DN used when Harbor queries the LDAP Server
LDAP search password		Password of "cn=admin,dc=goharbor,dc=io". It can obtained through the following command: $ kubectl get secret --namespace default openldap -o jsonpath="{.data. LDAP_ADMIN_PASSWORD}" | base64 --decode; echo
LDAP base DN	ou=Users,dc=goharbor, dc=io	Base DN used during search for LDAP users. It can also be set to "dc=goharbor,dc=io".
LDAP UID	cn	Prefix of a relative DN used to identify entries during search for LDAP users
LDAP filter		It is used with UID and base DN to further search for LDAP users.
Base DN of LDAP group	ou=Groups, dc=goharbor,dc=io	Base DN used during search for LDAP groups
DN of LDAP group administrator	cn=administrator, ou=groups, dc=goharbor,dc=io	Members of the group are set to the role of Harbor system administrators.
LDAP group member	memberof	Membership attribute of LDAP group members

attribute *member* of the group and the attribute memberof of the entry are updated synchronously; if the two attributes are not in sync, the memberof overlay function is not enabled.

3.2.3 OIDC Provider Authentication

OIDC is a simple identity layer on top of OAuth 2.0 protocol. OAuth 2.0 introduces an authorization layer to distinguish two different roles: resource owner and client. The token obtained by the client from the resource server can replace the credential of the resource owner to access protected resources. Essentially, OAuth 2.0 indicates that the client obtains the token from a third-party application. It specifies four modes for obtaining the token:

- Authorization code
- Implicit
- Password
- Client credentials

With the help of OAuth 2.0 authorization service, OIDC provides third-party clients with the user identity authentication and transmits authentication information

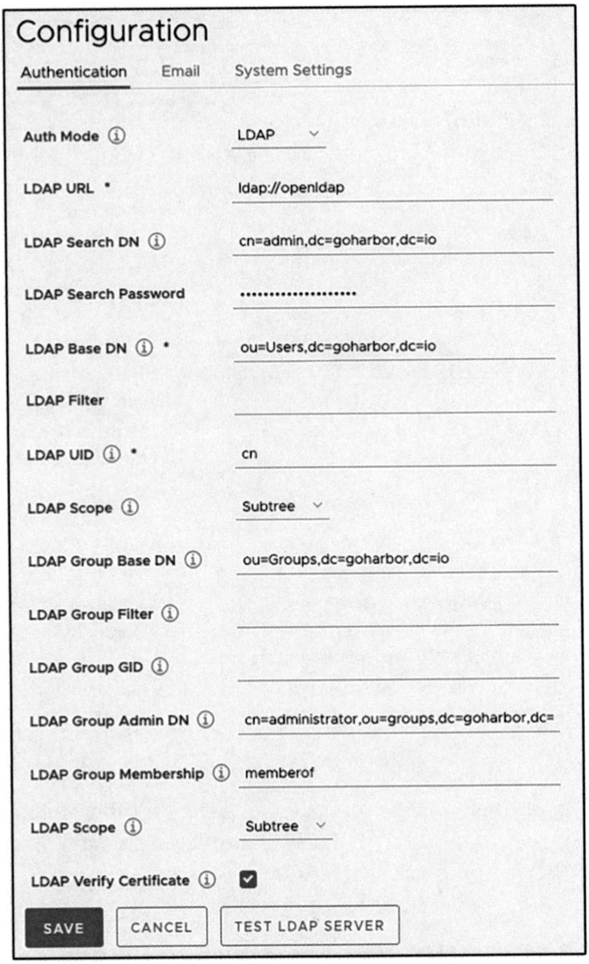

Fig. 3.6 The configuration of LDAP authentication

to the clients. Based on OAuth 2.0, OIDC provides an ID token for the authentication of third-party clients. It also provides the UserInfo interface for third-party clients to obtain more user information.

Harbor can authenticate a user using an OIDC-enabled OAuth service provider and obtain the token using the mode of authorization code. Figure 3.7 shows the steps of the flow.

1. A user accesses the login page of Harbor through the browser and clicks the **Login via OIDC Provider** button. The button appears only when Harbor uses OIDC authentication.
2. The user is redirected to the OIDC provider's authentication page.
3. After the user passes authentication, the OIDC provider redirects the user to Harbor with the authorization code.

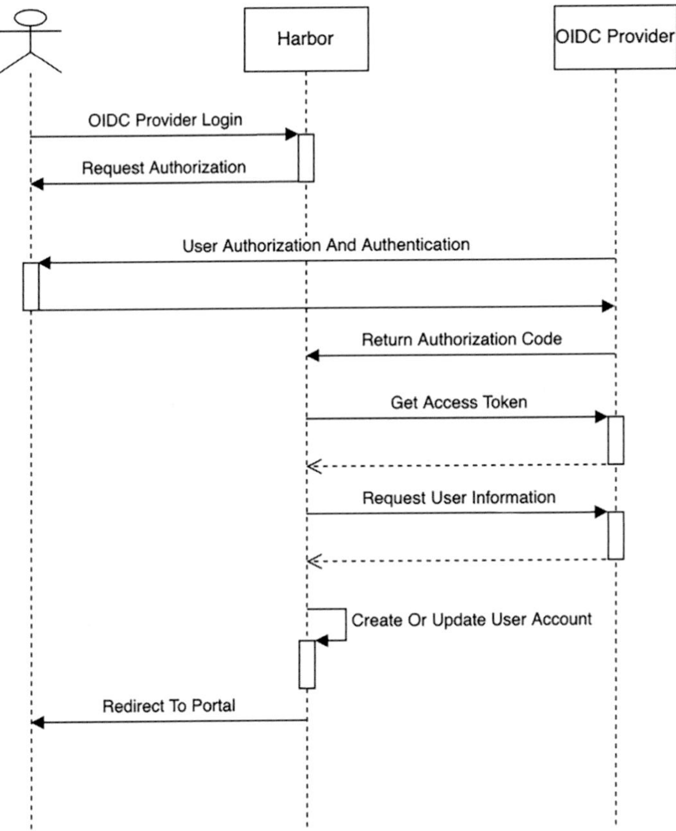

Fig. 3.7 The authentication flow between a user and an OIDC provider

4. Harbor exchanges the authorization code with the OIDC provider to obtain an access token.
5. Harbor uses the access token to obtain user information via the UserInfo interface.
6. Harbor creates or updates the user account and redirects the user to the admin console's home page.

The following are some OAuth service providers supporting OIDC:

- Apple
- GitLab
- Google
- Google App Engine
- Keycloak
- Microsoft (Hotmail, Windows Live, Messenger, Active Directory and Xbox)
- NetIQ
- Okta

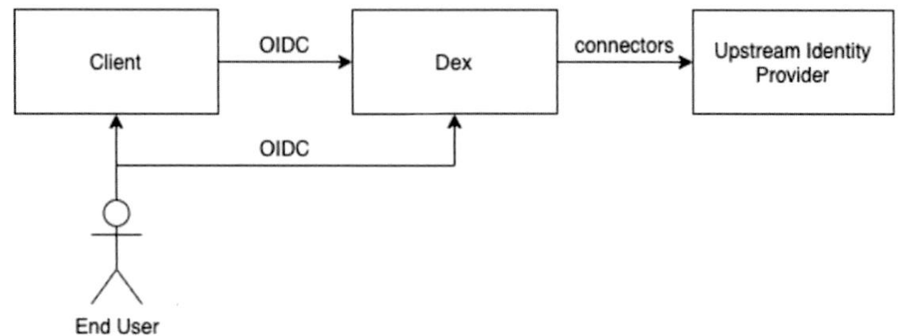

Fig. 3.8 Dex as the intermediate layer between clients and identity providers

Table 3.5 Connectors of Dex 2.24.0

Name	Token Refresh	Group	Preferred User Name
LDAP	Supported	Supported	Supported
GitHub	Supported	Supported	Supported
SAML 2.0	Not supported	Supported	Not supported
GitLab	Supported	Supported	Supported
OpenID Connect	Supported	Not supported	Not supported
Google	Supported	Supported	Supported
LinkedIn	Supported	Not supported	Not supported
Microsoft	Supported	Supported	Not supported
AuthProxy	Not supported	Not supported	Not supported
Bitbucket Cloud	Supported	Supported	Not supported
OpenShift	Not supported	Supported	Not supported
Atlassian Crowd	Supported	Supported	Supported

- Salesforce.com
- WSO2 Identity Server

In addition to these OAuth service providers, we can also create our own OIDC provider through Dex. Dex is a federated OIDC identity service. It provides clients or end users with an OIDC service. The actual user authentication function is done by the upstream identity provider through connectors. As shown in Fig. 3.8, as the intermediate layer, Dex connects clients and upstream identity providers.

Connector is the policy used by Dex to call an identity provider for user authentication. Table 3.5 lists the connectors implemented by Dex 2.24.0.

The following describes how Harbor works with Dex's OIDC authentication service using OpenLDAP as the upstream identity provider.

1. Install Harbor and OpenLDAP by referring to Sect. 3.2.2 and prepare the data in OpenLDAP.
2. Use cert-manager to prepare a certificate for Dex.

   Create a namespace for cert-manager.

```
$ kubectl create namespace cert-manager
```

Add a jetstack repository.

```
$ helm repo add jetstack https://charts.jetstack.io
```

Update the Helm repository.

```
$ helm repo update
```

Install cert-manager.

```
$ helm install cert-manager jetstack/cert-manager --namespace
cert-manager --set installCRDs=true --version=v0.16.0
```

Generate the HTTPS certificate required by Dex.

```
$ cat <<EOF | kubectl apply -f -
apiVersion:cert-manager.io/v1alpha2
kind:Issuer
metadata:
 name:dex-selfsigned
spec:
 selfSigned:{}
---
apiVersion:cert-manager.io/v1alpha2
kind:Certificate
metadata:
 name:dex-ca-key-pair
spec:
 secretName:dex-ca-key-pair
 isCA:true
 commonName:dex-ca
 issuerRef:
  name:dex-selfsigned
  kind:Issuer
---
apiVersion:cert-manager.io/v1alpha2
kind:Issuer
metadata:
 name:dex-ca-issuer
spec:
```

(continued)

```
  ca:
   secretName:dex-ca-key-pair
---
apiVersion:cert-manager.io/v1alpha2
kind:Certificate
metadata:
 name:dex-tls
spec:
 secretName:dex-tls
 issuerRef:
  name:dex-ca-issuer
  kind:Issuer
 dnsNames:
 - dex.192.168.1.2.nip.io
EOF
```

3. Install Dex. The following example configures a client named Harbor. The client ID is "harbor", the secret of the client is "secretforclient" and identity provider at the back end is OpenLDAP. In the LDAP directory tree, the users who have the "objectClass=person" attribute and are under the base DN "ou=Users, dc=goharbor,dc=io" can log in through their email addresses. The LDAP group information of the users can be provided by OIDC to Harbor.

```
$ cat <<EOF | helm install dex stable/dex --version=2.13.0 --
values=-
ingress:
 enabled:true
 hosts:
  - dex.192.168.1.2.nip.io
 tls:
 - secretName:dex-tls
  hosts:
  - dex.192.168.1.2.nip.io
config:
 issuer:https://dex.192.168.1.2.nip.io
 storage:
  type:kubernetes
  config:
   inCluster:true
 expiry:
  signingKeys:"6h"
  idTokens:"24h"
 connectors:
 - type:ldap
  name:OpenLDAP
  id:ldap
```

(continued)

```
  config:
   host:openldap:389

   # No TLS for this setup.
   insecureNoSSL:true

   # This would normally be a read-only user.
   bindDN:cn=admin,dc=goharbor,dc=io
   bindPW:'kubectl get secret --namespace default openldap -o
jsonpath="{.data.LDAP_ADMIN_PASSWORD}" | base64 --decode; echo'

   usernamePrompt:Email Address

   userSearch:
    baseDN:ou=Users,dc=goharbor,dc=io
    filter:"(objectClass=person)"
    username:mail
   # "DN" (case sensitive) is a special attribute name. It indicates
that
   # this value should be taken from the entity's DN not an attribute
on
    # the entity.
    idAttr:DN
    emailAttr:mail
    nameAttr:cn

   groupSearch:
    baseDN:ou=Groups,dc=goharbor,dc=io
    filter:"(objectClass=groupOfUniqueNames)"

    userMatchers:
    - userAttr:DN
     groupAttr:uniqueMember

    # The group name should be the "cn" value.
    nameAttr:cn
 staticClients:
 - id:harbor
  redirectURIs:
  - 'https://harbor.192.168.1.2.nip.io/c/oidc/callback'
  name:'Harbor'
  secret:secretforclient
EOF
```

4. Log in to Harbor by using the system administrator, choose **Administration > Configuration > Authentication** and configure the LDAP authentication mode. Table 3.6 lists the main configuration items and Fig. 3.9 shows the configuration dialogue.

Table 3.6 The configuration items of OIDC authentication

Configuration Item	Value	Description
OIDC Provider Name	Dex	The OIDC provider's name.
OIDC Endpoint	https://dex.192.168.1.2.nip.io	Access address of the OIDC provider, which must be the same as the issuer of the provider. Only HTTPS is supported.
OIDC Client ID	harbor	The Client ID configured by the OIDC provider for Harbor.
OIDC Client Secret	secretforclient	The Client Secret configured by the OIDC for Harbor.
Group Claim Name	groups	The name of the attribute for obtaining user group information from the claim of IDToken.
OIDC Scope	openid, profile, email, groups, offline_access	The scope that is sent to the OIDC server during authentication. It must include **openid**. In Dex, **profile**, **email** and **groups** are used to obtain the name, the email address and the group of the user; **offline_access** is used for the Harbor system to call the interface of the OIDC provider to refresh the token and update the user information of OIDC to the local system when the user accesses Harbor through the CLI password and the OIDC token has been invalidated.

5. After the configuration is completed, access the login page of Harbor and click **Log in via OIDC Provider**. Harbor jumps to the Dex authentication page, as shown in Fig. 3.10.

   On the Dex authentication page, click **Log in with OpenLDAP**. The OpenLDAP login page is displayed. Log in to Dex by using the email address "kate@goharbor.io" and password "Harbor12345", as shown in Fig. 3.11.

After you log in to Dex successfully, the page is redirected to the OIDC callback page of Harbor. On the page shown in Fig. 3.12, set the name of the OIDC user to access the system.

The above describes the steps to integrate Harbor the upstream LDAP identity providers through Dex. The following section describes how Harbor authenticates against GitHub using OIDC protocol through Dex.

1. Install Harbor by referring to Sect. 3.2.2.
2. Log in to the website of GitHub, choose **Settings** > **Developer settings** > **OAuth Apps** and click **New OAuth App** or **Register a new application**. Create an application named Dex, as shown in Fig. 3.13, and obtain the application ID (Client ID) and application key (Client Secret) on the page shown in Fig. 3.14.
3. Prepare the certificate required by Dex by referring to the above steps in the example of OpenLADP and Dex.

Configuration
Authentication Email System Settings
Auth Mode OIDC More info...
OIDC Provider Name * Dex
OIDC Endpoint * https://dex.192.168.1.2.nip.io
OIDC Client ID * harbor
OIDC Client Secret * ••••••••••••••••••••
Group Claim Name groups
OIDC Scope * openid,profile,email,groups,offline_access
Verify Certificate
Please make sure the Redirect URI on the OIDC provider is set to https://10.193.59.96/c/oidc/callback
SAVE CANCEL TEST OIDC SERVER

Fig. 3.9 The configuration of OIDC authentication

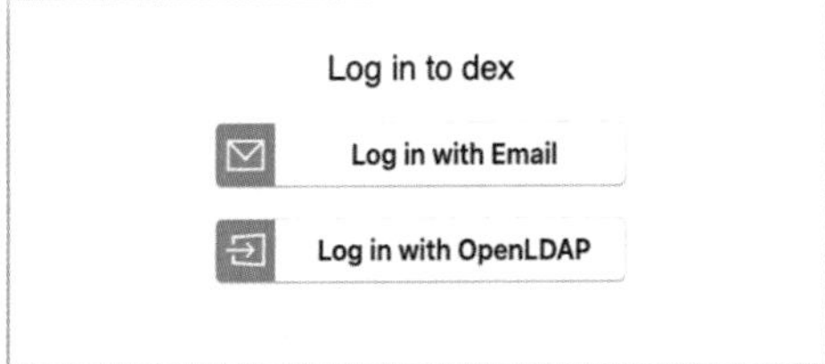

Fig. 3.10 The Dex authentication page

Fig. 3.11 Log in Dex by email address and password

4. Install Dex, configure a client with the name of "Harbor", the Client ID of "harbor" and the Client Secret of "secretforclient" and configure a GitHub connector.

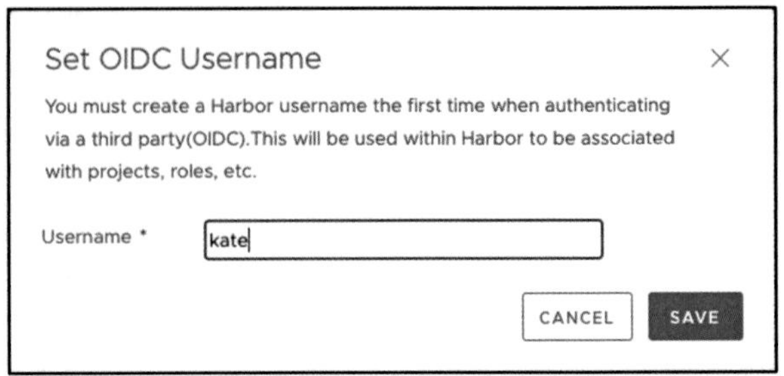

Fig. 3.12 The OIDC callback page of Harbor

```
$ cat <<EOF | helm install dex stable/dex --version=2.13.0 --
values=-
ingress:
 enabled:true
 hosts:
  - dex.192.168.1.2.nip.io
 tls:
 - secretName:dex-tls
  hosts:
  - dex.192.168.1.2.nip.io
config:
 issuer:https://dex.192.168.1.2.nip.io
 storage:
  type:kubernetes
  config:
   inCluster:true
 expiry:
  signingKeys:"6h"
  idTokens:"24h"
 connectors:
 - type:github
  name:Github
  id:github
  config:
   clientID:e1335491fe7419d33e4b
   clientSecret:6502ccd62247fd3943a4efe29111d90f8ec811e9
   redirectURI:https://dex.192.168.1.2.nip.io/callback

 staticClients:
 - id:harbor
  redirectURIs:
  - 'https://harbor.192.168.1.2.nip.io/c/oidc/callback'
  name:'Harbor'
  secret:secretforclient
EOF
```

5. Configure the OIDC authentication mode of Harbor by referring to Step 4 in the example of LDAP and Dex, setting the **OIDC Scope** to “**openid,profile**”.

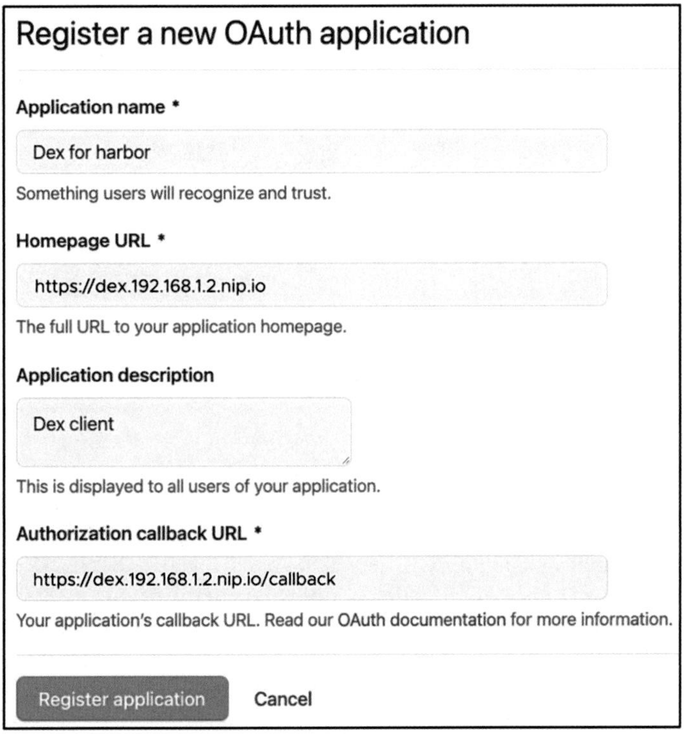

Fig. 3.13 Register a new OAuth application page on Github

Fig. 3.14 OAuth Client ID and Client Secret

6. On the Dex authentication page, click **Log in with GitHub** to access the GitHub authentication page. Refer to Step 5 in the example of LDAP and Dex.

The above describes how to log in to the Harbor user interface via the OIDC authentication mode. However, this method can only be used in the browser. Users cannot log in to Harbor by using the user name and password of the OIDC provider

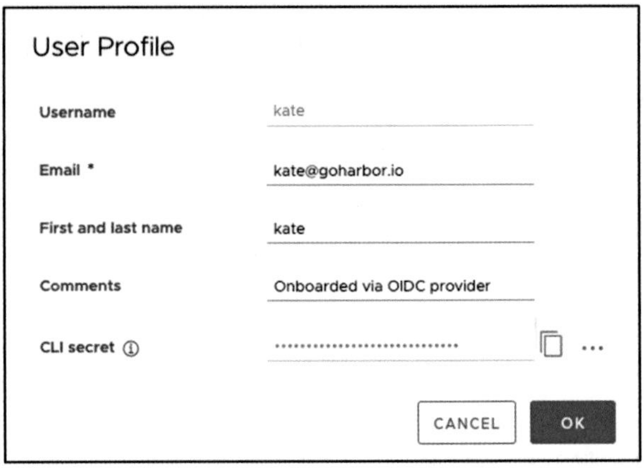

Fig. 3.15 User Profile page

in the command line client (for example, Docker client). In this scenario, Harbor provides an authentication mode based on CLI secret. The command line client is given a CLI secret, which is associated with the OIDC token obtained by the user. When the user logs in using the CLI secret, the oidcCli generator checks whether the OIDC token saved in user information is still valid after verifying the user name and CLI secret. If the OIDC token is still valid, the user information can be retrieved and updated by using the token; if the OIDC token is invalid, Harbor calls the interface of the OIDC provider to refresh the token and updates its local user information to keep it the same as the user information in the OIDC provider.

On the **User Profile** page of the management interface, you can obtain and reset your CLI secret, as shown in Fig. 3.15.

3.3 Access Control and Authorization

Access control is an issue that must be considered in enterprise applications. Different users should have different permissions when they use system functions, or they need to be authorized before performing certain operations. The most common authorization model is role-based access control. Harbor defines five roles. Users can determine the permissions that can be used in Harbor depending on their roles in a project.

3.3.1 Role-based Access Policy

Harbor manages artifacts such as images and Helm Charts based on project. Except for public artifacts (such as images in public projects) which can be accessed anonymously, users must be a member of a project before they can access resources of the project. In Harbor, the system administrator is a special role. It owns the permissions of a "super user" and can manage all projects and system-level resources and configurations. In addition to the default system administrator "admin" created during initial installation of Harbor, users with the system administrator role can assign the system administrator role to other users. In LDAP authentication mode, an administrator group in LDAP can be designated to have the system administrator role.

Project members are divided into five roles: Project Admin, Master(renamed as Maintainer since Harbor 2.1), Developer, Guest and Limited Guest. Users can have one of the member roles in a project. Different member roles have different rights to access resources in the project. The user who creates a project automatically has the project administrator role of the project and can add other users as project members and grant a project role to access resources in the project. The access rights of projects are mutually independent, that is, one user can have different member roles in different projects. Table 3.7 lists complete permissions of roles in Harbor.

Table 3.7 Permissions of different roles

Permission	Project Admin	Master (Maintainer)	Developer	Guest	Limited Guest
View a project repository.	✓	✓	✓	✓	✓
Create a project repository.	✓	✓	✓		
Edit and delete a project repository.	✓	✓			
View, copy and pull an artifact.	✓	✓	✓	✓	✓
Push an artifact.	✓	✓	✓		
Scan and delete an artifact.	✓	✓			
View and pull a Helm Chart.	✓	✓	✓	✓	✓
Push a Helm Chart.	✓	✓	✓		
Delete a Helm Chart.	✓	✓			
View members of a project.	✓	✓	✓	✓	
Create, edit and delete a member in a project.	✓				
Create, edit, delete and view a label in a project.	✓	✓			
View a scanner.	✓	✓	✓	✓	✓
Modify a scanner.	✓				
View a policy.	✓	✓			
Add, delete and modify a policy.	✓	✓			
View a robot account.	✓	✓	✓	✓	
Create, edit and delete a robot account.	✓				
View a Webhook.	✓	✓			
Create, edit, disable and delete a Webhook.	✓				
View the log of a project.	✓	✓	✓	✓	
View a project's configuration.	✓	✓	✓	✓	✓
Edit a project's configuration.	✓				

3.3.2 *Users and Groups*

On the **Administration** > **Users** page, the system administrator can view, create and delete a user (the user creation and deletion functions are available only in the local database authentication mode) and set users to administrators or cancel users as administrators.

When the LDAP and OIDC authentication modes are used, a **Groups** function appears under the menu item of **Administration**, as shown in Fig. 3.16. On the **Groups** page, the system administrator can view, add, edit and delete a group.

In LDAP authentication mode, click **New Group** button on the **Groups** page. In the **Import LDAP Group** dialog box, enter the group DN and the name of the LDAP group to import the LDAP group into the system. In the example shown in Fig. 3.17, the "cn=developer,ou=Groups,dc=goharbor,dc=io" group of LDAP is imported into Harbor and is named as the Developer group of Harbor. In Fig. 3.18, the Developer role is assigned to the Developer group in a Harbor project. All members of the LDAP group "cn=developer,ou=Groups,dc=goharbor,dc=io" are added to a project and have the Developer role.

In OIDC authentication mode, click New Group button on the Groups page. In the **New OIDC Group** dialog box, enter an OIDC group name to create an OIDC group. As shown in Fig. 3.19, a developer group of Harbor is created. In Fig. 3.20,

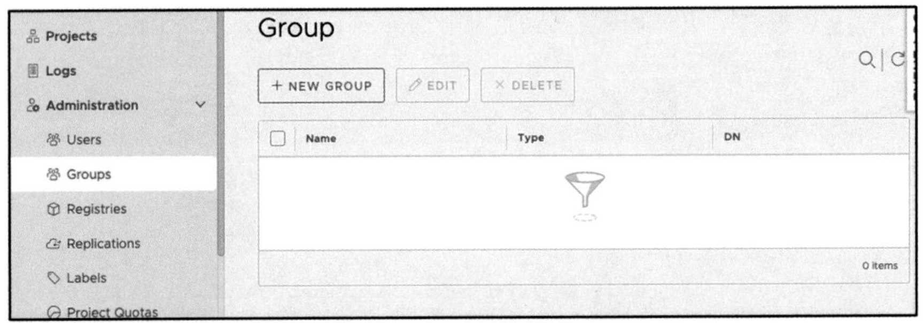

Fig. 3.16 Groups page

Fig. 3.17 Import LDAP Group dialog box

Import LDAP Group

Ldap Group DN * cn=developer,ou=Grou

Type LDAP

Name * Developer

CANCEL SAVE

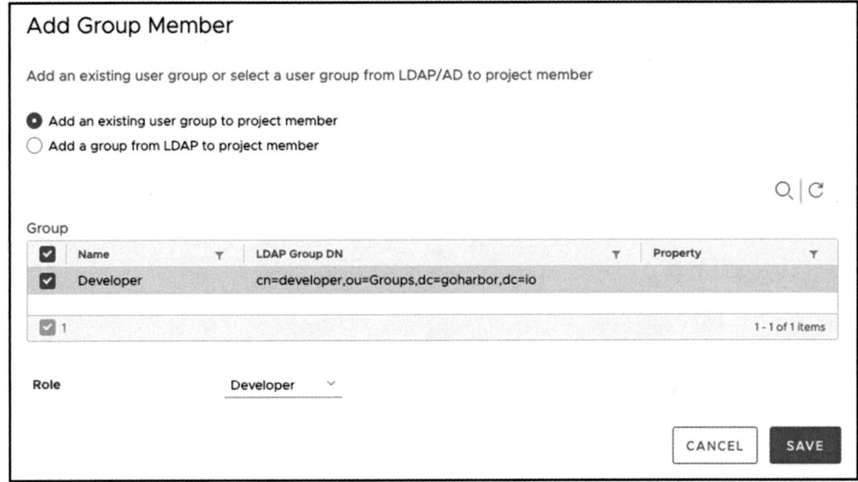

Fig. 3.18 Add Group Member dialog box

Fig. 3.19 New OIDC Group dialog box

Fig. 3.20 New Group Member dialog box

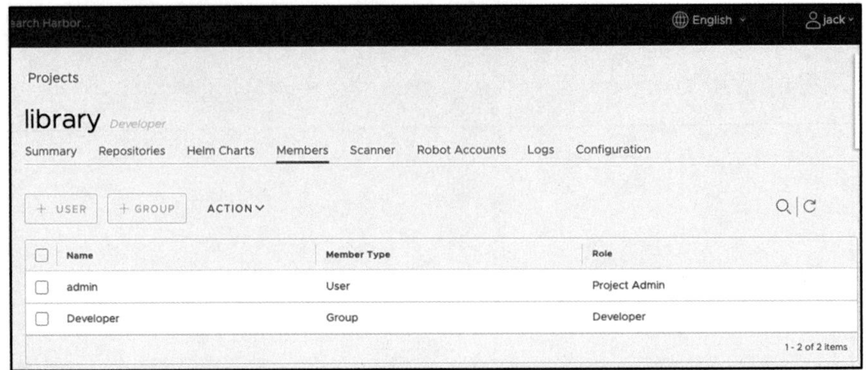

Fig. 3.21 Library project page

the Developer role is assigned to the developer group in a project, that is, the group in OIDC is added as a project member and has the Developer role.

After a group member is added successfully, the user can use the group role to access the corresponding project after logging in to Harbor. For example, after logging in to Harbor, the user jack has the permission of project Developer role, as shown in Fig. 3.21.

3.4 Robot Account

Other application systems often need to access Harbor, for example, the continuous integration/continuous delivery (CI/CD) system needs to access artifacts of a Harbor project. When these systems access Harbor, the systems must have user accounts for authentication. However, because these systems are not bound to people in the real world, they usually do not have accounts in identity providers such as LDAP. To solve this issue, Harbor designs the robot account to allow the authentication between systems. Using the robot account has many advantages: the user password of a real person is not exposed; the validity period of the access account can be defined; the robot account can be disabled at any time.

On the **Robot Accounts** tab of a project, you can add, disable, delete and view the robot account of the project, as shown in Fig. 3.22.

On the **Robot Accounts** page, click **New Robot Account button**. In the **Create Robot Account** dialog box, enter a name to create a robot account. As shown in Fig. 3.23, a robot account named "gitlab-ci" is created, which has the permission to push and pull artifacts and never expires.

After a robot account is successfully created, you can copy the token of the robot account to the clipboard or export the robot account to a file, as shown in Fig. 3.24. In the **docker login** command, use the prefix "robot$" plus the robot account name as the user name and the token as the password for login.

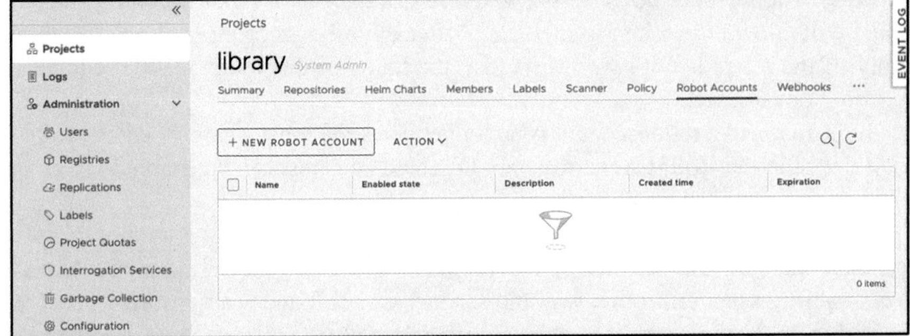

Fig. 3.22 Robot Account tab of the library project

Fig. 3.23 Create Robto Account dialog box

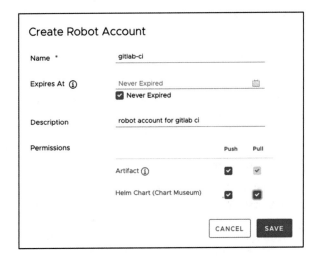

Fig. 3.24 Token of a robot account

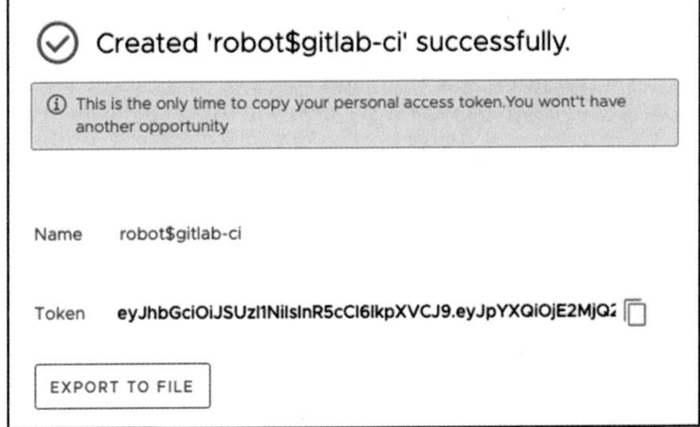

Note: Harbor does not save the token information of a robot account. The user must write down the token immediately after the robot account is created successfully. If the token is not saved or is lost, the token of this robot account cannot be restored or retrieved.

If the token of a robot account is no longer used, the robot account can be disabled or deleted on the **Robot Accounts** tab. Disabled accounts can be enabled again, but deleted accounts cannot be restored.

When the vulnerability scanner scans artifacts, Harbor creates a temporary robot account that has the scanner-pull permission and gives the robot account to the vulnerability scanner. In this way the scanner can pull and scan artifacts. After the scanning, the robot account is deleted immediately.

3.5 FAQ

1. Why doesn't newly installed Harbor allow self-registration by default?

   When the local database authentication mode is in use, Harbor provides the user with the self-registration function. In most cases, Harbor is set up as a private registry of an enterprise. For security reasons, Harbor does not enable the self-registration by default. If the self-registration function is needed, you can enable the **Allow Self-registration** function (this option is available only when the local database authentication mode is used) under **Administration**> **Configuration** > **Authentication**.

2. I want to change the user authentication mode of Harbor from the default local database mode to the LDAP provider or the OIDC mode. Why is the authentication mode read-only and cannot be modified in **Administration** > **Configuration** > **Authentication**?

   Harbor does not automatically migrate existing users to a new authentication mode. Therefore, if user accounts (except for the default admin account) already exist in the system, switching the authentication mode is not allowed.

3. After a user is removed from the LDAP administrator group, why is the user still a system administrator when the user logs in to Harbor?

   When an LDAP user logs in, the system checks whether the user is in the LDAP administrator group. If the user is not in the administrator group, Harbor checks whether the administrator flag is set for the user. If the administrator flag is set, the user can still access Harbor as the system administrator. To solve this problem, you are advised to delete the user from the LDAP administrator group and remove the corresponding system administrator flag on the **Users** management page of Harbor.

4. Why is the following message displayed when the command **docker login -u username -p password server** is used to log in to Harbor through a robot account: unauthorized: authentication required?

   The name of the robot account contains the "$" symbol. When the **docker login** command is used to log in to Harbor in a shell terminal or a script, use the "\" to escape the "$" character in the robot account name. For example, replace "robot$gitlab-ci" with "robot\$gitlab-ci". the other way is to wrap the user name with single quotation marks, for example, replace robot$gitlab-ci with 'robot$gitlab-ci'.

5. Can one robot account access resources in multiple different projects at the same time?

   In Harbor 2.0, a robot account does not have the permission to access multiple projects at the same time. In the future release of Harbor, a robot account can be used to access multiple projects.

6. Two different Harbor instances use the same private key file. Can a robot account of a project in a Harbor instance gain access to resources of the same project in the other Harbor instance?

   Because the two Harbor instances use the same private key file, the token of a robot account in one instance can be decrypted by the other instance to obtain the information of the token. However, the robot Security Context generator compares the information obtained from the token with the data its database. The token of one Harbor instance can be accepted by the other Harbor instance only when the robot account with the same ID and name exists in both instances.

7. In OIDC authentication mode, a user can pull and push images by using the CLI secret. Why can't the CLI secret be used in the remote replication policy?

   Because the CLI secret supports only the operations of pulling and pushing artifacts. It does not support calling an API, thus the CLI secret cannot be used in the remote replication policy.

8. In the configuration of the OIDC authentication mode, how to correctly obtain the OIDC endpoint?

   According to the OIDC specification, the URL of the configuration file must be "$ENDPONT_URI/.well-known/openid-configuration". Therefore, in the configuration of the OIDC endpoint, the user can use the **curl** command to test and confirm the URL of the OIDC configuration file. Then the "$ENDPONT_URI" can be extracted from the URL and it can be used in the configuration of Harbor OIDC (see Table 3.6).

Chapter 4
Security Policy

As a cloud native artifact registry, Harbor manages and distributes artifacts of applications. The security of the content directly affects the operation of the platform and environment where the content is distributed or deployed. Therefore, in addition to the security of Harbor itself, the security of the content managed by Harbor is particularly important. This chapter describes the capabilities provided by Harbor from the perspective of content security, including the content trust function for preventing content tampering and the static scanning mechanism for discovering security vulnerabilities. In addition, this chapter describes how to configure the security policy and the whitelist system of vulnerability based on content trust and vulnerability scanning. Finally, it shares some FAQs about the content security in Harbor.

4.1 Trusted Content Distribution

As a pioneer of container technology, Docker, the company, introduced the concept of Docker content trust (DCT) in Docker 1.8.0, which implemented the content trust mechanism of container images and supported the trusted distribution of images. DCT used strongly encrypted digital signatures for the data sent to or received from remote image registries. These digital signatures allowed container clients or container runtime to verify the issuer and integrity of images. In general, when an issuer enables DCT to push an image to a remote registry, Docker uses the private key of the issuer to digitally sign the images locally. When a user pulls images subsequently, Docker obtains the public key of the issuer in a secure way and verifies using the public key to find out whether or not the images were created by the issuer, have been tampered, or they are the latest version.

DCT uses the open source project Notary to provide the content trust function. Notary is implemented based on another open source project, namely The Updating Framework (TUF). To maintain the same flow and user experience as the Docker

H. Zhang, Y. Wang, *The Authoritative Guide on Harbor*,
https://doi.org/10.1007/978-981-19-2727-0_4

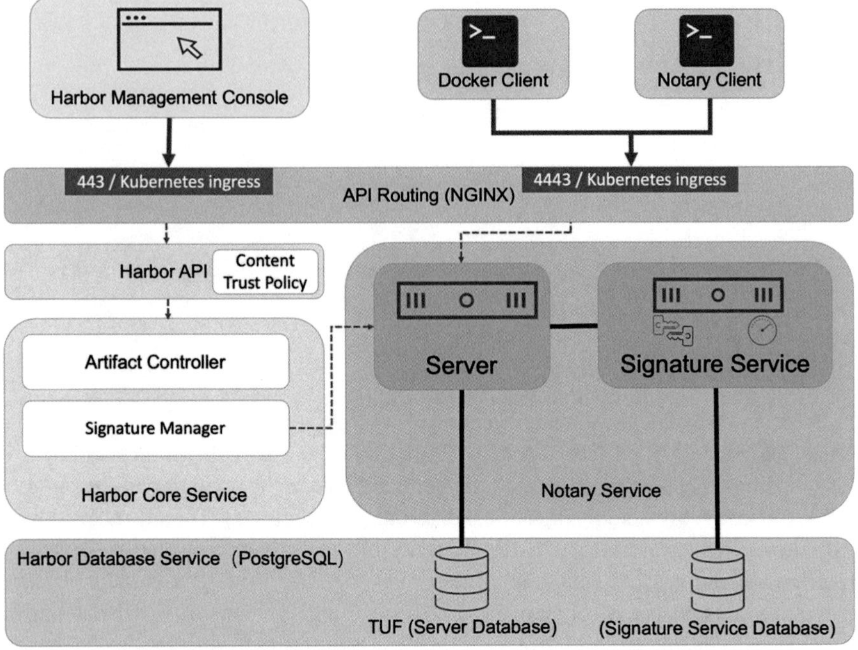

Fig. 4.1 Notary service in Harbor

tool chain, Harbor registry also implements the support of content trust through the Notary project. Both TUF and Notary are open source projects hosted by CNCF. Readers can understand the basic elements and mechanisms through the documents about the two projects.

4.1.1 Content Trust

This section explains how to implement the content trust mechanism in Harbor so as to improve the credibility and security of the managed content.

4.1.1.1 Integrating Notary

Notary is an optional component in Harbor. Whether Notary is installed and enabled is determined by the user through installation parameters during the installation of Harbor. When Notary is enabled, Harbor integrates the Notary service based on the structure shown in Fig. 4.1.

The Notary server and the Signature Service are deployed on the Harbor service network with other components of Harbor. The database on which the Notary server and the Signature Service depend is provided by the Harbor database service component. When Notary is installed through the **docker-compose** command, the Notary service is exposed on port 4443 for clients to access through the API routing layer (Nginx); when Notary is deployed on Kubernetes, Notary provides the endpoint for clients to access through the ingress of Kubernetes. This structure follows the basic architecture pattern of Notary and is compatible with Docker and Notary clients. Therefore, it retains the same pattern, flow and mechanism as the DCT.

The Signature Manager is a component of the core service of Harbor and the Notary server can be used to manage digital signatures of artifacts. The Signature Manager is used only when Notary is enabled. The Signature Manager provides the upper-layer artifact controller with metadata related to artifact signatures. If the artifact requested by a client is signed, the artifact controller first obtains the signature information of the artifact through the Signature Manager, then obtains other metadata and merges into the artifact metadata model before returns them to the client.

In addition, after Harbor enables the content trust policy, if a request for pulling an artifact is received, the middleware processor of the content trust policy in the core components determines whether the request is allowed based on the signature of the requested artifact. If the signature does not exist, the pull request is rejected; if the signature does exist and is valid, the pull request is allowed. The function of content trust ensures that the artifact pulled by a client or a container runtime is authentic and trustable. The content trust policy of Harbor enforces the client can only pull signed artifacts, so that it can better enhance the system security.

The last thing to mention is that the content trust mechanism of Harbor is currently based on and compatible with DCT. Therefore, the type of artifacts supported by the content trust mechanism is limited only to container images.

4.1.1.2 Using Notary to Sign Artifacts

This section describes how to sign Docker images with Notary. The Notary service must be installed and enabled in Harbor.

First set the following environment variables in the command line to enable the content trust mechanism:

```
$ export DOCKER_CONTENT_TRUST=1
$ export DOCKER_CONTENT_TRUST_SERVER=https://<Harbor host
address>:4443
```

If TLS is enabled and a self-signed certificate is used in Harbor, ensure that the CA certificate is copied to the following location in the operating system of the Docker client:

```
/etc/docker/certs.d/<Harbor host address>
$HOME/.docker/tls/<Harbor host address>:4443/
```

In this case, use the **docker** command to push images to Harbor. After the images are successfully pushed, the signature steps of the content trust will proceed. If a root key has not been created, the system asks for a strong password to create the root key. Later, this password is required for pushing images when content trust enabled. Meanwhile, the system asks for another strong password to create the target key of the registry being pushed. These generated keys are stored in the path **$HOME/.docker/trust/private/<digest>.key** and the corresponding TUF metadata file is stored in the following directory: **$HOME/.docker/trust/tuf/<Harbor_host_address>/<repository_name>/metadata**. The following shows an example of pushing an image:

```
$ docker push 192.168.1.2/sz/nginx:latest
The push refers to repository [192.168.1.2/sz/nginx]
787328500ad5:Layer already exists
077ae58ac205:Layer already exists
8c7fd6263c1f:Layer already exists
d9c0b16c8d5b:Layer already exists
ffc9b21953f4:Layer already exists
latest:digest:sha256:d9002da0297bcd090
9b394c26bd0fc9d8c466caf2b7396f58948cac5318d0
d0b size:1362
Signing and pushing trust metadata
You are about to create a new root signing key passphrase. This
passphrase
will be used to protect the most sensitive key in your signing
system. Please
choose a long, complex passphrase and be careful to keep the
password and the
key file itself secure and backed up. It is highly recommended that
you use a
password manager to generate the passphrase and keep it safe. There
will be no
way to recover this key. You can find the key in your config directory.
Enter passphrase for new root key with ID affd4a6:
Repeat passphrase for new root key with ID affd4a6:
Enter passphrase for new repository key with ID 15a6800:
Repeat passphrase for new repository key with ID 15a6800:
Finished initializing "192.168.1.2/sz/nginx"
Successfully signed 192.168.1.2/sz/nginx:latest
```

After the signing was successful, log in to the Harbor web management console and click on **Projects** on the navigation menu on the left. Select the project containing the image and then choose the **Repositories** tab. Click on the name of

Fig. 4.2 Signed tags of an image

an image and then click on its digest. The image details page is displayed. As shown in Fig. 4.2, the list of tags indicates that the image has been signed.

If the **docker** command is used to pull an unsigned image, Harbor directly rejects the pulling request. Note: This operation requires the client to set the above environment variables to enable the content trust function. If the client does not set the environment variables, the content trust function is not enabled and unsigned images can still be pulled. The following shows an example:

```
$ docker pull 192.168.1.2/sz/redis:latest
Error: remote trust data does not exist for 192.168.1.2/sz/
redis:192.168.1.2:4443 does not have trust data for 192.168.1.2/
sz/redis
```

Harbor provides a security policy based on the signature of content trust, through which the operation of pulling unsigned images is prohibited. The policy is not depended on the client side settings and greatly improves security.

Log in to the web management console as the project administrator and choose **Project** > **{Project Name}** > **Configuration** tab. In the setting of **Deployment Security**, select **Enable content trust** to enable the deployment of only verified (signed) images and save the configuration, as shown in Fig. 4.3.

Later on even if the client does not set any environment variables related to the content trust, the requests of pulling unsigned images will be rejected. The following shows an example:

```
$ env | grep DOCKER_CONTENT_TRUST
$ docker pull 192.168.1.2/sz/redis:latest
Error response from daemon:unknown:The image is not signed in
Notary.
```

In Harbor, signed image tags cannot be directly deleted. These tags can be deleted only after their signatures are removed. Otherwise, the system displays an error and

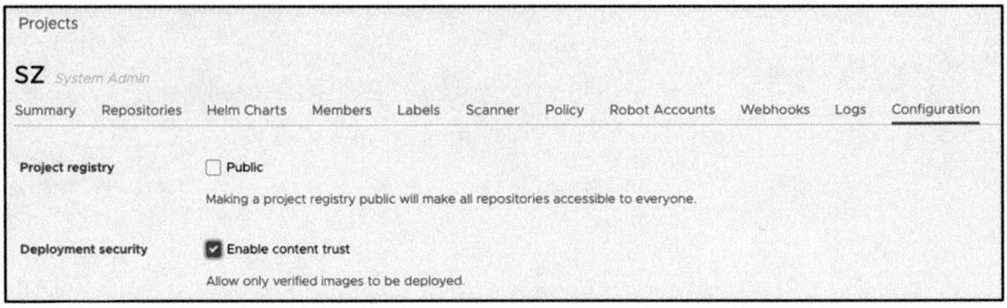

Fig. 4.3 Enabling content trust in the project configuration

prompts you to use the following command (this command requires the Notary command line tool) to remove the signatures on the tags first.

```
$ notary -s https://<harbor host address>:4443 -d ~/.docker/trust
remove -p 192.168.1.2/nginx:1.19
```

4.1.2 Signature of Helm 2 Chart

Before Harbor 2.0, Helm 2 Chart is supported through the open source project ChartMuseum. Harbor 2.0 directly supports the Helm 3 Chart as the OCI artifact but still retains the support of Helm 2 Chart via ChartMuseum. Harbor does not rely on Notary to support the signature of Helm 2 Chart. Instead, it follows the tool chain used by the Helm community. Helm provides the provenance verification tool chain based on the industry standard tools such as GnuPG (GPG). As such, Helm can generate and verify related signature files.

The integrity of a chart is determined through the comparison of the chart with its corresponding provenance record. The provenance record is stored in the provenance file and is stored in the repository with the associated chart. The chart repository must ensure that the provenance file can be accessed through a specific HTTP request and the provenance file is in the same URL path as the chart. For example, if the basic URL path of a chart is **https://<mywebsite>/charts/mychart-1.2.3.tgz**, the provenance file must be accessed under the URL path **https://<mywebsite>/charts/mychart-1.2.3.tgz.prov**. The provenance file is designed to be automatically generated and it includes the yaml file of the chart and multiple verification information. Its format is as follows:

```
----BEGIN PGP SIGNED MESSAGE----
name: nginx
description:The nginx web server as a replication controller and
service pair.
version:0.5.1
keywords:
  - https
  - http
  - web server
  - proxy
source:
- https://github.com/foo/bar
home:https://nginx.com

...
files:
    nginx-0.5.1.tgz:"sha256:9f5270f50fc842cfcb717f817e95178f"
----BEGIN PGP SIGNATURE----
Version: GnuPG v1.4.9 (GNU/Linux)

iEYEARECAAYFAkjilUEACgQkB01zfu119ZnHuQCdGCcg2YxF3
XFscJLS4lzHlvte
WkQAmQGHuuoLEJuKhRNo+Wy7mhE7u1YG
=eifq
----END PGP SIGNATURE----
```

The main data blocks included are as follows:

- Metadata file (**Chart.yaml**) of chart package: used to specify the content of the chart package.
- Signature digest (.tgz file) of chart package: used to verify the integrity of the chart package.
- GPG algorithm: used to encrypt and sign the entire content of the chart package.

Through the combination of the above mechanism, users are provided with the following security assurance:

- The chart package is not tampered (by verifying the tgz file).
- The entity that issues the package is known and trusted (through GnuPG and PGP signature).

To sign Helm 2 Chart, ensure that the **helm** command is installed and a valid binary (non-ASCII format) PGP key pair exists. GnuPG 2.1 or later can also be used to facilitate the management of keys. The key pair is generally stored in the path **~/.gnupg/**. The command **gpg --list-secret-keys** can be used to view the current keys. It should be noted that if a password is set for a key, the password must be entered every time when the key is used. To avoid frequent password entering, set the environment variable **HELM_KEY_PASSPHRASE**. In addition, the key file format is changed in GnuPG 2.1. The newly introduced .kbx format is not supported by

Helm. Therefore, the GnuPG command must be used to convert the key file format. The following shows a simple example:

```
$ gpg --export-secret-keys >~/.gnupg/secring.gpg
```

For the chart that is ready for packaging, add the **--sign** parameter for the signing operation when calling the **helm package** command for packaging. Moreover, specify a known signature key (--key) and a key ring (--keyring) containing the corresponding key.

```
$ helm package --sign --key 'my signing key' --keyring path/to/
keyring.secret mychart
```

After the packaging is completed, a chart file **mychart-0.1.0.tgz** and a provenance file **mychart-0.1.0.tgz.prov** are generated. These two files must be uploaded to the same directory in the chart repository. They can be uploaded through the web management console of Harbor. Choose **Project** > {**Project Name**} > **Helm Charts** > **Upload**. The chart upload dialog box is displayed, as shown in Fig. 4.4. Select the chart file to be uploaded and the corresponding provenance file and click **Upload**.

After the files are successfully uploaded, you can view the state of the signature in **Security** on the chart details page. A chart with the provenance file is displays as "Ready", as shown in Fig. 4.5. Click **Continue** to download the corresponding provenance file.

To verify the chart package, execute the **helm verify** command. If the verification failed, the system will display an error message.

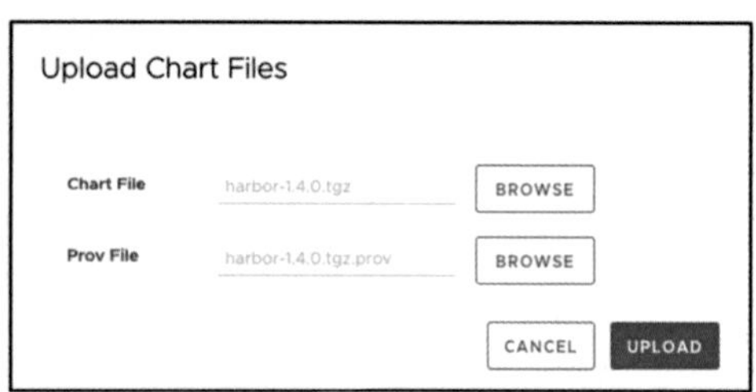

Fig. 4.4 Upload Chart Files dialog box

Fig. 4.5 Provenance file on the chart detail page

```
$ helm verify topchart-0.1.0.tgz
Error: sha256 sum does not match for topchart-0.1.0.tgz:"sha256:
1939fbf7c1023d2f6b865d137bbb600e0c42061c3235528b1e8c
82f4450c12a7" != "sha256:
5a391a90de56778dd3274e47d789a2c84e0e106e1a37ef8cfa
51fd60ac9e623a"
```

During installation of a Helm Chart, you can also use the "--verify" flag to verify the chart package to be installed.

```
$ helm install --verify mychart-0.1.0.tgz
```

If verification fails, the installation process of the chart package is terminated before the package is installed onto the Kubernetes cluster.

4.2 Pluggable Vulnerability Scanning

Code and software usually have defects. As a packaging form of applications and their dependent software packages and operating systems, container images are of no exceptions. During coding and building, errors are inevitable. The errors left in software packages are usually defects. These defects will become technical weaknesses of the software packages. Malicious attackers take advantage of these defects to illegally invade the system, destroy the operation of the system or steal confidential information. These defects are known as vulnerabilities.

Once a defect is identified as a vulnerability, the defect can be registered as a common vulnerabilities and exposures (CVE), a list of publicly disclosed computer security vulnerabilities, through the company MITRE. A CVE is usually referenced through the CVE ID assigned to each security vulnerability. CVE entries are simple and do not include technical data, related risks, impacts or remedy information. Details of the information are maintained in other databases, including the U.-S. National Vulnerability Database (NVD), CERT/CC Vulnerability Notes Database and various lists maintained by vendors and other organizations. In these different database systems, CVE IDs provide a reliable way for users to distinguish different security vulnerabilities.

The potential severity of registered CVEs is assessed in many ways, the most common of which is the Common Vulnerability Scoring System (CVSS). The CVSS scores vulnerabilities based on a set of open standards to measure and assess the level and the severity of vulnerabilities. NVD, CERT and other organizations all use the CVSS to assess the impact of vulnerabilities. The score ranges from 0.0 to 10.0. The larger the number is, the higher the severity of the vulnerability is. Within the range, 0.0 indicates none (no vulnerability), 0.1-3.9 indicates the severity level is low, 4.0-6.9 means the medium level, 7.0-8.9 and 9.0-10.0 stand for the high and the critical level, respectively.

The vulnerability database provides known vulnerability information of software packages. Based on the database, it is easy to find out vulnerability of software packages in container images. The database can be provided to software developers or maintainers as the important reference basis for modification and improvement. This process is also called vulnerability scanning. Vulnerability scanning is done by a special application, namely vulnerability scanner or vulnerability scanning tool. The vulnerability scanner identifies all software packages and operating systems on which software packages depend and creates a list. Based on the list, the vulnerability scanner checks each item against one or more known checklists of vulnerability databases to see if any item is affected by these vulnerabilities. The purpose of vulnerability scanning is to identify software packages in all systems and display known vulnerabilities that may need attention.

Harbor v1.1 has introduced Clair, an open source project of CoreOS, as a vulnerability scanning engine for container images stored and managed by Harbor. Users may choose to install and enable Clair when they install Harbor. The support of the image vulnerability scanning function enhances the security of images to a great extent and improves the security of Harbor in some enterprise-grade application scenarios. It is welcomed and trusted by many community users.

In addition, many vendors provide vulnerability scanning tools and services, including open source tools and commercial software. Although different vulnerability scanning tools or services provide similar vulnerability scanning capabilities, different implementations and dependent data make these tools and services different. Differences also exist in the aspects such as code sharing mode, service mode and service plan. This makes enterprises choose different scanning tools. Some enterprises may also have their own security platforms to provide security assurance, including image scanning. Therefore, enterprises or users prefer to integrate the registry service based on Harbor with their existing scanning tools and services so as to avoid additional maintenance costs.

All of the above considerations make it necessary to introduce a more flexible image scanning mechanism in Harbor. In Harbor 1.10, through efforts of the community, members from Aqua Security, Anchor, VMware and HPE jointly set up the scanning workgroup, designed and implemented a pluggable vulnerability scanning framework.

Through the pluggable vulnerability scanning framework, scanning tools or services are decoupled from Harbor and the system administrator can configure, monitor and manage scanning tools or services. The framework supports configuration management of multiple scanning tools or services, one of which can be set to the default scanning engine of the system. Project administrators can set other scanning engines that could be different from the default scanning engine of the system for their projects. If no scanning engine is set for a project, the default scanning engine of the system is used to scan images of the project. Obviously, the installation and configuration of scanning tools are independent of the installation and configuration of Harbor. Operators can install new scanning tools or services when necessary and configure them for use in Harbor. The pluggable vulnerability scanning framework makes it easy for enterprises to integrate existing tools or services, which brings in great convenience and saves integration costs.

Next, we will explain the design principle of the pluggable vulnerability scanning framework.

4.2.1 Overall Design

Figure 4.6 shows the overall architecture of the pluggable vulnerability scanning framework. Its main component modules are included in the Core service of Harbor, and the scheduling and execution of asynchronous scanning tasks are undertaken by JobService(the asynchronous task system).

First of all, different scanning tools or services have different functional interfaces. To shield these differences, the pluggable vulnerability scanning framework provides the scanning API specification and defines the functional interface of a scanner that can be identified, managed and invoked by the pluggable vulnerability scanning framework. If a scanning tool or service needs to be accessed via the pluggable vulnerability scanning framework, the scanning tool or the service must implement and expose the related functional interface defined in this scanning API specification. Clearly, to reduce the dependency on the underlying scanning tools or services, a reasonable approach is to implement an adapter for a particular scanning tool or service based on the scanning API specification. This approach introduces the capabilities of the scanning tools or services into the framework through the adapter. This specification decouples the scanning tools or services completely from Harbor and makes the pluggable vulnerability scanning framework more open. The specification fosters a good ecosystem with organizations and companies focusing on the security of containers and images, thus promoting the development of the Harbor community.

The pluggable vulnerability scanning framework introduces APIs for managing pluggable scanners, starting scanning tasks and obtaining scanning reports in Harbor to support the tasks related to scanning.

First of all, scanners are configured and managed through API. Management requests are fulfilled by calling the interface provided by the scanner controller through the API processor. The scanner controller relies on the scanner registry to maintain the scanner information. The metadata of a scanner in the scanner registry can be given to the scanning module to complete the scanning operations.

Secondly, a scanning API request is sent to the scanning controller responsible for the main flow control and the scheduling through the corresponding API processor. The scanning controller obtains the basic configuration of the current scanner through the scanner registry and selects a scanner as the execution engine. After that, the scanning controller submits an asynchronous scanning task to start the scanning flow. After the scanning task is launched, the scanning controller monitors the Webhook of JobService to obtain the progress of the scanning task and the final

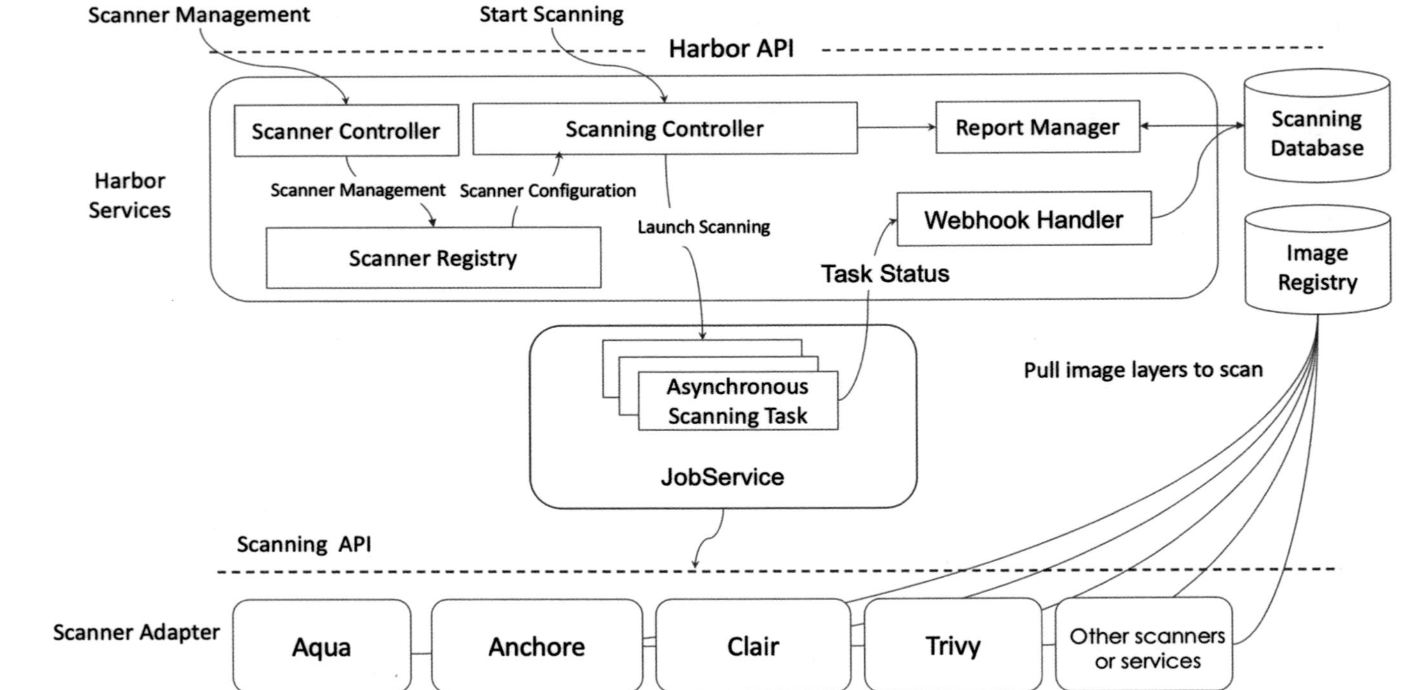

Fig. 4.6 Architecture of pluggable vulnerability scanning framework

scanning result. If the scanning flow is finished normally, the controller stores the scanning report through the report manager.

The asynchronous scanning task uses the adapter that implements the scanning API specification to execute the scanning process. The asynchronous scanning task obtains and encapsulates scanning information from its parameters and submits the information to the adapter of the scanner through the scanning API. The scanner uses information in the request to pull the content to be scanned from Harbor and performs corresponding vulnerability scanning. After the scanning request is submitted, the scanning task periodically queries the scanning status to confirm the scanning progress of the scanner until the whole scanning process is done and a report is generated. After that, the report is sent to the listener in Harbor by means of Webhook notification for subsequent processing.

Based on the above overall design, the following section explains the design details of some important components and modules in the pluggable vulnerability scanning framework.

4.2.2 Scanner Management

Scanner management is used to manage the registration objects that contain basic information of scanners, including metadata such as the name, description, URL, authentication mode (auth) and authentication credential (access_credential).

Note: The pluggable vulnerability scanning framework does not restrict the deployment and networking configuration of the scanner. It only needs to ensure that the scanner and Harbor can connect to each other via network. Under some circumstances, the administrator can install the scanner and Harbor service in the same network (namely the intree mode). The scanner can be accessed through the internal address of Harbor, which avoids the potential problems of external network connection between service components.

Scanner management can configure multiple types of scanner. For the same scanner type, there may be multiple different instances. As mentioned previously, one of the available scanners can be specified as the default scanner of the system. If no scanner is set in a project, the default settings of the system can be directly inherited. Scanners in the list can also be disabled, enabled or removed and scanner information can be updated.

Scanner management is coordinated by the scanner controller, and the actual storage operations are carried out by the scanner registry. The scanner registry is actually an encapsulation interface of the scanner data access object (DAO) methods. In DAOs, the basic methods such as add, delete, modify and query for connecting and operating the database are implemented.

The functions of the scanning controller are declared in the controller interface of "src/controller/scanner/controller.go". The registry interface and implementation of the scanner can be found in the "src/pkg/scan/scanner" package. The basic DAO operations of the scanner can be found in the "src/pkg/scan/dao/scanner" package. Readers can refer to the source code for details.

4.2.3 Scanning API Specification

Currently, the scanning API specification V1 defines three RESTful APIs: the API that returns scanner metadata, the API that initiates scanning requests and the API for obtaining scanning reports. The specific definitions of the three APIs are as follows:

1. the Metadata API: In addition to basic metadata such as the scanner name, vendor and version, this API returns the function set of a specific scanner, including the declaration of the types (mediaType) of artifacts that can be scanned (capabilities. consumes_mime_types[]), the declaration of the formats of scanning reports (the mediaType of the self-defined content) that can be returned (capabilities. produces_mime_types[]) and other scanner attributes such as the update timestamp of the vulnerability database (properties{}). Table 4.1 describes the design of the API.
2. the API that initiates scanning requests: This API accepts parameters that include the basic information about the artifact to be scanned, the address of the registry where the artifact is stored and the authentication credential. Then it starts the back-end adaptive scanning tool or service in a non-blocking mode for vulnerability scanning and immediately returns the ID that can uniquely identified the related scanning report. Table 4.2 describes the specific design of the API.
3. the API for obtaining scanning reports: Through this API, the scanning report of a request ID is retrieved. Note: It usually takes some time to complete the vulnerability scanning. A longer time is required for scanning a larger artifact. Therefore, when the scanning process is still in progress, this API returns the status code of 302 to inform the caller that the requested scanning report is not yet ready and need to retry the same call later. The returned header may contain the attribute "Refresh-After" to recommend the time of the next attempt. When a report is not ready, attempts must be made continuously until the scanning report is ready or an unresumable system error occurs. The scanner supports one or more formats of scanning reports according to its own implementation, and the supported formats can be declared in its metadata API. Table 4.3 describes the specific design of the API.

If readers want to know more about the scanning API specification, refer to the **README.md** file of the scanning API specification project under Harbor and the OpenAPI document **api/spec/scanner-adapter-openapi-v1.0.yaml** defined by the project.

Table 4.1 Scanning API to obtain the scanner's metadata

HTTP method		GET
URI		/api/v1/metadata
Request parameter		None
Response	200	Content-type:application/vnd.scanner.adapter.metadata+json; version=1.0

		Successful response. The declaration of scanner metadata and capability set was returned.
		Example of the response:
		{
		"scanner": {
		"name": "Trivy",
		"vendor": "Aqua Security",
		"version": "0.7.0"
		},
		"capabilities": [
		{
		"consumes_mime_types": [
		"application/vnd.oci.image.manifest.v1+json",
		"application/vnd.docker.distribution.manifest.v2+json"
		],
		"produces_mime_types": [
		"application/vnd.scanner.adapter.vuln.report.harbor+json; version=1.0"
		]
		}
		],
		"properties": {
		"harbor.scanner-adapter/scanner-type": "os-package-vulnerability",
		"harbor.scanner-adapter/vulnerability-database-updated-at": "2019-08-13T08:16:33.345Z"
		}
		}

	500	Content-type: application/vnd.scanner.adapter.error+json; version=1.0
		An internal error occurred in the server.
		Example of the response:
		{
		"error": {
		"message": "Some unexpected error"
		}
		}

4.2.4 Scanning Management

Scanning management focuses on the initiation of scanning requests and the access of scanning reports. The scanning controller manages the flow and provides the functional interface.

The operation of initiating a scanning task is actually to determine which scanner is to be used to scan the specified artifact. Because scanners have multi-level settings

Table 4.2 Scanning API to initiate scanning requests

HTTP method		POST
URI		/api/v1/scan
Request parameter		Content-type:application/vnd.scanner.adapter.scan.request+json; version=1.0
		Scanning request object. Example:

Request parameter		{
		"registry": {
		"url": "https://core.harbor.domain",
		"authorization": "Basic BASE64_ENCODED_CREDENTIALS"
		},
		"artifact": {
		"repository": "library/mongo",
		"digest": "sha256:
		6c3c624b58dbbcd3c0dd82b4c53f04194d1247c6eebdaab7c610cf7d66709b3b",
		"tag": "3.14-xenial",
		"mime_type": "application/vnd.docker.distribution.manifest.v2+json"
		}
		}

Response	201	Content-type:application/vnd.scanner.adapter.scan.response+json; version=1.0

		Successful response. The scanning response object was returned.
		Example of the response:
		{
		"id": "3fa85f64-5717-4562-b3fc-2c963f66afa6"
		}

	400	Content-type:application/vnd.scanner.adapter.error+json; version=1.0

		Invalid JSON data was received or data contained an incorrect type.
		Example of the response:
		{
		"error": {
		"message": "Some unexpected error"
		}
		}

	422	Content-type:application/vnd.scanner.adapter.error+json; version=1.0

		The data included an invalid field.
		Example of the response:
		{
		"error": {
		"message": "Some unexpected error"
		}
		}

	500	Content-type:application/vnd.scanner.adapter.error+json; version=1.0

		An internal error occurred in the server.
		Example of the response:
		{
		"error": {
		"message": "Some unexpected error"
		}
		}

Table 4.3 Scanning API to obtain the scanning reports

HTTP method		GET
URI		/scan/{scan_request_id}/report
Request parameter		scan_request_id: index ID of the scanning request Format of the requested report (request header): Accept:application/vnd.scanner.adapter.vuln.report.harbor+json; version=1.0
Response	200	Content-type:application/vnd.scanner.adapter.vuln.report.harbor+json; version=1.0

		Successful response. The JSON object of the scanning report was returned.
		Example of the response:
		{
		"generated_at": "2020-08-25T15:19:14.528Z",
		"artifact": {
		"repository": "library/mongo",
		"digest": "sha256:
		6c3c624b58dbbcd3c0dd82b4c53f04194d1247c6eebdaab7c610cf7d66709b3b",
		"tag": "3.14-xenial",
		"mime_type": "application/vnd.docker.distribution.manifest.v2+json"
		},
		"scanner": {
		"name": "Trivy",
		"vendor": "Aqua Security",
		"version": "0.4.0"
		},
		"severity": "Low",
		"vulnerabilities": [
		{
		"id": "CVE-2017-8283",
		"package": "dpkg",
		"version": "1.17.27",

		"fix_version": "1.18.0", "severity": "Low", "description": "dpkg-source in dpkg 1.3.0 through 1.18.23 is able to use a non-GNU patch program\nand does not offer a protection mechanism for blank-indented diff hunks, which\nallows remote attackers to conduct directory traversal attacks via a crafted\nDebian source package, as demonstrated by using of dpkg-source on NetBSD.\n", "links": ["https://security-tracker.debian.org/tracker/CVE-2017-8283"] }] }
	302	Refresh-After:15
		The scanning report was still not ready. Please access again 15s later.
	404	Content-type:application/vnd.scanner.adapter.error+json; version=1.0

		The report corresponding to the scanning request ID was not found.
		Example of the response:
		{
		"error": {
		"message": "Some unexpected error"
		}
		}

	500	Content-type:application/vnd.scanner.adapter.error+json; version=1.0
		An internal error occurred in the server. The response is the same as 404 above.

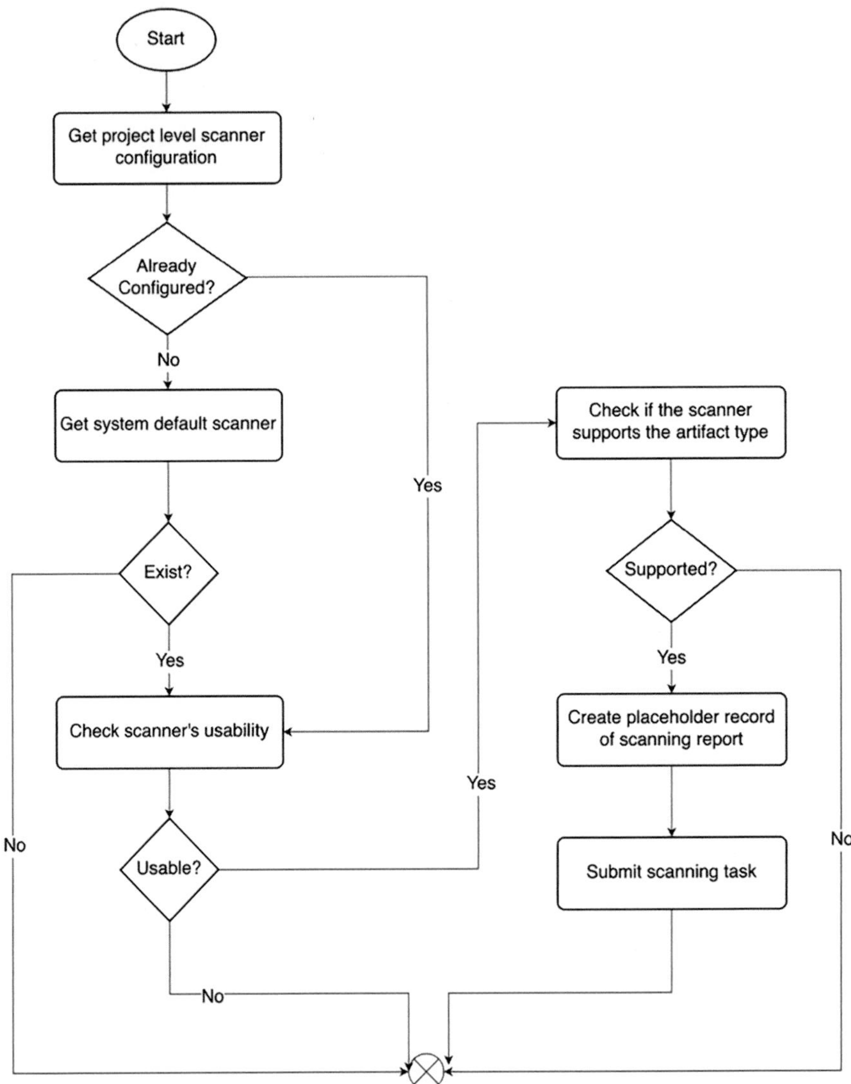

Fig. 4.7 Processing flow of a scanning request

like system-level and project-level, certain rules are required for the selection of a scanner. In addition, artifacts have many types and not all of the types can be scanned. Therefore, before starting the actual scanning, a judging process is also required, as shown in Fig. 4.7.

It can be seen from Fig. 4.7 that, during the request for scanning, the scanning controller first obtains scanner settings under the project of the corresponding artifact. If a scanner is already assigned to the project, the scanner can be used directly; if no scanner is available, the default scanner of the system is then used; if there is no default scanner of the system, the process is terminated due to no available scanner.

After a usable scanner is picked, the system continues to check whether the scanner is available. If not, the flow is terminated; if the scanner is available, the system needs to determine whether the scanner supports the currently given artifact type according to the capabilities declared in its metadata. If the scanner does not support the artifact type, the flow directly exits; if the scanner supports the artifact type, the system creates a placeholder record of the scanning report for the current scanning task before submitting an asynchronous task to the JobService component, so as to receive the content of the scanning report when the scanning is finished.

As mentioned in Sect. 4.2.3, the scanner returns a scanning report that includes a specific mediaType (for example, "application/vnd.scanner.adapter.vuln.report.harbor+json; version=1.0"). Considering the integrity of data and convenience of subsequent format reading, the data schema corresponding to this type of JSON data is not created in Harbor's database. Instead, the JSON data is persisted as a whole. Meanwhile, for the purposes of tracking and controlling the scanning progress, other auxiliary information is added to Harbor's database and the scanning report data schema shown in Fig. 4.8 is designed.

Data records of a scanning report can be uniquely mapped through the structural index. The structural index contains the default system auto-increment ID and the UUID assigned during the creation of the record. The ID is only used as the primary key of data records. In the related APIs and interface, UUID is used as the unique index of scanning report data records.

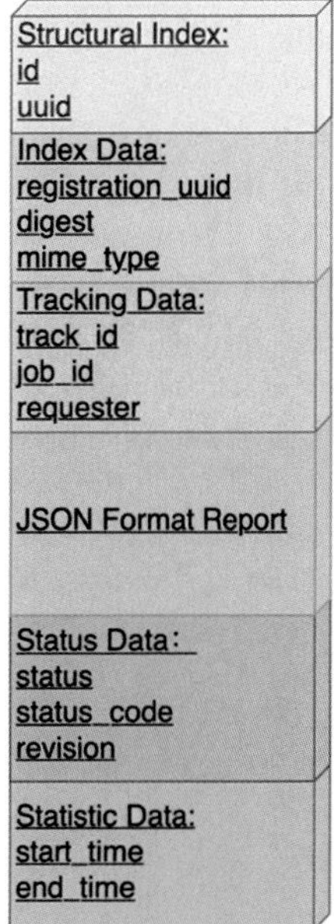

Fig. 4.8 Data schema of scanning report

In addition, each data record of a scanning report corresponds to three attributes (registration_uuid, digest and mime_type) of the index data, that is, a corresponding scanning report data record can be uniquely determined by these three attributes . If the scanner supports multiple types of report, the scanner generates multiple reports for the scanned objects in a round of scanning. However, only one report of a particular object is generated by the scanner and saved in the system. The same scanning repeated subsequently overwrites the previous report. As a result, only data of the latest scanning report is retained in the system.

In the report data schema, three tracking fields are introduced: **track_ id**, **job_id** and **requester**, to track scanning report data more easily. **track_id** determines the callback address of the Webhook of the asynchronous scanning task in the form of UUID, so as to receive the status changes of the corresponding task and the returned raw report data. **job_id** is only used to mark which scanning task provides this report, so that task information can be retrieved through job_id later. **requester** is used to aggregate multiple scanning tasks initiated to achieve the same goal. Tasks with the same requester belong to the same group. **requester** is generally used in the scanning process of composite artifacts built based on images, for example, scanning of the Manifest List and CNAB. During the scanning of a composite artifact, the scanning controller creates a scanning task for each sub-artifact of the artifact (recursion is supported but is not common). The report of each scanning task is aggregated as a final report of the artifact. The raw report data is still saved in the database in the JSON format.

As mentioned in the previous section, it takes some time to execute a scanning task and the execution process is reflected by different states. Therefore, a scanning report that depends on a scanning task also has a variety of corresponding states. In the scanning report schema, a data field describing the state of the report is introduced. The changes of a scanning task state can be captured by the monitoring Webhook, so that the corresponding data field of the scanning report can be updated. The state of a scanning report can reflect the overall progress of scanning. As such, the user can understand the whole scanning process through monitoring the related API. The initial state is pending, which can be switched to the running state. Finally, when a report is successfully generated, it is in the success state. Otherwise it will be put into the error state which indicates a failure of the scanning task.

The data schema of a scanning report also provides simple statistical data fields, which can provide the starting and ending time of the scanning operation.

After the basic flow of scanning and the basic structure of a generated report are introduced, more information can be found in the interface of the scanning controller in the following file: **src/controller/scan/controller.go**.

4.2.5 Asynchronous Scanning Task

The asynchronous scanning task is the implementer of the specific scanning operation and is implemented based on the task specification of the JobService. The specific flow is as follows

1. After Harbor receives a scanning request, Harbor integrates related information and submits it to the JobService to start a scanning task.
2. The JobService queues an asynchronous scanning task after getting a request for starting the task.
3. When an executor is available, the JobService pulls the scanning task from the queue and runs it.
4. The scanning task first checks whether the parameters needed to run the task exist and are valid.
5. The scanner needs a valid credential to access Harbor to retrieve the specific scanning content. Therefore, the scanning task needs to generate a reasonable access credential for the scanner.
6. The scanning task encapsulates the related parameters and access credential into a request object according to the scanning API specification and then sends the request object to the scanner for execution. The scanner returns an index ID for the scanning task to later query and obtain the corresponding scanning report.
7. The scanning report is obtained by means of scheduled attempt until the report is ready or an error occurs.
8. After the scanning report is ready, it is sent to the Harbor (core) service through the Webhook of the JobService.
9. The Harbor (core) service converts and persists the scanning report for later use.

The specific implementation of the task can be found in the source file **src/pkg/scan/job.go**.

4.2.6 APIs Related to Scanning

This section briefly sorts out the APIs related to the scanning function of Harbor. For the instructions of more APIs, refer to Chap. 8. The APIs related to scanning covers two aspects: the scanner management and the scanning operation management.

For the APIs related to the scanner management, the OpenAPI declaration description (Swagger) is located in the **api/v2.0/legacy_swagger.yaml** file of Harbor code repository and is marked with the "Scanner" label.

1. The API that lists the scanners configured by the current system. Table 4.4 describes the API.
2. The API that registers and configures a new scanner to the system. Table 4.5 describes the API.
3. The API that is used to test the connectivity of the specified scanner, Table 4.6 describes the API.
4. The API that is used to obtain the basic information about the registration object of the specified scanner. Table 4.7 describes the API.
5. The API that is used to update information about the registration object of the specified scanner. Table 4.8 describes the API.

Table 4.4 API to get a list of scanners

API	GET /api/v2.0/scanners
Description	This API supports the following query parameters: (1) Pagination (**page** and **page_size**). Example: /api/v2.0/scanners?page=1&page_size=25 (2) Fuzzy query for name, description and URL. Example: /api/v2.0/scanners?name=cla or /api/v2.0/scanners?url=clair (3) Exact query for name and URL. Example: /api/v2.0/scanners?ex_name=clair or /api/v2.0/scanners?ex_url=http%3A%2F%2Fharbor-scanner-clair%3A8080

Table 4.5 API to register and configure a new scanner

API	POST /api/v2.0/scanners

Description	The registration object of the scanner must be provided.
	{
	"name": "Clair",
	"description": "A free-to-use tool that scans container images for package vulnerabilities.\n",
	"url": "http://harbor-scanner-clair:8080",
	"auth": "Bearer",
	"access_credential": "Bearer:JWTTOKENGOESHERE",
	"skip_certVerify": false,
	"use_internal_addr": false,
	}

Table 4.6 API to test connectivity of a scanner

API	POST /api/v2.0/scanners/ping

Description	The basic information about the scanner to be tested must be provided.
	{
	"name": "Clair",
	"url": "http://harbor-scanner-clair:8080",
	"auth": "string",
	"access_credential": "Bearer:JWTTOKENGOESHERE"
	}

Table 4.7 API to obtain the registration object of a scanner

API	GET /api/v2.0/scanners/{registration_id}
Description	**registration_id** indicates the unique index value of the registration object.

6. The API that is used to delete the registration object of the specified scanner. Table 4.9 describes the API.
7. The API that sets the specified scanner to the default scanner of the system. Table 4.10 describes the API.
8. The API that is used to obtain the metadata about the specified scanner. Table 4.11 describes the API.

Table 4.8 API to update the registration object of a scanner

API	PUT /api/v2.0/scanners/{registration_id}

Description	**registration_id** indicates the index value of the registration object.
	The registration object to be updated must be provided.
	{
	"name": "Clair-Updated",
	"description": "A free-to-use tool that scans container images for package vulnerabilities.\n",
	"url": "http://harbor-scanner-clair:8080",
	"auth": "Bearer",
	"access_credential": "Bearer:JWTTOKENGOESHERE",
	"skip_certVerify": false,
	"use_internal_addr": false,
	"disabled": false
	}

Table 4.9 API to delete the registration object of a scanner

API	DELETE /api/v2.0/scanners/{registration_id}
Description	**registration_id** indicates the index value of the registration object. If the registration object is successfully deleted, the deleted object of the scanner is returned in the response of the API.

Table 4.10 API to set the default scanner of Harbor

API	PATCH /api/v2.0/scanners/{registration_id}

Description	**registration_id** indicates the index value of the registration object.
	A scanner is specified through the following attribute:
	{
	"is_default": true
	}

Table 4.11 API to obtain the meta data of the registration object of a scanner

API	GET /api/v2.0/scanners/{registration_id}/metadata
Description	**registration_id** indicates the index value of the registration object.

9. The API that is used to obtain the scanner associated with a specified project. Table 4.12 describes the API.
10. The API that is used to set a scanner associated with the specified project. Table 4.13 describes the API.

The following describes the APIs related to scanning management. APIs of this type actually cover two dimensions: the scanning initiation and the progress control as well as the viewing of the corresponding report or report overview. The following section briefly sorts out such APIs.

In the OpenAPI document of **api/v2.0/swagger.yaml**, two APIs are related to scanning initiation and progress control. They are marked with the "scan" label.

Table 4.12 API to obtain the scanner associated with a project

API	GET /api/v2.0/projects/{project_id}/scanner
Description	**project_id** indicates the unique index ID of a project. As mentioned previously, if the project administrator does not set a scanner for the project and the system has a default scanner, the default scanner of the system is returned here. Otherwise, the scanner associated with this project is retrieved.

Table 4.13 API to set the scanner associated with a project

API	PUT /api/v2.0/projects/{project_id}/scanner
Description	**project_id** indicates the unique index ID of a project.

Table 4.14 API to initiate a scanning of an artifact

API	POST /api/v2.0/projects/{project_name}/repositories/{repository_name}/artifacts/{reference}/scan
Description	**project_name** indicates the name of the project. **repository_name** indicates the name of the repository. **reference** indicates the index of the artifact. The artifact's digital digest of sha256 is used.

Table 4.15 API to obtain the log of a scanning operation

API	GET /api/v2.0/projects/{project_name}/repositories/{repository_name}/artifacts/{reference}/scan/{report_id}/log
Description	**project_name** indicates the name of the project. **repository_name** indicates the name of the repository. **reference** indicates the index of the artifact. The artifact's digital digest of sha256 is used. **report_id** indicates the unique index of the corresponding report.

1. The API that is used to initiate the scanning for the specified artifact. Table 4.14 describes the API.
2. The API that is used to obtain the log information of the scanning operation. Table 4.15 describes the API.

Two APIs are related to retrieving report and report overview information, which are included in the related APIs of artifacts. The APIs are marked with the "artifact" label.

1. The API that is used to obtain the summary of the vulnerability report of the given artifact. Table 4.16 describes the API.
2. The API that is used to obtain the details of the vulnerability report of the given artifact. Table 4.17 describes the API.

The APIs related to the global scanning operation are in the OpenAPI document **api/v2.0/legacy_swagger.yaml**, including the following:

Table 4.16 API to obtain the summary of the vulnerability report of an artifact

API	GET /api/v2.0/projects/{project_name}/repositories/{repository_name}/artifacts/{reference}
Description	**project_name** indicates the name of the project. **repository_name** indicates the name of the repository. **reference** indicates the index of the artifact. The artifact's digital digest of sha256 is used. Report overview information can be obtained through the **scan_overview** field of the artifact data model. If the report is not ready, this field is null.

Table 4.17 API to obtain the details of the vulnerability report of an artifact

API	GET /api/v2.0/projects/{project_name}/repositories/{repository_name}/artifacts/{reference}/additions/vulnerabilities
Description	**project_name** indicates the name of the project. **repository_name** indicates the name of the repository. **reference** indicates the index of the artifact. The artifact's digital digest of sha256 is used. The returned vulnerability detail report includes the list of all found vulnerabilities.

Table 4.18 API to create a global scanning task

API	POST /api/v2.0/system/scanAll/schedule
Description	The API is used to create a global scanning task. If no specified schedule parameter exists in the parameter object, the task is executed immediately. If the schedule parameter is set, the task is executed periodically according to the specified schedule setting.

Table 4.19 API to obtain the schedule of a global scanning task

API	GET /api/v2.0/system/scanAll/schedule
Description	If the schedule parameter is specified for the created global scanning task, the schedule in the system is returned through this API.

1. The API that is used to create a global scanning task. Table 4.18 describes the API.
2. The API that is used to obtain the schedule set by the global scanning task. Table 4.19 describes the API.
3. The API that is used to update the schedule set by the global scanning task. Table 4.20 describes the API.
4. The API that is used to obtain the progress statistical report of the latest global scanning task executed according to the specified schedule. Table 4.21 describes the API.
5. The API that is used to obtain the progress statistical report of the latest global scanning task executed manually. Table 4.22 describes the API.

Table 4.20 API to update the schedule of a global scanning task

API	PUT /api/v2.0/system/scanAll/schedule
Description	If the schedule parameter is specified for the created global scanning task, the schedule in the system is updated through this API.

Table 4.21 API to obtain the progress of statistics report of a scheduled global scanning task

API	GET /api/v2.0/scans/schedule/metrics

Description	The progress statistical information in the following format is returned:
	{
	"total": 100,
	"completed": 90,
	"requester": "28",
	"metrics": {
	"Success": 5,
	"Error": "2,",
	"Running": 3
	}
	}

Table 4.22 API to obtain the progress of statistics report of a manually-triggered global scanning task

API	GET /api/v2.0/scans/all/metrics
Description	The format of the progress statistical report is the same as that of the report returned by the API in (4) above.

4.3 Using the Vulnerability Scanning Function

This section describes how to use the vulnerability scanning function to enhance the security of managed and distributed content. The illustration and description of these functions are based on the web management console of Harbor.

4.3.1 System Scanner

To use vulnerability scanning, the system first needs to configure at least one scanner. You can install the default scanners (only Trivy and Clair scanners are supported) during installation of Harbor or you can install and configure a selected scanner separately after installing Harbor. The scanner management and configuration can be done on the scanner management page.

In the left navigation menu, choose **Administrations** > **Interrogation Services** as the system administrator. The scanner management page is displayed, as shown in Fig. 4.9.

Interrogation Services

Scanners Vulnerability

Image Scanners

+ NEW SCANNER SET AS DEFAULT ACTION

Name	Endpoint	Health	Enabled	Authorization
Trivy Default	http://trivy-adapter:8080	Healthy	true	None
Clair	http://clair-adapter:8080	Healthy	true	None

1 - 2 of 2 items

Fig. 4.9 Scanner management

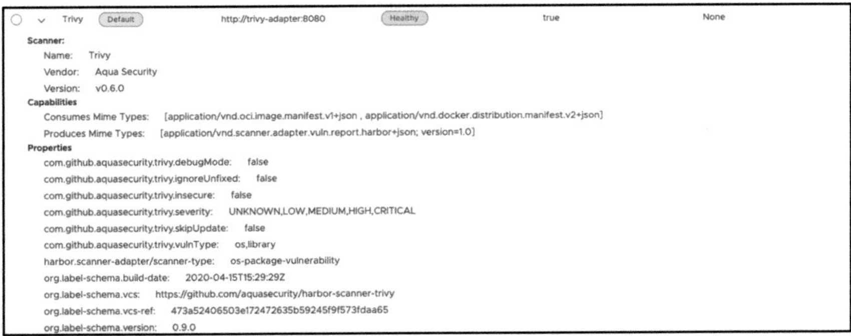

Fig. 4.10 Metadata of Trivy scanner

All configured scanners are listed on the page. Each record contains the scanner name, connection address, health status, enabled or not and authentication mode. The default scanner of the system is displayed by the "Default" label. Meanwhile, for these configured scanners, you can click **Set as Default** to set a selected scanner to the new default scanner of the system. In the **Action** dropdown box, click the **Disable** or **Enable** menu to change the enabled flag of the selected scanner; in the **Action** dropdown box, click the **Edit** menu. In the editing window, update basic information about the scanner; in the **Action** dropdown box, click the **Delete** menu to remove the selected scanner.

Click the leftmost arrow of an item in the list. All metadata of the corresponding scanner is listed in the form of key-value pair. It should be noted that metadata is obtained in real time. If a scanner is in an unhealthy state, the metadata cannot be obtained. Figure 4.10 shows the metadata of the Trivy scanner.

To configure a new scanner, click **New Scanner**. The dialog box for creating a scanner is displayed, as shown in Fig. 4.11. Enter a name and connection address of a scanner to configure the scanner. In addition, the optional description text and authentication mode of a scanner can be entered. At present, the following authentication modes are supported:

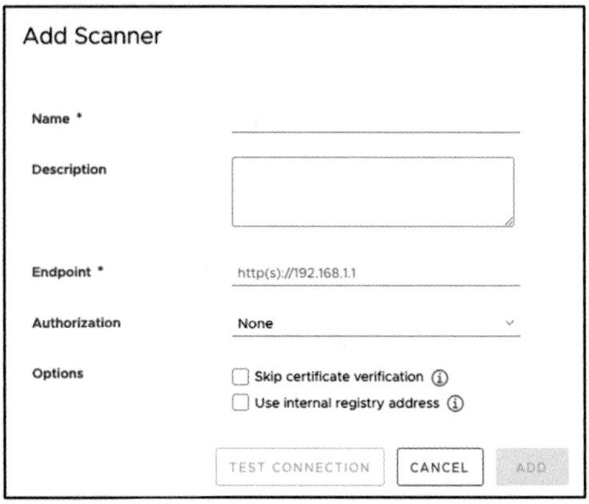

Fig. 4.11 Add Scanner dialog box

1. None: The scanner does not enable any authentication mode.
2. Basic: the HTTP Basic mode. In this mode, the user name and password must be provided.
3. Bearer: the HTTP bearer token mode. In this mode, the corresponding token information must be provided.
4. APIKey: the API token mode. In this mode, the API token recognized by the scanner must be provided.

In addition, two options are available for how to connect the scanner to be configured.

1. Skip certificate verification: If the remote scanner uses a self-signed or untrusted certificate, select this option to skip the verification of its certificate.
2. Use internal address of Harbor: If the remote scanner to be added is in the same network as Harbor , check this option to use an internal address of Harbor.

After providing the necessary information, click the button of **Test Connection** at the bottom of the dialog box to check whether the scanner to add is available. Only scanners that pass the connection test can be added to the system. If you add a scanner that cannot be connected, an internal system error is returned.

After entering the required information, click **Add** button to add the verified scanner to the scanner list. If adding a scanner fails due to any problem that occurs during this process, an error message is displayed to troubleshoot the error. For internal errors of the system, other information such as logs may be required to help identify the error.

4.3.2 Project Scanner

By default, a project uses the default scanner of the system. However, a project may also have a dedicated scanner that is different from the default scanner of the system.

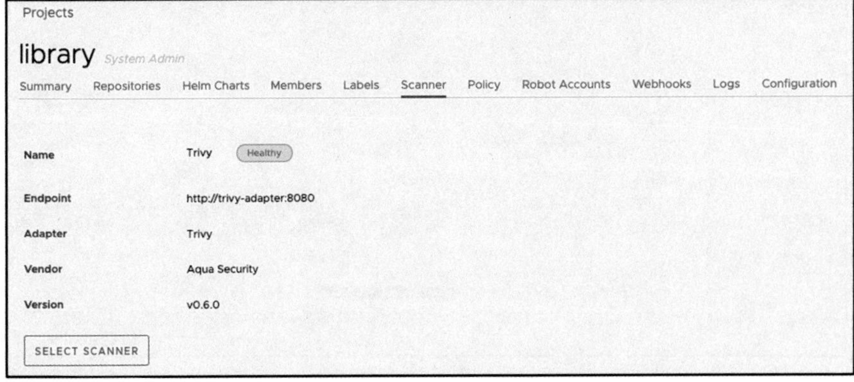

Fig. 4.12 Scanner tab of the library project

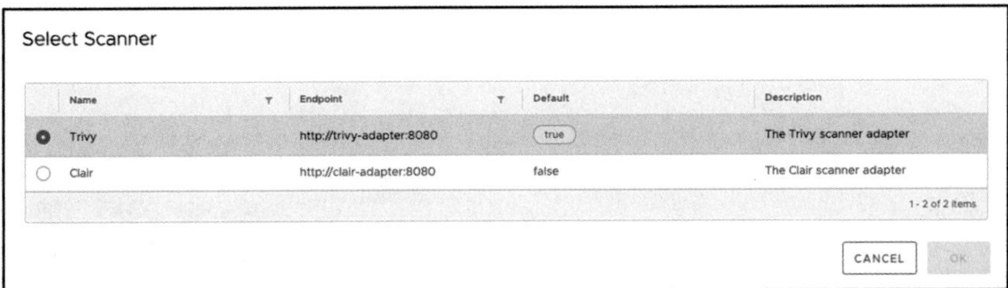

Fig. 4.13 Select Scanner dialog box

In the left navigation menu, click on the **Project** menu as the project administrator. The project list is displayed. Click on a project and the project page is displayed. Switch to the **Scanner** tab. The settings page of the scanner is displayed, as shown in Fig. 4.12.

By default, the information and health status of the default scanner of the system are displayed. Click on **Select Scanner** in the lower left corner. A dialog box is displayed, as shown in Fig. 4.13. In this dialog box, all scanners that are configured in the system are listed for selection.

Select an alternative scanner and click on **OK** button to complete the setting of the project scanner. At this point, the scanner page of the project displays the basic information and health status of the newly selected scanner. After that, the new scanner will be used for scanning artifacts in this project.

4.3.3 Project Vulnerability Scanning

After a scanner is configured, a scanning operation can be initiated for the content of a project. It should be noted that the configurable scanners supported by the system

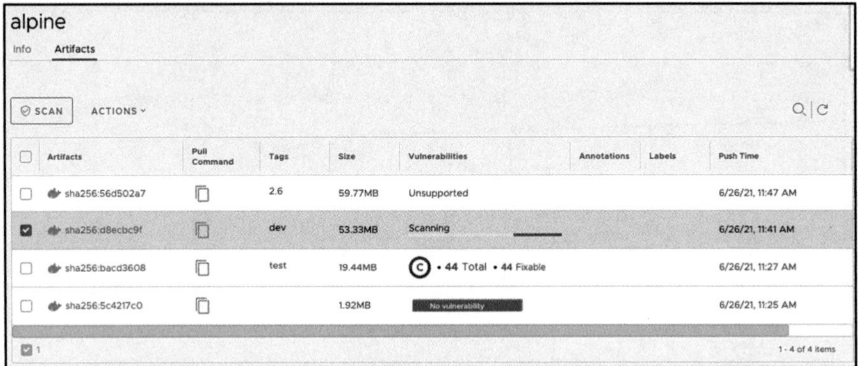

Fig. 4.14 Scan an artifact for vulnerability

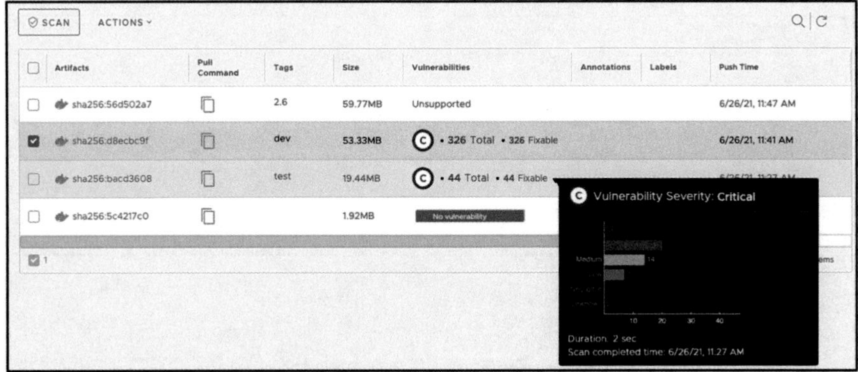

Fig. 4.15 Severity chart of vulnerability report

currently are only for container images. Therefore, in addition to container images, only OCI artifacts built based on container images can support scanning, such as OCI index and CNAB. Moreover, scanning can be started only when the current user has at least the developer role of the project.

Choose **Project** > **{Project Name}** > **Repository** > **{Repository Name}**. The list of artifacts in a specific repository is displayed. Select the artifact to be scanned and click on **Scan** in the upper left corner to start content vulnerability scanning, as shown in Fig. 4.14.

The mediaType of some artifacts may not be supported by the currently set scanner. In such a case, the vulnerability status column shows Unsupported. For this type of artifacts, even if they are selected, the scan button is still unavailable.

Move the mouse over to the **Vulnerabilities** column. The vulnerability report severity chart is displayed, as shown in Fig. 4.15.

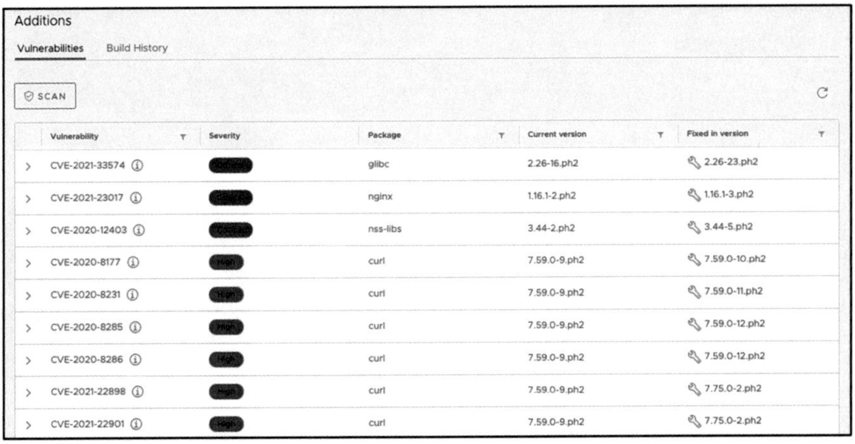

Additions

Vulnerabilities Build History

SCAN

	Vulnerability	Severity	Package	Current version	Fixed in version
>	CVE-2021-33574	[illegible]	glibc	2.26-16.ph2	2.26-23.ph2
>	CVE-2021-23017	[illegible]	nginx	1.16.1-2.ph2	1.16.1-3.ph2
>	CVE-2020-12403	[illegible]	nss-libs	3.44-2.ph2	3.44-5.ph2
>	CVE-2020-8177	High	curl	7.59.0-9.ph2	7.59.0-10.ph2
>	CVE-2020-8231	High	curl	7.59.0-9.ph2	7.59.0-11.ph2
>	CVE-2020-8285	High	curl	7.59.0-9.ph2	7.59.0-12.ph2
>	CVE-2020-8286	High	curl	7.59.0-9.ph2	7.59.0-12.ph2
>	CVE-2021-22898	High	curl	7.59.0-9.ph2	7.75.0-2.ph2
>	CVE-2021-22901	High	curl	7.59.0-9.ph2	7.75.0-2.ph2

Fig. 4.16 The complete report of the vulnerabilities of an artifact

Click on the hyperlink of the digest of the corresponding artifact. The detailed information page is displayed. In the **Additions** section of the page, a complete report of the vulnerabilities found in this artifact is displayed as in Fig. 4.16.

If an artifact in the repository is built based on container images such as CNAB or OCI index, the vulnerability scanning report is a simple aggregation result of all child artifact vulnerability reports. Click on the **Folder** icon on the right of the artifact digest column. The list view of the artifact is displayed. The same as the parent artifact, the detailed vulnerability reports of child artifacts can be viewed when clicking on the hyperlinks of their digests, as shown in Fig. 4.17.

4.3.4 Global Vulnerability Scanning

Scanning within a project is performed only for the selected artifacts in a specific repository. If the system administrator needs to scan all artifacts managed by Harbor, the global vulnerability scanning function can be used. Global vulnerability scanning can be triggered manually or through a configured timer.

Choose **Administration > Interrogation Services > Vulnerability** as the system administrator. The global vulnerability scanning management page is displayed. Click **Scan** to start global vulnerability scanning. During scanning, a progress bar is displayed on the right, including the total number of artifacts to be scanned, the number of artifacts that have been scanned and the number of artifacts that are being scanned, as shown in Fig. 4.18.

In addition to the global vulnerability scanning triggered after you click on a button, the global vulnerability scanning operation can also be run periodically by setting a timer. Click **Edit** on the page shown in Fig. 4.18 to set a timer. The timer is

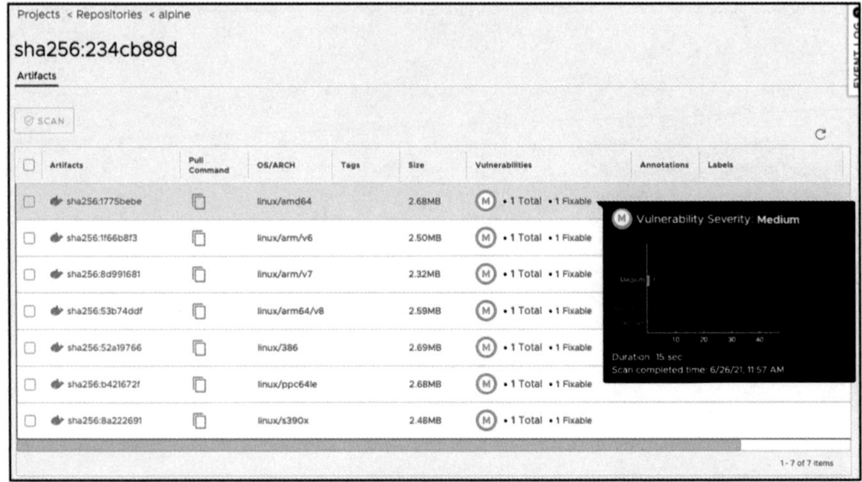

Fig. 4.17 The report of the vulnerabilities of child artifacts

Fig. 4.18 Start scanning all artifacts

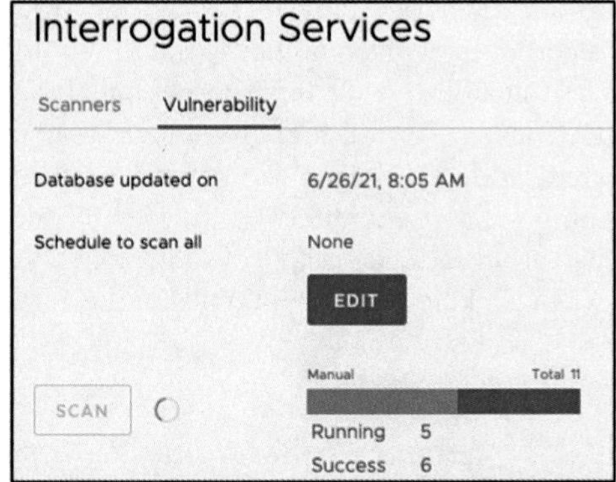

set based on the Cron format. Through the drop-down box, select a predefined mode such as **hourly**, **daily** and **weekly**. You can also set a custom value by selecting **Custom** from the drop-down box. As shown in Fig. 4.19, "0 0 8 * * *" indicates that the global vulnerability scanning task is started at 8 o'clock (UTC time) every morning. If you do not know the meanings of fields in the Cron format, you can move the mouse pointer to the small icon on the right. Related tooltips are displayed so that you can get help quickly.

4.3.5 Automatic Scanning

Choose **Project** > {**Project Name**} > **Configuration** as the project administrator. The configuration page of the project is displayed, as shown in Fig. 4.20. Under

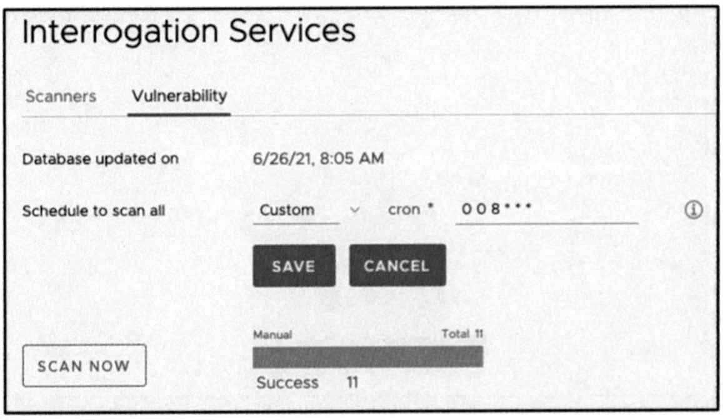

Fig. 4.19 Scheduled scanning of all artifacts

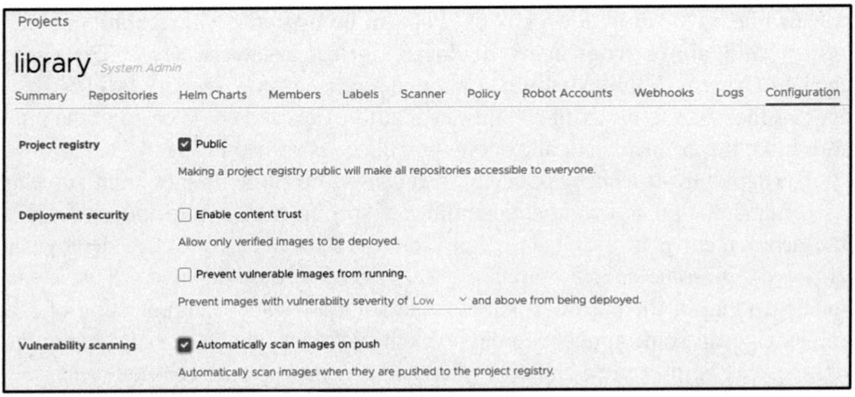

Fig. 4.20 Option of automatically scan image on push

Vulnerability scanning, select the "**Automatically scan image on push**" option to enable the automatic scanning function. After an image has been pushed successfully, the system scans the image automatically and generates a report.

4.3.6 Security Policy of Deployment Associated with Vulnerability

Through vulnerability scanning, we can find vulnerabilities of different severity in the content of artifacts. Based on the information, we can set whether the deployment of the artifacts with these vulnerabilities is allowed and the security policy of the deployment. Choose **Project > {Project Name} > Configuration** as the project administrator. The configuration page of the project is displayed. In **Deployment security**, select the option of "**Prevent potential vulnerable images from running**" to enable the security policy of deployment associated with vulnerability.

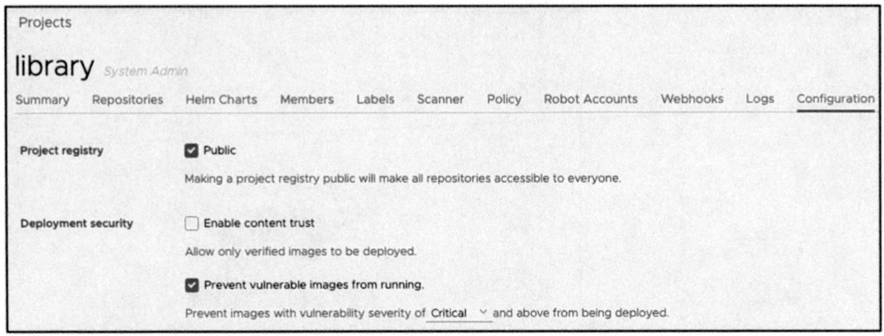
Projects
library System Admin
Summary Repositories Helm Charts Members Labels Scanner Policy Robot Accounts Webhooks Logs Configuration
Project registry
Public
Making a project registry public will make all repositories accessible to everyone.
Deployment security
Enable content trust
Allow only verified images to be deployed.
Prevent vulnerable images from running.
Prevent images with vulnerability severity of Critical and above from being deployed.

Fig. 4.21 Setting severity threshold to prevent downloading valnerable images

Meanwhile, in the drop-down box of "**Prevent images with vulnerability severity of ___ and above from being deployed**", select a severity level. The options include **Critical**, **High**, **Medium**, **Low** and **None**. After a severity level is set, as long as the severity of a vulnerability in an artifact exceeds or is equal to the preset threshold, the artifact is not allowed to be pulled, as shown in Fig. 4.21.

The deployment security policy of "**Prevent vulnerable images from running**" ensures that the images with vulnerabilities of specific severity are not distributed to the deployment platform. This greatly improves the security of the deployment. However, in some specific circumstances, organizers or deployers have a clear understanding of the hazard of some vulnerabilities. Under the protection of other measures or in some application deployment scenarios, the hazard of these vulnerabilities can be prevented and controlled and no unacceptable consequences occur. Therefore, a vulnerability allowlist (used to be called whitelist in Harbor 2.0 and earlier) can be created to exclude these vulnerabilities from the security policy.

In the current design of Harbor, the vulnerability allowlist covers two dimensions: one is at the system level, which is visible to and shared by all projects in the system; the other is a custom list at the project level. The project administrator can choose to directly reference the allowlist defined at the system level or customize a allowlist.

For the system vulnerability allowlist, choose **Administration** > **Configuration** > **System Settings** as the administrator. The system settings page is displayed. The section of **Deployment security is** shown in Fig. 4.22. The allowlist is composed of unique vulnerability IDs. You can click on **Add** to add one or more vulnerability IDs to the list or click on **Delete** icon on the right of a vulnerability ID to remove the vulnerability ID. In addition, setting the validity period of the allowlist is supported. The default value is **Never expire**.

For the vulnerability white list of a project, choose **Project** > {**Project Name**} > **Configuration** as the project administrator. The configuration page of the project is displayed and white list can be edited in the section of **CVE allowlist**, as shown in Fig. 4.23.

As mentioned above, for the allowlist of a project, you can choose to use the system allowlist by selecting "**System allowlist**". You can also customize the

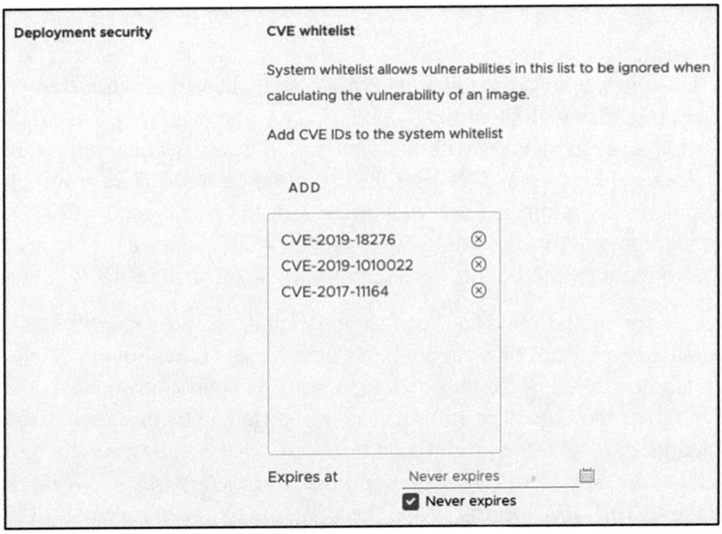

Deployment security

CVE whitelist

System whitelist allows vulnerabilities in this list to be ignored when calculating the vulnerability of an image.

Add CVE IDs to the system whitelist

ADD

CVE-2019-18276
CVE-2019-1010022
CVE-2017-11164

Expires at Never expires

Never expires

Fig. 4.22 System level allowlist (whitelist) of CVEs

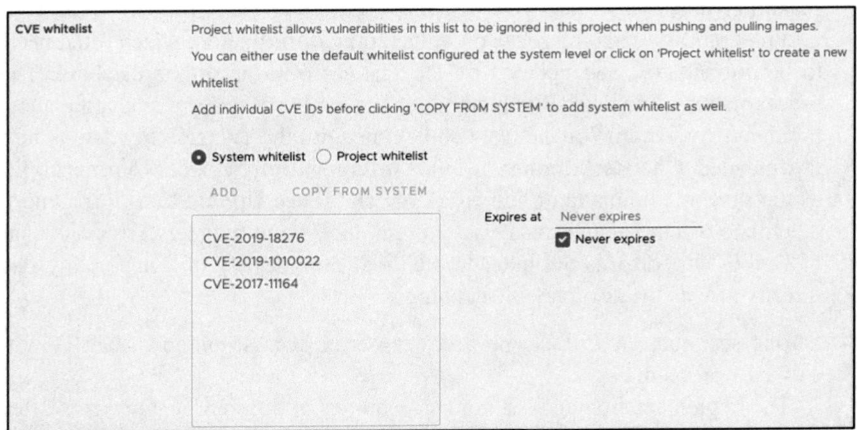

Fig. 4.23 Project level allowlist (whitelist) of CVEs

allowlist of a project by selecting "**Project allowlist**". In the custom mode, you can choose to set from scratch or you can edit the system allowlist after copying it. When a custom allowlist is used, the validity period needs to be customized at the same time. However, the default value is still **Never expire**.

4.4 FAQ

1. Can the signature information of an artifact be replicated to other Harbor registry services together with the artifact content?

   Artifacts are associated with the access path, registry path and tag in Harbor. Therefore, replicating and sharing the signature between Harbor instances with different access paths are not supported. However, the good news is that the Notary community is discussing how to refactor and enhance the Notary function so that signatures can be transferred with their associated artifacts.

2. When a tag of the specified artifact is deleted, the system displays an error indicating that signed tags cannot be deleted. In this case, how to delete the tag?

   In Harbor, deleting the tags of signed artifacts is not allowed. To delete a tag, first remove the signature information associated with the tag. In the Notary command line, execute a command similar to the following to remove the signature: **notary -s https://<harbor host address>:4443 -d ~/. docker/trust remove -p 10.1.10.20/nginx** . After the signature has been successfully removed, the specific tag of the artifact can be deleted. An example of this command is also provided in the error prompt of **Event Log** on the page.

3. Vulnerabilities exist in artifacts, but no vulnerability is found by the Harbor after scanning. Why?

   Vulnerability scanning relies on vulnerability information, which often needs to be downloaded and updated by the scanner from an online database. This process takes some time. If vulnerability data is not completely ready, the above problem may occur. You can wait some time until the vulnerability data is fully downloaded. Choose **Administration > Interrogation Service > Vulnerability** as the system administrator and check the **Database Updated on** timestamp to determine whether data is ready. At present, the default scanners Trivy and Clair of Harbor support this attribute. In addition, the integrity of vulnerability data directly affects the accuracy of scanning.

4. During scanning an artifact, the following error occurs: unknown OS. How to solve the problem?

   The implementation and scanning capabilities of different scanners are different, and the base operating systems (OSs) of the image structures that can be identifies are also limited. If an OS is unknown to a scanner, the OS cannot be scanned. In this case, if multiple scanners are configured, the current scanner can be switched to other scanner for scanning.

5. When the current scanner is switched to another one, which is used to scan the same artifact, the scanning results are different. Why?

   As mentioned previously, the accuracy of the scanning results of a scanner is based on the vulnerability database on which the scanner relies. The vulnerability data of different scanners are different, and the final scanning results could also be different.

6. Duplicate items appear in the scanning results of the manifest list or CNAB. Is that right?

   This complies with the current design because currently the scanners supported by Harbor scan only container images. The manifest list or the CNAB actually corresponds to a group of images. The scanning for such composite artifacts is implemented through scanning of their child images. The generation of a report is simply the aggregation of scanning reports of child images. During the aggregation, deduplication is not performed. Therefore, duplicate vulnerabilities or vulnerability counts may appear in the aggregated report or summary.

Chapter 5
Remote Replication of Content

The replication and distribution of artifacts have always been a pain point due to the lack of good tools. To tackle this issue, Harbor provides the policy-based artifact replication. Users can replicate and distribute artifacts among different types of registry services by making different replication rules based on operational modes, triggering modes and filtering rules. Remote replication of Harbor is one of the most used functions. It is applicable to a variety of different scenarios. This chapter introduces the remote replication function of Harbor, including basic principles, usage modes and applicable scenarios, to help readers design replication policies and cope with various scenarios of artifact replication and distribution.

5.1 Basic Principles

During the day-to-day development and operation, multiple registry services are often needed to fulfill different tasks. For example, the development and testing work may require a registry service instance while the production environment needs another instance. An artifact needs to be pushed from the development registry to the production registry after the development and testing of the artifact. To increase the local download speed, multiple registry services may be deployed in different data centers. After an artifact is pushed to one of the registry services, the artifact is automatically distributed to the rest of other registry services.

In some simple scenarios, the tasks of pushing and distributing images can be completed through an automation script or manual operation. However, if there are many repositories or artifacts such as images which need to be replicated between heterogeneous registry services, it could be challenging to manage and implement.

The remote replication provided by Harbor helps users meet the requirements of above scenarios and reliably move cloud native artifacts such as images across systems. In addition to allow the replication between different Harbor instances,

H. Zhang, Y. Wang, *The Authoritative Guide on Harbor*,
https://doi.org/10.1007/978-981-19-2727-0_5

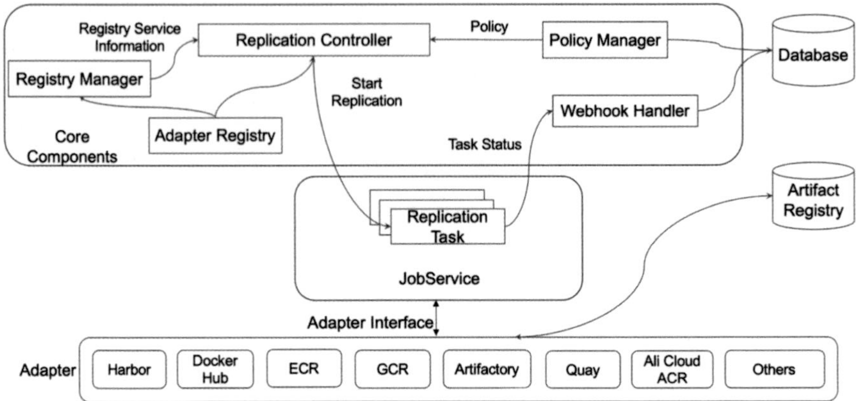

Fig. 5.1 Architecture of the remote replication module

the remote replication supports replication between Harbor and other registry services (such as Amazon Elastic Container Registry and Google Container Registry).

The remote replication is defined by replication policy. The user describes the desired replication logic by setting a replication policy (see Sect. 5.3 for replication policies). An execution record is generated for the execution of each replication policy. Each execution may be composed of several tasks. A task is responsible for the replication of all artifacts in the same repository.

Because different registry services have their own management modes (for example, namespace management) for artifacts, the remote replication uses adapters to abstract these different behaviors. Each type of registry service requires an implementation of the adapter, so as to shield the underlying differences and provide a consistent interface upward.

Figure 5.1 shows the overall architecture of the remote replication module. The control flow, coordination, scheduling and basic functional logic are implemented in the Core component. The time-consuming data transmission tasks are completed by the JobService component. Specifically, the Adapter Registry registers the information about all registry service adapters of Harbor and selects an adapter of the configured registry service type when it executes a remote replication task. The Policy Manager is responsible for creating, modifying, viewing, and deleting a policy. User-defined replication policies are eventually persisted to the database. The Registry Manager is responsible for the management operation of registry services. The Replication Controller constructs a workflow according to the user-defined policies and registry service information to trigger a remote replication task. The replication task is finally scheduled and executed by the JobService component, and its operating status is reported to the Core component in real time through Webhook. The Core component persists the status to the database so that the user can know about the status at any time.

The following briefly introduces the basic workflow of remote replication by taking images as an example.

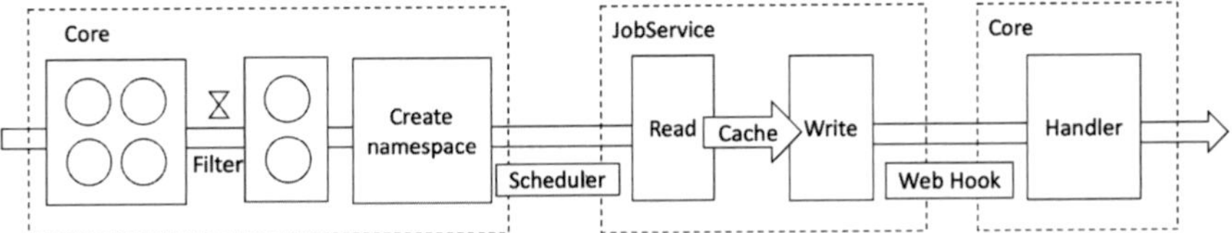

Fig. 5.2 The replication workflow

After a replication policy is triggered, depending on the triggering mode and the replicating operation, one of the two workflows is created: replication and deletion. The replication workflow synchronizes artifacts from the source repository to a remote repository; the deletion workflow is to delete in the remote repository the images which have been removed in the source repository.

Figure 5.2 shows the replication workflow, in which the Core component appears twice.

After the replication workflow is triggered, the workflow first pulls images from the source repository specified by the replication policy and filters out the list of images to be replicated by the filtering rules. Because different registry services have different namespace management modes, before images are pushed to a remote registry, the replication workflow first checks whether the corresponding namespace already exists in the remote registry. If it does not exist, the workflow creates the corresponding namespace. Then the workflow groups the images by the repository. All images in the same repository are placed in the same group. Each group is associated with a replication task, which is finally executed by the JobService component. After the replication task is submitted to the JobService component, the task enters the task queue and waits for scheduling of the JobService component, so as to complete the actual replication work. By default, up to 10 replication tasks can be executed concurrently. The number of concurrent tasks can be modified for the JobService component.

The following section describes the replication workflow of an image executed in the JobService component:

1. Pull the manifest of a source image.
2. Check whether the source image exists in the remote repository. If the source image exists, the workflow ends directly; otherwise, proceed with the following steps.
3. Check whether the image with the same name but of different content exists in the remote repository. If the image exists and the replication policy prohibits overwriting such images, the workflow ends directly; otherwise, continue with the following steps.

4. If the manifest type is list, the manifest is an image index. For each child manifest referenced by the list, jump to Step (1) and continue. Otherwise, replicate the layers referenced by the manifest. During the replication of layers, if a layer is a foreign layer (a layer not stored locally), skip the replication of this layer directly; otherwise, check whether the layer exists in the remote repository. If it does exist, skip the replication of this layer directly; otherwise, pull the layer from the source repository and then push it to the remote repository.
5. Push the manifest to the remote repository.

If an error occurs during the execution of a replication task, the task is placed at the end of the execution queue of the JobService component again and waits for the next scheduling and execution. This process is repeated for a maximum of three times to retry the task for a possible successful execution. After the replication task in the JobService component is completed, the JobService component reports the status of the replication task to the Core component through Webhook. Finally, the whole replication workflow is done.

When an artifact in the source repository is deleted, the deletion workflow is triggered. The deletion workflow is similar to the replication workflow: Check whether the current artifact meets the filtering conditions according to the filtering rules in the replication policy. If the artifact meets the filtering conditions, create a deletion task, and submit the task to the JobService component to complete the actual deletion; otherwise, the deletion of the artifact is not synchronized to the remote registry service.

In addition, a replication or deletion task in execution can be stopped. Several checkpoints are inserted in the execution logic of a task. When the checkpoints are executed, they check whether the current task should be stopped. If the task should be stopped, the execution terminates; otherwise, continue with the execution. That is, after the user sends a request to stop an execution, the task keeps being executed until the first checkpoint is reached.

5.2 Setting up a Registry Endpoint

Many public or private cloud providers offer artifact registry products or online registry services. The remote replication function of Harbor already supports many registry products and services that are widely used. In Harbor 2.0, the supported registry services can be divided into two categories in terms of the type of managed artifacts: image registry services and Helm Chart registry services.

The supported image registry services include Harbor, Docker Hub, Docker Registry, Amazon Elastic Container Registry, Azure Container Registry, AliCloud Container Registry, Google Container Registry, Huawei SWR, GitLab, Quay.io and JFrog Artifactory.

The supported Helm Chart registry services include Harbor and Helm Hub.

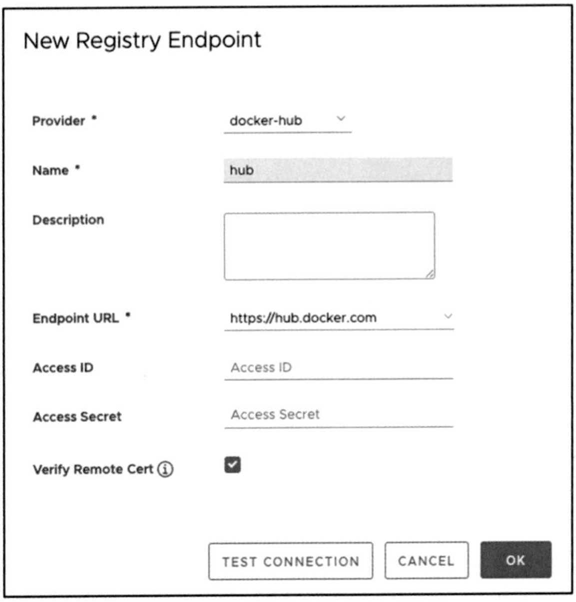

Fig. 5.3 New Registry Endpoint dialog box

Before using the remote replication function, first create in Harbor an instance of the remote registry service. The registry service must be already up and running properly.

Log in to Harbor by using the system administrator account, choose **Administration** > **Registries** and click **New Endpoint** to create a registry endpoint, as shown in Fig. 5.3.

According to the type of remote artifact registry, select corresponding options from the **Provider** drop-down list, enter the registry name and the description information, provide the endpoint URL, the access ID and the access secret of the remote registry service and choose whether to enable "Verify Remote Cert" option according to the protocol used by the remote registry service. Click on **Test Connection** to test the connection between the current Harbor instance and the remote registry service. If the connection is successful, click **OK** to complete the creation of the registry service.

If no access permission control (for example, to pull images under the public repository of Docker Hub) is enabled for the artifact to be replicated, the access ID and access secret can be blank. For different registry services, the access IDs and access secret have different forms, which are described in detail in Sect. 5.5.

When the access ID and access secret are blank, click on **Test Connection** to test only the network connectivity between the current Harbor instance and the remote registry service; when the access ID and access secret are not blank, the provided authentication credential is also verified.

For registry services using HTTP or HTTPS with self-signed certificates, do not select the option of "Verify Remote Cert".

5.3 Replication Policy

The system administrator needs to create a replication policy for artifact replication and distribution. This section describes the modes, filters and triggering modes of replication policies, as well as the steps to create a replication policy and view the execution status of a replication policy.

5.3.1 Replication Mode

A replication policy supports the push and pull modes. Push mode refers to the replication of artifacts from the current Harbor instance to a remote registry service; pull mode refers to the replication of artifacts from other remote registry services to the current Harbor instance. In push mode, the current Harbor instance is the source registry and the target registry is the remote registry. On the contrary, in pull mode, remote artifact registries are source registries and the current Harbor instance is the target registry. In the view of other artifact registries, the current Harbor instance is the remote registry. These two modes apply to different scenarios. For example, in an environment with a firewall restricting inbound network connections, the registry service instance behind the firewall must obtain remote artifacts through the pull mode.

5.3.2 Filter

A project in the source registry may have many artifacts, but not all artifacts are needed to be replicated to the target registry. Therefore, multiple filtering rules can be set in the replication policy to filter artifacts to be replicated. Harbor supports four types of filters: name filter, tag filter, label filter and resource filter, which filter artifacts by different attributes of artifacts. The following section introduces the four types of filters.

The name filter checks the registry part of the "artifact" name, and the tag filter examines the tag part. For example, if "library/hello-world:latest" is the full name of a container image, the name filter looks at the "library/hello-world" part and the tag filter checks the "latest" part. The name filter and tag filter support the following matching patterns (special characters used in the matching patterns must be escaped with a backslash "\").

- "*": matches all characters except for the separator "/".
- "**": matches all characters, including the separator "/".
- "?": matches all single characters except for the separator "/".
- "{alt1,alt2,...}": matches a character sequence that can be matched by any matching pattern separated by comma in braces.

The following are examples of some matching patterns.

- "library/hello-world": matches only library/hello-world.
- "library/*": matches library/hello-world but does not match library/my/hello-world.
- "library/**": matches both library/hello-world and library/my/hello-world.
- "{library,goharbor}/*": matches library/hello-world and goharbor/core but does not match google/hello-world.
- "1.?": matches 1.0 but does not match 1.01.

You can use labels in Harbor to classify artifacts. The label filter checks the labels marked on artifacts. The label filter can have multiple labels. Artifacts can be selected only when the artifacts are marked with all labels contained in the filter.

Harbor 2.0 provides two types of artifact storage management services: one is provided for OCI artifacts such as image, Helm Chart and Cloud Native Application Bundle (CNAB). The other is provided for Helm Chart served by the integrated ChartMuseum component.

The two storage management services both provide support for Helm Chart. However, they are different in terms of usage. The Helm 3 client provides the experimental function of pushing Helm Chart to the OCI registry service. Therefore, if the Helm 3 client is used, charts can be pushed to Harbor and managed as an OCI artifact. On the other hand, Harbor still retains the support for the Helm 2 client through the ChartMuseum component. Charts can be pushed to Harbor through Helm 2 client.

The resource filter works by checking artifact types. When a replication policy is created, you may choose to replicate only Charts in the ChartMuseum, images or OCI artifacts or all of the above. When you choose to replicate all resource types, the current registry service and remote registry service must both support all resource types. Otherwise, the tasks of replicating unsupported resource types will fail.

5.3.3 Triggering Mode

When creating replication policies, you can select different triggering modes. Harbor currently supports three different triggering modes: manual triggering, scheduled triggering and event-based triggering.

Manual triggering indicates that the system administrator needs to manually click on **Replication** to trigger a replication process, in which all artifacts satisfying the filtering conditions are replicated.

Scheduled triggering refers to performing a periodical replication operation by defining a Cron-like task. A Cron expression adopts the format of "* * * * *". Table 5.1 lists the meanings of fields. Note: The time in the Cron expression set here is the UTC time of the server instead of the time of the browser.

The meanings of special characters are as follows:

Table 5.1 Cron expression

Field Name	Mandatory	Allowed Values	Allowed Special Characters
Second	Yes	0–59	*/,-
Minute	Yes	0–59	*/,-
Hour	Yes	0–23	*/,-
A day within a month	Yes	1–31	*/,-?
Month	Yes	1 to 12 or JAN to DEC	*/,-
A day within a week	Yes	0–6 or SUN-SAT	*/,-?

- "*": indicates any possible value.
- "/": indicates that some given values are skipped.
- ",": indicates enumeration.
- "-": indicates the range.
- "?": is used in "A day within a month" and "A day within a week" and can replace "*".

Some examples of Cron expressions are as follows:

- "0 0/5 * * * ?": performed every five minutes.
- "10 0/5 * * * ?": performed every five minutes. The operation is performed at the 10th second of each minute every time.
- "0 30 10-13 ? * Wed,Fri": performed at 10:30, 11:30, 12:30 and 13:30 every Wednesday and Friday.
- "0 0/30 8-9 5,20 * ?": performed at 8:00, 8:30, 9:00 and 9:30 on the 5th day and 20th day of each month.

The same as the manual triggering mode, the timed triggering mode also replicates all artifacts that satisfy the filtering conditions in the current Harbor instance.

The event-based triggering mode indicates that the replication is automatically triggered when an event occurs in Harbor as the source registry. Harbor supports two types of events: artifact pushing and artifact deletion. After the two events occur, if the resource of the operation meet the conditions set in the filter, the same operation is immediately synchronized to the remote registry service and the operation of pushing or deleting corresponding artifacts is completed. The event-driven mode can deal with the real-time synchronization scenario to a certain extent, but the transfer delay likely occurs depending on network environments. If the replication task fails, the task is retried for up to three times. However, a successful replication cannot be guaranteed (for example, the remote registry service fails). Therefore, if the environment requires high data consistency, other solutions need to be considered. Synchronizing the artifact deletion operation is optional and can be enabled or disabled in a replication policy. When the target repository is a production environment, you can choose not to synchronize the deletion operation to avoid mistaken deletion.

5.3.4 Creating a Replication Policy

Log in to Harbor using the system administrator account, choose **Administration > Replications** and click **New Replication Rule** to create a replication policy, as shown in Fig. 5.4.

Enter a policy name and description, select the replication mode, select the corresponding source registry (pull mode) and destination registry (push mode), set the source resource filter, enter the destination namespace, select a triggering mode, choose whether to select the "Override" option and click **Save**. A replication policy is created.

The destination namespace specifies the namespace in which the replicated artifacts are stored in the target registry. If it is blank, artifacts are stored in the same namespace as the source artifact. Table 5.2 lists several examples.

After "Override" is selected, if an artifact has the same name as this artifact but has different content in the destination artifact repository, the artifact will be overwritten. Otherwise, the system skips the replication process of this artifact.

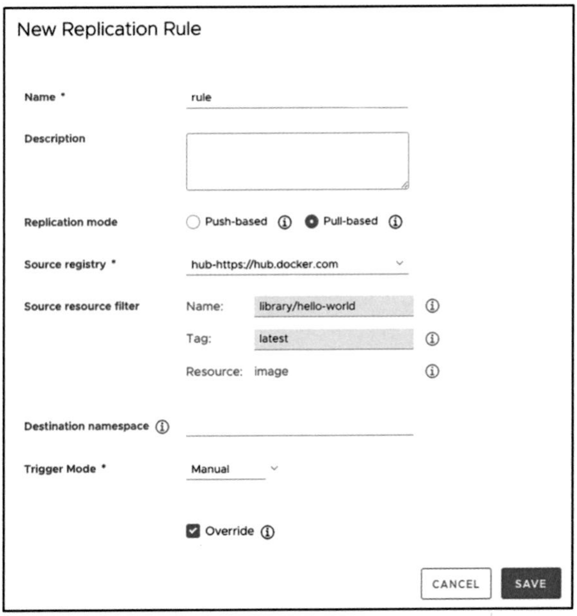

Fig. 5.4 New Replication Rule dialog box

Table 5.2 Source and destination namespaces

Source Artifact	Destination Namespace	Destination Artifact
hello-world:latest	destination	destination/hello-world:latest
library/hello-world:latest	destination	destination/hello-world:latest
library/my/hello-world:latest	destination	destination/hello-world:latest
library/hello-world:latest	Blank	library/hello-world:latest

You can view all created replication policies, modify and delete policies on the replication management page. A replication policy can be modified and deleted only when all execution records of the replication policy are in the terminated status (stopped, successful or failed).

5.3.5 Executing a Replication Policy

After a replication policy is triggered, you can see the execution records of all replication policies on the replication management page, including the triggering mode, starting time, duration, status, total number of tasks and success rate of tasks, as shown in Fig. 5.5.

Click on the ID (serial number) of the execution record shown in Fig. 5.5. The details of the currently executing task are displayed. You can see the execution of all sub-tasks in the current execution record. Click on the log icon of a sub-task. You can see the execution log of the subtask, as shown in Figs. 5.6 and 5.7.

Select an execution record on the page shown in Fig. 5.5 and click on the **Stop** button to stop the execution of the selected task in the non-terminated status (waiting, running and retrying).

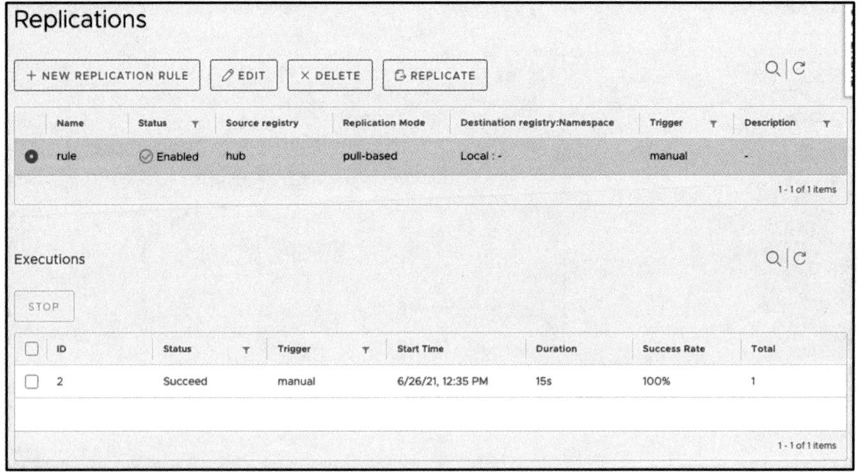

Fig. 5.5 Execution records of all replication policies

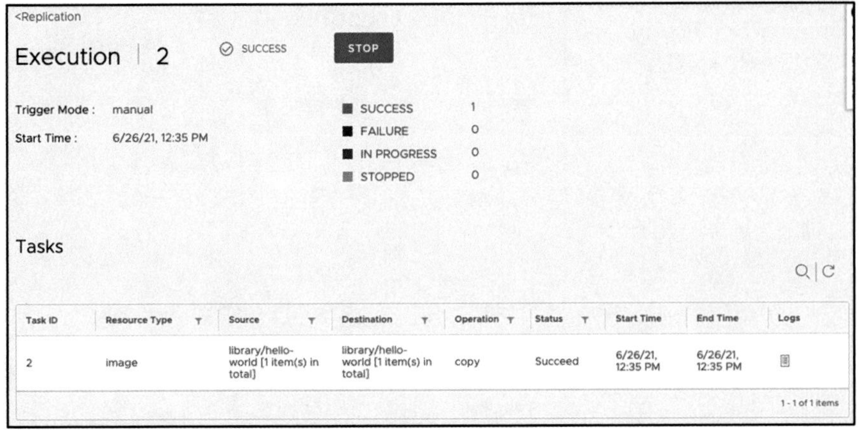

Fig. 5.6 Summary of the execution of a sub task

```
2021-06-26T04:35:08Z [INFO] [/replication/transfer/image/transfer.go:115]: client for source registry [type: docker-hub, URL: https://hub.docker.com, insecure: false]
created
2021-06-26T04:35:08Z [INFO] [/replication/transfer/image/transfer.go:125]: client for destination registry [type: harbor, URL: http://core:8080, insecure: true]
created
2021-06-26T04:35:08Z [INFO] [/replication/transfer/image/transfer.go:158]: copying library/hello-world:[latest](source registry) to library/hello-world:[latest]
(destination registry)...
2021-06-26T04:35:08Z [INFO] [/replication/transfer/image/transfer.go:179]: copying library/hello-world:latest(source registry) to library/hello-
world:latest(destination registry)...
2021-06-26T04:35:08Z [INFO] [/replication/transfer/image/transfer.go:285]: pulling the manifest of artifact library/hello-world:latest ...
2021-06-26T04:35:11Z [INFO] [/replication/transfer/image/transfer.go:291]: the manifest of artifact library/hello-world:latest pulled
2021-06-26T04:35:11Z [INFO] [/replication/transfer/image/transfer.go:179]: copying library/hello-
world:sha256:1b26826f602946860c279fce658f31050cff2c596583af237d971f4629b57792(source registry) to library/hello-
world:sha256:1b26826f602946860c279fce658f31050cff2c596583af237d971f4629b57792(destination registry)...
2021-06-26T04:35:11Z [INFO] [/replication/transfer/image/transfer.go:285]: pulling the manifest of artifact library/hello-
world:sha256:1b26826f602946860c279fce658f31050cff2c596583af237d971f4629b57792 ...
2021-06-26T04:35:11Z [INFO] [/replication/transfer/image/transfer.go:291]: the manifest of artifact library/hello-
world:sha256:1b26826f602946860c279fce658f31050cff2c596583af237d971f4629b57792 pulled
2021-06-26T04:35:11Z [INFO] [/replication/transfer/image/transfer.go:255]: copying the blob sha256:d1165f2212346b2bab48cb01c1e39ee8ad1be46b87873d9ca7a4e434980a7726...
2021-06-26T04:35:13Z [INFO] [/replication/transfer/image/transfer.go:276]: copy the blob sha256:d1165f2212346b2bab48cb01c1e39ee8ad1be46b87873d9ca7a4e434980a7726
completed
2021-06-26T04:35:13Z [INFO] [/replication/transfer/image/transfer.go:255]: copying the blob sha256:b8dfde127a2919ff59ad3fd4a0776de178a555a76fff77a506e128aea3ed41e3...
2021-06-26T04:35:14Z [INFO] [/replication/transfer/image/transfer.go:276]: copy the blob sha256:b8dfde127a2919ff59ad3fd4a0776de178a555a76fff77a506e128aea3ed41e3
completed
2021-06-26T04:35:14Z [INFO] [/replication/transfer/image/transfer.go:310]: pushing the manifest of artifact library/hello-
world:sha256:1b26826f602946860c279fce658f31050cff2c596583af237d971f4629b57792 ...
2021-06-26T04:35:14Z [INFO] [/replication/transfer/image/transfer.go:322]: the manifest of artifact library/hello-
world:sha256:1b26826f602946860c279fce658f31050cff2c596583af237d971f4629b57792 pushed
2021-06-26T04:35:14Z [INFO] [/replication/transfer/image/transfer.go:222]: copy library/hello-
world:sha256:1b26826f602946860c279fce658f31050cff2c596583af237d971f4629b57792(source registry) to library/hello-
world:sha256:1b26826f602946860c279fce658f31050cff2c596583af237d971f4629b57792(destination registry) completed
2021-06-26T04:35:14Z [INFO] [/replication/transfer/image/transfer.go:179]: copying library/hello-
world:sha256:e5785cb0c62cebbed4965129bae371f0589cadd6d84798fb58c2c5f9e237efd9(source registry) to library/hello-
world:sha256:e5785cb0c62cebbed4965129bae371f0589cadd6d84798fb58c2c5f9e237efd9(destination registry)...
2021-06-26T04:35:14Z [INFO] [/replication/transfer/image/transfer.go:285]: pulling the manifest of artifact library/hello-
world:sha256:e5785cb0c62cebbed4965129bae371f0589cadd6d84798fb58c2c5f9e237efd9 ...
2021-06-26T04:35:14Z [INFO] [/replication/transfer/image/transfer.go:291]: the manifest of artifact library/hello-
world:sha256:e5785cb0c62cebbed4965129bae371f0589cadd6d84798fb58c2c5f9e237efd9 pulled
2021-06-26T04:35:14Z [INFO] [/replication/transfer/image/transfer.go:255]: copying the blob sha256:cfdb1bf11e4ca3676dddbd756e478e5394ae31dca507bd5c4b4497852d7fd24b...
2021-06-26T04:35:14Z [INFO] [/replication/transfer/image/transfer.go:276]: copy the blob sha256:cfdb1bf11e4ca3676dddbd756e478e5394ae31dca507bd5c4b4497852d7fd24b
completed
```

Fig. 5.7 Log of the execution of a sub task

5.4 Content Replication Between Harbor Instances

Because the APIs may be different in different Harbor versions, the remote replication between different versions of Harbor instances may not work properly. You are advised to configure the replication policy only between the same version of Harbor instances so as to avoid unforeseeable circumstances.

First, create an instance of the Harbor registry service. Log in to Harbor by using the system administrator account, choose **Administration** > **Registries**, click on **New Registry Endpoint**, and select **harbor** for **Provider**, as shown in Fig. 5.8.

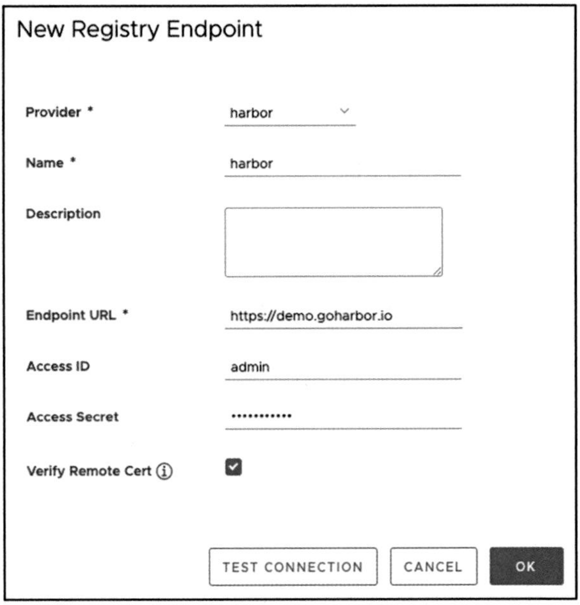

Fig. 5.8 Select harbor provider in New Registry Endpoint dialog box

The access ID and access secret are the name and password of a local user (the database authentication mode) of the target repository or a user in an LDAP/AD (the LDAP authentication mode). When the OIDC authentication mode is used, the user credential of OIDC cannot be used for remote replication. In this case, configure the replication policy by using the local system administrator account of the target repository. Note: In any authentication mode, the robot account cannot be used in the remote replication.

Enter other necessary information to complete the creation of a registry service.

Choose **Administration** > **Replications**, click on **New Replication Rule** to create a replication policy and select the corresponding replication mode, filter, and triggering mode based as needed, as shown in Fig. 5.9.

The list of resource types in **Source Resource Filter** varies depending on whether the current instance (in push mode) or the remote Harbor instance (in pull mode) enables the Helm Chart service. When Helm Chart is not enabled, the **Chart** option is unavailable in the list.

Enter other necessary information to complete the creation of a replication policy.

According to its triggering mode, the replication policy is triggered either manually or automatically to launch remote replication between Harbor instances.

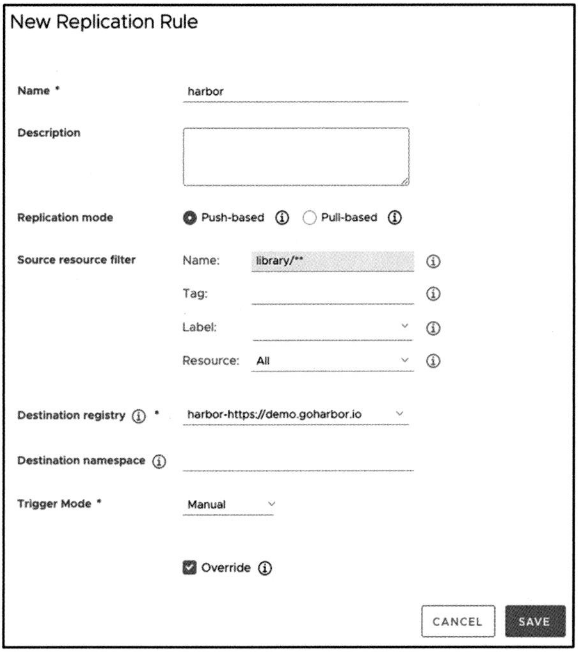

Fig. 5.9 Select harbor endpoint in New Replication Rule dialog box

5.5 Content Replication Between Third-party Registry Services

Because the configuration may vary for the remote replication between Harbor and different third-party registry services, this section helps readers understand how to configure the remote replication for different registry services by going through the configuration of several typical registry services.

5.5.1 Content Replication with Docker Hub

Docker Hub is a public registry service officially maintained by Docker Inc.. Image replication with Docker Hub is of great significance to daily development and testing.

First, create a registry service instance of Docker Hub and select **docker-hub** for **Provider**. The **Endpoint URL** is automatically generated, as shown in Fig. 5.10.

When only public images need to be pulled from Docker Hub, because there is no access control for these images, **Access ID** and **Access Secret** can be blank. In other circumstances, you need to enter a valid user name and password of Docker Hub, make sure that **Verify Remote Cert** is selected and click **OK** to complete the creation of the registry service.

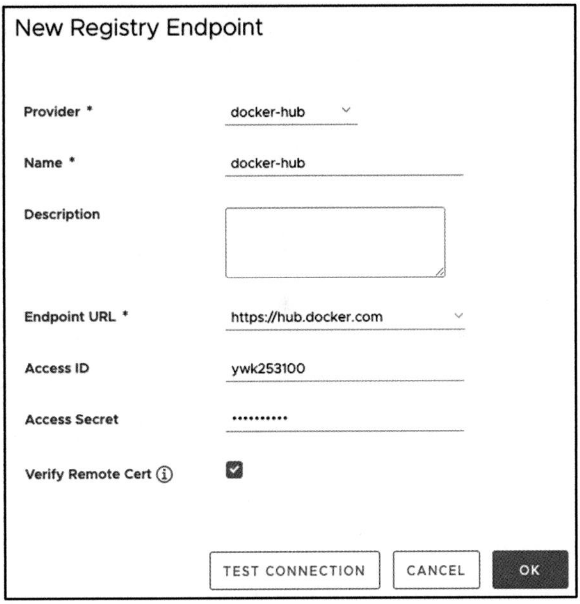

Fig. 5.10 Select docker-hub provider in New Registry Endpoint dialog box

During the creation of a replication policy, if you want to pull official images of Docker Hub, such as hello-world and busybox, you need to prefix the **Name** filter of the **Source Resource Filter** with "library/". For example, "library/hello-world", "library/busybox" or "library/**". If the **Name** filter is blank or "**", and other filters retain the default values, the replication policy pulls all images under the user account, as shown in Fig. 5.11.

Enter other necessary information to complete the creation of a replication policy.

5.5.2 *Content Replication with Docker Registry*

Docker Registry is an open source private registry maintained by Docker Inc.. The name of the open source project is Docker Distribution, which provides the basic registry management functions.

First create a registry service instance of Docker Registry and select **docker-registry** for **Provider**, as shown in Fig. 5.12.

At present, Harbor can replicate content with Docker registries that do not enable authentication or use token-based authentication. Docker registries with the authentication modes of silly or basic auth are not supported.

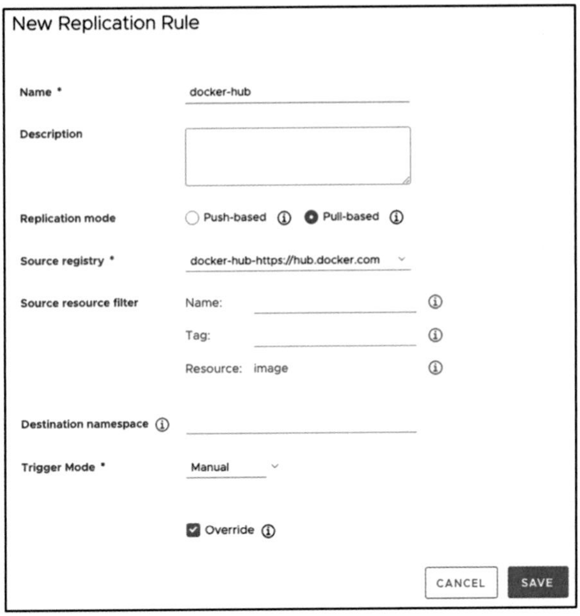

Fig. 5.11 Select docker-hub endpoint in New Replication Rule dialog box

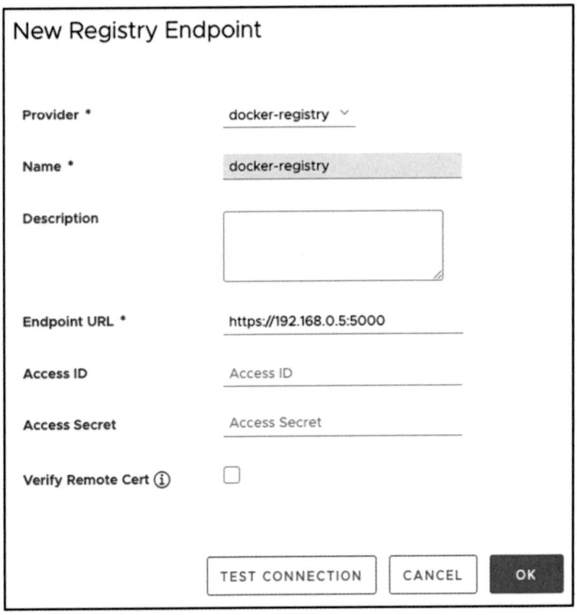

New Replication Rule

Name *	docker-hub
Description	
Replication mode	○ Push-based ⓘ ● Pull-based ⓘ
Source registry *	docker-hub-https://hub.docker.com
Source resource filter	Name: ⓘ
	Tag: ⓘ
	Resource: image ⓘ
Destination namespace ⓘ	
Trigger Mode *	Manual
	☑ Override ⓘ

CANCEL SAVE

Fig. 5.12 Select docker-registry provider in New Registry Endpoint dialog box

New Registry Endpoint

Provider *	docker-registry
Name *	docker-registry
Description	
Endpoint URL *	https://192.168.0.5:5000
Access ID	Access ID
Access Secret	Access Secret
Verify Remote Cert ⓘ	☐

TEST CONNECTION CANCEL OK

During the creation of a replication policy, if the **Name** filter in **Source Resource Filter** is blank or "**", and other filters retain the default values, this policy replicates all images under the user account in the source registry service.

Enter other necessary information to complete the creation of a replication policy.

5.5.3 Content Replication with Amazon ECR

Amazon Elastic Container Registry (ECR) is a public registry service hosted by Amazon.

First, create a registry service instance of ECR, select **aws-ecr** for **Provider**, select the region in the **Endpoint URL** list and enter the **Access ID** and **Access Secret**. Note: The **Access ID** and **Access Secret** here are not the user name and password. The Access ID should have sufficient permissions for the resources in ECR, as shown in Fig. 5.13.

Enter other necessary information to complete the creation of a replication policy.

5.5.4 Content Replication with GCR

Google Container Registry (GCR) is an online registry service hosted by Google Cloud.

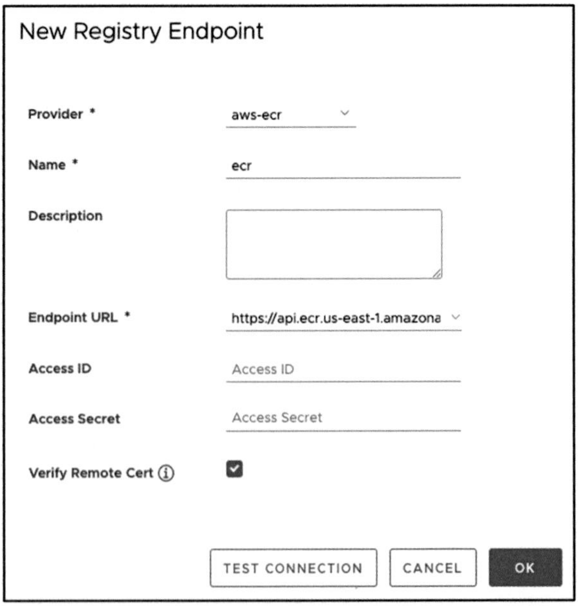

Fig. 5.13 Select aws-ecr provider in New Registry Endpoint dialog box

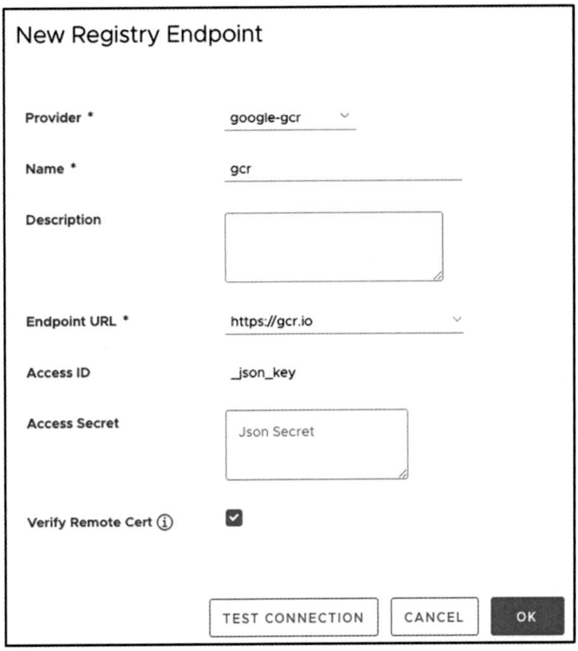

Fig. 5.14 Select google-gcr provider in New Registry Endpoint dialog box

First create a registry service instance of GCR, select **google-gcr** for **Provider**, select a URL in the **Endpoint URL**, and enter the **Access Secret**. Note: The **Access Secret** must use the JSON key file generated by the Service Account, as shown in Fig. 5.14. In addition, the account should have the permissions of the storage administrator.

Enter other necessary information to complete the creation of a replication policy.

5.5.5 Content Replication with Helm Hub

Helm Hub is a public Helm Chart registry service. It references many public third-party Helm Chart registries and provides a unified registry view of chart.

First create a registry service instance of Helm Hub and select **helm-hub** for **Provider**. The **Endpoint URL** is automatically generated, as shown in Fig. 5.15.

Because Helm Hub does not enable any authentication mode, you do not need to enter the Access ID and Access Secret. Make sure that **Verify Remote Cert** is selected and click on **OK** to complete the creation of a registry service.

Because Helm Hub currently only supports pulling Helm Chart, select **Pull-based** for the replication mode when creating a replication policy. If the **Name** filter is blank or "**" and other filters retain the default values, the replication policy pulls all charts on Helm Hub, as shown in Fig. 5.16.

Enter other necessary information to complete the creation of a replication policy.

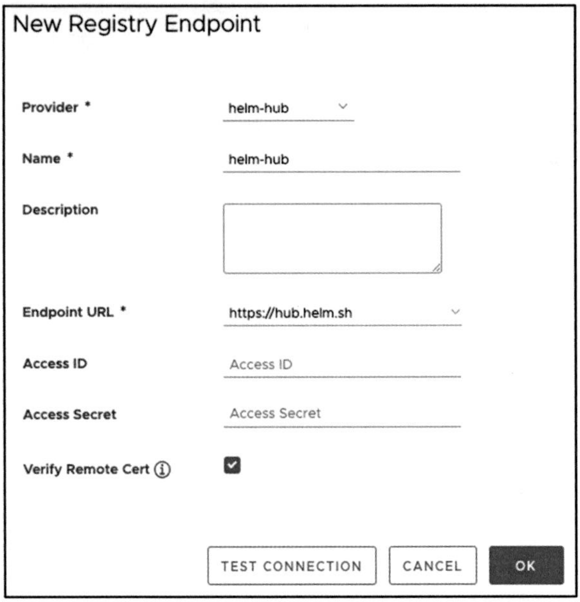

Fig. 5.15 Select helm-hub provider in New Registry Endpoint dialog box

Fig. 5.16 Select helm-hub endpoint in New Replication Rule dialog box

5.6 Typical Usage Scenarios

As introduced in previous sections, readers should understand the basic principles and usage of remote replication. This section introduces some typical usage scenarios of remote replication to help readers further understand the principles and flexibility of remote replication.

5.6.1 Artifact Distribution

In a large-scale cluster environment, if all Docker hosts pull images from a single registry instance, the registry probably becomes a bottleneck of image distribution. This issue can be solved in some degree by using remote replication to set up multiple registries.

Figure 5.17 shows the topology of the registry service. The registry in the figure is divided into two levels: master registry and child registries. A remote replication policy is configured between the master registry and each child registry. After images of an application are pushed to the master registry, the images can be immediately distributed to child registries according to the replication policy. Docker hosts in the cluster can pull the images from any child registry nearby to reduce the pressure of the master registry. If the cluster scale is large or the geographical distribution of the hosts is wide, the child registries could also be deployed in a multi-level hierarchy. Primary child registries distribute images to secondary child registries, and Docker hosts pull the images from the nearest secondary child registries.

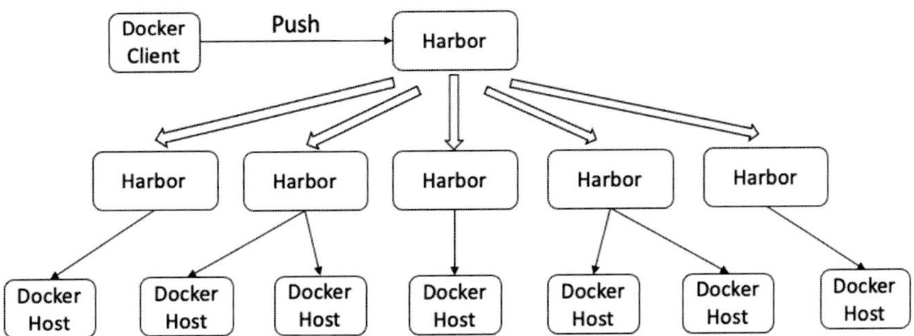

Fig. 5.17 Image distribution through the replication across multiple Harbor instances

5.6.2 *Two-way Synchronization*

Remote replication can also be used to implement simple synchronization across different geographic locations or between the public cloud and private cloud.

Figure 5.18 shows the topology of a registry service.

In Fig. 5.18, there are two Harbor instances: Harbor A and Harbor B. Harbor A replicates the images pushed to it to Harbor B in near real-time by a replication policy; meanwhile, a similar policy is configured on Harbor B to replicate the images pushed to it to Harbor A in almost real-time. In this way, when an image is pushed to one of the registries, the image is pushed to the other registry right away. This approach creates two Harbor instances with almost the same content. The topology can also include more than two registries, which are synchronized with each other through a two-way replication policy.

Note: Although the replication policy can configure the real-time image pushing, the actual time when an image arrives at the destination registry depends on the latency of network transmission. Therefore, the impact of this latency must be taken into account. Although the retry mechanism is provided in the replication, no strong consistency algorithm is used. As a result, the failure of image replication could be unavoidable. Therefore, it is recommended that this approach be used in development and testing environments instead of a production environment.

5.6.3 *Transfer of DevOps Images*

During the lifecycle of an application, it often goes through multiple steps: development, testing, staging, and production. The corresponding images also go through multiple steps of the transfer. The image replication function can be used to set up the DevOps pipeline shown in Fig. 5.19 for publishing images.

In Fig. 5.19, remote replication policies are configured between the Development, Testing, Staging and Production registries. After the source code is submitted to the code repository (such as Git), the continuous integration (CI) system can be triggered to build application images and push the images to the Development Registry. Next

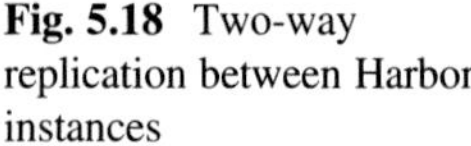

Fig. 5.18 Two-way replication between Harbor instances

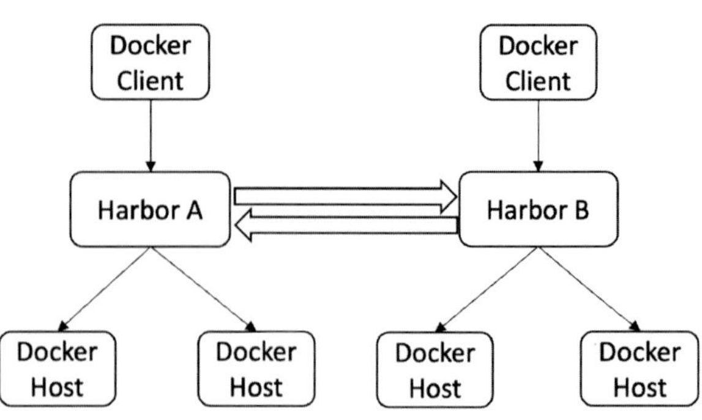

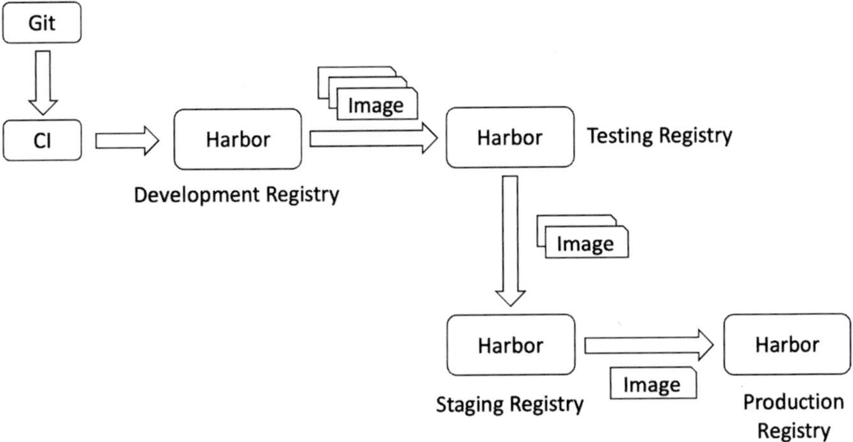

Fig. 5.19 Transferring images across different environments

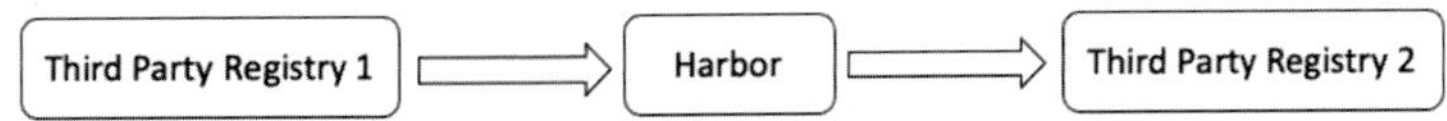

Fig. 5.20 Harbor as an intermediate repository for image migration

the images are replicated to the Testing Registry for testing. After passing the testing, the images are moved to the Staging Registry and finally the images reach the Production Registry after the verification in a staging environment. The transfer of images can be done by using remote replication with different policies, so as to achieve a controllable, flexible and automatic image releasing pipeline.

5.6.4 Other Scenarios

The remote replication of Harbor can also be used to migrate images. When you want to switch from an existing registry service to Harbor, you can configure a replication policy in pull mode to move image data of other repositories to Harbor. When data need to be migrated between two third-party repositories, Harbor can also serve as an intermediate repository to facilitate data migration using the replication policy, as shown in Fig. 5.20.

The remote replication function can also be used for data backup. Refer to Chap. 7 for more details.

Chapter 6
Advanced Management

This chapter introduces multiple advanced features of Harbor, including resource quota management, garbage collection, immutable artifacts, artifact retention policy, Webhook notification and multi-language support. Harbor 2.0 extends the image related functions to OCI artifacts. For example, the remote replication of images supports other artifacts. This chapter mentions both images and artifacts in different scenarios. In most cases, we can consider images as special cases of artifacts. Because images are the type of artifact mostly used, for the ease of understanding, the term "image" is sometimes used when the functions of artifacts are described. Therefore, image and artifact are treated as synonyms in this chapter.

6.1 Resource Quota Management

During daily operation and maintenance, the allocation and management of system resources is an important part. To prevent a project from consuming too much system resource, Harbor provides the resource quota management of each project. The system administrator can allocate or limit the storage space of a project by the resource quota management of Harbor.

This section introduces the resource quota management of Harbor including the principles, the configuration and the client interaction.

6.1.1 Principles

In Harbor, resource quota refers to the total usable storage of a project. Resource quota is calculated based on project. The resource quota management has always been one of the pain points of artifact repositories. The main challenge comes from the fact that the storage of artifacts is shared by layer. Different artifacts of different

H. Zhang, Y. Wang, *The Authoritative Guide on Harbor*,
https://doi.org/10.1007/978-981-19-2727-0_6

projects can share one or more layers. The resource quota management needs to allocate quota for shared resources and determines which project the shared resource quota belong to.

Before introducing the basic principles of Harbor's resource quota management, this section first explains several fundamental concepts. Knowing these concepts helps understand the principles of the resource quota management of Harbor.

6.1.1.1 Composition of an OCI Artifact

As mentioned in Chap. 1, OCI artifacts are data packaged according to the OCI image specification. A typical OCI artifact includes the following parts:

- Configuration: the configuration file of the OCI artifact, including the metadata of the image. For example, the architecture, the configuration and the configuration of building the image.
- Layers: layers of the OCI artifact. Generally, an artifact may include a group of layers.

Manifest: the manifest file of the OCI artifact. The file is an OCI artifact description file in the JSON format and provides a configuration and a set of layers for a single container image of a specific architecture.

Let's take the image hello-world:latest as an example. As shown in the following manifest file, hello-world:latest has a layer and a configuration file. Together with the manifest file, the hello-world:latest image consists of three files. The **config** section indicates the media type, the size and the digest value of the configuration file; the **layers** section contains an array of layers referenced by the manifest and specifies the media type, the size and the digest value of each layer.

```
{
  "schemaVersion": 2,
  "mediaType": "application/vnd.docker.distribution.manifest.
v2+json",
  "config": {
    "mediaType": "application/vnd.docker.container.image.
v1+json",
    "size": 1510,
    "digest": "sha256:fce289e99eb9bca977dae136fbe2a82b6b7d4c372
474c9235adc1741675f587e"
  },
  "layers": [
    {
      "mediaType": "application/vnd.docker.image.rootfs.diff.
tar.gzip",
      "size": 977,
      "digest": "sha256:
```

(continued)

```
1b930d010525941c1d56ec53b97bd057a67ae1865eebf042686d2a2d1
8271ced"
    }
  ]
}
```


6.1.1.2 Pushing an Artifact to an Artifact Repository

When a client pushes an artifact to an artifact repository, the following steps are performed in order: the layers making up the artifact are uploaded first, followed by the manifest.

1. Push the configuration file.
2. Push layers in turn. The client determines whether a layer exists in the repository according to the digest of the layer. If a layer does not exist, the client pushes the layer. The client pushes a large layer in chunks through a PATCH Blob request. After all chunk files are successfully pushed, the client initiates a PUT Blob request to close the session.
3. Push the manifest file. Without the manifest file, the repository does not know which artifact the pushed layers in the previous step belongs to. After the PUT Manifest request succeeded, the repository indexes the artifact by layers according to the manifest file.

6.1.1.3 Layer Management and Sharing of Docker Distribution

When using the **docker pull** command to pull an image from a registry, you may notice that Docker pulls the image by layer and each layer is independent, as shown in Fig. 6.1.

An ID can be generated for the data in the image layer using the hash algorithm SHA256. It is the unique ID of the layer and is also the digest value in the manifest file. The manifest file of an OCI artifact includes a group of layers and the ID (digest) of each layer. In this way, when a Docker client initiates a pull request, the client only needs to specify and pull the corresponding layers by the digests in the manifest file.

```
18.04: Pulling from library/ubuntu
5bed26d33875: Pull complete
f11b29a9c730: Pull complete
930bda195c84: Pull complete
78bf9a5ad49e: Pull complete
Digest: sha256:bec5a2727be7fff3d308193cfde3491f8fba1a2ba392b7546b43a051853a341d
Status: Downloaded newer image for ubuntu:18.04
docker.io/library/ubuntu:18.04
```

Fig. 6.1 Docker pull image by layer

Docker Distribution manages artifacts in layer to optimize the storage structure, so as to improve the storage efficiency. For each layer with a distinct digest value, a copy of the layer is saved in the artifact repository, which optimizes the use of the storage space. The sharing of layer storage reduces storage space but causes a lot of troubles in the resource quota management. For example, when a layer is referenced by different artifacts under multiple projects, because only one layer exists in the storage, which project's quota should the storage of the layer belong to?

The following example explains how Harbor obtains the size of an OCI artifact and allocates quota to it.

6.1.1.4 PATCH Blob

When Harbor receives a PATCH Blob request, it records in Redis the number of bytes that are written into the storage. Docker Distribution allocates a Session ID to each layer. When a layer is divided into multiple PATCH Blob requests, the PATCH requests share the same Session ID. In Redis, the Session ID is used as a key. Harbor obtains the chunk size from each PATCH request and updates it as the value associated with the key Session ID. After all PATCH requests end, the size of the layer stored in Redis is the final layer size, as shown in Fig. 6.2.

6.1.1.5 PUT Blob

After Harbor receives the PUT Blob request, it means that the all layers have been uploaded. At this point, Harbor applies for a quota of the project based on the layer size recorded in Redis. If Harbor can apply for enough quota, the quota of the project is updated and the Blob data is persisted; if Harbor cannot apply for enough quota, the PUT Blob request is rejected, as shown in Fig. 6.3.

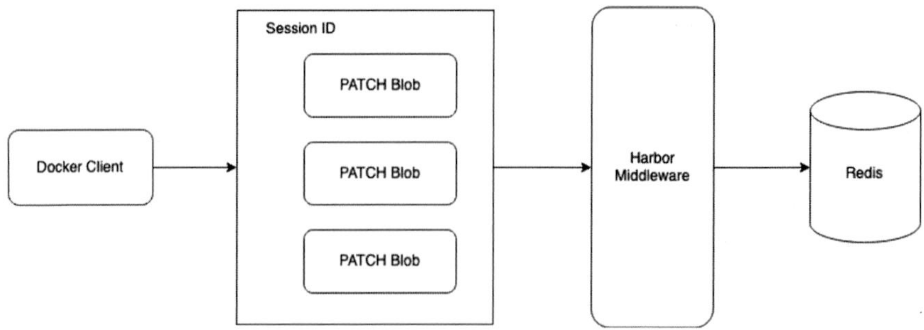

Fig. 6.2 Quota middleware injects patch blob request

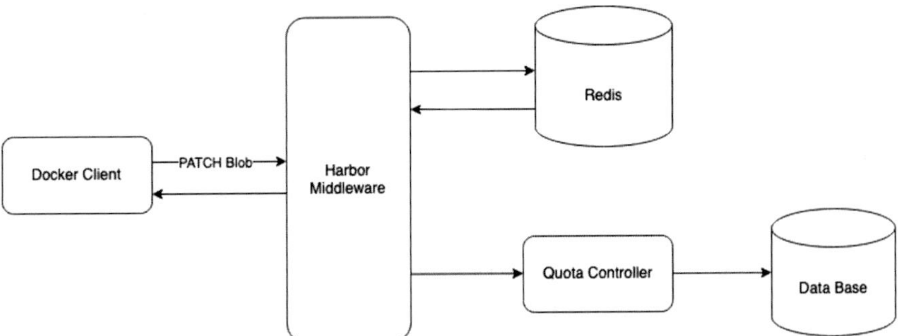

Fig. 6.3 Quota middleware injects put blob request

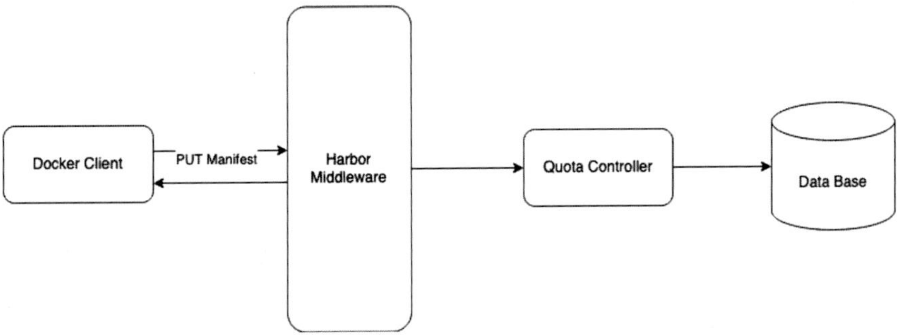

Fig. 6.4 Quota middleware injects put manifest request

6.1.1.6 PUT Manifest

When Harbor receives a PUT Manifest request, Harbor applies for a quota of the project based on the requested data size. If Harbor can apply for enough quota, the quota of the project is updated and the Manifest and the Blob data are persisted; if Harbor cannot apply for enough quota, the PUT Manifest request is rejected, as shown in Fig. 6.4.

Through the above explanation, readers can roughly understand how Harbor obtains the size of an artifact and applies for its quota. The quota of Harbor works at the project level, while layers of Docker Distribution are shared at the system level. In Harbor, the quota is calculated at the project level. That is, when artifacts under different projects reference the same layer, the size of the layer is added up to the quota of all projects that reference the layer. When different artifacts under the same project reference the same layer, the size of the layer will not be double counted to the available quota of the project. Therefore, the sum of the quota of all projects in Harbor could be greater than the usage of actual storage.

Fig. 6.5 New project dialog box

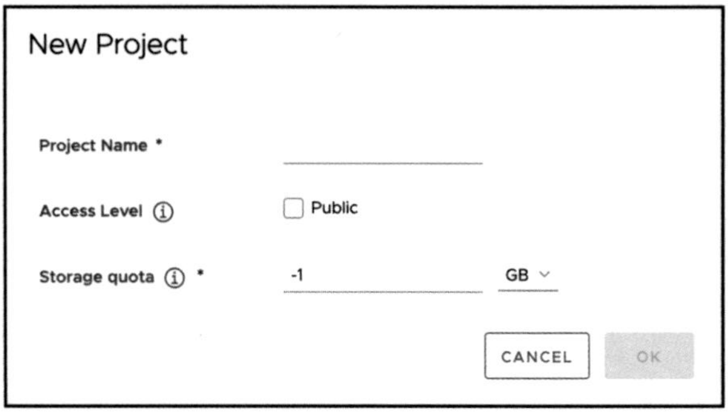

6.1.2 Setting Project Quota

This section illustrates how to set up the quota of a project and control the project resources in Harbor.

When a project is created, you can specify the storage capacity required by the project, as shown in Fig. 6.5.

The **Storage quota** is a mandatory field. Generally, the default quota of the system can be used, where **-1** indicates unlimited capacity. Enter the capacity value, selecting MB, GB, or TB from the drop-down menu, and click **OK**. A project is then successfully created and its resource quota has been allocated.

After the project is successfully created, you can view the capacity usage on the project summary page, as shown in Fig. 6.6.

6.1.3 Setting System Quota

The system administrator can set the default quota value of the system, that is, the default quota value of every new project. In addition, most importantly, the system

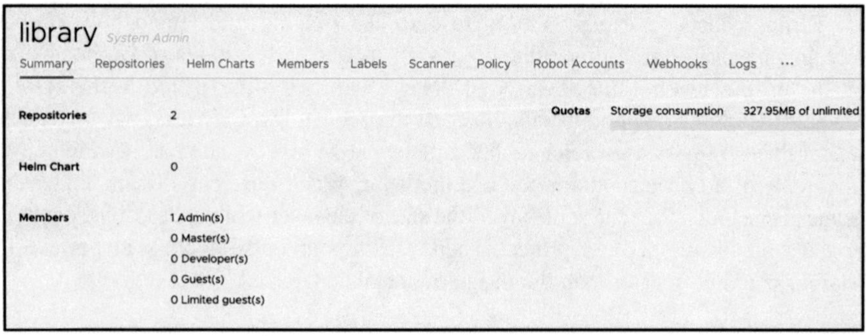

Fig. 6.6 Project summary page

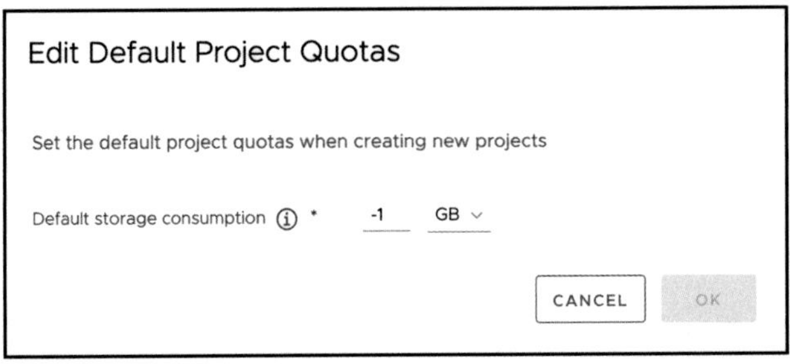

Fig. 6.7 Edit default project quotas dialog box

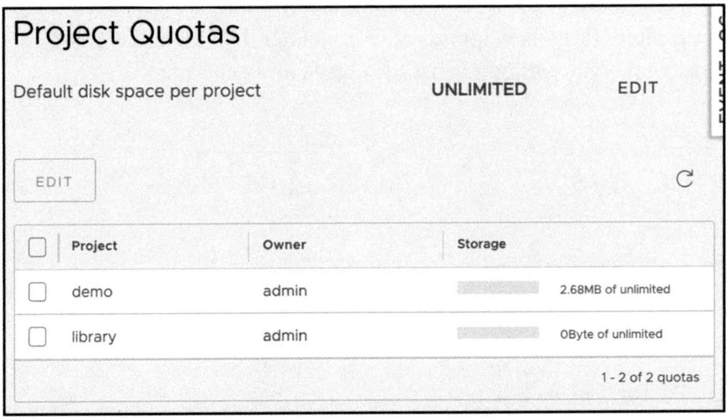

Fig. 6.8 Project quotas overview page

administrator can increase or decrease the quota of any project for the overall system quota management.

On the quota management page, expand **Administration** and select **Project Quotas** and click **Edit**. The dialog box of **Edit Default Project Quotas** is displayed as shown in Fig. 6.7.

For **Default storage consumption**, enter the maximum quantity of storage that any project can consume, selecting MB, GB, or TB from the drop-down menu, or enter -1 to set the default to unlimited. After the default project quota is set successfully, new projects will use this default value but existing projects are not affected.

When the system administrator needs to adjust the system resources, the system administrator can view the quota usage on the **Project Quotas** page and set the quota of any project, as shown in Fig. 6.8.

Select the checkbox of any project and click on **Edit** button. The **Edit Project Quotas** dialog box is displayed, as shown in Fig. 6.9.

Enter a desired value in **Storage consumption**, selecting the storage unit (MB, GB, or TB), and click **OK**. After the project quota is set successfully, it takes effect

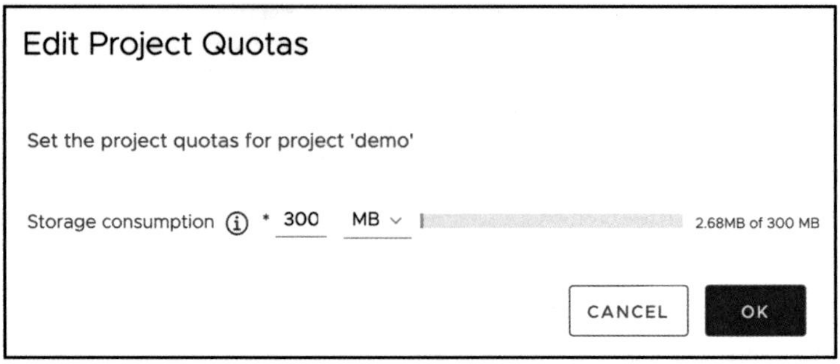

Edit Project Quotas

Set the project quotas for project 'demo'

Storage consumption ⓘ * 300 MB ∨ 2.68MB of 300 MB

CANCEL OK

Fig. 6.9 Edit project quotas dialog box

right away. Note: If the new quota value is smaller than the project storage currently allocated, the project will be unable to receive any new image.

6.1.4 *Use of Quota*

This section explains in detail the operations which can affect the available quota of a project.

6.1.4.1 Pushing of Artifacts

After you push an artifact to a project, Harbor deducts the size of the artifact from the available project quota.

Take a Docker image as an example. After you push the hello-world:latest image to the project library, the project consumption is updated to the size of the hello-world:latest image, as shown in Fig. 6.10.

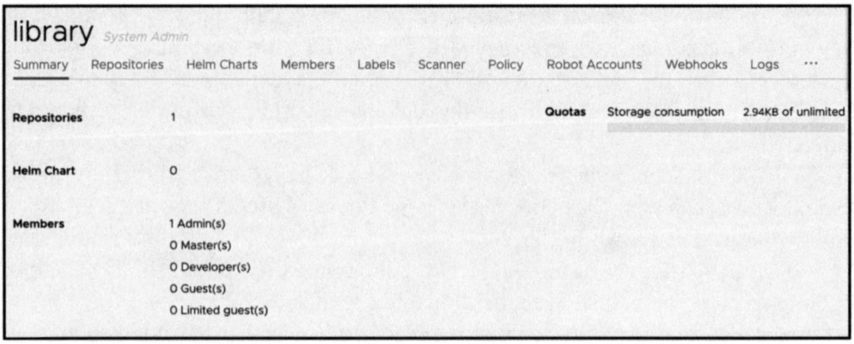

library System Admin

Summary Repositories Helm Charts Members Labels Scanner Policy Robot Accounts Webhooks Logs ···

Repositories	1	**Quotas**	Storage consumption	2.94KB of unlimited
Helm Chart	0			
Members	1 Admin(s) 0 Master(s) 0 Developer(s) 0 Guest(s) 0 Limited guest(s)			

Fig. 6.10 Project summary page

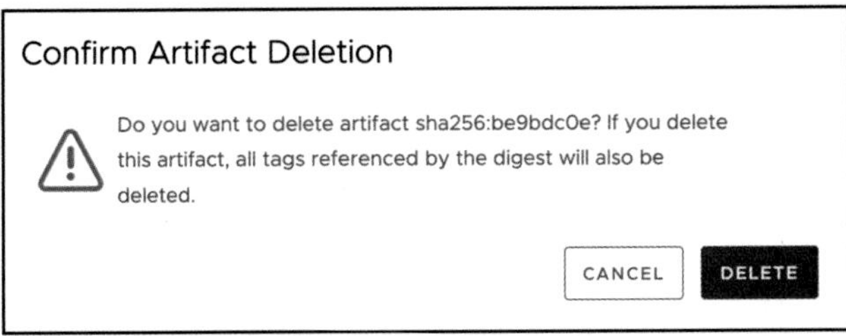

Fig. 6.11 Artifact deletion dialog box

Note: When the newly pushed artifact shares a layer with an existing artifact in the same project, the quota is not deducted.

6.1.4.2 Deletion of Artifacts

When any artifact is deleted from the project, Harbor adds the size of the artifact to the available quota of the project, as shown in Fig. 6.11. Note: When the artifact shares a layer with other artifacts in the same project, the available quota remains unchanged.

6.1.4.3 Copying of Artifacts

When an artifact is copied to another project, Harbor deducts the available quota of the target project accordingly, as shown in Fig. 6.12. Note: The quota is deducted only when the target project and the current project are not the same project. Otherwise, the project quota remains unchanged.

6.1.4.4 Remote Replication of Artifacts

When a remote replication policy is created to replicate artifacts to the current Harbor system from other registries, the available quota of the corresponding project is deducted accordingly.

Fig. 6.12 Artifact copy dialog box

6.1.4.5 Operations of Untagged Artifact

In Harbor, an artifact that is not associated with any tag is called an untagged artifact. An untagged artifact can be generated in the following ways:

- After a user deletes all tags of an artifact, the artifact becomes an untagged artifact.
- A new artifact is pushed to Harbor, it overwrites an existing artifact with the same repository and tag name. When the digest of the newly pushed artifact is different from the digest of the existing artifact, the existing artifact becomes an untagged artifact.
- When the index of an artifact is being pushed, the client first pushes its child artifacts and waits until all child artifacts have been pushed successfully before pushing the index. Before the index is pushed successfully, the child artifacts already pushed into Harbor are untagged artifacts.

Harbor has two features related to untagged artifacts: tag retention and garbage collection.

In the configuration of a tag retention policy, the **untagged artifacts** option can be selected as shown in Fig. 6.13. Harbor decides whether to delete untagged artifacts according to the retention policy. When untagged artifacts are deleted, the quota of the untagged artifacts are recycled.

When you execute a garbage collection task and select the option of **Delete Untagged Artifacts**, as shown in Fig. 6.14, the garbage collection task deletes untagged artifacts and recycles the corresponding quota.

Add Tag Retention Rule
Specify a tag retention rule for this project. All tag retention rules are independently calculated and each rule can be applied to a selected list of repositories.
For the repositories
matching
**
Enter multiple comma separated repos,repo*,or **
By artifact count or number of days
Tags
matching
**
untagged artifacts
Enter multiple comma separated tags, tag*, or **. Optionally include all untagged artifacts when applying the 'including' or 'excluding' selector by checking the box above.
CANCEL
ADD

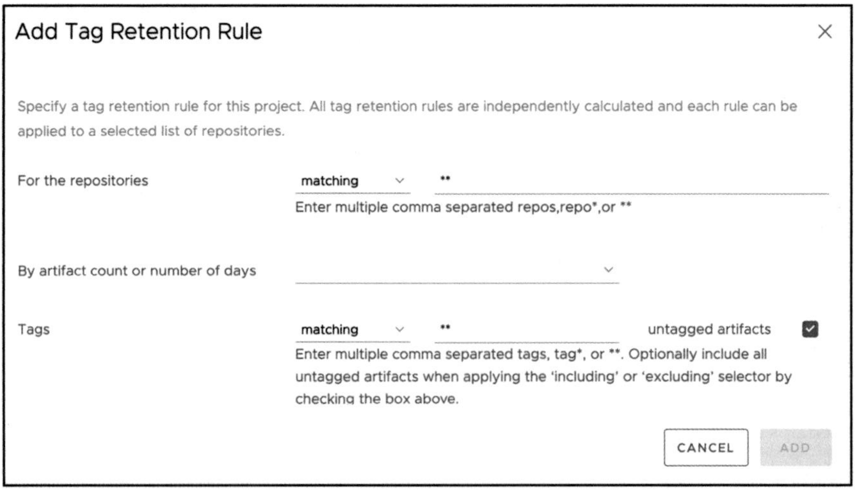

Fig. 6.13 Create tag retention rule dialog box

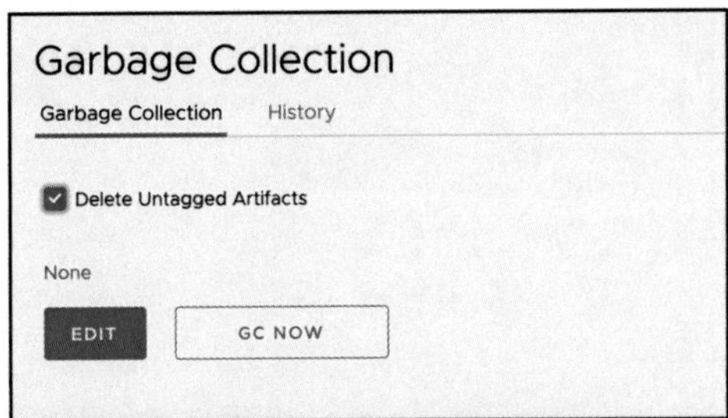

Fig. 6.14 System garbage collection page

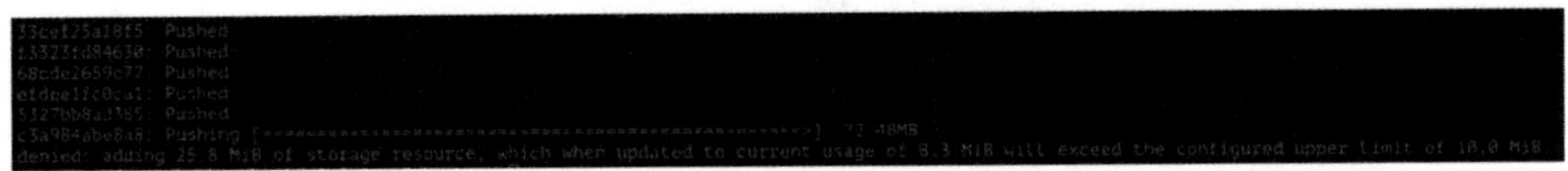

Fig. 6.15 Client warning message for project quota is close to the upper limit

6.1.5 Message of Out-of-Quota

If the project quota reaches the upper limit when an artifact is being pushed, Harbor prompts the users with some error messages.

6.1.5.1 Insufficient Quota When a Docker Client Pushes Images

During the pushing of image layers, if the push request of a layer cannot apply for sufficient quota, an error message is displayed, as shown in Fig. 6.15. The Docker client receives an error message indicating the invalid quota application with an error code of 412, which means that the current project quota is close to or exceeds the upper limit and no sufficient quota can be allocated to the current request. The system administrator can be informed to set more quota for the project.

6.1.5.2 Insufficient Quota of Other Projects

When an artifact is copied from one project to another in Harbor, if the target project does not have sufficient quota, a system prompt will be displayed, as shown in Fig. 6.16.

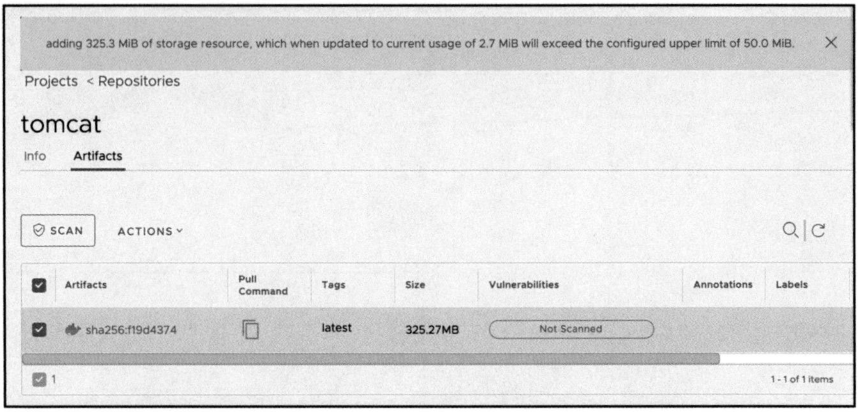

Fig. 6.16 GUI warning message for project quota is close to the upper limit

6.2 Garbage Collection

To save the storage space in the system, the storage occupied by artifacts must be released after the artifacts are deleted. Garbage collection is essentially the automatic management of storage resources, that is, the recycling of storage space occupied by artifacts that are no longer used in Harbor.

This section explains the principles, usage methods and policy setting of garbage collection.

6.2.1 Principles

Before explaining the basic principles of garbage collection, let's understand the lifecycle of an artifact in Harbor.

- After a user pushes an artifact to Harbor, the system inserts a record in the artifact data table. The artifact data table records valid artifacts that exist in Harbor.
- After a user deletes an artifact from Harbor, the system deletes the record of the artifact from the artifact data table and inserts a record into the artifact trash data table. The artifact trash data table keeps track of all artifacts that have been deleted by the system.

In Harbor, the deletion of artifacts is "soft deletion". Soft deletion means that only data records corresponding to the artifacts are deleted and the artifacts are not physically deleted from the storage. The actual deletion in storage is completed by the garbage collection task. The following section breaks down the garbage collection task and describes step by step.

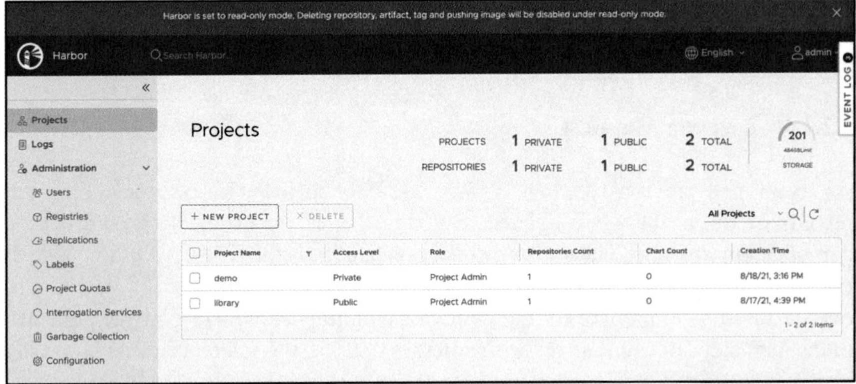

Fig. 6.17 Read only mode enabled

6.2.1.1 Setting the Read-Only Mode

During the execution of the garbage collection task, the reference of each layer in physical storage is counted. The counting process cannot be affected by any push request. Therefore, Harbor must be set to the read-only mode. Any request to modify the system will be rejected. You can only pull artifacts and view system data, as shown in Fig. 6.17.

6.2.1.2 Marking Alternative Artifacts

When you execute a garbage collection task and select **Delete Untagged Artifacts**, as shown in Fig. 6.18, the garbage collection task deletes all untagged artifacts in the system. The deletion operation records the untagged artifacts in the artifact trash data table.

In this way, all artifacts to be deleted in Harbor are kept in the artifact trash data table. However, not all records in the trash data table indicate the artifacts that really need to be deleted. Imagine this scenario: A deleted artifact is pushed to Harbor again. Although the artifact is recorded in the artifact trash data table, the artifact

Fig. 6.18 System garbage collection page

Garbage Collection
Garbage Collection History
Delete Untagged Artifacts
None
EDIT GC NOW

should not be deleted. The garbage collection task filters data in the artifact trash data table to obtain the artifacts that eventually need to be deleted.

6.2.1.3 Deleting Manifest

As mentioned previously when artifacts are deleted from Harbor, only their data records of the artifacts are deleted. Deleting the actual manifest of an artifact is completed in this step. The garbage collection task calls the registry API to delete the manifest of the artifacts obtained in the last step. The purpose of deleting the manifest here is to prepare for the reference counting of registry garbage collection in the next step. Because after the manifest is deleted, the reference of its layers also becomes invalid.

6.2.1.4 Performing Registry Garbage Collection

The garbage collection task relies on the garbage collection mechanism of the Registry (Docker Distribution). It calls the CLI of the Registry to execute the garbage collection command and complete final release of storage space.

Note: When the garbage collection command of Registry is executed, **--delete-untagged=true** or the **-d** parameter cannot be used. The parameter is used to delete the manifest of an untagged artifact during the Registry garbage collection. This function must be disabled because the tags of artifacts are fully managed by Harbor instead of the Registry. In other words, all artifacts stored in Harbor have tags but all artifacts stored in the Registry do not, as shown in Fig. 6.19. Image pull requests using tags are converted by Harbor to image pull requests using digests. Therefore, once this parameter is enabled, the garbage collection mechanism of the registry deletes all valid artifacts in Harbor.

The garbage collection of the Registry covers two steps: mark and recycling, which are used to release storage space.

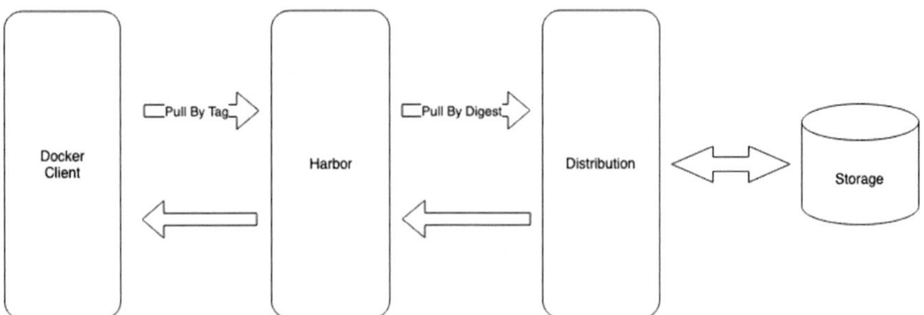

Fig. 6.19 Docker pull image flow chart

1. Mark: Perform reference counting for each layer and consider the layers with the reference count of 0 as the candidates to be deleted.
2. Sweep: Delete the candidate layers through the API of the storage system.

6.2.1.5 Releasing Quota Space

The quota management is described in detail previously. In most cases, the release of quota does not need to go through the garbage collection task except the following circumstance. When the pushing of an artifact failed due to quota restriction, the quota requested by layers during the push cannot be released through the deletion of the artifact. This requires the garbage collection task to release this part of the quota. The garbage collection task retrieves the layers based on database records, then deletes the layers and releases the quota of the layers.

6.2.1.6 Cleaning Up the Cache

After the garbage collection task cleans up the storage, the cache of the Registry needs to be flushed. This is mainly because of a problem of the Registry itself: After the garbage collection command is executed, the Registry does not clean up its cache. As a result, you cannot push again the images that have been cleaned up because the Registry thinks the images exist by checking data in the cache. Harbor configures Redis as the cache of the registry and clears the cache after the garbage collection task recycle the storage.

6.2.1.7 Restoring the Read/Write Status

After the garbage collection task finishes, the read/write status of Harbor is restored. Users can continue to push artifacts to Harbor. If Harbor was in read-only mode before the garbage collection task is executed, the status is not changed here.

6.2.2 Triggering Mode

On the management page of Harbor, the system administrator clicks **Garbage Collection**. The garbage collection page is displayed, as shown in Fig. 6.20.

The garbage collection of Harbor can be triggered manually or by schedule.

- Manual: the system administrator clicks **GC Now** button to trigger the garbage collection task immediately.
- Schedule: the garbage collection task is executed periodically by defining a Cron task.

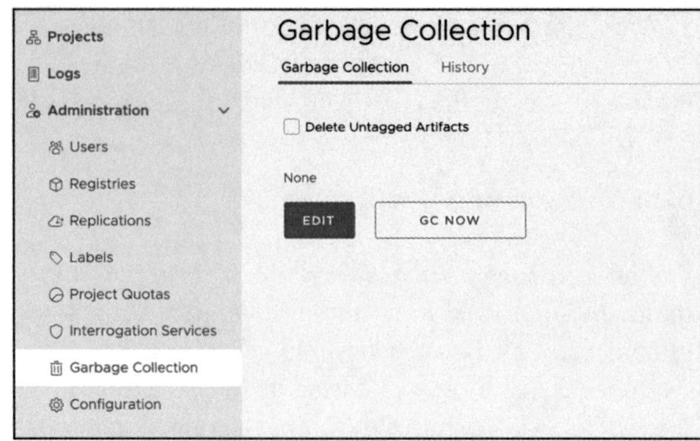

Fig. 6.20 System garbage collection page

Table 6.1 The cron expression

Field name	Mandatory	Allowed Values	Allowed Special Characters
Second	Yes	0 to 59	*/,-
Minute	Yes	0 to 59	*/,-
Hour	Yes	0 to 23	*/,-
A day within a month	Yes	1 to 31	*/,-?
Month	Yes	1 to 12 or JAN to DEC	*/,-
A day within a week	Yes	0 to 6 or SUN to SAT	*/,-?

A Cron expression adopts the format of "* * * * *". Table 6.1 lists the meanings of fields in the format. Note: The time in the Cron expression is the time of the server instead of the time of the browser.

Refer to Sect. 5.3.3 for more information about the Cron expression.

6.2.3 *Execution of Garbage Collection*

After the garbage collection process is triggered, Harbor starts a garbage collection task. The system administrator can view the execution of garbage collection tasks in **History**, as shown in Fig. 6.21.

When the garbage collection task is completed, the system administrator can click on the icon in the column of **Logs** to view the log of the garbage collection task, as shown in Fig. 6.22.

Note: When there is a large amount of artifact data in Harbor or cloud storage such as S3 is used as the storage, it may take a long time to finish the garbage collection task. Sometimes the task may last more than 24 hours. It is recommended to schedule the garbage collection task at night or during non-working days.

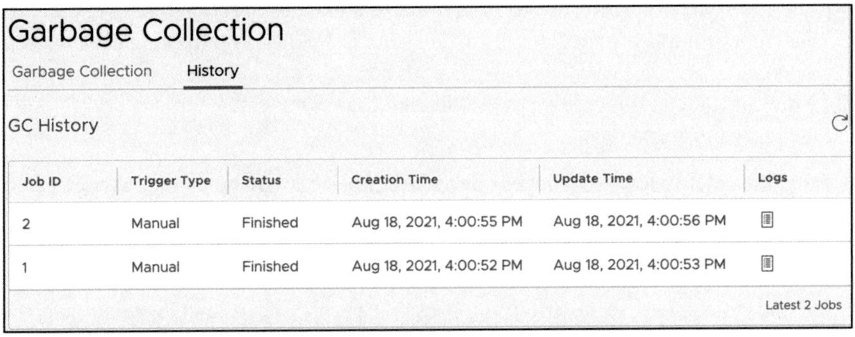

Garbage Collection

Garbage Collection   History

GC History

Job ID	Trigger Type	Status	Creation Time	Update Time	Logs
2	Manual	Finished	Aug 18, 2021, 4:00:55 PM	Aug 18, 2021, 4:00:56 PM	
1	Manual	Finished	Aug 18, 2021, 4:00:52 PM	Aug 18, 2021, 4:00:53 PM	

Latest 2 Jobs

Fig. 6.21 Garbage collection history page

```
2020-06-15T09:06:11Z [INFO] [/jobservice/job/impl/gc/garbage_collection.go:131]: start to run gc in job.
2020-06-15T09:06:11Z [INFO] [/jobservice/job/impl/gc/garbage_collection.go:271]: required candidate: %+v[]
2020-06-15T09:06:11Z [INFO] [/jobservice/job/impl/gc/garbage_collection.go:279]: end to delete required artifact.
2020-06-15T09:06:11Z [INFO] [/jobservice/job/impl/gc/garbage_collection.go:236]: flush artifact trash
2020-06-15T09:06:11Z [INFO] [/jobservice/job/impl/gc/garbage_collection.go:144]: GC results: status: true, message: demo/redis
demo/redis: marking manifest sha256:86edeb058fb97b7e9441515a5f1bb57f1547432fedbaf3513117ba521d99ef9d
demo/redis: marking blob sha256:4cdbec704e477aab9d249262e60b9a8a25cbef48f0ff23ac5eae879a98a7ebd0
demo/redis: marking blob sha256:c499e6d256d6d4a546f1c141e04b5b4951983ba7581e39deaf5cc595289ee70f
demo/redis: marking blob sha256:bf1bc8a5a7e4b2529c9f893946e08a020b961ff8b2682807987f407e6da2f266
demo/redis: marking blob sha256:7564fb795604548fde45efccac7008b17ac86faf01f7fd393a6b9ecfb31d0889
demo/redis: marking blob sha256:ec6e86f783e4327c9957a6fc3ba1079aac5adf4c60bd0af15204508ca4b885d9
demo/redis: marking blob sha256:1371d6223f46d8d18bfee5f54db873d03a116e0d02e2b7887e32d50db56af58a
demo/redis: marking blob sha256:021fd554320fb855c449e33fe30fe134f781409c5da4f78683f8ebd80e0188c1

8 blobs marked, 0 blobs and 0 manifests eligible for deletion
, start: 2020-06-15 09:06:11.5387112 +0000 UTC, end: 2020-06-15 09:06:11.601464316 +0000 UTC.
2020-06-15T09:06:11Z [INFO] [/jobservice/job/impl/gc/garbage_collection.go:145]: success to run gc in job.
```

Fig. 6.22 Garbage collection log datails page

6.2.4 Non-blocking Garbage Collection[1]

In Harbor 2.0 and earlier versions, the garbage collection is always blocking. That is, when Harbor executes the garbage collection task, the system is read-only and cannot allow any pushing of new images. In some production environments, blocking garbage collection is unacceptable because it forces the system into the blocking state for a period between a few minutes to dozens of hours.

The main reasons for the blocking and the long execution time of garbage collection tasks are as follows:

6.2.4.1 Counting Reference of Layers

In a blocking garbage collection task, the garbage collection function provided by Docker Distribution (hereinafter referred to as Distribution) is used. The implementation flow is roughly as follows.

[1]The original book introduced the garbage collection function based on Harbor 2.0. The non-blocking garbage collection function was implemented in Harbor 2.1 and later versions. This section is added when this book is being translated.

1. The file system is traversed to obtain the reference number of each shared layer. When the number of references of a layer is 0, the layer is a candidate to be deleted.
2. After all the candidate layers are obtained, the storage system is called to delete the layers in turn.

During the calculation of the layer reference count, if an image upload happens at the same time, the garbage collection process may delete the layer that is being uploaded, thus destroying the image. Therefore, image pushing must be blocked when the garbage collection task is being executed.

Meanwhile, because Distribution does not record the reference relationship of layers in the database, Distribution needs to traverse the path of the whole storage system to obtain the reference count of each layer. This traversal mode causes much overhead in time and the required time increases linearly with the number of layers.

6.2.4.2 Using the Cloud Storage

During the traversal of the layer reference relationship and the deletion of layers, the interface of the storage system must be invoked. If cloud storage (such as S3) is used as Harbor's storage system, the time overhead for calling the interface of the storage system is greater than that of the local storage.

To overcome the above challenges, Harbor 2.1 implements a non-blocking garbage collection solution to eliminate the system blocking during the execution of garbage collection tasks. The following briefly introduces the high-level ideas of the non-blocking garbage collection solution.

Artifact Database

In Harbor 2.0, after an image is pushed to the registry, Harbor records all its meta data in the database, as shown in Fig. 6.23.

It can be seen from Fig. 6.23 that the layers of an image and their reference relationship are saved in the artifact database. Accordingly, after an image is deleted, the reference relationship of its layers is also deleted. In this way, the non-blocking garbage collection task can calculate from the database the reference count of all layers in the storage system. When the reference count of any layer is 0, the layer is a candidate to be deleted. Compared with the traversal of the storage system, the calculation using the database saves a lot of time.

API for Deleting Layers and Manifest files

After candidate layers to be deleted are obtained through the database, the next steps is to physically delete the layers. Distribution does not provide an API for deleting

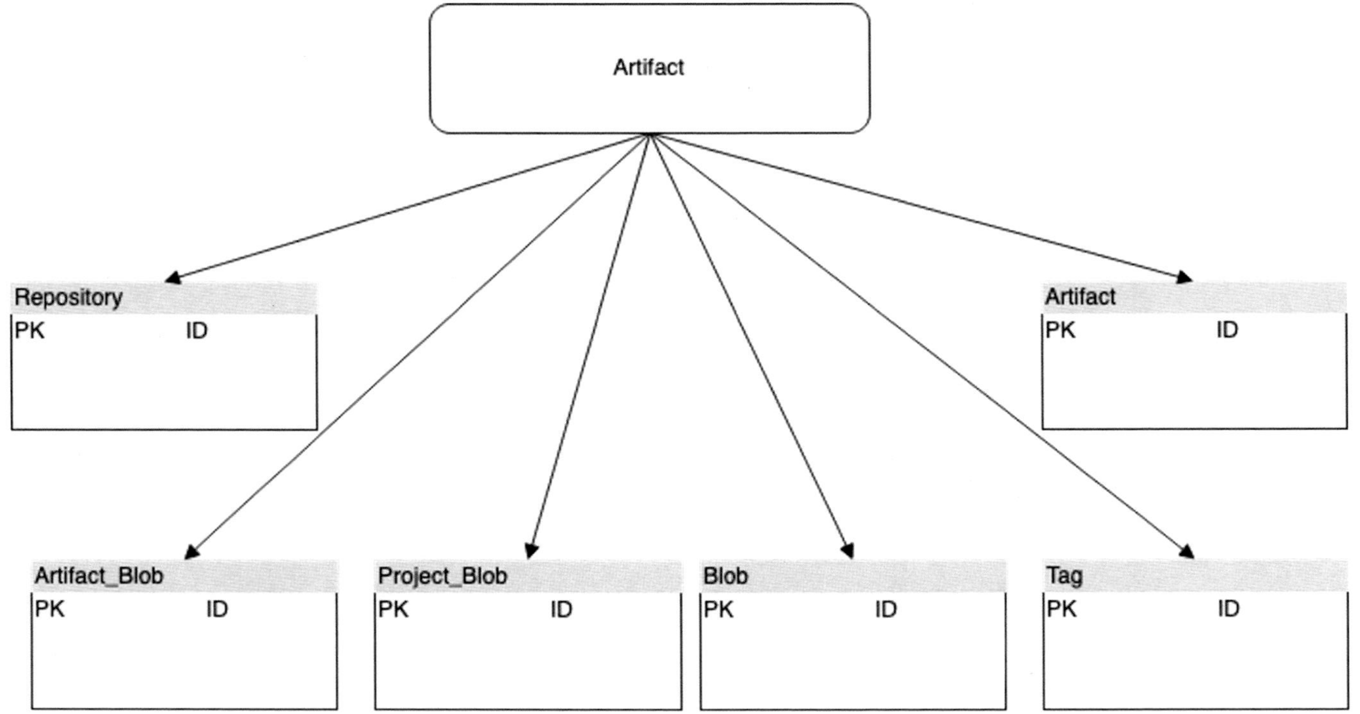

Fig. 6.23 The entity relationship diagram of artifact

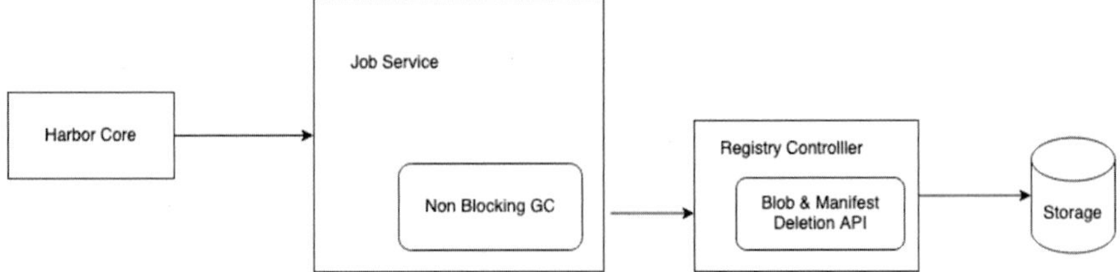

Fig. 6.24 API for deleting blobs and manifests in non-blocking GC

layers and manifest files but expose a public function for its garbage collection task. In Harbor's implementation of the non-blocking garbage collection task, the code of Distribution must be referenced to implement the API for deleting layers and manifest files. The API is only used by the non-blocking garbage collection task and is not exposed to external users, as shown in Fig. 6.24.

Non-blocking

The essence of non-blocking garbage collection is to allow the pushing of artifacts such as user's images when the garbage collection task is executed. To achieve this goal, the mechanisms of the state control and the time window are introduced here. The following section takes images as an example.

State Control

The version and state columns are added to the database table of layers. Every state change of layers add a version. In this way, the optimistic locking can be achieved through the versioning. When the non-blocking garbage collection task performs a deletion operation, the task attempts to mark the layers to be deleted as the "deleting" state. If the layers to be marked are referenced by the image being pushed, the marking of the "deleting" state fails. This is because the HEAD Blob request during the pushing process is intercepted by Harbor middleware, which adds a version of layers. When the non-blocking garbage collection task updates the layer state to "deleting", the version of the layers does not comply with the latest version in the database, causing the update to fail, as shown in Fig. 6.25.

Time Window

During the pushing process, the Docker client first pushes layers. At this time, the reference count of layers in the system is 0. Harbor creates a reference relationship only after the manifest file has been pushed successfully, so that the reference count of these layers is no longer 0. To ensure that the layers being pushed are not deleted during the execution of a non-blocking garbage collection task, the time window concept needs to be introduced. The update time column is added to the database

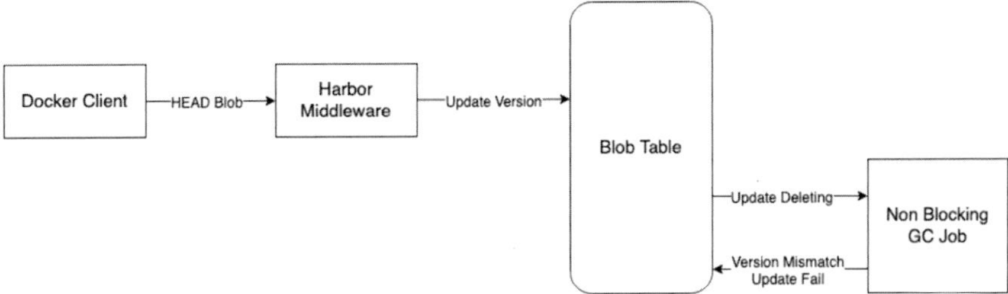

Fig. 6.25 State control in non-blocking GC

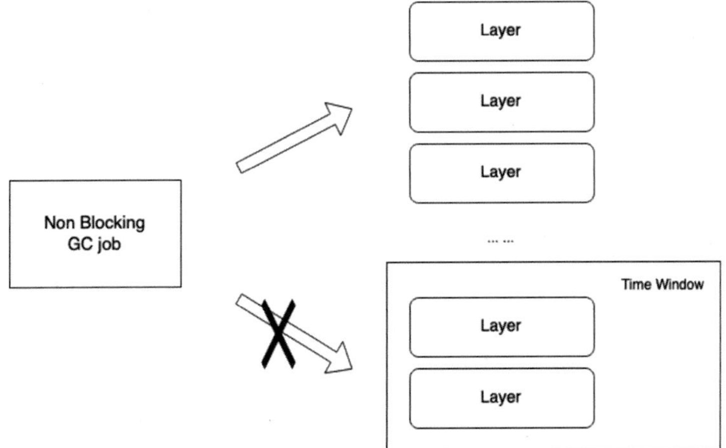

Fig. 6.26 Time window in non-blocking GC

table of layers. Non-blocking garbage collection applies to only layers whose update time is two hours earlier than the start time of non-blocking garbage collection. All layers pushed during the time window are retained, as shown in Fig. 6.26.

6.3 Immutable Artifact

In Harbor, any user with the write permission of a project can push artifacts to the project. In most cases, a user pushes artifacts through tags, which makes it hard to ensure the artifacts are not overwritten by other users. Once the artifacts are overwritten, it is difficult to track the source of the problem.

The Harbor feature of immutable artifacts protects one or more artifacts from being modified. Once an artifact is set as immutable, Harbor does not allow any user to push artifacts with the same name of the artifact.

The function of immutable artifact was called “immutable image” in versions earlier than Harbor 2.0. It protects image resources from being overwritten by accidental operations. In Harbor 2.0, immutable functions are extended to cover artifacts. Therefore, the immutable image function is called “immutable artifact” since Harbor 2.0. The immutable artifact function applies to the tag of artifacts, therefore, the function is also displayed as “immutable tag” on the management page.

6.3.1 Principles

The objective of immutable artifact is to ensure the same artifact can always be pulled from the same repository by using the same tag. This requires that immutable artifacts cannot be overwritten or deleted.

6.3.1.1 Not Overwritable

When an artifact is pushed to the repository from the client, the last step is for the client to initiate a PUT Manifest request to push the manifest file of the artifact to complete the whole pushing process. Harbor protects immutable artifacts by intercepting PUT Manifest requests of the client, as shown in Fig. 6.27.

After Harbor receives a PUT Manifest request from the client, Harbor matches the current artifact based on immutable artifact rules of the project. If the artifact successfully matches any rule, it means the user is pushing an artifact to overwrite an immutable artifact. In this case, the request is blocked. However, there is an exception for applying the rule of immutable artifacts. When the immutable artifact does not exist in the registry, the artifact can still be pushed properly.

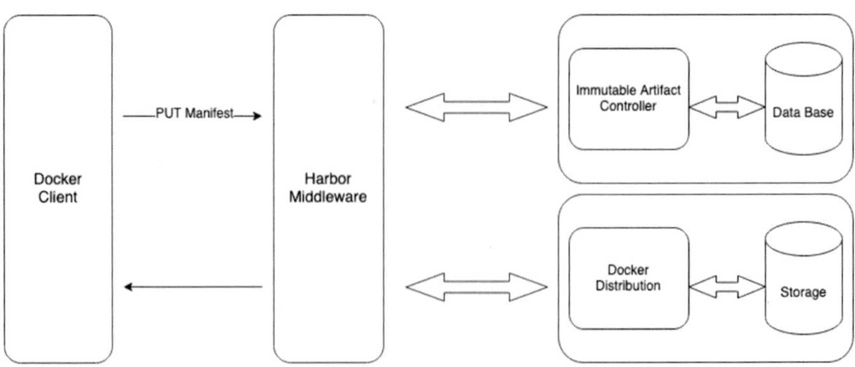

Fig. 6.27 Basic schematic of the immutable tag

6.3.1.2 Not Deletable

When the user requests the tag list of an artifact in Harbor, the system marks the immutable attribute for each tag according to the immutable artifact rules. When the user chooses to delete a tag with the immutable attribute, Harbor blocks the deletion request.

The purpose of immutable artifacts can be achieved through the above processes.

6.3.2 Setting Rules of Immutable Artifacts

The rules of immutable artifacts are actually a filter matching repository name and tag name. Under a project, the project administrator or the system administrator can create up to 15 immutable artifact rules. Harbor uses the OR relationship to apply the rules to artifacts. If an artifact successfully matches any rule, the artifact is an immutable artifact.

Click **Tag Immutability** on the project policy page to view the immutable tag rules of the project, as shown in Fig. 6.28.

Click **Add Rule**. The window for setting immutable rules is displayed, as shown in Fig. 6.29.

An immutable artifact rule consists of two parts: repository and tag. Each part includes actions and name expressions.

1. Actions: include matching and excluding.
    - Matching: includes the repository or tag matched by the rule's expression.
    - Excluding: excludes the repository or tag matched by the rule's expression.
2. Name expression: indicates the name expression of the repository or tag for which the immutable artifact attribute must be set.

The name expression filters artifacts based on their repository and tag. It supports the following matching patterns (special characters used in the matching patterns must be escaped by a backslash "\").

- "*": matches all characters except the delimiter "/".
- "**": matches all characters, including the delimiter "/".

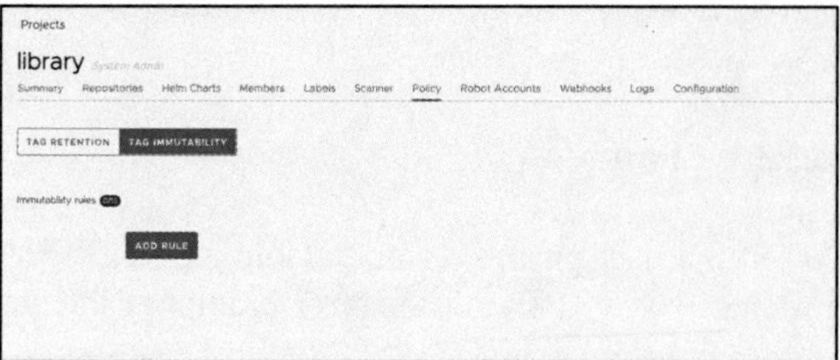

Fig. 6.28 Project tag immutability page

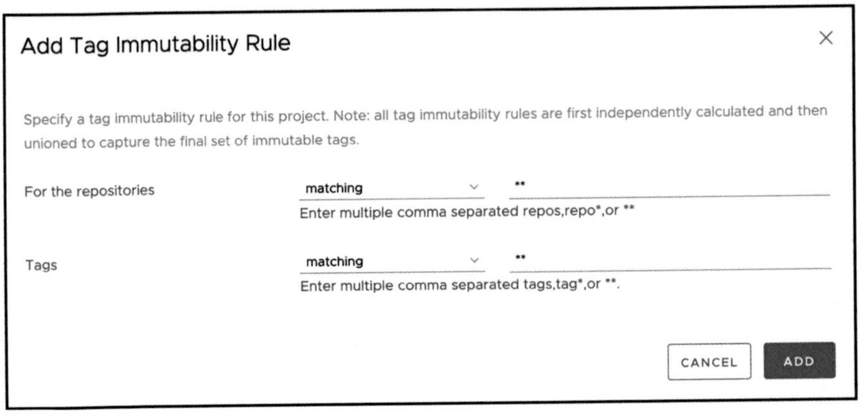

Add Tag Immutability Rule

Specify a tag immutability rule for this project. Note: all tag immutability rules are first independently calculated and then unioned to capture the final set of immutable tags.

For the repositories matching **
Enter multiple comma separated repos,repo*,or **

Tags matching **
Enter multiple comma separated tags,tag*,or **.

CANCEL ADD

Fig. 6.29 Create tag immutability rule dialog box

- "?": matches all single characters except the delimiter "/".
- "{alt1,...}": matches any pattern separated by commas (for example, alt1).

The following are examples of the patterns:

- "library/hello-world": matches only library/hello-world.
- "library/*": matches library/hello-world but does not match library/my/hello-world.
- "library/**": matches both library/hello-world and library/my/hello-world.
- "{library,goharbor}/*": matches library/hello-world and goharbor/core but does not match google/hello-world.
- "1.?": matches 1.0 but does not match 1.01.

6.3.3 *Using Rules of Immutable Artifacts*

Once the rules of immutable artifacts are created successfully, the rules become effective immediately. Multiple rules are evaluated independently and the artifacts matching each rule are independent. Because the OR relationship is used, an artifact can be an immutable artifact so long as it matches any rule.

You can check whether a tag is immutable by the tag list of the artifact, as shown in Fig. 6.30.

6.3.3.1 Push

When the user pushes an immutable artifact to Harbor, the client obtains an error prompt. Fig. 6.31 shows the error prompt of the Docker client.

Tags

+ ADD TAG | REMOVE TAG

Name	Signed	Pull Time	Push Time
test	⊗		8/18/21, 6:32 PM
latest Immutable	⊗		8/18/21, 3:45 PM

1 - 2 of 2 items

Fig. 6.30 Artifact tag details page

```
33cef25a18f5: Layer already exists
f3323fd84630: Layer already exists
68cde2659c77: Layer already exists
efdee1fc0ca1: Layer already exists
5327bb8ad385: Layer already exists
c3a984abe8a8: Layer already exists
[DEPRECATION NOTICE] registry v2 schema1 support will be removed in an upcoming release. Please
contact admins of the 10.92.103.227 registry NOW to avoid future disruption.
unknown: Failed to process request due to 'redis:latest' configured as immutable.
```

Fig. 6.31 Client warning message for tag immutability

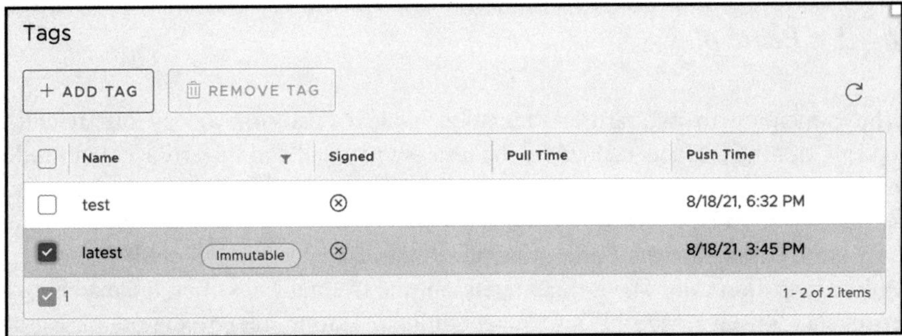

Fig. 6.32 Artifact tag details page

6.3.3.2 Delete

When a user wants to delete an immutable artifact, the system disables the **Remove Tag** button, as shown in Fig. 6.32.

When the tag retention policy deletes an immutable artifact, an error is generated in the system execution log, as shown in Fig. 6.33.

```
2020-05-06T08:23:30Z [INFO] [/pkg/retention/job.go:83]: Run retention process.
 Repository: library/hello-world
 Rule Algorithm: or
 Dry Run: true
2020-05-06T08:23:31Z [INFO] [/pkg/retention/job.go:98]: Load 1 candidates from repository library/hello-world
2020-05-06T08:23:31Z [INFO] [/pkg/retention/job.go:201]:
|                                Digest                                   |     Tag     | Kind  | Labels |     PushedTime      | PulledTime |     CreatedTime     | Retention |
|-------------------------------------------------------------------------|-------------|-------|--------|---------------------|------------|---------------------|-----------|
| sha256:92c7f9c92844bbbb5d0a101b22f7c2a7949e40f8ea90c8b3bc396879d95e899a | test,latest | image |        | 2020/05/06 07:47:26 |            | 2020/05/06 07:46:54 | IMMUTABLE |
2020-05-06T08:23:31Z [INFO] [/pkg/retention/job.go:206]: Retention error for artifact image:library/hello-
world:sha256:92c7f9c92844bbbb5d0a101b22f7c2a7949e40f8ea90c8b3bc396879d95e899a : Immutable tag
```

Fig. 6.33 Retention policy execution log details

6.4 Artifact Retention Policy

Harbor can manage a large number of container images which usually have different versions. Facing the increasing amount of images, the administrator needs to have a flexible automatic control capability for different versions of images. Harbor 1.9 introduced the image retention policy to help solve the issue of batch deletion of redundant images. In Harbor 2.0, the retention policy can also be applied to artifacts. Harbor automatically deletes the artifacts based on the retention policies.

This section introduces the functions of the retention policy from the aspects such as basic principles, usage modes and applicable scenarios, so as to help readers design corresponding policies to automatically delete historical images or other artifacts based on the understanding of the principles behind the scenes.

6.4.1 Principles

The principles of the artifact retention policy (also known as tag retention policy) are: the artifacts needed by the user are retained and the artifacts not needed are deleted according to the retention rules. This requires Harbor to calculate which artifacts need to be retained or deleted.

Before explaining the basic principles, first of all, we should clarify a concept: artifact retention rule. The artifact retention rule is a filter based on the matching of repository or tag, and the artifact conditions. During the execution of Harbor retention policy task, each artifact is verified by the retention rules. If an artifact successfully matches any rule, the artifact is to be retained; otherwise, the artifact is to be deleted.

In Harbor, the retention policy is applied by the artifact retention task. The following section introduces the task.

1. The retention API controller provides a unified REST API at the outermost layer and is responsible for interacting with the Scheduler module.
2. The retention manager is responsible for creating and modifying policies, keeping track of the task execution and saving data through the DAO layer.
3. The Scheduler module can define and cancel a scheduled task, which can be defined in the Cron format.
4. The launcher starts a Retention Job after it receives a scheduled task or a manual task triggered by the user.

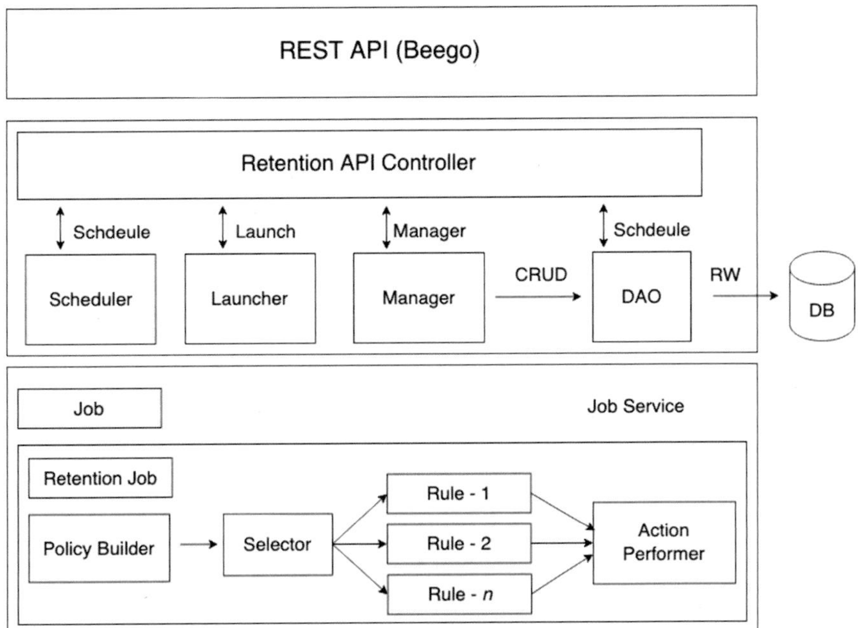

Fig. 6.34 The architecture design of the artifact retention policy

5. The Retention Job first matches the list of repositories according to the repository filter condition (Repo Selector) and creates a sub-task for each repository to execute, so that the Retention Job can operate on each repository in a parallel and efficient way.
6. The task first applies the Tag Selector on the corresponding repository to filter out candidate artifacts, which are called the Candidate list.
7. The Candidate list is transferred to the Ruler.
8. Different Rulers filter out the artifacts that can be retained according to their respective algorithms and the user's input parameters and then merge the calculation result sets to obtain the Retained list.
9. The Retained list is subtracted from the Candidate list to obtain the Delete list and then pass it to the Performer.
10. The Performer checks whether an artifact is immutable, and determines whether to delete the artifact if it is not a Dryrun.
11. The JobService component obtains the execution result, outputs the log and sends it to the Webhook module for notification.

Fig. 6.34 shows the architecture design of the artifact retention policy.

6.4.2 Setting a Retention Policy

The same as the function of immutable artifact, the artifact retention policy is set based on project. Tags are used as the identifiers of artifacts to determine whether artifacts need to be retained. Therefore, **Tag Retention** is displayed on the management page. The system administrator clicks **Tag Retention** on the project policy page to view the retention rules of the project, as shown in Fig. 6.35.

Click **Add Rule** and the **Add Tag Retention Rule** page is displayed, as shown in Fig. 6.36.

An artifact retention rule consists of three parts: repository, artifact condition and tag.

1. The repository to which the rule needs to be applied can be configured. You can select **Matching** or **Excluding** to configure the repository. The repository name supports the following matching patterns (the special characters used in the matching patterns are escaped by a backslash "\").

   - "*": matches all characters except the delimiter "/".
   - "**": matches all characters, including the delimiter "/".
   - "?": matches all single characters except the delimiter "/".
   - "{alt1,...}": matches any pattern separated by commas (for example, alt1).

   The following are examples of the patterns:

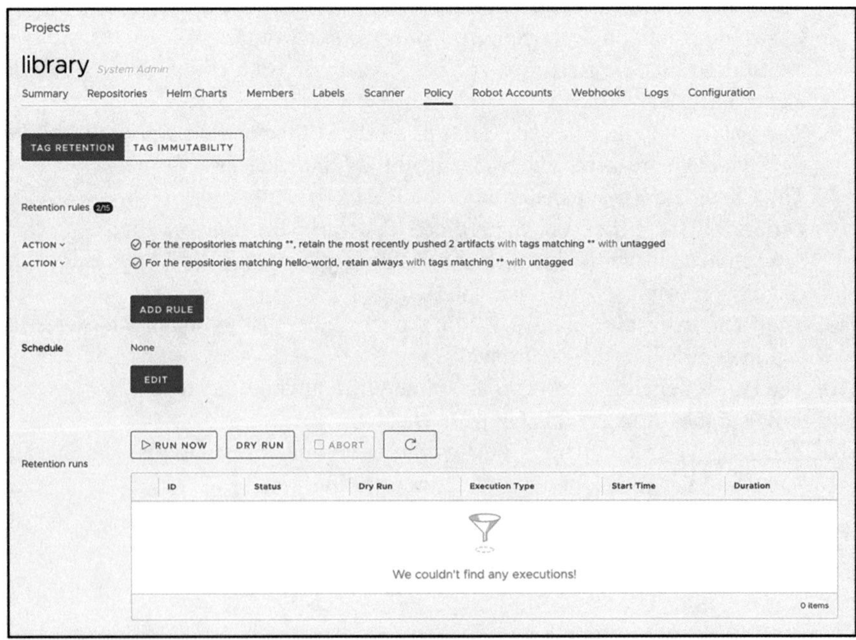

Fig. 6.35 Project tag retention page

Add Tag Retention Rule

Specify a tag retention rule for this project. All tag retention rules are independently calculated and each rule can be applied to a selected list of repositories.

For the repositories matching **

Enter multiple comma separated repos,repo*,or **

By artifact count or number of days

Tags matching ** untagged artifacts

Enter multiple comma separated tags, tag*, or **. Optionally include all untagged artifacts when applying the 'including' or 'excluding' selector by checking the box above.

CANCEL ADD

Fig. 6.36 Create tag retention rule dialog box

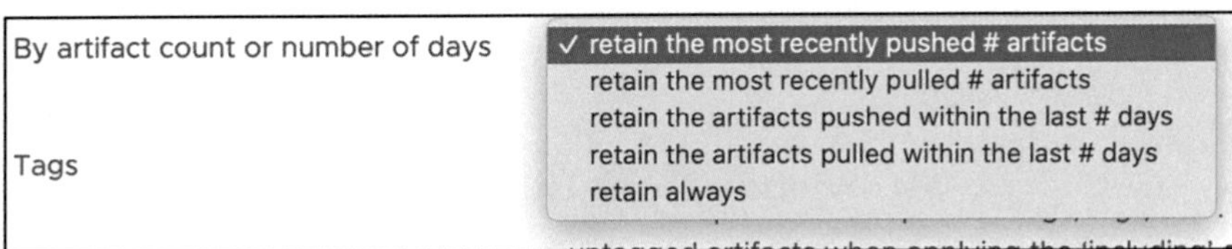

Fig. 6.37 The artifact retention conditions drop down box

- "library/hello-world": matches only library/hello-world.
- "library/*": matches library/hello-world but does not match library/my/hello-world.
- "library/**": matches both library/hello-world and library/my/hello-world.
- "{library,goharbor}/*": matches library/hello-world and goharbor/core but does not match google/hello-world.
- "1.?": matches 1.0 but does not match 1.01.

2. When setting the artifact retention conditions, you can choose to set the conditions based on the number of artifacts pushed or pulled, or the number of days in the recent past the artifacts have been pushed or pulled, as shown in Fig. 6.37.
3. To filter the tags to which this rule needs to be applied, you can select **Matching** or **Excluding** the tags. The matching pattern is the same as that of the repository. If untagged images need to be retained, select the **untagged artifacts** option (see Fig. 6.36).

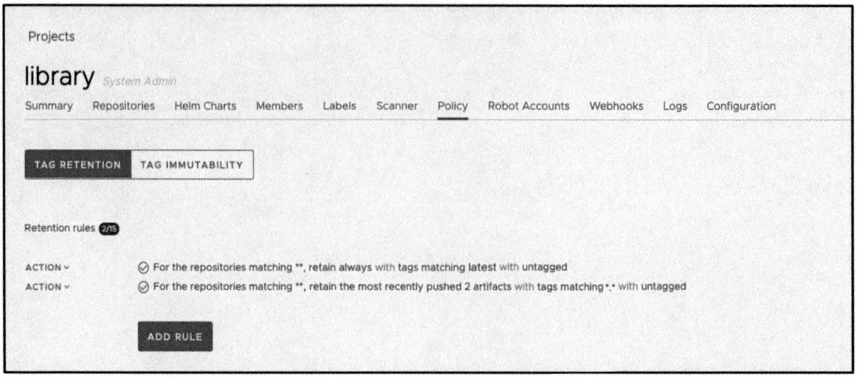

Fig. 6.38 Project tag retention page

We can learn how to set the retention policy through the above flow. Next, an example is used to illustrate how the retention policy works. As shown in Fig. 6.38, the following two tag retention rules are created under the library project.

The tag retention rule 1 is as follows:

- Repository matching: **.
- Retain always.
- Matching condition of artifacts: The tag is "latest".
- Including: untagged images.

The tag retention rule 2 is as follows:

- Repository matching: **.
- Retain the most recently pushed 2 artifacts.
- Matching condition of artifacts: The tag is "*.*".
- Including: untagged images.

In addition, the following images and tags exist under the library project. The images in the same repository are listed in the ascending order of the upload time.

1. repo1:1.0, 2.0, 3.0, dev, latest. The digests of the dev and latest tags are the same.
2. repo2:1.0, 2.0, latest.
3. repo3:dev.
4. repo4:userful (immutable artifact).

After the retention policy is run, the matching rules of images are as follows, as shown in Fig. 6.39.

Figure 6.39 describes the matching conditions of the two retention rules and the images (white boxes) matching the two retention rules. They will be retained, as described below.

- All images whose tags are "latest"
- Two newly uploaded images in each repository

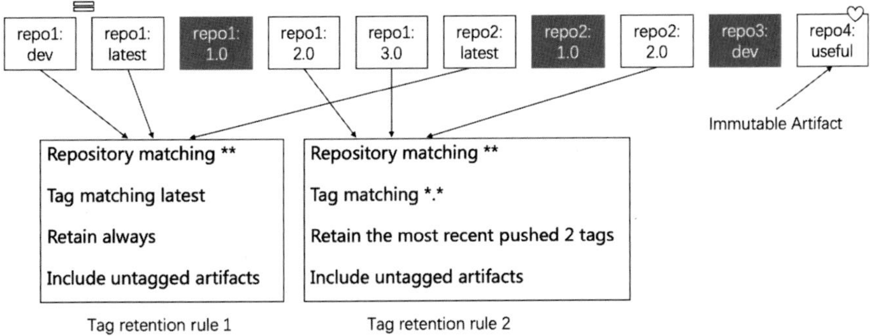

Fig. 6.39 The matching conditions of the two example rules

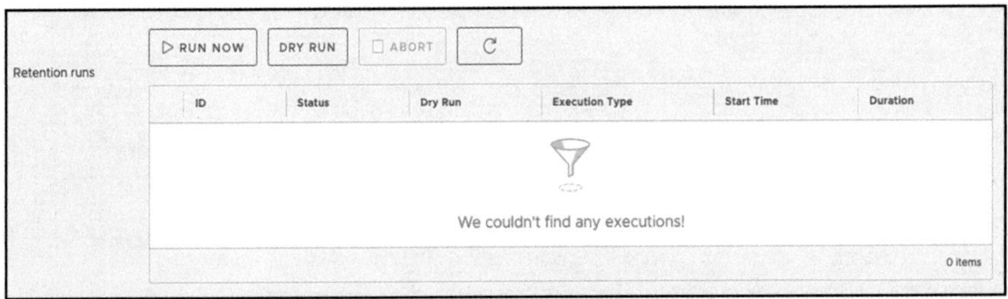

Fig. 6.40 Dry run page of the retention policy

- The repo1:dev image which has the same digest as that of the image repo1:latest
- repo4:useful with the immutable attribute

Unmatched images are depicted in dark colors and will be deleted by the retention policy: repo1:1.0, repo2:1.0, and repo3: dev.

6.4.3 Dry Run of the Retention Policy

After configuring the retention policy, the dry run of the retention policy can be used to verify the configuration, as shown in Fig. 6.40.

The dry run simulates the execution of the retention rules and provides simulation results to show the artifacts to be retained or deleted. It does not actually delete the artifacts. After a dry run of the retention policy task, you can view the detailed execution status, as shown in Fig. 6.41.

Each repository corresponds to a subtask. The status of the main task can be one of the followings: InProgress, Succeed, Failed or Stopped. The status of subtasks can be one of the followings: Pending, Running, Success, Error, Stopped or Scheduled. The status of the main task is dynamically calculated according to the status of its subtasks.

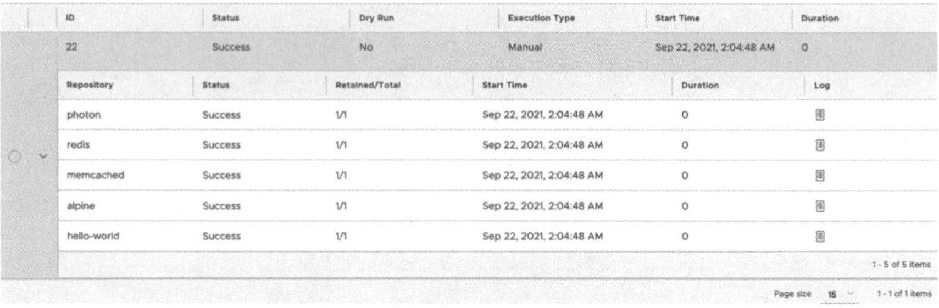

ID	Status	Dry Run	Execution Type	Start Time	Duration
22	Success	No	Manual	Sep 22, 2021, 2:04:48 AM	0

Repository	Status	Retained/Total	Start Time	Duration	Log
photon	Success	1/1	Sep 22, 2021, 2:04:48 AM	0	
redis	Success	1/1	Sep 22, 2021, 2:04:48 AM	0	
memcached	Success	1/1	Sep 22, 2021, 2:04:48 AM	0	
alpine	Success	1/1	Sep 22, 2021, 2:04:48 AM	0	
hello-world	Success	1/1	Sep 22, 2021, 2:04:48 AM	0	

1 - 5 of 5 items

Page size 15 1 - 1 of 1 items

Fig. 6.41 Dry run results details of the retention policy

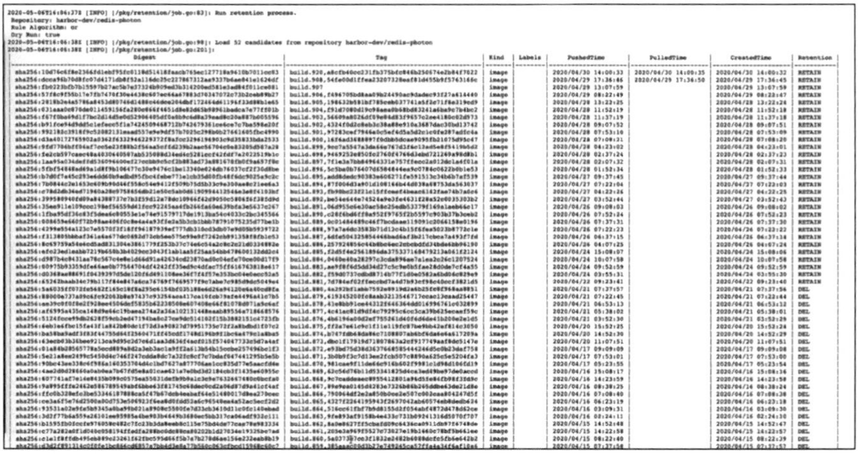

Fig. 6.42 The retention policy execution logs in detail

- If none of the subtasks ends, the status of the main task is InProgress.
- If the status of subtasks is Pending, Running or Scheduled, the status of the main task is Running.
- If the status of subtasks is Stopped, the status of the main task is Stopped.
- If the status of subtasks is Error, the status of the main task is Failed. Otherwise, the status of the main task is Succeed.

The retention policy can be triggered either manually or by schedule. After the status of the task becomes Running, the log can be viewed, as shown in Fig. 6.42. You can see the digests, tags and other information of artifacts in the log and see which artifacts are retained from the **Retention** column. **RETAIN** indicates the artifacts will be retained and **DEL** indicates the artifacts will be deleted.

Note: If an artifact is set to be immutable, the artifact is retained regardless of the retention rules.

6.4.4 Triggering the Retention Policy

The artifact retention policy of Harbor provides two triggering modes: manual and scheduled.

6.4.4.1 Manual

On the page shown in Fig. 6.40, click **Run Now** to launch a real execution of the retention policy. Because the execution will directly delete artifacts according to the retention rules, a dialog box is displayed to remind the risk of the operation, as shown in Fig. 6.43.

Click **Run** and the artifact retention process is executed. Check the execution log to see if there is any error.

6.4.4.2 Scheduled

Scheduled mode allows the retention policy to be executed periodically by defining a Cron task. Note: The time in the Crontab expression set here is the time of the server instead of the time of the browser.

The scheduled tasks can occur hourly, daily and weekly. Furthermore, customized scheduled tasks can be configured, as shown in Fig. 6.44. To create a custom scheduled task, you need to customize the execution time according to the Crontab syntax. As shown in Fig. 6.45, the task runs once half an hour. Refer to Sect. 5.3.3 for details of the Crontab expression.

After configuring the scheduled execution, click **Save**. A dialog box is displayed, as shown in Fig. 6.46. Click **OK**. A scheduled task is set up successfully.

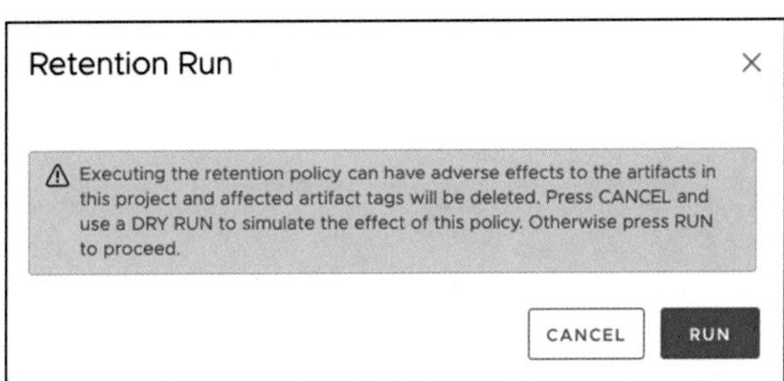

Fig. 6.43 Retention run warning dialog box

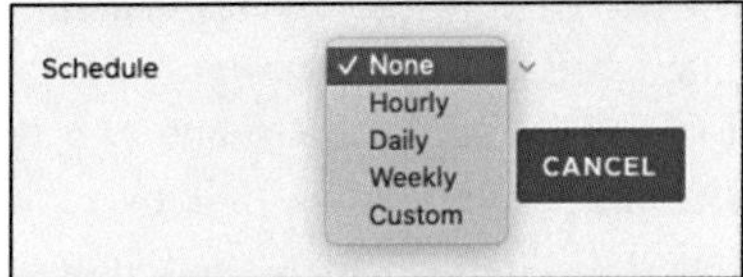

Fig. 6.44 The customized schedule of retention policy

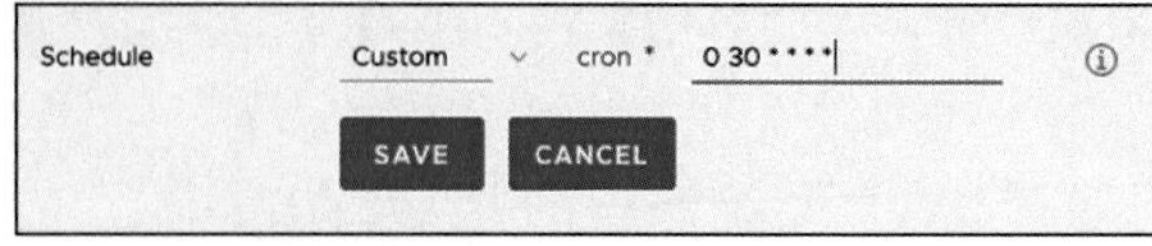

Fig. 6.45 Custom retention policy schedule

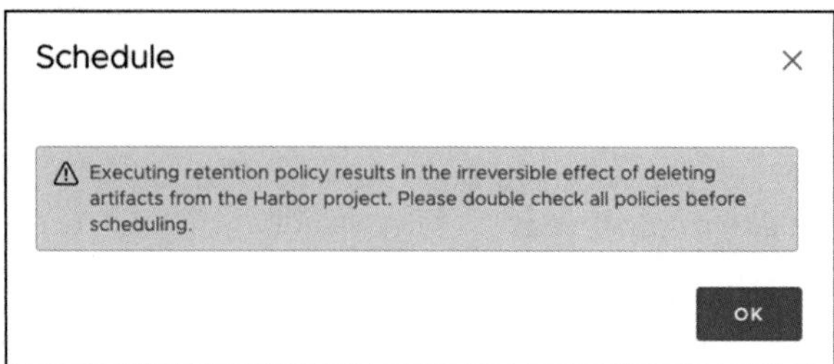

Fig. 6.46 Warning dialog box on saving retention policy schedule

ID	Status	Dry Run	Execution Type	Start Time	Duration
2	Succeed	NO	Schedule	Aug 18, 2021, 7:30:02 PM	0
1	Succeed	YES	Manual	Aug 18, 2021, 6:52:15 PM	0

1 - 2 of 2 items

Fig. 6.47 Scheduled retention policy execution history

After the first scheduled task is executed, a record with the execution type of Schedule can be seen in the task list, as shown in Fig. 6.47.

Note: The artifact retention policy should not be executed simultaneously with the garbage collection. Because when the garbage collection task is executed, Harbor is set to the read-only status and cannot delete any artifacts.

The same as the manual artifact deletion, the retention policy also performs the "soft deletion" of artifact, i.e., only the database records corresponding to artifacts are deleted and the artifacts are not physically deleted from the storage.

6.5 Webhook

Webhook is an important part of the system. It is generally used to notify subscribers of events that occur in the system. Strictly speaking, Webhook of Harbor should be called the notification system because it can not only support the web-based callback function but also other functions such as Slack subscription.

The design idea of the Webhook is to send the events in which users may be interested in to third-party systems. At present, Webhook provides up to 11 events for users to subscribe to and two types of hook modes: the HTTP callback and the Incoming Webhook of Slack. The continuous delivery process can employ the automatic deployment of container applications based on Webhook. The alarm function can be implemented through the notification mechanism of Webhook; Third-party platforms can integrate with Harbor through Webhook to display the statistical and operation data of Harbor artifacts.

6.5.1 Principles

The Webhook system design needs to consider a few issues. For example, how to successfully send an event to subscribers after the event is triggered? In the scenario that involves a large number of events, how can we guarantee the performance and the success rate of message delivery? This section describes how Webhook's design solve these issues.

6.5.1.1 Overall Architecture

Figure 6.48 shows the architecture of Webhook.

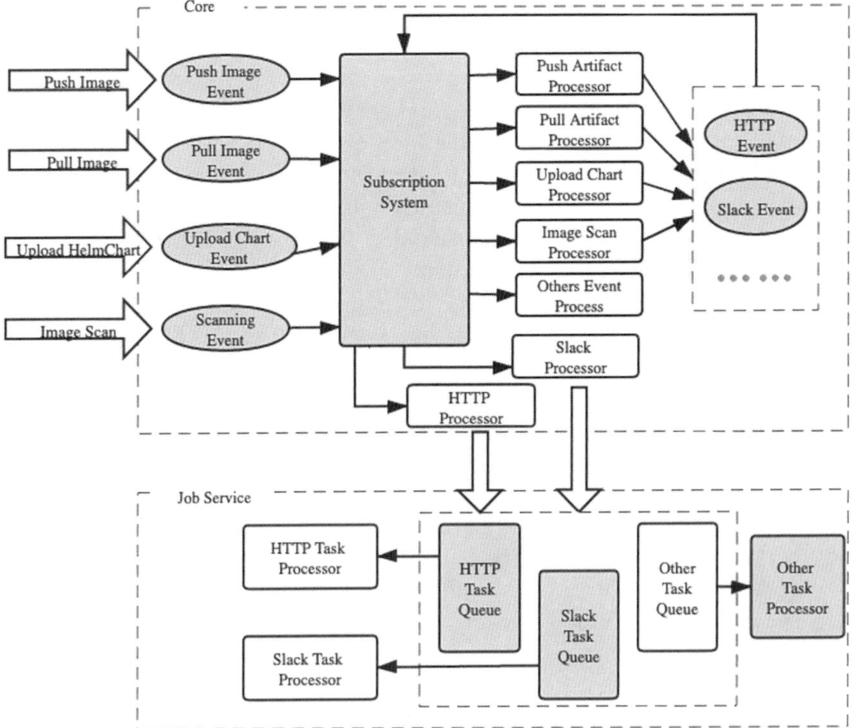

Fig. 6.48 The architecture design of the webhook

Webhook is an asynchronous task processing system. With the help of the cache function of Redis and the JobService component, Webhook has the powerful task distribution and processing capabilities.

Based on the architecture design shown in Fig. 6.48, the process from the generation of an event to the final sending of the event to the configured Webhook can be decomposed into the following steps:

1. Harbor triggers an event that can be subscribed to by Webhook.
2. The source information of the event is extracted and a source event body is generated.
3. The source event body of the event is processed and converted into a general event type of the message subscription framework and is sent to the processing framework.
4. The corresponding processor in the framework receives the event data and starts to process it.
5. The processor first checks whether any Webhook policies are defined under the project where the event occurs.
6. If no policy is defined, the processing flow ends. Otherwise, the policies are evaluated one by one.
7. The processor checks whether a policy is enabled. If not, it continues to evaluate the next policy.
8. If the policy is enabled, the processor continues to check whether the policy subscribes to the event. If not, the processor continues to evaluate the next policy.
9. If the policy subscribes to the event, the processor starts to assemble an asynchronous task (to be sent to the JobService).
10. The asynchronous task includes all information to be sent to subscribers. Some content needs to be queried depending on the source information.
11. After the asynchronous task is assembled, the processor starts to evaluate the Hook type (Notify type) of the policy.
12. Based on different Hook types, the processor generates different events containing the asynchronous task message and delivers it in the message subscription framework.
13. The corresponding processor (HTTP processor or Slack processor) in the framework further processes the asynchronous task generated above and sends the task to the JobService.
14. After receiving the asynchronous task, the JobService puts the task in different task queues based on the type and let it wait for the scheduling.
15. When an idle task processor is available, the task is scheduled and is processed by the processor of the corresponding type.
16. The asynchronous task processor extracts the content of the task and sends the information to a third-party subscription system based on the processing logic defined for the type.
17. After the task is processed, the status of the asynchronous task is written back to the Core service of Harbor via the callback mechanism.

18. The Core service of Harbor receives the callback information of the asynchronous task and writes the status into the database.

Now, the entire Webhook flow is completed.

6.5.1.2 Message Structure

A Webhook message consists of message meta information and event data. Event data includes the repository and resources which generated the event. The core resources of Harbor are artifacts. Therefore, Harbor puts events of the same artifact in a message body. This also complies with the processing logic of Harbor service.

The message structure of Webhook is designed as follows:

```
{
    "type": "PUSH_ARTIFACT",
    "occur_at": 1586922308,
    "operator": "admin",
    "event_data": {
        "resources": [{
          "digest": "sha256:8a9e9863dbb6e10edb5adfe917c00da84e170
0fa76e7ed02476aa6e6fb8ee0d8",
          "tag": "latest",
          "resource_url": "hub.harbor.com/test-webhook/debian:
latest"
        }],
        "repository": {
            "date_created": 1586922308,
            "name": "debian",
            "namespace": "test-webhook",
            "repo_full_name": "test-webhook/debian",
            "repo_type": "private"
        }
    }
}
```

Table 6.2 describes the attributes of the message body.

For different types of events, attributes of the message body are different. For example, for Helm Chart resources, the digest attribute is not included in the section of resources.

6.5.1.3 Message Retry

During the execution of a Webhook task, Harbor ensures that messages are correctly delivered to third-party systems through the configurable number of retries. The

Table 6.2 The attributes of the webhook message

Attribute	Description
type	Event type
occur_at	The time when the event occurred
operator	Operator of the event
event_data. repository. date_created	Creation time of the repository where the event originated
event_data. repository. name	Name of the repository where the event originated
event_data. repository. namespace	Namespace of the repository where the event source originated (namely Harbor project name)
event_data. repository. repo_full_name	Full name of the repository where the event originated
event_data. repository. repo_type	Type of the repository where the event originated (**private** indicates private repository and **public** indicates public repository)
event_data. resources. digest	Digest of the event source
event_data. resources. tag	Tag of the event source
event_data. resources. resource_url	URL of the event source resources (that is, storage path of the resources in Harbor)

asynchronous framework ensures high throughput of the system while the failure retry mechanism ensures the reliability of message delivery.

During they deployment of Harbor, the number of Webhook failure retries can be configured in the configuration file **harbor.yml**. The default value is 10. It is a tradeoff of picking the value of the retry. If too many retries are set to ensure the reliability, the JobService component may be overloaded. The relevant section in the configuration is as follows:

```
notification:
 # Maximum retry count for Webhook job
 webhook_job_max_retry: 10
```

6.5.2 *Configuring Webhook*

The configuration of Webhook is based on project. The project administrator or system administrator can create, delete and view a Webhook.

6.5.2.1 Creating a Webhook

On the project page, click **Webhooks** to view the Webhooks of the project, as shown in Fig. 6.49.

The Webhooks page provides the functions of creating a Webhook, enabling or disabling a Webhook, editing a Webhook, deleting a Webhook and viewing triggering events. You can create a new Webhook by clicking **Add Webhook**, as shown in Fig. 6.50.

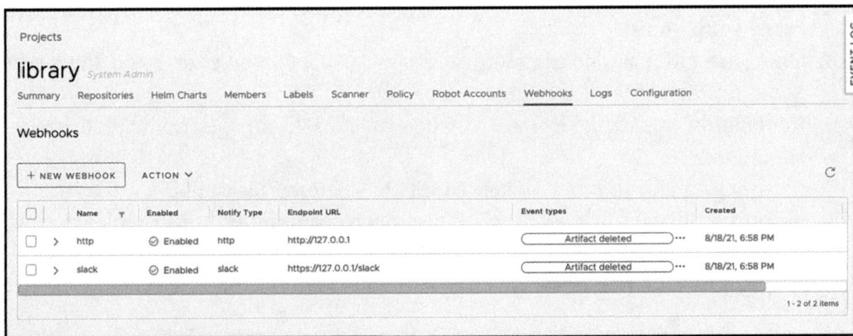

Fig. 6.49 Project webhook page

Fig. 6.50 Create webhook dialog box

Add Webhook

Specify the endpoint for receiving webhook notifications

Name *

Description

Notify Type * http

Event Type * Artifact deleted, Artifact pulled, Artifact pushed, Chart deleted, Chart downloaded, Chart uploaded, Quota exceed, Quota near threshold, Replication finished, Scanning failed, Scanning finished

Endpoint URL * http(s)://192.168.1.1

Auth Header

Verify Remote Certificate

TEST ENDPOINT CANCEL ADD

The core of Webhook functions is the Webhook policy, which consists of two parts: event type and notify type.

The event types supported by Webhook are as follows.

1. Artifact deleted: triggered when an artifact is deleted.
2. Artifact pulled: triggered when an artifact is pulled.
3. Artifact pushed: triggered when an artifact is pushed.
4. Chart deleted: triggered when a Helm Chart is deleted.
5. Chart downloaded: triggered when a Helm Chart is downloaded.
6. Chart uploaded: triggered when a Helm Chart is uploaded.
7. Quota exceed: triggered when an artifact is uploaded and the project quota exceeds the limit.
8. Quota near threshold: triggered when an artifact is uploaded and the project quota reaches 85% of the limit.
9. Replication finished: triggered when a remote image replication task is completed.
10. Scanning failed: triggered when an image scanning task fails.
11. Scanning finished: triggered when an image scanning task is completed.

The notify types supported by Webhook include HTTP and Slack, as shown in Fig. 6.51.

1. HTTP mode: This mode is provided as the general Webhook mode. Users can choose the HTTP mode and enter the URL and the authentication header of the subscription system. When an event occurs, a message is sent to the subscription system and the authentication header is written into the Authorization header of the HTTP request.
2. Slack mode: Messages are sent to slack accounts through Slack's Incoming Webhook. Because Slack's Incoming Webhook limits the frequency of message reception to one message per second, the JobService of Harbor also limits the frequency of sending out messages. The interval between message sending exceeds 1 second.

After the project administrator sets the Webhook policy, if an event specified by the Webhook occurs in Harbor, the subscription system immediately receives a message. At present, the number of policies that can be configured under each project is unlimited.

6.5.2.2 Managing Webhook

On the Webhooks page, a webhook can be enabled, disabled, edited or deleted, as shown in Fig. 6.52.

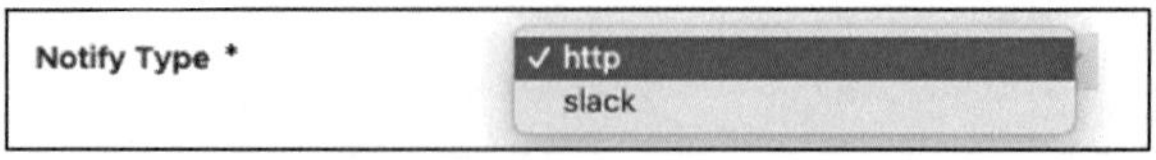

Fig. 6.51 Webhook notify typy drop down box

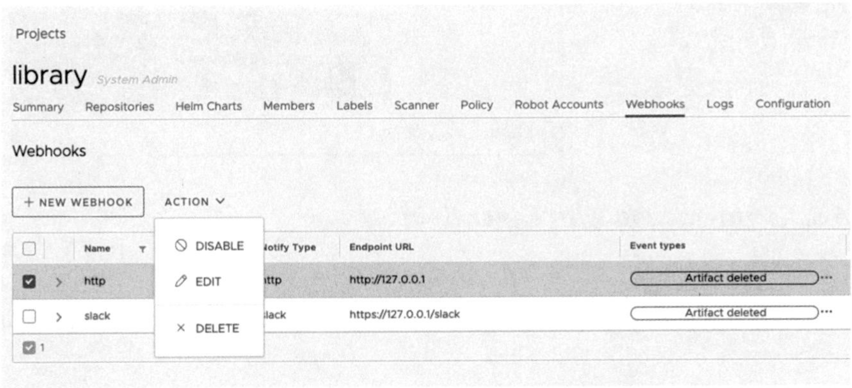

Fig. 6.52 Webhook action drop down box

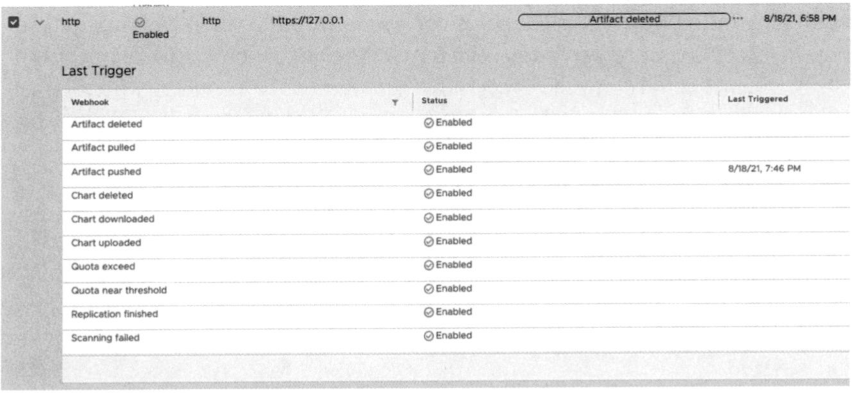

Fig. 6.53 Webhook last trigger page

6.5.2.3 Viewing a Webhook Policy

You can unfold the policy to view the last triggered time of different events, as shown in Fig. 6.53.

6.5.2.4 Flag to Enable or Disable Webhook

On the page of system settings, the system administrator can set the flag to enable or disable Webhook globally. If **Webhooks enabled** is unchecked, Webhook is disabled for all projects in the system, as shown in Fig. 6.54.

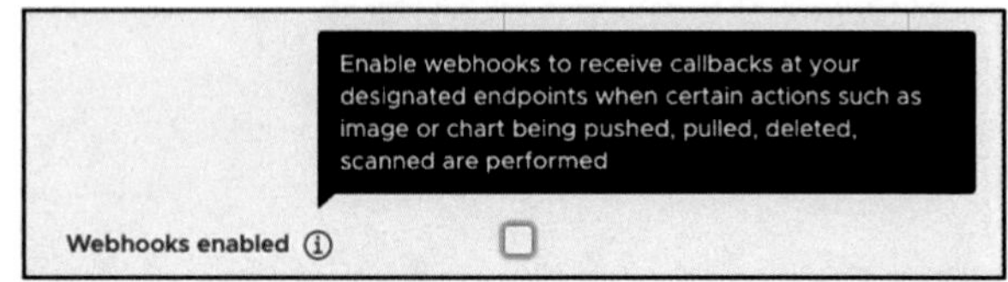

Fig. 6.54 Webhook enabled checkbox

6.5.3 Interaction with Other Systems

This section introduces how to view received events in the system configured with Webhook and how to make use of the received message of an event. The example describes the interaction with Slack.

After the project administrator creates a Slack Webhook and subscribes to all event types, when an image is pushed to the corresponding project in Harbor, the channel in Slack soon receives a message, as shown in Fig. 6.55.

In the triggering records of a Webhook in Harbor, the last triggered time of **Artifact pushed** shows the time when the event occurred, as shown in Fig. 6.56.

The Slack message can be considered as a "notification". All members in the Slack channel can receive the event message in time. The members who follow the channel can complete the follow-up work according to the content of the message.

#skiffdevops
1 | Add a topic

Webhooks APP 11:59 AM
Harbor webhook events

Wednesday, April 15th

event_type: PUSH_ARTIFACT

occur_at: April 15th at 11:59 AM

operator: admin

event_data:


```
{
    "resources": [
        {
            "digest":
"sha256:8a9e9863dbb6e10edb5adfe917c00da84e1700fa76e7ed02476aa6e6fb8ee0d8",
            "tag": "latest",
            "resource_url": "10.219.192.104/test-webhook/debian:latest"
        }
    ],
    "repository": {
        "date_created": 1586922308,
        "name": "debian",
        "namespace": "test-webhook",
        "repo_full_name": "test-webhook/debian",
        "repo_type": "private"
    }
}
```


Fig. 6.55 Webhook message in Slack

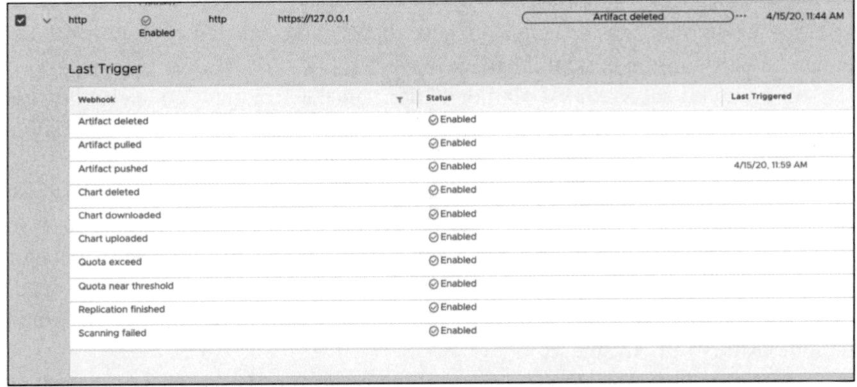

Fig. 6.56 Webhook last trigger page

6.6 Multiple Languages

The Harbor project provides the support of multiple languages since its inception. This section describes how to switch a language and how to add a new language to Harbor.

Harbor 2.0 supports six languages, including English, Simplified Chinese, French, Spanish, Portuguese and Turkish. English and Simplified Chinese are maintained by the Harbor team and the rest languages are maintained by the community.

To switch the language in Harbor, follow the following steps:

1. Click the **Language** menu in the management console. The menu is on the right of the navigation bar at the top of the Harbor page. In Fig. 6.57, the drop-down menu shows **English** on the left of the user name (**admin**).
2. Pick a desired language from the drop-down list.
3. The page will be refreshed automatically with the selected language.

Fig. 6.57 Switch language drop down box

If the languages supported by Harbor still cannot meet your needs or some translations of the current language have flaws, you can create your own new language or repair the current language.

The internationalization of Harbor is done in the front-end code. Harbor uses Google's open source front-end framework Angular and VMware's open source front-end component Clarity to achieve the internationalization function.

To display the content in different languages, Harbor does not directly output the original content on the page. Instead, it first defines a series of index keys and associates a string value to each index key in different languages. The front end of Harbor generates pages by using the special index keys initially, and then render them into the user interface according to the string values in the internationalization definition file of the language.

It is relatively simple to create a new language for Harbor. Take Spanish (its language code is "es" and the region code is "es") as an example. To add in the Spanish language, perform the following steps:

1. In the **src/portal/src/i18n/lang** folder of Harbor source code, locate the **en-us-lang.json** file, copy and rename it as **es-es-lang.json**. This file contains the keys required for internationalization of Harbor and the corresponding values in English. Then translate the English values into the desire language (Spanish in this case). Note: Do not modify key names in the file.
2. Add the new language to the list of supported languages: find the variable **supportedLangs** in the file **src/portal/src/app/shared/shared.const.ts** and add the new language to its list (e.g., export const supportedLangs = ['en-us', 'zh-cn', 'es-es']). Define the displayed name of the newly added language in the variable **supportedLangs**, which is of a dictionary type. Add in the item **"es-es": " Español"** to the variable.
3. Add a new language list in the front-end template file: find the file **src/portal/src/app/base/navigator/navigator.component.html**, then in the file look for the HTML tag that defines the language supported by Harbor and add in a new item. The code is as follows:

```
    <clr-dropdown-menu *clrIfOpen>
    <a href="javascript:void(0)" clrDropdownItem (click)
='switchLanguage("en-us")' [class.lang-selected]='matchLang
("en-us")'>English</a>
      <a href="javascript:void(0)" clrDropdownItem (click)
='switchLanguage("zh-cn")' [class.lang-selected]='matchLang
("zh-cn")'>中文简体</a>

      <!- - Take Spanish as an example. Add in the following line of code -->
    <a href="javascript:void(0)" clrDropdownItem (click)
='switchLanguage("es-es")' [class.lang-selected]='matchLang
("es-es")'>Español</a>
```

(continued)

```
    <a href="javascript:void(0)" clrDropdownItem (click)
='switchLanguage("fr-fr")' [class.lang-selected]='matchLang
("fr-fr")'>Français</a>
    <a href="javascript:void(0)" clrDropdownItem (click)
='switchLanguage("pt-br")' [class.lang-selected]='matchLang
("pt-br")'>Português do Brasil</a>
    <a href="javascript:void(0)" clrDropdownItem (click)
='switchLanguage("tr-tr")' [class.lang-selected]='matchLang
("tr-tr")'>Türkçe</a>
    </clr-dropdown-menu>
```

4. Recompile the code.

   Compile the local source code:

```
$ make build <parameters for the compilation of Harbor>
```

   If you want to install the newly compiled Harbor onto other hosts, you need to create an offline installation package.

```
$ make package_offline
```

In this way, the steps for adding a new language are completed. Of course, if you just want to modify the content of an existing language, you only need to update the relevant language JSON file and recompile the code.

Readers may wonder how to configure the date formats of different languages. In fact, the date component of the Clarity library automatically switches the date format according to the language and region code. Thanks to Angular and Clarity, Harbor can automatically display an appropriate language by detecting the preferred languages of the browser. If none of the preferred languages is supported by Harbor, Harbor displays the user interface in English.

6.7 FAQ

1. Why is Harbor still in read-only mode after the garbage collection is finished?

   The garbage collection task retains the system status before it is executed. If before the garbage collection, Harbor is in the read-only mode, Harbor remains in the read-only mode after the garbage collection.

2. Why does Harbor automatically enter the read-only mode regularly?

   If you set and cancel the task of garbage collection, in some cases, the scheduling of the garbage collection task is successfully removed from the database. However, it is not removed from Redis. As a result, JobService still executes the garbage collection task regularly and sets Harbor to read-only mode. To solve this problem, refer to github.com/goharbor/harbor/issues/12209#issuecomment-657952180 to manually delete the task from Redis.

3. Why is the actual usage of storage lower than the total quota of all projects?

   Due to the sharing of layers between artifacts, only one copy of each shared layer is saved in the storage. In Harbor, the quota of a project is calculated based on the layers that the project references. If a layer is referenced by multiple projects, the size of the layer is repeatedly calculated by these projects. This leads to the fact that the total quota of all projects may be higher than the total usage of the storage.

4. Why can new images still be pushed after "**" is set in the immutable artifact policy to match repositories and tags?

   Immutable artifacts are applied to only existing artifacts (images). New images can be pushed successfully for the first time. Once images are pushed successfully, the images become immutable artifacts and cannot be pushed again later.

5. Why isn't a Webhook message received immediately after an event is triggered?

   In Harbor, all tasks are processed by the JobService. When a large number of tasks need to be processed in the system, JobService puts the tasks in the waiting queue. This causes the delay between the event triggering time and the event receiving time.

Chapter 7
Lifecycle Management

After Harbor is deployed in the production environment, it continuously provides users the registry service. At this time, Harbor enters the operation and maintenance phase. In the production environment, the user needs to be familiar with the lifecycle management knowledge of Harbor to prevent and control risks.

Starting from the architecture and historical evolution of Harbor, this chapter introduces the way to effectively manage the whole lifecycle of Harbor based on common scenarios such as backup, restoration, upgrade and online troubleshooting.

7.1 Backup and Restoration

Backup and restoration are routine operations in maintenance. Their importance is obvious: when a system file is corrupted and cannot be repaired, the backup file can be used to restore the system.

7.1.1 Data Backup

Backup refers to replicating one or more copies of data and storing them in other locations. When data is lost due to a system failure, these copies can be used to restore the system to the previous state.

This shows that the operations of backup and restore are all performed around data. The prerequisite for the backup of Harbor is that we need to know which data should be backed up. As shown in Fig. 7.1, the data on which Harbor depends can be divided into two categories: temporary data and persistent data.

1. Temporary data is the data generated via the configuration file during the installation of Harbor and is mainly the configuration files and environment variables

H. Zhang, Y. Wang, *The Authoritative Guide on Harbor*,
https://doi.org/10.1007/978-981-19-2727-0_7

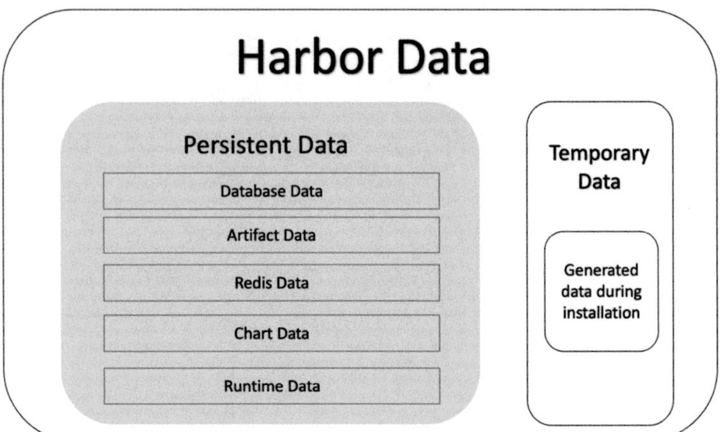

Fig. 7.1 Persistent data and temporary data in Harbor

on which Harbor components depend. The data is usually stored in the **common/** directory of the Harbor installation directory (if Harbosr is installed through source code, the data is in the **make/common** directory of the source code directory) and is mounted to corresponding containers when Harbor components are started. Although temporary data is crucial to the smooth operation of services, the installer reads the configuration file of Harbor every time and regenerates a copy of the temporary data. Therefore, we only need to back up the configuration file instead of the whole **common** directory.

2. Persistent data is stored under a directory specified by the value of the **data_volume** configuration item. The data mainly includes database data of Harbor, artifact data, Redis data, chart data and runtime data on which Harbor components rely.

The folders contained in the **data** directory and their corresponding functions are as follows:

- **ca_download**: stores the CA required when a user accesses Harbor.
- **cert**: certificates and keys required when Harbor starts the HTTPS service.
- **chart_storage**: stores the data of Helm v2 Chart.
- **database**: directory for storing the database. Harbor, Clair and Notary databases are in this directory.
- **job_logs**: stores logs of JobService.
- **redis**: stores Redis data.
- **registry**: stores the data of OCI artifacts (e.g., image data for most users).
- **secret**: stores the encryption information required for communication of internal components of Harbor.
- **trivy-adapter**: stores the data related to Trivy runtime.

Note: Harbor needs to mount the files under these directories into containers when it starts. Most containers of Harbor components, except for the log container which must be run as root, are run as a user other than root. The user group and permission of the files do not match those in the containers. As a result, errors related to the permission may occur in the containers. Therefore, these directories and files must be set to the specific users and user groups of the containers on the host. The users and permission of these files cover the following two categories:

- Database and Redis: Containers are run as the 999:999 (user id : group id).
- Other containers of Harbor: Containers are run based on the 10000:10000 (user id : group id).

Restored data must be consistent with the backup data. Many users cannot start Harbor after restoring data and find error messages related to file permissions in the log. This was likely caused by the incorrect file permission of the backup data.

Next, start backing up the data.

1. Back up the Harbor installation directory to the **/my_backup_dir** directory.

```
$ cp ./harbor /my_backup_dir/harbor
```

   If you did not modify the generated files and do not want to back up Harbor images and related files (you can always download them again when necessary), you can only back up the configuration file.
2. Back up the Harbor **data** directory to the **/my_backup_dir** directory.

```
$ cp ./harbor/harbor.yml /my_backup_dir/harbor.yml
```

3. Back up the external data (this step is required only when the external data is used): if an external database, Redis or block storage is used, back up their data by referring to the backup solution provided by the software or the external storage.

```
$ cp -r/data /my_backup_dir/data
```

The above steps complete the backup process.

7.1.2 Restoration of Harbor

This section describes how to restore to the previous version of Harbor by using the backup files created in Sect. 7.1.1.

We all know that online services will always encounter emergencies. In the situations of fire, earthquake, mistaken data deletion or serious bugs in the new version, we may need to restore the current version to the previous version that runs stably. The following describes how to restore Harbor.

1. If Harbor is still running, first stop Harbor.

```
$ cd harbor
$ docker-compose down
```

2. Delete the current Harbor directory.

```
$ rm -rf harbor
```

3. Restore the Harbor directory of the previous version.

```
$ mv /my_backup_dir/harbor harbor
```

4. If the Harbor directory is not backed up but the configuration file is backed up, you can download and decompress the installation package of Harbor again and restore the configuration file (**xxx** in the following command indicates the version of Harbor).

```
$ tar xvf harbor-offline-installer-xxx.tgz
$ mv /my_backup_dir/harbor.yml ./harbor/harbor.yaml
```

5. Restore the **data** directory.

   • If the **data** directory exists, you need to delete the directory (or rename the directory) first.

```
$ rm -rf /data
```

   • Restore the directory.

```
$ mv /my_backup_dir/data /data
```

6. Restore data of the external storage. If an external database, Redis or storage is used, perform corresponding restoration for different storage and services.
7. Restart Harbor by using the following command:

```
$ cd harbor
$ ./install.sh
```

Wait a few minutes until Harbor restarts.

7.1.3 Backup and Restoration of Helm Deployment

Many Harbor clusters are deployed by Helm Chart on the Kubernetes platform in the production environment to achieve high availability.

In this scenario, you are advised not to save data on local nodes of Harbor. Instead, you should use an external storage. For example, databases and Redis use an external PostgreSQL service or Redis high-availability solution, or directly use cloud storage or services. In this way, external components or services are responsible for data backup and restoration. Harbor does not actually need to back up any other data except for the configuration file **values.yaml**. The backup procedure is as follows:

1. Back up **values.yaml**.
2. Back up the database.
3. Back up Redis.
4. Back up external storage.

Run the **helm install** command to restore data.

In the following commands, <**Harborname**> indicates the name identifier for the deployment of Helm and **harbor-backup.yaml** indicates the **values.yaml** file used during backup.

The command in Helm V3 is as follows:

```
$ helm install -f harbor-backup.yaml <Harborname> harbor/harbor
```

The command in Helm V2 is as follows:

```
$ helm install -f harbor-backup.yaml --name <Harborname> harbor/
harbor
```

If you did not use any third-party storage but directly deployed Harbor in the local Kubernetes cluster, you are advised not to back up data by yourself. You can refer to third-party backup tools such as velero.io.

7.1.4 Backup and Restoration Using Image Replication

In addition to the above conventional backup modes, you can also back up by using the image replication of Harbor. As we all know, the image replication function of Harbor can be used for image distribution and workflow integration with DevOps. In essence, it uses the JobService component to start an asynchronous task to transfer local images to other endpoints or pull the images of other endpoints to the local node. In the scenario shown in Fig. 7.2, a Harbor instance is used as a node to back up the images (or other artifacts) of other nodes and then replicate the images over to this node.

When the original instance fails and needs to be recovered, as shown in Fig. 7.3, restore the images of the backup node to the newly established Harbor instance.

The configuration flow during backup is as follows:

1. Start the Harbor service instance and backup instance.
2. Configure the backup instance as the replication target of the Harbor service instance. Log in to the Harbor service instance, select **New Registry Endpoint** on the repository management page and add information of the backup instance: Select **harbor** as the **Provider**; enter a target name as **Name** ; enter the address of the Harbor backup node as **Endpoint URL**; enter values of **Access ID** and **Access Secret** and determine whether to select the **Verify Remote Cert** option according to the configuration during installation, as shown in Fig. 7.4.
3. Create a replication rule to back up images periodically. In the **Replication Management** of the Harbor administrator page, create a rule for replicating images to the backup node. As shown in Fig. 7.5, select **Push-based** as **Replication mode**; enter a value of **Source Resource Filter** to filter out the objects to be replicated. If you want to back up all image data, enter ** for **Name** and **Tag**; enter the target created previously for **Destination Registry** and leave **Destination Namespace** blank so that the backup node can be consistent with the namespace of the source node; select **Scheduled** for **Trigger Mode** so that the backup task can be run periodically.

Fig. 7.2 Using image replication for backup

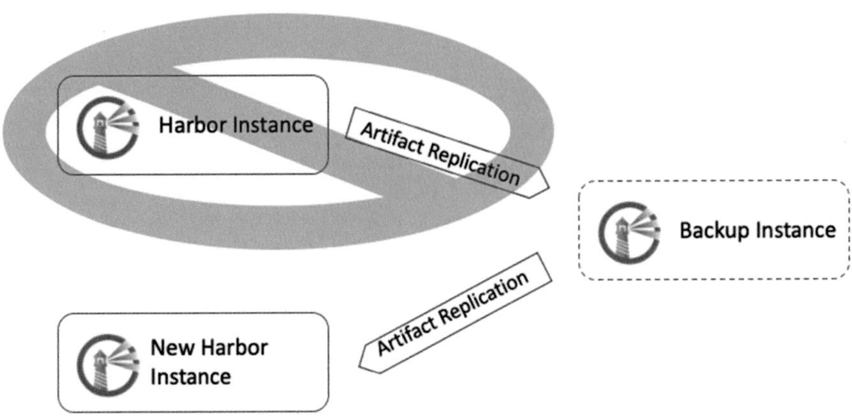

Fig. 7.3 Using image replication for restore

Fig. 7.4 New Registry Endpoint dialog box

New Registry Endpoint

Provider * harbor

Name * harbor-backup

Description

Endpoint URL * https://10.193.59.96

Access ID admin

Access Secret ••••••••••••

Verify Remote Cert

TEST CONNECTION CANCEL OK

The configuration flow during recovery is as follows:

1. Start the new instance of Harbor.
2. Create a registry endpoint of the Harbor backup instance, with its content corresponding to the registry endpoint created in Step (2) of the configuration flow during backup in this section.

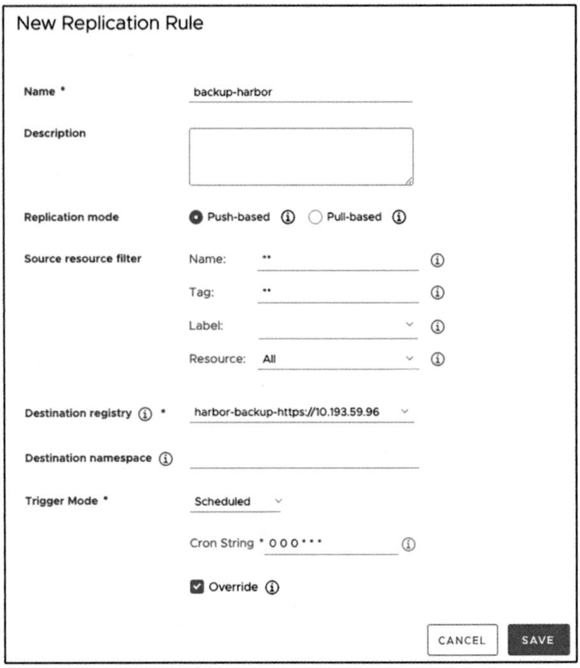

Fig. 7.5 Create a backup rule in New Replication Rule dialog box

3. Create a recovery (replication) rule. As shown in Fig. 7.6, enter a policy name in **Name**; select **Pull-based** for **Replication mode**; select the Harbor backup node as **Source Registry**; leave **Destination Namespace** blank so that the namespace of images can be consistent with the backup node; select a mode for **Trigger Mode** based on the requirement of recovery.

It should be pointed out that this method has its limitations. Because remote replication in Harbor only backs up artifacts such as images and Helm Charts, the users' permissions and labels in a project are not replicated to the backup instance. Therefore, during the recovery, only artifact data is replicated and in contrast data such as user permission is not restored. The administrator still needs to manually restore the permissions of every project. If an external authentication service (such as LDAP) is used, the authentication of the recovered Harbor instance may still work. This is a simple backup approach, which replicates images that are the most important to the user and have the largest amount of data. It helpful in environments which the user permission model (such as a production environment) is simple.

7.2 Upgrading Harbor Version

Harbor supports only the current version and the latest two minor versions of the current version. For example, after Harbor 2.0 is released, Harbor supports only three versions: 2.0, 1.10 and 1.9. There is no support of 1.8 and versions earlier than 1.8. If

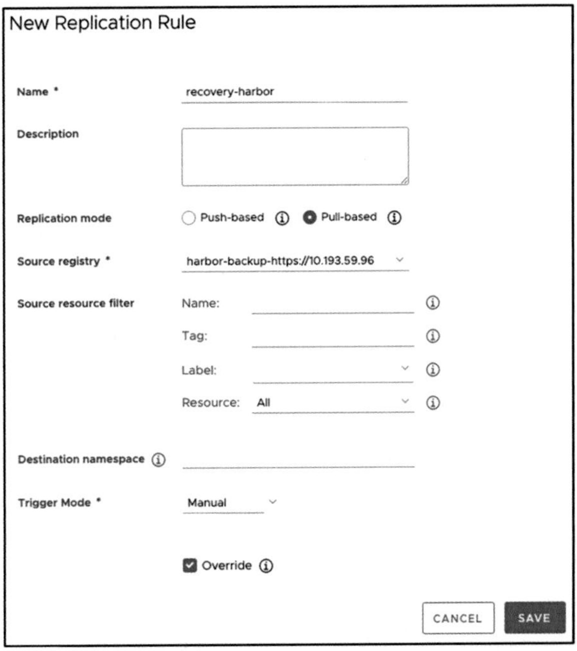

Fig. 7.6 Create a recovery rule in New Replication Rule dialog box

you continue to use Harbor versions that are no longer supported, the system may be at risk because vulnerabilities or defects in these versions cannot be repaired by official patches. Therefore, you should update Harbor to a supported version timely. Because upgrading version may incur errors due to misoperation, this section describes the upgrade approach of Harbor from the aspects such as Harbor architecture, implementation details and historical background.

7.2.1 Data Migration

Before upgrading a Harbor service, you need to migrate its data to adapt to the new version. Data of the following two types needs to be migrated: database schema and configuration file data.

- The database schema is the structure of tables in the database. Each time when a new version is released, new functions and the refactoring of old functions and codes lead to the change of the database schema. Therefore, the database schema must be updated during each upgrade.
- Configuration file data, as the name suggests, refers to the configuration file of Harbor components. When some new functions or new components appear, their parameters must be added to the configuration file. The configuration file will also be updated when old functions and components are refactored or discarded.

If data migration is not performed during upgrade, the data will be incompatible with the new version, thereby causing problems. Data migration is a high-risk operation. When any problem occurs during the operation, severe consequences such as data loss will occur. Therefore, you must first back up the data by following the steps in Sect. 7.1.

The following section describes the data migration. You only need to pay attention to the configuration file instead of database migration because the database schema is automatically upgraded every time when the instance is started. The principle is as follows: Harbor calls the third-party library "golang-migrate" to check the version of the current database schema every time when it is started. If the version of the Harbor instance is later than that of the current database, the database is automatically upgraded. The upgrade of the configuration file requires the manual execution of the command line toolkit. This toolkit is released with Harbor and is included in the "goharbor/prepare:v2.0.0" image. You can find it in the offline installation package of Harbor or obtain it from Docker Hub. The command is as follows:

```
$ docker pull goharbor/prepare:v2.0.0
```

Harbor 2.0 supports data migration from 1.9.*x* or 1.10.*x*. To upgrade Harbor 1.9 to Harbor 2.0, execute the following migration command:

```
$ docker run -v /:/hostfs goharbor/prepare:v2.0.0 migrate --input
/home/harbor/upgrade/harbor-19.yml --output /home/harbor/
upgrade/harbor-20.yml --target 2.0.0
```

In the command, **-v /:/hostfs** is used to mount the root directory **/** of the host to the **/hostfs** directory in the container. The command is executed in the container and files are stored on the host. The mounting allows the files on the host can be accessed in the container. Note: The path of files on the host cannot contain any soft link. Otherwise, the correct path cannot be found in the container.

The **migrate** command contains three parameters.

- **--input** (abbreviated as **-i**): indicates the absolute path of the input file, namely the original configuration file to be upgraded.
- **--output** (abbreviated as **-o**): indicates the absolute path of the output file, namely the configuration file after upgrade. This parameter is optional. If the default value is used, the upgrade file is written back to the input file.
- **--target** (abbreviated as **-t**): indicates the target version, namely the version to which you want to upgrade. This parameter is optional. If the default value is used, the version is the latest supported version.

Therefore, the above command is used to upgrade the configuration file **/home/harbor/upgrade/harbor-19.yml** from Harbor 1.9 to 2.0 and save it to the directory **/**

home/harbor/upgrade/harbor-20.yml. If the abbreviations and default values are used, the command can be simplified as follows:

```
$ docker run -v /:/hostfs goharbor/prepare:v2.0.0 migrate -i /
home/harbor/upgrade/harbor.yml
```

If the data migration is successful, the results are as follows:

```
migrating to version 1.10.0
migrating to version 2.0.0
Written new values to /home/harbor/upgrade/harbor-20.yml
```

The above shows how to upgrade Harbor 1.9 and Harbor 1.10 to version 2.0. If you want to upgrade an earlier version of Harbor to 2.0, you need to upgrade to version 1.9 or 1.10 first and then upgrade it to version 2.0.

Many differences exist in the upgrade procedure between versions earlier than Harbor 2.0 and versions later than Harbor 2.0. The evolution of Harbor went through many changes in the database, configuration file format and migration tool. As shown in Fig. 7.7, the changes introduced in Harbor versions 1.5, 1.7, 1.8 and 2.0 affect the data migration behavior.

The following lists the changes and their impacts:

- **1.5**: In versions earlier than 1.5, Harbor used MySQL as the underlying database and later switched to PostgreSQL. If you use the internal database component of Harbor, the data migration tool automatically processes database upgrades and changes. However, if you use the external MySQL service, you need to manually migrate the data.
- **1.7**: In versions earlier than 1.7, Harbor used the Alembic library of Python as the database migration tool and later switched to golang-migrate. Therefore, versions earlier than 1.7 must first be migrated using the migration tool. In version 1.7 and subsequent versions, only configuration data needs to be migrated and no manual migration on the database is needed. The data migration of the database is completed automatically when the instance is started.
- **1.8**: In this version, the configuration file format had been changed. Previously, the Microsoft INI configuration file format was used. Since version 1.8, the format has been changed to yaml. The migration of previous versions'

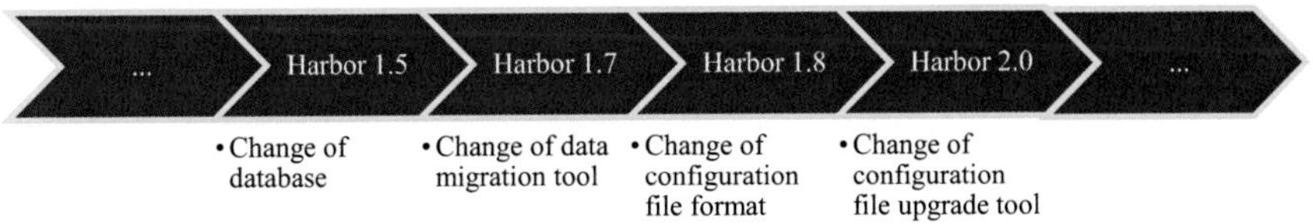

Fig. 7.7 Change history of Harbor

configuration file was to modify the file directly. However, in version 1.8, the format of the input file differs from that of the output file. Therefore, the input file and the output file must both be specified for the migration of the configuration file.

- **2.0**: In this version, Harbor goes through major upgrade and refactoring. It only supports the upgrade from versions 1.9.*x* and 1.10.*x*. In addition, the previous migration tool is implemented by Python 2.7. However, Python 2.7 has been sunset since 2020. As a result, the migration tool was abandoned in Harbor 2.0. The data migration functions of versions 1.9 and 1.10 are migrated to the prepare toolkit. From Harbor 2.0 on, the upgrade tool of Harbor has been changed. If you want to upgrade an early version of Harbor to 2.0, you need to first upgrade the version to 1.9 or 1.10.

A secure upgrade path is shown Fig. 7.8.

The upgrade commands corresponding to the numbers in Fig. 7.8 are as follows.

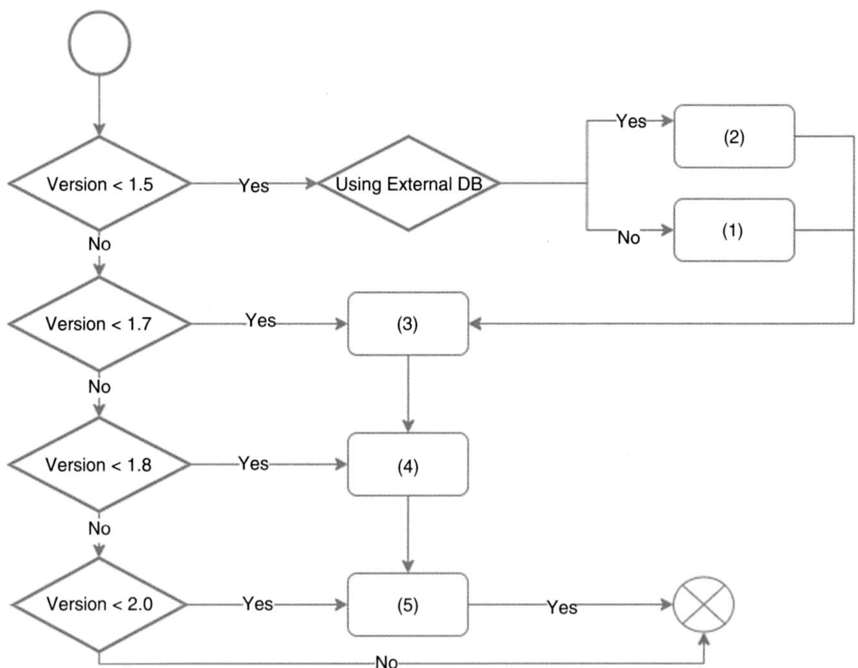

Fig. 7.8 The upgrade path of different versions of Harbor

1. Upgrade data to version 1.6.

```
    $ docker run -it --rm -e DB_USR=root -e DB_PWD=<database
password> -v <database folder path>:/var/lib/mysql -v
<configuration file address>:/harbor-migration/harbor-cfg/
harbor.cfg goharbor/harbor-migrator:1.6 up
   $ docker run -it --rm -e DB_USR=root -v <notary database path> /
:/var/lib/mysql -v <harbor database path>:/var/lib/postgresql/
data goharbor/harbor-migrator:1.6 --db up
    $ docker run -it --rm -v <clair database path>:/clair-db -v
<harbor database path>:/var/lib/postgresql/data goharbor/
harbor-migrator:1.6 --db up
```

2. Refer to the implementation of Harbor to upgrade and migrate external databases.
3. Upgrade the configuration file to version 1.8.

```
$ docker run -it --rm -v <path of harbor.cfg>:/harbor-migration/
harbor-cfg/harbor.cfg -v <path of harbor.yml>:/harbor-
migration/ harbor-cfg-out/harbor.yml goharbor/harbor-
migrator:1.8 --cfg up
```

4. Upgrade the configuration file to version 1.10.

```
$ docker run -it --rm -v <path of harbor.yml>:/harbor-migration/
harbor-cfg/harbor.yml goharbor/harbor-migrator:1.10 --cfg up
```

5. Upgrade the configuration file to version 2.0.

```
$ docker run -v /:/hostfs goharbor/prepare:v2.0.0 migrate -i
<path of harbor.yml>
```

7.2.2 Upgrading Harbor

This section describes how to upgrade Harbor. At present, Harbor supports upgrading versions 1.9 and 1.10 to version 2.0. For earlier versions, refer to Sect. 7.2.1 to migrate data to version 1.9 or 1.10 first. This section only describes how to migrate Harbor 1.9 and 1.10 to Harbor 2.0.

1. If Harbor is still running, first stop Harbor.

```
$ cd harbor
$ docker-compose down
```

2. Back up the current **Harbor** folder (optional).

```
$ mv harbor /my_backup_dir/harbor
```

3. Back up the data.

```
$ cp -r /data/database /my_backup_dir/
```

4. Obtain the latest installation package of Harbor from **github.com/goharbor/harbor/releases**.
5. Migrate the data (if the current Harbor version is earlier than 1.9, see Sect. 7.2.1 to migrate data).

```
$ docker run -v /:/hostfs goharbor/prepare:v2.0.0 migrate -i
<path of harbor.yml>
```

6. Use the new configuration file to install Harbor.

```
$ cd <decompressed folder of new Harbor version>
# Install Harbor based on actual requirements.
$ ./install.sh --with-notary -with-clair -with-chartmuseum
```

Now the upgrade of Harbor is completed. You may wonder: The patch version upgrade (for example, upgrade from version 1.7.1 to 1.7.2) of Harbor is not mentioned in this document. In fact, the development of Harbor follows a principle: The upgrade of a patch version does not involve the change of the configuration file and database. Therefore, we do not need to consider this circumstance.

If the above upgrade is successful, you can see that Harbor starts properly and provides services. If Harbor does not start properly, you can perform system troubleshooting. For details, see Sect. 7.3.

7.3 System Troubleshooting

Harbor has many components which makes it hard to identify errors. Based on the architecture of Harbor, this section provides the basic idea of troubleshooting.

The source of an error can be determined by observation. An error can be resolved or bypassed. First, observe the operational status of services and then analyze the logs. To locate the source of an error, you need to understand the communication relationship between Harbor components so that you can trace the error along the data flow. Fig. 7.9 shows the data flow of Harbor.

It can be seen from Fig. 7.9 that all user requests go through the Proxy first. After the Proxy intercepts the requests, it redirects the requests to the Core component, the Notary component or the Portal component. When the Core component processes different API requests, invocations between different components and the accessing to the database and Redis are also involved.

Harbor components expose their status through logs and the health API. When the command **docker-compose** is used to run Harbor, logs are collected and processed by the harbor-log component. The harbor-log component first adds a consistent prefix to the log content collected by each component. The prefix includes the collection time, the IP address of the source component, the process name and the ID of the source component. Then harbor-log component writes the logs to the file system with the process name of the component as the file name. If Harbor is deployed on Kubernetes, you can use a command like **kubectl logs** to view the logs of the containers of the corresponding components.

Table 7.1 lists log files of Harbor components.

The following takes a log of the Core component as an example to explain the meaning of each field.

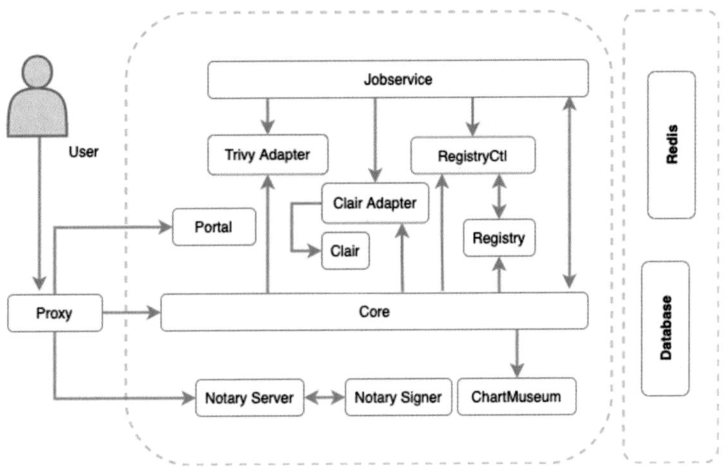

Fig. 7.9 Data flow of Harbor

Table 7.1 Log files of Harbor components

Component Name	Log File Name	Component Name	Log File Name
ChartMuseum	chartmuseum.log	Portal	portal.log
ClairAdapter	clair-adapter.log	Harbor-DB	postgresql.log
Clair	clair.log	Proxy	proxy.log
Core	core.log	Redis	redis.log
JobService	jobservice.log	RegistryCtl	registryctl.log
NotaryServer	notary-server.log	Registry	registry.log
NotarySigner	notary-signer.log	TrivyAdapter	trivy-adapter.log

Table 7.2 Healthcheck function of Harbor components

Component Name	Health Check Method	Component Name	Health Check Method
ChartMuseum	API: /health	Portal	API: /
ClairAdapter	API: /probe/healthy	Harbor-DB	Script: /docker-entrypoint.sh
Clair	API: /health	Proxy	API: /
Core	API: /api/v2.0/ping	Redis	Script: docker-healthcheck
JobService	API: /api/v1/stats	RegistryCtl	API: /api/health
NotaryServer	None	Registry	API: /
NotarySigner	None	TrivyAdapter	API: /probe/healthy

```
Apr 26 08:55:37 172.18.0.1 core[5166]: 2020-04-26T08:55:37Z
[INFO] [/replication/adapter/harbor/adaper.go:31]: the factory
for adapter harbor registered
```

In the prefix added by the harbor-log component: the first field **Apr 26 08:55:37** indicates the time when the harbor-log component collects the log; the second field **172.18.0.1** indicates the IP address of the Core component in the container network; the third field **core[5166]** indicates that the process name is **core** and the process ID is **5166**.

In the log generated by the Core component (the log structures of other core components of Harbor are similar): the first field **2020-04-26T08:55:37Z** indicates the timestamp when the log is generated; the second field **[INFO]** indicates the log level; the third field **[/replication/adapter/harbor/adaper.go:31]** indicates the source file name and the row number in the source file; the fourth field **the factory for adapter harbor registered** indicates the specific content of the log.

In addition to core components, see relevant documents for the log formats of third-party components referenced by Harbor, such as Redis, Postgres and Nginx.

Most Harbor components provide the health check function. Table 7.2 describes these functions.

The health status is mainly tested through the health status APIs of components or some specific scripts. If the test results of these test scripts or APIs are healthy, the

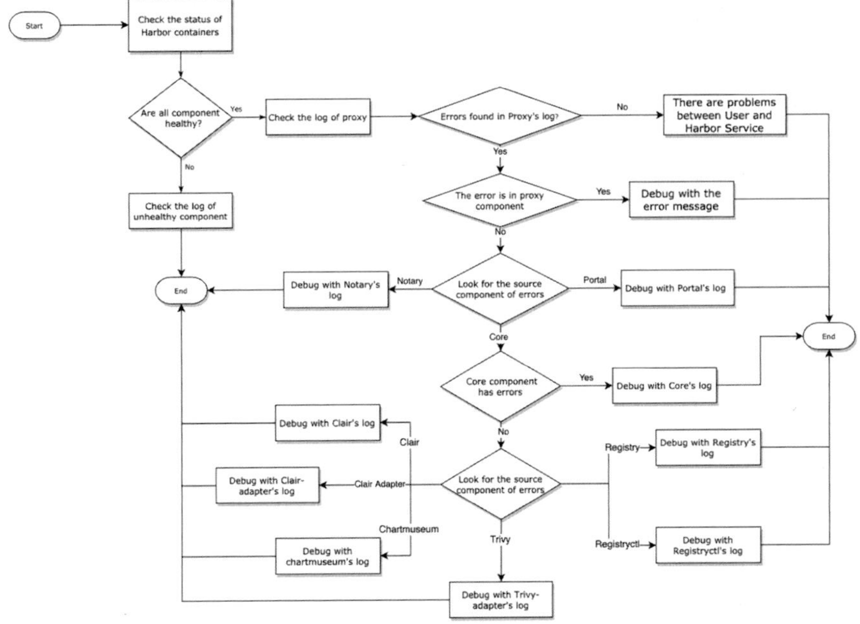

Fig. 7.10 Workflow to identify the error source

container status is considered "healthy". Otherwise, the container status is "unhealthy".

After the above background is introduced, the following flow describes how to locate the source of an error through observation. Figure 7.10 shows the flowchart of locating the source components of an error.

Based on the flowchart, the steps for tracing the error source of Harbor are as follows.

1. Check whether the container status on the Harbor host is healthy.

```
$ docker ps
```

2. If a container is found to be unhealthy or constantly restarting, the container is probably the source of the error. After the tracing of the error source ends, solve the problem based on the log.
3. If all components are healthy, continue to view the log of the upstream Proxy component.
4. If the log of the Proxy component is normal and no user access log exists, the network between the user and Harbor probably fails. In this case, the tracing of the error source in Harbor ends. Next, check the network problem.

5. If an error message is found in the log of the Proxy component and the error source is the Proxy component, the tracing of the error source ends. Next, troubleshoot the proxy problem based on the error in the log.
6. If the error information or the error status code in the log of the Proxy component originates from other components (such as the Core component, the Notary component or the Portal component), the root source of the error is the component which generated the error.
7. If the error in the log of the Proxy component originates from the Portal component, troubleshoot the Portal component. The tracing of the error source in Harbor ends.
8. If the error in the log of the Proxy component originates from Notary, troubleshoot the Notary component. The tracing of the error source in Harbor ends.
9. If the error in the log of the Proxy component originates from Core, continue to analyze the log of the Core component to proceed with the next step of the tracing.
10. If the error in the log of the Core component is caused by the component itself, troubleshoot the Core component. The tracing of the error source in Harbor ends.
11. If the error in the log of the Core component originates from other components, continue to troubleshoot upstream components.
12. If the error in the log of the Proxy component originates from Registry, troubleshoot the Registry component. The tracing of the error source in Harbor ends.
13. If the error in the log of the Proxy component originates from Clair, troubleshoot the Clair component. The tracing of the error source in Harbor ends.
14. If the error in the log of the Proxy component originates from Trivy, troubleshoot the Trivy component. The tracing of the error source in Harbor ends.
15. If the error in the log of the Proxy component originates from ChartMuseum, troubleshoot the ChartMuseum component. The tracing of the error source in Harbor ends.
16. If the error involves functions of JobService, for example, garbage collection, content replication and vulnerability scanning, find the log entry of the corresponding task on the page for triggering the task and perform troubleshooting based on the log.

Through the above steps, you can locate the error source of Harbor. In addition to the error of Harbor, many tasks are executed in an asynchronous fashion. Both garbage collection and image replication trigger asynchronous tasks. The errors of asynchronous tasks can be found from the task logs in the task history (shown in Fig. 7.11).

Through the above analysis of the error source , we can determine the accurate source of the error. Next, we will enter the troubleshooting phase. Generally, troubleshooting is performed from the following aspects:

1. Network: Repair network devices, the network configuration and the DNS configuration.

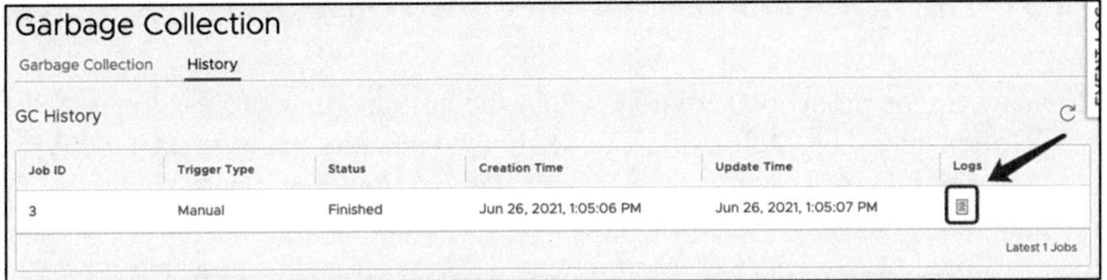

Fig. 7.11 Task logs in the task history (garbage collection and remte replication)

2. Environment: Upgrade the software version of the operating environment, install the software on which Harbor relies, modify the file permissions on which Harbor runtime depends and make sure dependent files such as certificates are correct.
3. Configuration: Upgrade the configuration file to the correct version, modify the wrong configuration and make sure that the configuration file takes effect (you need to manually run the scripts such as prepare and install).
4. Data: Solve the issue of compatibility between database, Redis, third-party storage and Harbor and make sure that the version of the data model matches to the required version of Harbor.
5. Hardware: Replace damaged devices such as CPU, hard disk and memory.

Problems that occur in the production environment vary greatly. It is difficult to have a standard troubleshooting method to cover all errors. Although some errors are exposed in Harbor, but their sources may be other services.

Through the above troubleshooting directions, we can find out some problems. However, if you meet some unsolvable problems or bugs, go to the GitHub repository of Harbor to submit the issues (problems) and provide the community with error description to seek for help. You are advised to also attach logs of relevant components. By default, the log file is in the **/var/log/harbor** directory. Use the following command to package all logs, and then upload **harbor.log.tar.gz** to the issue content or directly copy and paste the log content to the issue, so that community members can help locate the root cause of the problem. Note: Because GitHub is accessible to all users, the sensitive information in the log should be removed before the log is uploaded.

```
$ tar -zxvf harbor.log.tar.gz /var/log/harbor
```

7.4 Common Problems

This section lists several common problems and the related solutions.

7.4.1 The Configuration File Does Not Take Effect

No matter in the production environment or the test environment, the configuration file is often modified. After stopping Harbor containers, many users modify the configuration file of Harbor and then restart Harbor. However, the users find that the configuration remains unchanged. This is because the configuration file of Harbor does not directly take effect after it is modified. Many Harbor components have their own configuration files and environment variables. Users need to run the prepare command to render the configuration files on which Harbor components depend. After Harbor's configuration file is modified, run the following command to update the configuration of all components:

```
$ docker-compose down -v
$ ./prepare --with-notary --with-clair --with-trivy --with-
chartmuseum
$ docker-compose up -d
```

In this way, the configuration can take effect each time after a user modifies the configuration file of Harbor.

7.4.2 Harbor Cannot Be Started After Docker Is Restarted

After Harbor is deployed in the production environment, the Docker daemon on the Harbor host could be restarted from time to time. After the restart of Docker daemon, Harbor often fails to run and the containers of some components fall into a status of infinite restarting.

This is because dependencies exist between containers of Harbor components and the dependencies are defined in the file **docker-compose.yml**. The log container listens to port 1514 of the local IP address 127.0.0.1 to receive and summarize logs of other containers. Other containers send logs to the standard output and then Docker daemon forwards the logs to the log container. However, the launching sequence of the log container and the Docker daemon is random. If the log container is started first, the log container will find that the Docker daemon does not exist. Therefore, Harbor fails to be started. If other containers cannot connect to the log container, Harbor also fails to be started.

The root cause of this problem is that two interdependent processes cannot guarantee the start sequence because the start sequence is determined by scheduling of the operating system. Therefore, lifecycle management of the Docker daemon is beyond the capabilities of Harbor and cannot be resolved by Harbor itself. However, we can define the start sequence of services at the operating system level. In mainstream Linux systems such as Ubuntu and CentOS, we can use the systemd configuration to define the sequence of launching services. A sample configuration file is as follows and it can be saved to the systemd startup configuration folder, for example, the **/lib/systemd/system** directory in Ubuntu 18.04.

```
[Unit]
Description=Harbor
After=docker.service systemd-networkd.service systemd-
resolved.service
Requires=docker.service

[Service]
Type=simple
Restart=on-failure
RestartSec=5
ExecStart=/usr/local/bin/docker-compose -f <path of the docker-
compose.yml file> up
ExecStop=/usr/local/bin/docker-compose -f <path of the docker-
compose.yml file> down

[Install]
WantedBy=multi-user.target
```

7.4.3 A Signed Image Cannot Be Deleted When the Secret Key Is Lost

The image signature function of Harbor is an important function related to image security. It is provided by Notary. A signed image can be deleted only after it is verified and authorized by Notary. If the user loses the secret key of Notary, the signed image cannot be deleted. In this case, the administrator can bypass the restriction and delete the signed image. The steps are as follows.

1. Stop Harbor.

```
$ docker-compose down -v
```

2. Run the prepare script to generate a docker-compose file which does not contain the Notary service.

```
$ ./prepare --with-clair --with-chartmuseum --with-trivy
```

3. Restart Harbor.

```
$ docker-compose up -d
```

4. In this case, Harbor disables the Notary component. You can delete the signed image in Harbor.
5. Restore the previous configuration.

```
    $ docker-compose down -v
    $ ./prepare --with-clair --with-chartmuseum --with-trivy --
with-notary
    $ docker-compose up -d
```

7.4.4 The Password of the System Administrator Is Lost

The user admin is a system administrator of Harbor who has many privileges. If the password of admin is lost, the password can be reset through the following steps.

1. Connect the Harbor database and select the Harbor database.

```
$ docker exec -it harbor-db
$ psql -U postgres
postgres=# \c registry;
```

2. Execute the following command to reset the admin account:

```
registry=# select * from harbor_user update harbor_user set
salt='', password='' where user_id = 1;
```

3. Log in to Harbor. The system administrator admin can use the initial password configured in **harbor.yml** for login.

Note: After Harbor is restarted, change the default password of admin as soon as possible.

Chapter 8
Harbor APIs

Previous chapters introduce various management functions of Harbor. Most of the functions can be implemented through application programming interfaces (APIs). This chapter describes the main functions, authentication modes and usage of Harbor APIs and introduces how to interact with Harbor through APIs. Readers can develop various management tools or integrate Harbor into other systems on this basis. Harbor APIs play an important role in the practice of development, operation, and maintenance, which is reflected in the following aspects:

- Other systems (such as the CI/CD system) trigger Harbor functions by calling APIs, which improves the interoperability between systems and the automation capability.
- Other systems (such as the monitoring system) can obtain data of Harbor APIs and integrate, save or display the data.
- Users can create a script or use a command line tool to call Harbor APIs for interactive operations.

8.1 Overview of APIs

One of the criteria for measuring the maturity of software is whether the software provides rich and perfect APIs and whether the software can be easily and flexibly integrated with other systems to meet the requirements of various scenarios. Harbor provides comprehensive RESTful APIs to facilitate custom development such as system integration and process automation. Harbor implements core management functions of users, projects, scanning, replication and artifacts. In addition, Harbor leverages other open source components (such as Docker Distribution) to complete some of its functions. The APIs of these components are exposed to users through Harbor. The APIs provided by Harbor are divided into two categories: the core management APIs and the registry APIs. Figure 8.1 shows the composition of

H. Zhang, Y. Wang, *The Authoritative Guide on Harbor*,
https://doi.org/10.1007/978-981-19-2727-0_8

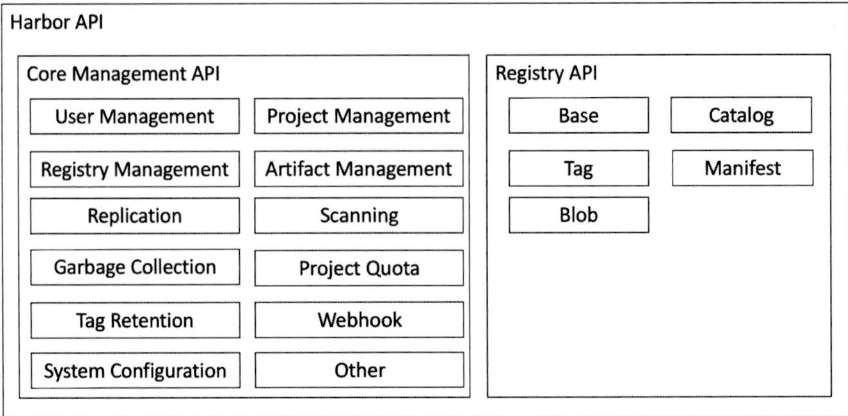

Fig. 8.1 Categories of Harbor's API

Harbor's APIs. The core management APIs are all implemented by Harbor itself. The functions of the registry APIs are mainly provided by the Docker Distribution and the registry API calls from users are directly passed through from Harbor to Docker Distribution.

8.1.1 Overview of the Core Management APIs

The core management APIs provide the programming interfaces for the core management functions of Harbor. The functions are categorized as follows.

- User management (**/users** and **/usergroups**): covers management functions related to users and user groups, including creating, modifying, searching for and deleting of users and user groups.
- Project management (**/projects**): covers management functions related to projects, including creating, modifying, deleting and searching for projects, obtaining project summary and managing project meta data.
- Repository management (**/projects/{project_name}/repositories**): covers the management functions related to repositories, including modifying, searching for and deleting repositories.
- Artifact management (**/projects/{project_name}/repositories/{repository_name}/artifacts**): covers the management functions related to artifacts, including searching for, deleting, and adding artifacts, removing labels, obtaining additional attributes and managing tags.
- Remote replication (**/replication** and **/registries**): covers the functions related to remote replication, including managing registry service instances, managing and executing remote replication policies.

Table 8.1 Harbor document directories on GitHub

Version	Branch	Document Location
2.0	release-2.0.0	/api/v2.0
1.10	release-1.10.0	/api/harbor
1.9 and earlier versions	release-1.9.0	/docs/swagger.yaml

- Scanning (**/scanners**, **/projects/{project_id}/scanner** and **/projects/{project_name}/ repositories/{repository_name}/artifacts/{reference}/scan**): covers functions related to scanning, including managing scanners, triggering scanning and viewing scanning results.
- Garbage collection (**/system/gc**): covers functions related to garbage collection, including triggering garbage collection and viewing execution results.
- Project quota (**/quotas**): covers functions related to project quotas, including setting, changing and viewing project quotas.
- Tag retention (**/retentions**): covers functions related to artifact retention policies, including creating, modifying, deleting and executing artifact retention policies.
- Immutable artifact management (**/projects/{project_id}/immutabletagrules**): covers functions related to immutable artifact policies in projects, including creating, modifying, deleting and executing immutable artifact policies.
- Webhook (**/projects/{project_id}/webhook**): covers functions related to Webhooks, including creating, modifying and deleting Webhooks.
- System configuration (**/configurations** and **/systeminfo**): covers functions related to system configuration and basic information, including viewing and modifying system configuration.

The core management APIs comply with the OpenAPI 2.0 specification. Refer to the Swagger document in the Harbor official repository on GitHub for details of the core management APIs. To view the API document of a specific version, you need to switch to the corresponding code branch first. Table 8.1 lists the document locations of a few branches.

You can also directly use the API Explorer to view and invoke APIs from a web page. For details, see Sect. 8.2.13.

8.1.1.1 API Version

Harbor 2.0 introduces the API version to better support the evolution of subsequent APIs. If code changes cannot guarantee forward compatibility, the APIs will be included into APIs of later versions. In a specific release, Harbor only maintains APIs of one version. Therefore, you need to pay attention to whether the API version has changed after an upgrade. You can send a request "GET /api/version" to obtain the API version supported by a Harbor instance.

```
$ curl https://demo.goharbor.io/api/version
```

The following result is returned:


```
{"version":"v2.0"}
```


You can see that the current version of Harbor API is v2.0. In this case, all core management APIs are prefixed with /api/v2.0.

8.1.1.2 Authentication Mode

The core management APIs adopt HTTP for basic authentication (Basic Auth). During basic authentication, the HTTP header of a request contains the authorization field in the form of "authorization: Basic <credential>". The credential is composed of a user and a password which are encoded by Base64.

In the following example, cURL is used to call the project list API by using the user name and password of Harbor system administrator admin. The code is as follows:

```
$ curl -u admin:xxxxx https://demo.goharbor.io/api/v2.0/projects
```

The following result is returned:


```
[
 {
  "project_id": 1,
  "owner_id": 1,
  "name": "library",
  "creation_time": "2020-04-30T20:46:40.359337Z",
  "update_time": "2020-04-30T20:46:40.359337Z",
  "deleted": false,
  "owner_name": "",
  "current_user_role_id": 1,
  "current_user_role_ids": [
   1
  ],
  "repo_count": 0,
  "chart_count": 0,
  "metadata": {
   "public": "true"
  },
```


(continued)

```
    "cve_whitelist": {
      "id": 0,
      "project_id": 0,
      "items": null,
      "creation_time": "0001-01-01T00:00:00Z",
      "update_time": "0001-01-01T00:00:00Z"
    }
  }
]
```


8.1.1.3 Error Format

An API call may fail due to an error of the client or the server. In this case, a standard API error is returned to explain the cause.

The format of the returned API error is an array. Each element in the array indicates a specific error message. Each error message is composed of the HTTP response status code and the error content. The error content contains two fields: the error code and the error information. For example, when the Repository API is invoked to obtain a Repository that does not exist, the request is as follows:

```
$ curl -u admin:xxxxx https://demo.goharbor.io/api/v2.0/
projects/library/repositories/hello-world
```

The following result is returned:

```
HTTP/1.1 404 Not Found
Server:nginx
Date: Sun, 03 May 2020 04:02:15 GMT
Content-Type: application/json; charset=utf-8
Content-Length:87
Connection:keep-alive
Set-Cookie:sid=9c31cb12979604d6df71b30536166dde; Path=/;
Secure; HttpOnly
X-Request-Id:544b8371-85f8-42b2-ab0f-7d06e38a681e

{
   "errors": [{
      "code": "NOT_FOUND",
      "message": "repository library/hello-world not found"
   }]
}
```

The status code of the response is 404 and the error content is {“errors”: [{“code”:”NOT_FOUND”, “message”:“repository library/hello-world not found”}]}. The returned error array (errors[]) contains only one element, in which "NOT_FOUND" is the error code and "repository library/hello-world not found" is the error message.

8.1.1.4 Query Keyword “q”

Since Harbor 2.0, some APIs introduce the support of the query keyword "q", providing a general way to filter query results.

The query keyword "q" supports five types of query syntax.

- Exact match: key=value.
- Fuzzy match: key=~value. “~” is added before the value to indicate the fuzzy match.
- Range: key=[min~max]. The inclusive range is specified by the minimum (min) value and the maximum value (max) with a delimiting character “~”. If the maximum value is omitted, i.e. key=[min~], it indicates the range with the value of key greater than or equal to the value of min; if the minimum value is omitted, i.e. key=[~max], it specifies the range with the value of key smaller than or equal to the value of max.
- The set of OR relationship: key={value1 value2 value3}. Query all results which have the value of key equal to any of the given values. Multiple values are delimited by spaces, for example, tag={‘v1’ ‘v2’ ‘v3’}.
- The set of AND relationship: key=(value1 value2 value3). Query all results which contain the values of key matching to all the given values at the same time. Multiple values are delimited by space, for example, label=(‘L1’ ‘L2’ ‘L3’).

The types of a range or a set can be strings (enclosed by single quotation marks or double quotation marks), integers or time (for example, the time format is "2020-04-09 02:36:00").

When an API is called, all query conditions must be placed in the query keyword “q” and are delimited by comma. For example, to query the Repository whose project ID is 1, whose name contains “hello” and whose creation time is not earlier than 2020-04-09 02:36:00, use the following API format:

```
$ curl -u admin:xxxxx -globoff https://demo.goharbor.io/api/
v2.0/projects/library/repositories?q=project_id=1,
name=~hello,creation_time=[2020-04-09%2002:36:00~]
```

8.1.2 Overview of Registry APIs

Docker Distribution is an implementation of the OCI Distribution Specification. Harbor provides basic artifact management functions through Docker Distribution. Therefore, it directly exposes the API of Docker Registry to users. For details of the registry APIs, see the official document of the OCI Distribution Specification.

Harbor provides two authentication modes for the registry APIs: HTTP Basic Auth and Bearer Token.

8.1.2.1 Basic Auth

The way to use HTTP Basic Auth is the same as that of the core management APIs. The API request to retrieve the manifest of an image by using HTTP Basic Auth mode is as follows:

```
$ curl -u admin:xxxxx https://demo.goharbor.io/v2/library/hello-
world/manifests/latest
```

The following result is returned:


```
{
  "schemaVersion": 2,
  "mediaType": "application/vnd.docker.distribution.manifest.
v2+json",
  "config": {
    "mediaType": "application/vnd.docker.container.image.
v1+json",
    "size": 1510,
    "digest": s"sha256:
fce289e99eb9bca977dae136fbe2a82b6b7d4c372474c9235adc174167
5f587e"
  },
  "layers": [
    {
      "mediaType": "application/vnd.docker.image.rootfs.diff.
tar.gzip",
      "size": 977,
      "digest": "sha256:
1b930d010525941c1d56ec53b97bd057a67ae1865eebf042
686d2a2d18271ced"
    }
  ]
}
```

8.1.2.2 Bearer Token Authentication

The bearer token authentication flow is introduced in Sect. 3.1.3. The following section introduces the details of the API authentication. Take the request to retrieve the manifest of an image as an example. The request with no authentication information is as follows:

```
$ curl -i https://demo.goharbor.io/v2/library/hello-world/
manifests/latest
```

The following result is returned:

```
HTTP/1.1 401 Unauthorized
...
Www-Authenticate:Bearer realm="https://demo.goharbor.io/
service/token",service="harbor-registry",scope="repository:
library/hello-world:pull"

{
   "errors": [{
      "code": "UNAUTHORIZED",
      "message": "unauthorized to access repository:library/
hello-world, action:pull:unauthorized to access repository:
library/hello-world, action:pull"
   }]
}
```

The response status code is 401 and the response header "Www-Authenticate" contains the address of the authentication service and the required permission to apply for.

A request to obtain a token is then sent based on the required permission (pull permission in the example).

```
$ curl -u admin:xxxxx https://demo.goharbor.io/service/token?
service=harbor-registry\&scope=repository:library/hello-
world:pull
```

The following result is returned:

```
{
 "token": "eyJ0eX...",
 "access_token": "",
```

(continued)

```
  "expires_in": 1800,
  "issued_at": "2020-08-04T12:52:28Z"
}
```


The request to retrieve the manifest is sent again with the returned token in the request header.

```
$ curl -H "Authorization:Bearer eyJ0eX..." https://demo.goharbor.
io/v2/library/hello-world/manifests/latest
```

The following result is returned:


```
{
  "schemaVersion": 2,
  "mediaType": "application/vnd.docker.distribution.manifest.
v2+json",
  "config": {
    "mediaType": "application/vnd.docker.container.image.
v1+json",
    "size": 1510,
    "digest": "sha256:
fce289e99eb9bca977dae136fbe2a82b6b7d4c372474c
9235adc1741675f587e"
},
  "layers": [
    {
      "mediaType": "application/vnd.docker.image.rootfs.diff.
tar.gzip",
      "size": 977,
      "digest": "sha256:
1b930d010525941c1d56ec53b97bd057a67ae1865eebf0426
86d2a2d18271ced"
    }
  ]
}
```


8.2 Core Management APIs

This section describes how to use the main core management APIs and gives some examples. For more information, see the OpenAPI (Swagger) document of Harbor or get it from the interactive API Explorer.

Table 8.2 APIs for user management

Endpoint	Method Description
/users	GET: obtains information of a registered user. POST: creates a user account.
/users/{user_id}	GET: obtains information of a user. PUT: updates information of a user. DELETE: deletes a user.
/users/{user_id}/password	PUT: updates the password of a user.
/users/{user_id}/sysadmin	PUT: updates the flag to indicate whether the user is a system administrator.
/users/{user_id}/cli_secret	PUT: generates a user's new CLI secret.
/users/search	GET: searches for a user.
/users/current	GET: obtains information of the current user.
/users/current/permission	GET: obtains the permission of the current user.
/ldap/users/search	GET: searches for a user in LDAP.
/ldap/users/import	POST: imports users from LDAP.
/usergroups	GET: obtains information of all user groups. POST: creates a user group.
/usergroups/{group_id}	GET: obtains information of a user group. PUT: updates information of a user group. DELETE: deletes a user group.

8.2.1 User Management APIs

The user management APIs (**/users** and **/usergroups**) cover management functions related to users and user groups, including creating, modifying, deleting, and searching for users and user groups. Table 8.2 lists the APIs.

The request to obtain the information of all existing users in the system is as follows:

```
$ curl -u admin:xxxxx https://demo.goharbor.io/api/v2.0/users
```

The following result is returned:

```
[
 {
  "user_id": 3,
  "username": "zhangsan",
  "email": "zhangsan@example.com",
  "password": "",
  "password_version": "sha256",
```

(continued)

```
    "realname": "San Zhang",
    "comment": "",
    "deleted": false,
    "role_name": "",
    "role_id": 0,
    "sysadmin_flag": false,
    "admin_role_in_auth": false,
    "reset_uuid": "",
    "creation_time": "2020-08-18T08:53:11Z",
    "update_time": "2020-08-18T08:53:11Z"
  }
]
```


8.2.2 Project Management APIs

The project management APIs (**/projects**) cover management functions related to projects, including creating, modifying, searching for and deleting projects, obtaining the summary and members of a project, and deleting and managing project meta data. Table 8.3 lists the APIs.

Table 8.3 APIs for project management

Endpoint	Method Description
`/projects`	GET: lists project information that meets the conditions. POST: creates a project. HEAD: checks whether a project exists.
`/projects/{project_id}`	GET: obtains details of a project. PUT: updates information of a project. DELETE: deletes a project.
`/projects/{project_id}/metadatas`	GET: obtains meta data of a project. POST: add meta data for a project.
`/projects/{project_id}/metadatas/{meta_name}`	GET: obtains the specified meta data of a project. PUT: updates the specified meta data of a project. DELETE: deletes the specified meta data of a project.
`/projects/{project_id}/members`	GET: obtains members of a project. POST: adds members for a project.
`/projects/{project_id}/members/{mid}`	GET: obtains the information of a member in a project. PUT: updates the information of a member in a project. DELETE: deletes a member from a project.

The request to create a public project named "test" is as follows:

```
$ curl -u admin:xxxxx -H "Content-Type:application/json" -d
'{"project_name":"test","metadata":{"public":"true"}}'
https://demo.goharbor.io/api/v2.0/projects
```

The request to obtain the project whose name contains "test" is as follows:

```
$ curl -u admin:xxx https://demo.goharbor.io/api/v2.0/projects?
q=name=~test
```

The following result is returned:


```
[
 {
  "project_id": 4,
  "owner_id": 1,
  "name": "test",
  "creation_time": "2020-08-18T09:20:30Z",
  "update_time": "2020-08-18T09:20:30Z",
  "deleted": false,
  "owner_name": "",
  "current_user_role_id": 1,
  "current_user_role_ids": [
   1
  ],
  "repo_count": 0,
  "chart_count": 0,
  "metadata": {
   "public": "true"
  },
  "cve_whitelist": {
   "id": 0,
   "project_id": 0,
   "items": null,
   "creation_time": "0001-01-01T00:00:00Z",
   "update_time": "0001-01-01T00:00:00Z"
  }
 }
]
```


The request to obtain the meta data of the project whose ID is 1 is as follows:

```
$ curl -u admin:xxxxx https://demo.goharbor.io/api/v2.0/
projects/1/metadatas
```

The following result is returned:


```
{
 "auto_scan": "false",
 "enable_content_trust": "false",
 "prevent_vul": "true",
 "public": "true",
 "reuse_sys_cve_whitelist": "true",
 "severity": "low"
}
```


The request to delete the project whose ID is 4 is as follows:

```
$ curl -u admin:xxxxx -X DELETE https://demo.goharbor.io/api/
v2.0/projects/4
```

8.2.3 Repository Management APIs

The repository management APIs (**/projects/{project_name}/repositories**) cover management functions related to repositories, including modifying, searching for and deleting repositories. Table 8.4 lists the APIs.

The request to obtain all repositories in the project named "library" is as follows:

```
$ curl -u admin:xxxxx https://demo.goharbor.io/api/v2.0/
projects/library/repositories
```

The following result is returned:

Table 8.4 APIs for repository management

Endpoint	Method Description
/projects/{project_name}/repositories	GET: lists repository information meeting conditions in a project.
/projects/{project_name}/repositories/{repository_name}	GET: obtains information of a repository in a project. PUT: updates information of a repository in a project. DELETE: deletes a repository from a project.

```
[
 {
  "artifact_count": 1,
  "creation_time": "2020-08-18T09:45:26.617Z",
  "id": 1,
  "name": "library/hello-world",
  "project_id": 1,
  "update_time": "2020-08-18T09:45:26.617Z"
 }
]
```

The request to delete the repository named "library/hello-world" is as follows:

```
$ curl -u admin:xxxxx -X DELETE https://demo.goharbor.io/api/
v2.0/projects/library/repositories/hello-world
```

8.2.4 Artifact Management APIs

The artifact management APIs (**/projects/{project_name}/repositories/{repository_name}/artifacts**) cover management functions related to artifacts, including obtaining, searching for, deleting and adding artifacts, managing labels, obtaining additional attributes and managing tags. Table 8.5 lists the APIs. Note: The **reference** parameter in the APIs is the digest value or the tag of an artifact.

The request to obtain all artifacts under the repository “library/hello-world” is as follows:

```
$ curl -u admin:xxxxx https://demo.goharbor.io/api/v2.0/
projects/library/repositories/hello-world/artifacts
```

Table 8.5 APIs for artifact management

Endpoint	Method Description
`/projects/{project_name}/repositories/{repository_name}/artifacts`	GET: lists artifact information meeting conditions under a repository of a project. POST: copies artifacts to a repository of a project.
`/projects/{project_name}/repositories/{repository_name}/artifacts/{reference}`	GET: obtains information of an artifact under a repository of a project. DELETE: deletes an artifact under a repository of a project.
`/projects/{project_name}/repositories/{repository_name}/artifacts/{reference}/labels`	POST: adds a label for an artifact.
`/projects/{project_name}/repositories/{repository_name}/artifacts/{reference}/labels/{label_id}`	DELETE: deletes a label of an artifact.
`/projects/{project_name}/repositories/{repository_name}/artifacts/{reference}/tags`	GET: obtains the tag of an artifact under a repository of a project. POST: adds a tag for an artifact.
`/projects/{project_name}/repositories/{repository_name}/artifacts/{reference}/tags/{tag_name}`	DELETE: deletes a tag of an artifact.

The following result is returned:


```
[
 {
  "addition_links": {
   "build_history": {
    "absolute": false,
    "href": "/api/v2.0/projects/library/repositories/hello-
world/artifacts/sha256:92c7f9c92844bbbb5d0a101b22f7c2a7949e4
0f8ea90c8b3bc396879d95e899a/additions/build_history"
   },
   "vulnerabilities": {
    "absolute": false,
    "href": "/api/v2.0/projects/library/repositories/hello-
world/artifacts/sha256:92c7f9c92844bbbb5d0a101b22f7c2a7949e
40f8ea90c8b3bc396879d95e899a/additions/vulnerabilities"
   }
  },
  "digest": "sha256:92c7f9c92844bbbb5d0a101b22f7c2a7949e40f8ea
90c8b3bc396879d95e899a",
  "extra_attrs": {
   "architecture": "amd64",
   "author": null,
   "created": "2019-01-01T01:29:27.650294696Z",
   "os": "linux"
```


(continued)

```
  },
  "id": 2,
  "labels": null,
  "manifest_media_type": "application/vnd.docker.distribution.
manifest.v2+json",
  "media_type": "application/vnd.docker.container.image.
v1+json",
  "project_id": 1,
  "pull_time": "0001-01-01T00:00:00.000Z",
  "push_time": "2020-08-18T10:11:35.453Z",
  "references": null,
  "repository_id": 2,
  "size": 3011,
  "tags": [
   {
    "artifact_id": 2,
    "id": 2,
    "immutable": false,
    "name": "latest",
    "pull_time": "0001-01-01T00:00:00.000Z",
    "push_time": "2020-08-18T10:11:35.472Z",
    "repository_id": 2,
    "signed": false
   }
  ],
  "type": "IMAGE"
 }
]
```

The request to obtain all tags of the artifact whose digest value is "sha256: 92c7f9c92844bbbb5d0a101b22f7c2a7949e40f8ea90c8b3bc396879d95e899a" under the above repository is as follows:

```
$ curl -u admin:xxxxx https://demo.goharbor.io/api/v2.0/
projects/library/repositories/hello-world/artifacts/sha256:
92c7f9c92844bbbb5d0a101b22f7c2a7949e40f8ea90c8b3bc396
879d95e899a/tags
[
 {
  "artifact_id": 2,
  "id": 2,
  "immutable": false,
  "name": "latest",
  "pull_time": "0001-01-01T00:00:00.000Z",
  "push_time": "2020-08-18T10:11:35.472Z",
  "repository_id": 2,
  "signed": false
 }
]
```

The request to add a tag named "dev" for the artifact whose digest value is "sha256:
92c7f9c92844bbbb5d0a101b22f7c2a7949e40f8ea90c8b3bc396879d95e899as" in the repository is as follows:

```
$ curl -u admin:xxxxx -H "Content-Type:application/json" -d
'{"name":"dev"}' https://demo.goharbor.io/api/v2.0/projects/
library/repositories/hello-world/artifacts/sha256:
92c7f9c92844bbbb5d0a101b22f7c2a7949e40f8ea90c8b3bc3968
79d95e899a/tags
```

8.2.5 Remote Replication APIs

The remote replication APIs (**/replication**) cover functions related to remote replication, including managing and executing remote replication policies. The registry management APIs (**/registries**) are responsible for managing the access endpoints of the remote image or artifact registry service and providing support for functions (e.g., remote replication) that depend on remote repository. Table 8.6 lists the APIs.

The request to obtain all remote replication policies is as follows:

```
$ curl -u admin:xxxxx https://demo.goharbor.io/api/v2.0/
replication/policies
[
 {
  "id": 2,
  "name": "rule01",
  "src_registry": {
   "type": "docker-hub",
   "url": "https://hub.docker.com",
   ...
  },
  "dest_registry": {
   "type": "harbor",
   "url": "http://core:8080",
   ...
  },
  "dest_namespace": "",
  "filters": [
   {
    "type": "name",
    "value": "library/hello-world"
   },
   ...
```

(continued)

```
    ],
    "trigger": {
     "type": "manual",
     ...
     }
    },
    "override": true,
    "enabled": true,
    ...
  }
]
```

Table 8.6 APIs for remote replication

Endpoint	Method Description
`/replication/executions`	GET: lists execution records of remote replication tasks. POST: starts executing a new remote replication task.
`/replication/executions/{id}`	GET: lists execution records of a remote replication task. PUT: stops execution of a remote replication task.
`/replication/executions/{id}/tasks`	GET: obtains the subtask of a remote replication.
`/replication/executions/{id}/tasks/{task_id}/log`	GET: obtains the log of a subtask of a remote replication.
`/replication/policies`	GET: lists remote replication policies. POST: creates a remote replication policy.
`/replication/policies/{id}`	GET: obtains a remote replication policy. PUT: updates a remote replication policy. DELETE: deletes a remote replication policy.
`/replication/adapters`	GET: lists supported remote replication adapters.
`/registries`	GET: lists the destination registry of remote replication. POST: creates a destination registry for remote replication.
`/registries/{id}`	GET: obtains a destination registry. PUT: modifies information of a destination registry. DELETE: deletes a destination registry.
`/registries/{id}/info`	GET: obtains information of a destination registry.

8.2.6 Scanning APIs

Chapter 4 introduces the details of scanning APIs. This section summarizes the purposes of scanning APIs and gives some examples. The scanning APIs (**/scanners**, **/projects/{project_id}/scanner** and **/projects/{project_name} /repositories/{repository_name}/artifacts/{reference}/scan**) cover functions related to scanning, including managing scanners, triggering scanning and viewing scanning logs. Table 8.7 lists the APIs. Note: The **reference** parameter in the APIs is the digest value or the tag of an artifact.

/scanners and **/projects/{project_id}/scanner** manage the system-level and the project-level scanners respectively. The request to obtain a system-level scanner is as follows:

Table 8.7 APIs for scanning

Endpoint	Method Description
`/scanners`	GET: obtains system-level scanners. POST: registers a new system-level scanner.
`/scanners/{registration_id}`	GET: obtains the registration information of a scanner. PUT: updates the registration information of a scanner. DELETE: deletes a scanner. PATCH: sets the default scanner of the system.
`/scanners/{registration_id}/metadata`	GET: obtains the metadata of a scanner.
`/scanners/ping`	POST: tests the configuration of scanners.
`/projects/{project_id}/scanner`	GET: obtains scanners of a project. PUT: updates scanners of a project.
`/projects/{project_id}/scanner/candidates`	GET: obtains candidate scanners of a project.
`/projects/{project_name}/repositories/{repository_name}/artifacts/{reference}/scan`	POST: scans an artifact.
`/projects/{project_name}/repositories/{repository_name}/artifacts/{reference}/scan/{report_id}/log`	GET: obtains the scanning operation log of an artifact.
`/system/scanAll/schedule`	GET: obtains the global scanning plan of the system. PUT: updates the global scanning plan of the system. POST: creates a global scanning plan of the system or manually triggers global scanning.

```
$ curl -u admin:xxxxx https://demo.goharbor.io/api/v2.0/scanners
```

The following result is returned:


```
[
 {
  "uuid": "de8aecb5-a87b-11ea-83ab-0242ac1e0004",
  "name": "Trivy",
  "description": "The Trivy scanner adapter",
  "url": "http://trivy-adapter:8080",
  "disabled": false,
  "is_default": true,
  "auth": "",
  "skip_certVerify": false,
  "use_internal_addr": true,
  "create_time": "2020-08-07T05:00:55.631199Z",
  "update_time": "2020-08-07T05:00:55.631202Z"
 },
 {
  "uuid": "de8b3143-a87b-11ea-83ab-0242ac1e0004",
  "name": "Clair",
  "description": "The Clair scanner adapter",
  "url": "http://clair-adapter:8080",
  "disabled": false,
  "is_default": false,
  "auth": "",
  "skip_certVerify": false,
  "use_internal_addr": true,
  "create_time": "2020-08-07T05:00:55.632944Z",
  "update_time": "2020-08-07T05:00:55.632946Z"
 }
]
```


/Projects/{project_name}/repositories/{repository_name}/artifacts/{reference}/scan is used to trigger scanning. The request to trigger the scanning of artifacts is as follows:

```
$ curl -u admin:xxxxx -X POST https://demo.goharbor.io/api/v2.0/
projects/library/repositories/hello-world/artifacts/sha256:
92c7f9c92844bbbb5d0a101b22f7c2a7949e40f8ea90c8b
3bc396879d95e899a/scan
```

/Projects/{project_name}/repositories/{repository_name}/artifacts/{reference}/scan/{report_id}/log can be used to view the scanning operation log. The request is as follows:

```
$ curl -u admin:xxxxx https://demo.goharbor.io/api/v2.0/
projects/library/repositories/hello-world/artifacts/sha256:
92c7f9c92844bbbb5d0a101b22f7c2a7949e40f8ea90c8b3
bc396879d95e899a/scan/f5981728-9640-4f1d-820e-c366afd3b70a/
log
```

The following result is returned:


```
2020-08-31T12:52:48Z [INFO] [/pkg/scan/job.go:325]:
registration:
2020-08-31T12:52:48Z [INFO] [/pkg/scan/job.go:336]: {
 "uuid": "b18f1069-ebda-11ea-a362-0242ac1c0009",
 "name": "Trivy",
 "description": "The Trivy scanner adapter",
 "url": "http://trivy-adapter:8080",
 "disabled": false,
 "is_default": true,
 "health": "healthy",
 "auth": "",
 "skip_certVerify": false,
 "use_internal_addr": true,
 "adapter": "Trivy",
 "vendor": "Aqua Security",
 "version": "v0.9.2",
 "create_time": "2020-08-30T22:38:30.256269Z",
 "update_time": "2020-08-30T22:38:30.256271Z"
}
2020-08-31T12:52:48Z [INFO] [/pkg/scan/job.go:325]:
scanRequest:
2020-08-31T12:52:48Z [INFO] [/pkg/scan/job.go:336]: {
 "registry": {
  "url": "http://core:8080",
  "authorization": "[HIDDEN]"
 },
 "artifact": {
  "namespace_id": 1,
  "repository": "library/hello-world",
  "tag": "",
  "digest": "sha256:
92c7f9c92844bbbb5d0a101b22f7c2a7949e40f8ea90c8b3bc
396879d95e899a",
  "mime_type": "application/vnd.docker.distribution.manifest.
v2+json"
 }
}
```

Table 8.8 APIs for garbage collection

Endpoint	Method Description
/system/gc	GET: obtains the latest garbage collection report.
/system/gc/{id}	GET: obtains the status of a garbage collection.
/system/gc/{id}/log	GET: obtains the report of a garbage collection.
/system/gc/schedule	POST: creates a plan of a garbage collection task. GET: obtains a plan of a garbage collection task. PUT: updates a plan of a garbage collection task.

8.2.7 Garbage Collection APIs

The garbage collection APIs (**/system/gc**) cover functions related to garbage collection, including triggering garbage collection and viewing execution results. Table 8.8 lists the APIs.

The request to view the garbage collection execution records is as follows:

```
$ curl -u admin:xxxxx https://demo.goharbor.io/api/v2.0/system/
gc
```

The following result is returned:


```
[
 {
  "schedule": {
   "type": "Manual",
   "cron": ""
  },
  "id": 1,
  "job_name": "IMAGE_GC",
  "job_kind": "Generic",
  "job_parameters": "{\"delete_untagged\":false,
\"redis_url_reg\":\"redis://redis:6379/1\"}",
  "job_status": "finished",
  "deleted": false,
  "creation_time": "2020-07-21T07:36:20Z",
  "update_time": "2020-07-21T07:36:23.177984Z"
 }
]
```

Table 8.9 APIs for project quota

Endpoint	Method Description
/quotas	GET: obtains project quotas.
/quotas/{id}	GET: obtains information of a quota. PUT: updates information of a quota.

8.2.8 Project Quota APIs

The project quota APIs (**/quotas**) cover functions related to project quotas, including setting, changing, and viewing project quotas. Table 8.9 lists the APIs.

The request to view all project quotas in the system is as follows:

```
$ curl -u admin:xxxxx https://demo.goharbor.io/api/v2.0/quotas
```

The following result is returned:


```
[
 {
  "id": 1,
  "ref": {
   "id": 1,
   "name": "library",
   "owner_name": "admin"
  },
  "creation_time": "2020-08-08T05:00:53.579175Z",
  "update_time": "2020-08-08T07:36:23.186501Z",
  "hard": {
   "storage": -1
  },
  "used": {
   "storage": 3011
  }
 }
]
```


8.2.9 Tag Retention APIs

The tag retention APIs (**/retentions**) cover functions related to artifact retention policies, including creating, modifying, deleting and executing artifact retention policies. Table 8.10 lists the APIs.

The request to execute the tag retention policy of an artifact is as follows:

Table 8.10 APIs for tag retention

Endpoint	Method Description
`/retentions`	POST: creates a retention policy.
`/retentions/{id}`	GET: obtains a retention policy. PUT: modifies a retention policy.
`/retentions/{id}/executions`	GET: obtains the execution status of a retention policy. POST: triggers the execution of a retention policy.
`/retentions/{id}/executions/{eid}`	PATCH: stops the execution of a retention policy.
`/retentions/{id}/executions/{eid}/tasks`	GET: obtains subtasks of an execution of retention policies.
`/retentions/{id}/executions/{eid}/tasks/{tid}`	GET: obtains the subtask log of the execution of a retention policy.
`/retentions/metadatas`	GET: obtains the metadata of a retention policy.

```
$ curl -u admin:xxxxx -H "Content-Type:application/json" -d
'{"dry_run":false}' https://demo.goharbor.io/api/v2.0/
retentions/2/executions
```

8.2.10 Immutable Artifact APIs

The immutable artifacts are also called immutable tags. The related APIs (**/projects/{project_id}/immutabletagrules**) cover functions related to immutable artifact policies, including creating, modifying, deleting and executing immutable artifact policies (Table 8.11).

Table 8.11 APIs for immutable artifact

Endpoint	Method Description
/projects/{project_id}/immutabletagrules	POST: creates policies of immutable tag under a project. GET: obtains policies of immutable tag under a project.
/projects/{project_id}/immutabletagrules/{id}	PUT: updates immutable tag policies under a project, including enable and disable. DELETE: deletes a policy of immutable tag under a project.

The request to obtain immutable tag policies with 1 as the project ID is as follows:

```
$ curl -u admin:xxxxx -H "accept:application/json" https://demo.
goharbor.io/api/v2.0/projects/1/immutabletagrules
```

The following result is returned:


```
[
 {
  "id": 1,
  "project_id": 1,
  "disabled": false,
  "priority": 0,
  "action": "immutable",
  "template": "immutable_template",
  "tag_selectors": [
   {
    "kind": "doublestar",
    "decoration": "matches",
    "pattern": "**"
   }
  ],
  "scope_selectors": {
   "repository": [
    {
     "kind": "doublestar",
     "decoration": "repoMatches",
     "pattern": "**"
    }
   ]
  }
 }
]
```


8.2.11 Webhook APIs

The Webhook APIs (**/projects/{project_id}/webhook**) cover functions related to Webhooks, including creating, modifying and deleting Webhooks. Table 8.12 lists the APIs.

The request to view all Webhooks with 1 as the project ID is as follows:

```
$ curl -u admin:xxxxx
https://demo.goharbor.io/api/v2.0/projects/1/webhook/policies
[
 {
  "id": 1,
  "name": "hook01",
  "description": "",
  "project_id": 1,
  "targets": [
   {
    "type": "http",
    "address": "https://192.168.0.2",
    "skip_cert_verify": true
   }
  ],
  "event_types": [
   "DELETE_ARTIFACT",
   "PULL_ARTIFACT",
   "PUSH_ARTIFACT",
   "DELETE_CHART",
   "DOWNLOAD_CHART",
   "UPLOAD_CHART",
   "QUOTA_EXCEED",
   "QUOTA_WARNING",
   "REPLICATION",
   "SCANNING_FAILED",
   "SCANNING_COMPLETED"
  ],
  "creator": "admin",
  "creation_time": "2020-08-08T09:18:04.716279Z",
  "update_time": "2020-08-08T09:18:04.716279Z",
  "enabled": true
 }
]
```

Table 8.12 APIs for webhook

Endpoint	Method Description
/projects/{project_id}/webhook/policies	POST: creates Webhook policies under a project. GET: obtains Webhook policies under a project.
/projects/{project_id}/webhook/policies/{id}	GET: obtains a Webhook policy under a project. PUT: modifies a Webhook policy under a project. DELETE: deletes a Webhook policy under a project.
/projects/{project_id}/webhook/policies/test	POST: tests Webhook policies under a project.
/projects/{project_id}/webhook/lasttrigger	GET: obtains information of the Webhook policy triggered recently under a project.
/projects/{project_id}/webhook/jobs	GET: obtains Webhook jobs of a project.
/projects/{project_id}/webhook/events	GET: obtains Webhook event and notification types supported by a project.

Table 8.13 APIs for system service

Endpoint	Method Description
/configurations	GET: obtains system configuration information. PUT: modifies system configuration information.
/systeminfo	GET: obtains system information such as the version and the authentication mode.
/systeminfo/volumes	GET: obtains information such as the system storage space and the remaining space.
/systeminfo/getcert	GET: downloads the default root certificate of the system.

8.2.12 System Service APIs

The system service APIs cover configuration (**/configurations**) and system information (**/systeminfo**). Table 8.13 lists the APIs.

The request to obtain the system configuration is as follows:

```
$ curl -u admin:xxxxx https://demo.goharbor.io/api/v2.0/
configurations
{
 "auth_mode": {
  "value": "db_auth",
  "editable": false
 },
 "count_per_project": {
  "value": -1,
  "editable": true
 },
 "email_from": {
  "value": "admin <sample_admin@mydomain.com>",
  "editable": true
 },
 "email_host": {
  "value": "smtp.mydomain.com",
  "editable": true
 },
 "email_identity": {
  "value": "",
  "editable": true
 },
 "email_insecure": {
  "value": false,
  "editable": true
 },
 "email_port": {
  "value": 25,
  "editable": true
```

(continued)

```
  },
  "email_ssl": {
   "value": false,
   "editable": true
  },
  "email_username": {
   "value": "sample_admin@mydomain.com",
   "editable": true
  },

 ......
}
```

The request to modify the system configuration to enable the self-registration function is as follows:

```
$ curl -u admin:xxxxx -H "Content-Type:application/json" -X PUT -d
'{"self_registration":true}' https://demo.goharbor.io/api/
v2.0/configurations
```

8.2.13 API Explorer

Since Harbor 1.8, Harbor adds in an API Explorer and provides the swagger interface for APIs. A user can directly view and call the core management APIs on web pages (registry APIs are not included in the API Explorer. For details of registry APIs, see Sect. 8.3). This feature facilitates the debugging and troubleshooting of the system.

Log in to Harbor as a user with any permission and click on the **Harbor API v2.0** menu item under **API Explorer** at the bottom of the left navigation bar, as shown in Fig. 8.2.

In the page that is displayed, you can browse the detailed instructions of all the core management APIs. Click on the row of each API in the list shown in Fig. 8.3 to unfold the detailed description of the API, including query parameters, output results and returned values.

You can test APIs directly on the page. During the testing, the current login account is used to call APIs by default. If you need to use another user identity to call APIs, click on **Authorize** in Fig. 8.3 and enter the required user account name and password. You can click to unfold the API that needs to be called, for example, the API "GET /users/search" to search users based on the user name, as shown in Fig. 8.4.

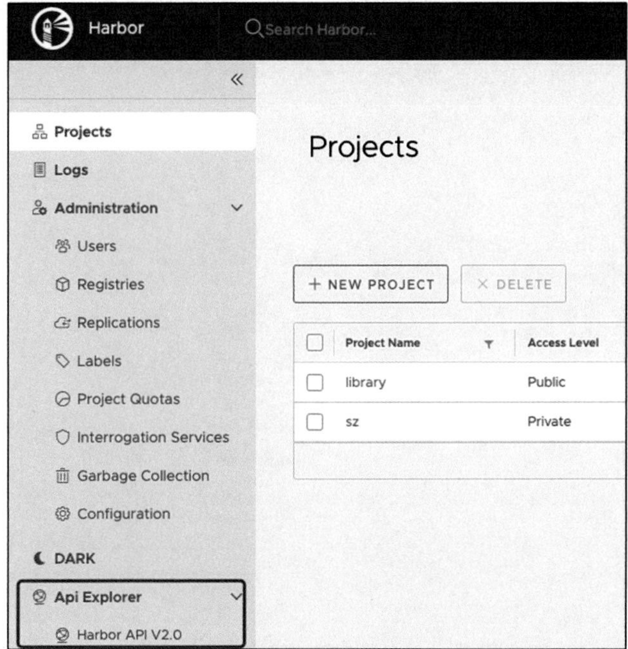

Fig. 8.2 API explorer at the navigation bar

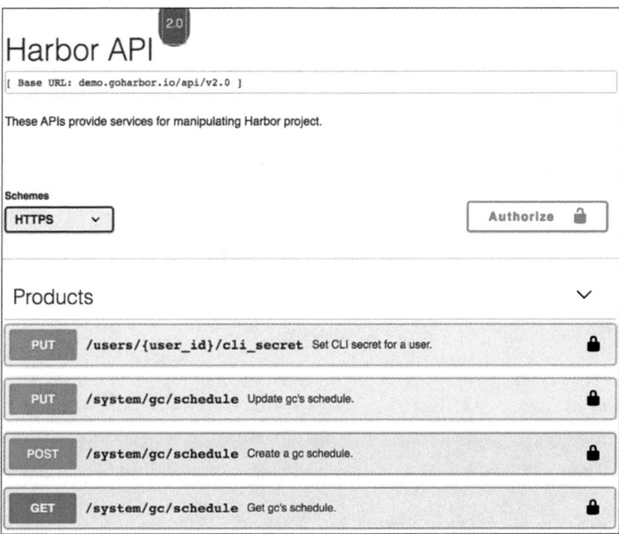

Fig. 8.3 API explorer (Embeded Swagger page)

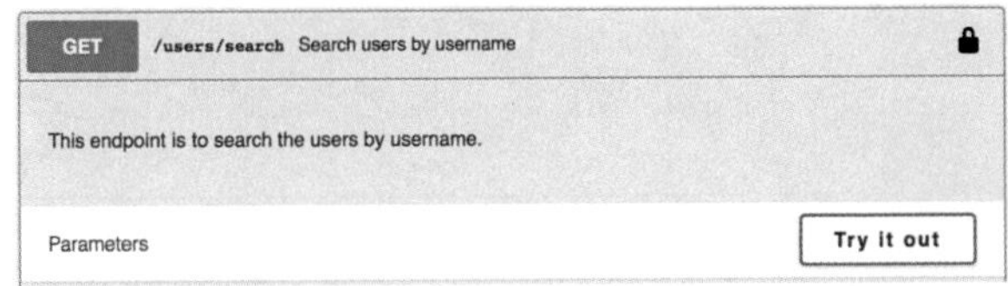

Fig. 8.4 API "GET /user/search"

Fig. 8.5 Parameters to invoke the API "GET /user/search"

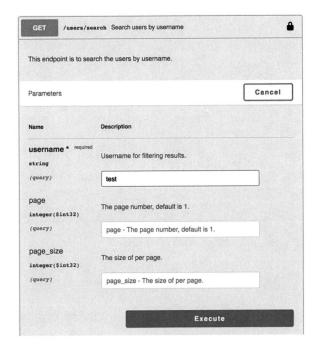

Click on **Try it out** to test the API function. Enter the required query parameter **username** in the **Parameters** column, as shown in Fig. 8.5. Enter the user name **test** to search for, and then click on **Execute** to invoke the API.

Figure 8.6 shows the execution result. You can see that the HTTP response code is 200 (success). From the content of the response, you can see a record with the username "test" and the **user_id** of 35. The information of the HTTP response header is also shown.

In addition, the **curl** command and the URL of Harbor API are displayed on the page so that they can be used as a command or in scripts, as shown in Fig. 8.7.

As shown in Fig. 8.8, the list of data models used by APIs is displayed at the bottom of the API page. You can click on the name of each data model to view their model definition. As shown in Fig. 8.9, you can see the data structure of UserGroup.

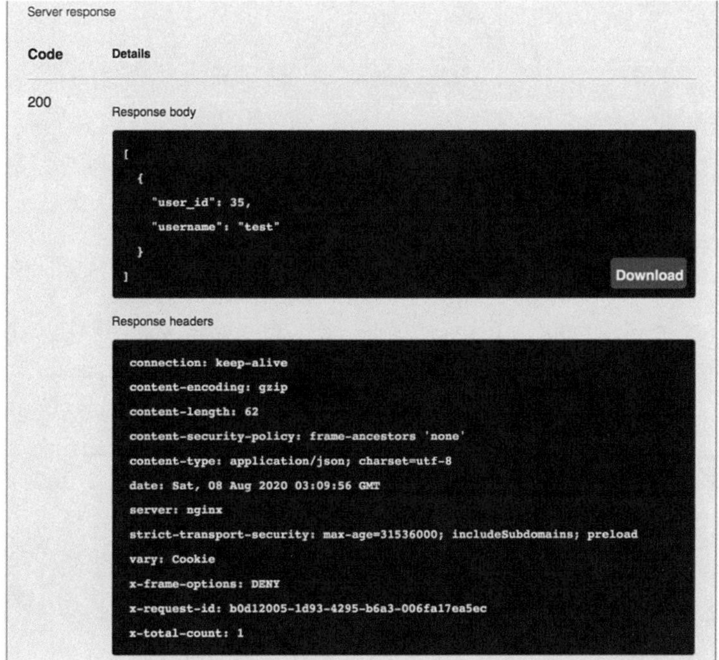

Fig. 8.6 Execution result of the API "GET /user/search"

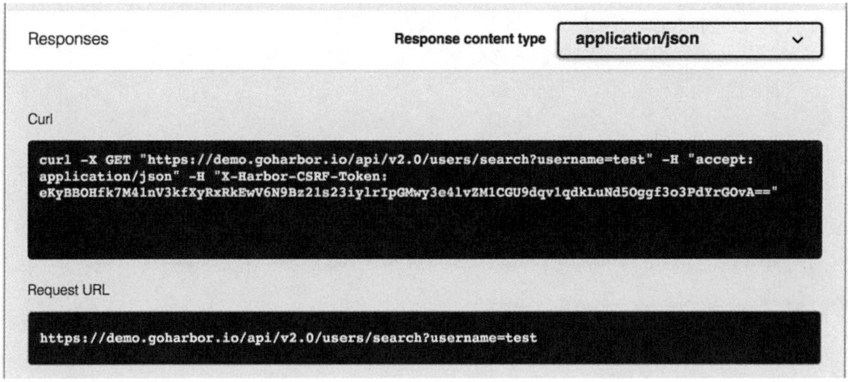

Fig. 8.7 curl command of the API call

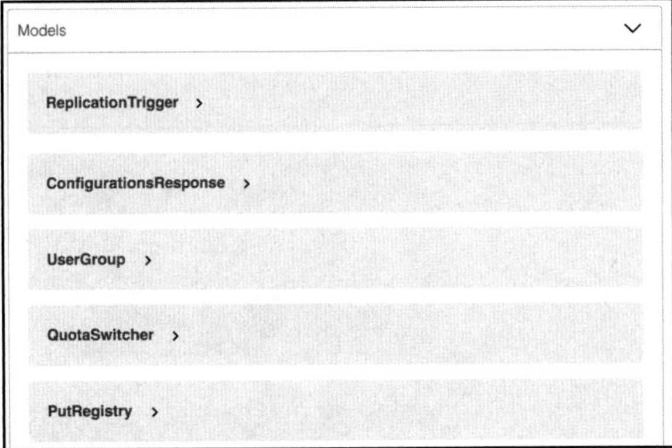

Fig. 8.8 Data model on the API page

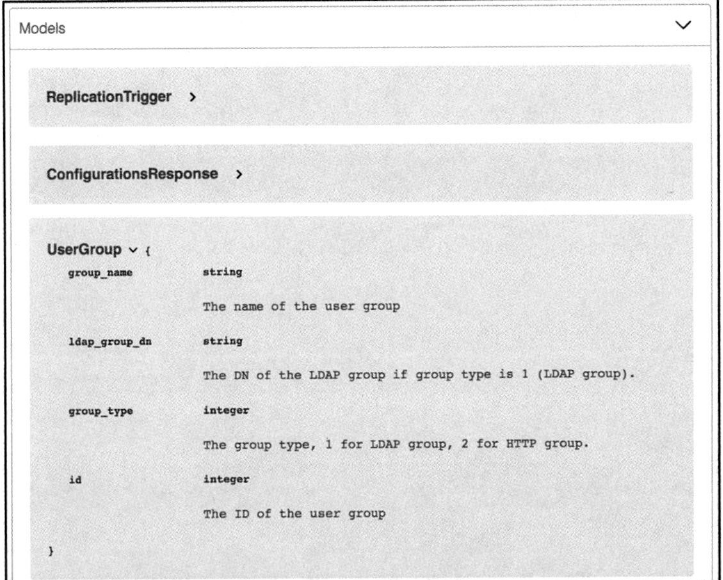

Fig. 8.9 Data structure of UserGroup

8.3 Registry APIs

This section sorts out how to use the registry APIs. The registry APIs are prefixed with "/v2/", and the API requests are passed through from Harbor to Docker Distribution for processing.

8.3.1 Base API

The base API ("/v2/") is used to check whether the server implements the registry v2 API. The request is shown as follows:

```
$ curl -I -u admin:xxxxx https://demo.goharbor.io/v2/
```

If the response status code is 200, the server implements the registry v2 API.

```
HTTP/1.1 200 OK
Server:nginx
Date: Fri, 08 Aug 2020 18:18:18 GMT
Content-Type: application/json; charset=utf-8
Content-Length:2
Connection:keep-alive
Docker-Distribution-Api-Version:registry/2.0
Set-Cookie:sid=630e22029853b760672aa0af7ec7b9bd; Path=/;
HttpOnly
X-Request-Id:b6e771f4-b78d-4c64-ae80-b67fb03fa9e3
Strict-Transport-Security:max-age=31536000;
includeSubdomains; preload
X-Frame-Options:DENY
Content-Security-Policy:frame-ancestors 'none'
```

8.3.2 Catalog API

The catalog API ("/v2/_catalog") is used to obtain all repositories in the system. Only the system administrator of Harbor can invoke this API:

```
$ curl -u admin:xxxxx https://demo.goharbor.io/v2/_catalog
```

The following result is returned:

```
{
 "repositories": [
  " library/hello-world"
 ]
}
```

8.3.3 Tag API

The tag API ("/v2/{repository}/tags/list") is used to retrieve all tags under a repository. If you want to list all tags under "/library/hello-world", the request can be sent as follows:

```
$ curl -u admin:xxxxx https://demo.goharbor.io/v2/library/hello-
world/tags/list
```

The following result is returned:

```
{
 "name": "library/hello-world",
 "tags": [
  "latest"
 ]
}
```

8.3.4 Manifest API

The manifest API ("/v2/{repository}/manifests/{reference}") is used to obtain the manifest of an artifact. If you want to obtain the manifest under "/library/hello-world: latest", the request can be sent as follows:

```
$ curl -u admin:xxxxx https://demo.goharbor.io/v2/library/hello-
world/manifests/latest
```

The following result is returned:

```
{
 "schemaVersion": 2,
 "mediaType": "application/vnd.docker.distribution.manifest.
v2+json",
 "config": {
  "mediaType": "application/vnd.docker.container.image.
v1+json",
  "size": 1510,
  "digest": "sha256:
```

(continued)

```
fce289e99eb9bca977dae136fbe2a82b6b7d4c372474c9235adc174167
5f587e"
 },
 "layers": [
  {
   "mediaType": "application/vnd.docker.image.rootfs.diff.tar.
gzip",
   "size": 977,
   "digest": "sha256:
1b930d010525941c1d56ec53b97bd057a67ae1865eebf042686d2
a2d18271ced"
  }
 ]
}
```


8.3.5 *Blob API*

The blob API ("/v2/{repository}/blobs/{digest}") is used to obtain the blob data of an artifact by digest. If you want to obtain the blob data under the repository "/library/hello-world", the request is as follows (a digest is used in the call):

```
$ curl -u admin:xxxxx
https://demo.goharbor.io/v2/library/hello-world/blobs/sha256:
fce289e99eb9bca977dae136fbe2a82b6b7d4c372474
c9235adc1741675f587e
```

The following result is returned:


```
{
 "architecture": "amd64",
 "config": {
  "Hostname": "",
  ...
  "Labels": null
 },
 "container":
"8e2caa5a514bb6d8b4f2a2553e9067498d261a0fd83a96aeaaf30394
3dff6ff9",
 ...
}
```

8.4 Programming Example

To help readers better understand the functions of Harbor APIs, this section shows a sample program written in Go language. The program first obtains all artifacts under the artifact repository "library/hello-world" and then deletes the artifacts that were last pulled more than a day ago. The sample code is as follows (the error handling part is omitted for simplicity):

```
//Define the URL, username and password.
url := "https://demo.goharbor.io"
username := "admin"
password := "xxxxx"

//Obtain the API version.
resp, _ := http.Get(url + "/api/version")
defer resp.Body.Close()

type Version struct {
  Version string `json:"version"`
}
encoder := json.NewDecoder(resp.Body)
version := &Version{}
_ = encoder.Decode(version)

//Obtain all artifacts under "library/hello-world".
req, _ := http.NewRequest(http.MethodGet,
  fmt.Sprintf("%s/api/%s/projects/library/repositories/
hello-world/artifacts",
    url, version.Version), nil)
req.SetBasicAuth(username, password)
resp, _ = http.DefaultClient.Do(req)
defer resp.Body.Close()

type Artifact struct {
  Digest  string  `json:"digest"`
  PullTime time.Time `json:"pull_time"`
}
encoder = json.NewDecoder(resp.Body)
artifacts := []*Artifact{}
_ = encoder.Decode(&artifacts)

t := time.Now().Add(-24 * time.Hour)
//Traverse all obtained artifacts.
for _, artifact := range artifacts {
 //Determine whether the artifacts are pulled recently a day ago.
  if artifact.PullTime.Before(t) {
    //If yes, deletes the artifacts.
```

(continued)

```
        req, _ := http.NewRequest(http.MethodDelete,
          fmt.Sprintf("%s/api/%s/projects/library/repositories/
hello-world/artifacts/%s",
            url, version.Version, artifact.Digest), nil)
        req.SetBasicAuth(username, password)
        resp, _ = http.DefaultClient.Do(req)
        defer resp.Body.Close()
      }
    }
```

8.5 Summary

This chapter introduces the APIs provided by Harbor, which are divided into two categories: the core management APIs and the registry APIs. The core management APIs provide management functions of Harbor and the registry APIs are mainly Docker Distribution APIs exposed by Harbor. The core management APIs of Harbor can also be tested in an interactive way through the API Explorer in the graphical user interface. The Harbor APIs can help achieve interoperability between Harbor and other systems and can be used in automation tools to improve the efficiency.

Chapter 9
Governance Model of Harbor Community

The users, contributors and maintainers in the open source community are the driving forces and the source of the development of the Harbor project. It is one of the important reasons why Harbor has been widely used in a relatively short period of time. The Harbor project and its community are an integrated and complementary partnership. This chapter introduces the governance model of the Harbor community and the guidelines for users and contributors to participate in community governance and contribution. Harbor users and distributors should also pay close attention to the security disclosure and response process.

9.1 Governance Model

Harbor is a CNCF hosted project, committed to building an open, inclusive, efficient and autonomous open source community to promote the development of high-quality cloud-native artifacts repository. CNCF is a sub-foundation of the Linux Foundation, hosting many open source projects in the cloud-native field, such as Kubernetes, Helm, and Harbor. Open source projects can become CNCF's hosted projects through the review and approval of the TOC (Technical Oversight Committee). CNCF provides many resources to promote the use and development of the managed projects. By retaining the independent website of a project and allowing the original maintainers to continue to be responsible for the development of the project, the continuity and progress of the project development are ensured.

After an open source project becomes a CNCF hosted project, its project trademark and logo assets are owned by the Linux Foundation and supervised by the Technical Advisory Committee, thus transforming into a vendor-neutral software project which can improve the willingness of enterprise software companies, start-ups and independent developers to cooperate and contribute in the project. At the beginning of Harbor's open source project, VMware led the development of the project. After joining CNCF, the project adopted a neutral, open and transparent

H. Zhang, Y. Wang, *The Authoritative Guide on Harbor*,
https://doi.org/10.1007/978-981-19-2727-0_9

governance model. The roadmap and development plan were jointly decided by the community, thus attracting more contribution from all over the world. Many contributors join the project. Some important functions, such as Webhook, retention policy, Harbor Operator, were initiated and contributed by community members.

In accordance with CNCF's governance principles and common practices in open source communities, the Harbor project has formulated community management (Governance) rules to determine the way community members collaborate. These rules include code repository, community roles, project decisions, proposal acceptance processes, lazy consensus and so on. Specific rules reference can be found at this address:

https://github.com/goharbor/community/blob/master/GOVERNANCE.md

9.2 Security Release Process

Harbor is a CNCF graduated level project, which means that the maturity of Harbor has been accepted by most users. There are many deployments and applications in the production environment. Like all software projects, Harbor may have some security issues from time to time. Although the Harbor project went through a security audit and fixed the problems found when applying for graduation, as a large open source community, the Harbor project has developed and adopted a security disclosure and response strategy to ensure that when security issues arise, the maintainers can quickly deal with and respond.

The Harbor community maintains the latest three minor versions. For example, when the latest version is 2.0.x, the community-maintained versions are 1.9.x, 1.10.x, and 2.0.x. When a security problem occurs, the applicable security fixes will be patched to these three versions based on the severity and feasibility. In order to obtain security patches, it is recommended that users adopt the version within the maintenance range. If the user is currently running an unsupported version, there could be potential security risks. The Harbor project team may not provide a remedy plan, so it is better to upgrade to the latest version.

Harbor users or vendors should pay close attention to Harbor's security announcements and security patches, and should promptly upgrade or install patches for the Harbor system they are running. If a security problem is found, it should be reported to the Harbor security team in time to confirm and provide a repair patch. Harbor distributors can also apply to join the security issue notification mailing group.

For detailed information, please refer to: https://github.com/goharbor/harbor/blob/master/SECURITY.md

9.3 Community Participation

After several years of development, Harbor has a large maintainer team from all over the world as well as countless contributors and users. All these community members repeatedly deploy, use and test on thousands of servers around the world. They provide feedback, report bugs, submit improvement proposals and contribute to bug fixes and feature development, making Harbor more and more mature and powerful.

Harbor and its community are still developing. This is an open and enthusiastic community. The project maintainers warmly welcome and look forward to more users and developers participating in the project to contribute and take certain roles, whether it is to discuss with the community, report problems or bugs encountered, propose good suggestions and ideas, fix defects for Harbor, add new features, or help with reviewing the code and documentation. Regardless of the size of the contribution, the contribution of every community member will be remembered. Harbor provides a variety of ways to connect community members to facilitate communication among participants. Community members can choose many suitable channels to participate according to their own situation.

Reporting issues to the Harbor open source project is a good way to participate. Project maintainers always welcome well-written and thorough error reports. Users can create an issue in "goharbor/harbor" on GitHub, fill in the required information according to the template, and upload relevant logs. Because the log is publicly visible, if there is user private information (such as internal IP address, domain name, account number) in the log, you need to hide it before uploading. Before creating any problem report, users can first check whether there is a similar problem reported before, so as to avoid duplicated reports. If you find a matching problem report, you can "subscribe" to it to get notifications of problem updates. You can also comment on the issue page with your specific information.

Users and developers can also propose design specifications of new functionalities of Harbor and submit proposals in the "goharbor/community" code repository. Harbor maintainers review these proposals regularly and arrange for discussion in community meetings.

The following ways can be used to interact with community members such as Harbor maintainers, developers, and users.

- Use Slack instant messaging software. Slack has users all over the world. It helps Harbor connect users in different regions of the world. You can join CNCF's Slack space "cloud-native.slack.com", and then select Harbor's channels "#harbor" and "#harbor-dev" to participate in discussions or consult related issues.
- Chinese users can join WeChat groups for the technical discussion of Harbor related topics. You can follow the official WeChat account "HarborChina" to get more information.
- Users can also join the harbor-users@lists.cncf.io mailing group to get update on Harbor's news, features, releases, suggestions and feedback. Harbor also has a harbor-dev@lists.cncf.io mailing group for developers to discuss Harbor development and contribution related stuffs.

- Harbor holds online community meetings every two weeks to allow users, developers, and project maintainers to discuss Harbor's latest progress and roaodmap. The schedule and agenda can be viewed in the "goharbor/community" repository on GitHub.
- Users can also follow the news posted by @project_harbor on Twitter.

9.4 Participating in Code Contribution

Harbor is an Open Source Project developed and grown in an open environment. The development of the project is inseparable from the continuous improvement by users, contributors and maintainers. In June 2020, Harbor became the first open source project originated in China and graduated from the Cloud Native Computing Foundation, reflecting the joint efforts of all community members. This section explains how to contribute open source code to the project.

9.4.1 Setting Up the Development Environment

When you need to customize some functions of Harbor or want to contribute code to Harbor, you need to first set up a local environment for code development, compilation, and testing.

Harbor's backend is written in Go language. Please refer to the official Go language guide to install and configure the Go language development environment. The software and version requirements required by Harbor in the development, compilation and operation stages are shown in Table 9.1. The software needs to be installed correctly according to the corresponding official documents. Considering the compatibility of the code, Linux should be used as the operating system of the development machine.

First, clone the source code from the Harbor official repository on GitHub to the local machine:

Table 9.1 Backend development environment of Harbor

Software	Version
Git	1.9.1 or later
Golang	1.13 or later
Docker	17.05 or later
Docker-compose	1.18.0 or later
Python	2.7 or later
Make	3.81 or later

```
$ git clone https://github.com/goharbor/harbor
$ cd harbor
```

Next, copy the template file "make/harbor.yml.tmpl" of the configuration file to "make/harbor.yml" and make necessary modifications to the configuration items (such as hostname and HTTPS-related certificates).

After modifying the code as needed, execute the following commands to compile, build, and run Harbor:

```
$ make install CHARTFLAG=true NOTARYFLAG=true CLAIRFLAG=true
TRIVYFLAG=true
```

This command compiles all the components of Harbor and builds images, and finally starts the Harbor service as containers. If you ignore the flags of "CHARTFLAG=true NOTARYFLAG=true CLAIRFLAG=true TRIVYFLAG=true", only the core components are compiled and installed.

The code and images are built every time the "make install" command is executed, which is very inefficient. If you need to make frequent code changes and do tests for specific component, you can directly compile the code, and then copy the compiled binary files into the container and restart the container to improve development efficiency. Take modifying the core component as an example, the following commands need to be executed:

```
$ go build github.com/goharbor/harbor/src/core
$ docker cp ./core harbor-core:/harbor/harbor_core
$ docker restart harbor-core
```

Note: If you compile in a non-Linux environment, you need to add related compilation parameters. The specific commands are as follows to compile for the 64-bit x86 architecture (amd64):

```
$ GOOS=linux GOARCH=amd64 go build github.com/goharbor/harbor/
src/core
```

By default, the logs of all components are in the "/var/log/harbor/" directory. They can be viewed for debugging. The log path and log level can be modified in the configuration file.

Harbor's front-end graphical management console is based on the open source frameworks Clarity and Angular. When setting up a front-end development environment, you need to confirm that the dependent development kits shown in Table 9.2 have been installed.

Table 9.2 Frontend development environment of Harbor

Framework/Toolkit	Version
Node.js	12.14 or later
npm	6.13 or later
Angular	8.2.0 or later

The front-end development relies heavily on the Node.js runtime environment and npm toolkit. The back-end service could be an environment with Harbor installed, and all the front-end service requests can be redirected to it through the proxy mode. In this way, modifications or changes can be tested in real time without going through the complicated steps of compiling, packaging and restarting. Developers can create a proxy.config.json file in the front-end home directory "src/portal" and point the proxy addresses of each back-end service to an existing Harbor environment. The sample code is as follows (the IP address of Harbor in the example is 10.10.0.1):

```
{
    "/api/*": {
     "target": "https://10.10.0.1",
     "secure": false,
     "changeOrigin": true,
     "logLevel": "debug"
    },
    "/service/*": {
     "target": "https://10.10.0.1",
     "secure": false,
     "logLevel": "debug"
    },
    "/c/login": {
     "target": "https://10.10.0.1",
     "secure": false,
     "logLevel": "debug"
    },
    "/c/oidc/login": {
     "target": "https://10.10.0.1",
     "secure": false,
     "logLevel": "debug"
    },
    "/sign_in": {
     "target": "https://10.10.0.1",
     "secure": false,
     "logLevel": "debug"
    },
    "/c/log_out": {
     "target": "https://10.10.0.1",
     "secure": false,
     "logLevel": "debug"
    },
```

(continued)

```
"/sendEmail": {
 "target": "https://10.10.0.1",
 "secure": false,
 "logLevel": "debug"
},
"/language": {
 "target": "https://10.10.0.1",
 "secure": false,
 "logLevel": "debug"
},
"/reset": {
 "target": "https://10.10.0.1",
 "secure": false,
 "logLevel": "debug"
},
"/c/userExists": {
 "target": "https://10.10.0.1",
 "secure": false,
 "logLevel": "debug"
},
"/reset_password": {
 "target": "https://10.10.0.1",
 "secure": false,
 "logLevel": "debug"
},
"/i18n/lang/*.json": {
 "target": "https://10.10.0.1",
 "secure": false,
 "logLevel": "debug",
 "pathRewrite": {
  "^/src$": ""
 }
},
"/swagger.json": {
 "target": "https://10.10.0.1",
 "secure": false,
 "logLevel": "debug"
},
"/swagger2.json": {
 "target": "https://10.10.0.1",
 "secure": false,
 "logLevel": "debug"
},
"/swagger3.json": {
 "target": "https://10.10.0.1",
 "secure": false,
 "logLevel": "debug"
},
"/LICENSE": {
```

(continued)

```
        "target": "https://10.10.0.1",
        "secure": false,

        "logLevel": "debug"
      },
      "/chartrepo/*": {
        "target": "https://10.10.0.1",
        "secure": false,
        "logLevel": "debug"
      }
}
```

Before starting the environment, go to the home directory and dependency directory of the front-end code and run the npm command to download the corresponding package dependencies. The specific commands are as follows ($REPO_DIR is the home directory of the code):

```
$ cd $REPO_DIR/src/portal
$ npm install
$ cd $REPO_DIR/src/portal/lib
$ npm install
```

Then run the following command to complete the compilation and packaging process of the front-end repository:

```
$ npm run postinstall
```

Next, run the following command to start the web server to serve the front-end page::

```
$ npm run start
```

After the server starts successfully, the front-end webpage can be accessed through the URL “https://localhost:4200” in the browser.

More operation commands can be found in the npm package management file package.json located in the front-end directory "src/portal".

9.4.2 *The Process of Contributing Code*

The Harbor project team welcomes community users to submit code via pull requests (PRs), even if they only contain some minor fixes, such as typos corrections or a few lines of code. If the contributed code is related to new features or major changes to existing features, it is recommended to submit an issue on GitHub before writing the code to describe the features and design ideas. In this way the project maintainers can evaluate and provide feedback as soon as possible and ensure that the contributed code conforms to the overall architecture and the technical development roadmap of the project.

When submitting a pull request, please try to break it down into small and independent changes. A pull request consisting of many features and code changes are difficult to conduct a code review. It is recommended that contributors submit pull requests in an incremental way.

Note: If the pull request is broken down into small changes, please ensure that any changes merged into the master development branch does not break the existing functionalities. Otherwise, it cannot be merged until the contributed functions are all completed.

9.4.2.1 Forking the Code Repository

The source code of Harbor is hosted on GitHub. Contributing code to Harbor requires a GitHub personal account. First, the developer forks the code of the "goharbor/harbor" project into their own personal GitHub account. Then clone the Harbor source code to the developer's local computer using the "git clone" command:

```
# Set up the Go language development environment
$ export GOPATH=$HOME/go
$ mkdir -p $GOPATH/src/github.com/goharbor

# Get the code
$ cd $GOPATH/src/github.com/goharbor
$ git clone git@github.com:goharbor/harbor.git
$ cd $GOPATH/src/github.com/goharbor/harbor

# Track the code repository under the personal account
# By default, avoid pushing any content to "goharbor/harbor"
$ git config push.default nothing
$ git remote rename origin goharbor
$ git remote add my_harbor git@github.com:$USER/harbor.git
$ git fetch my_harbor
```

Note: The "$USER" in the above command should be changed to the developer's own GitHub username, and "my_harbor" is the name of the remote code base on the developer's own GitHub account. $GOPATH can be any directory. In the above example it is the "$HOME/go" directory. According to the workspace of the Go language, put Harbor's code under $GOPATH.

Execute the following command to set local working directory:

```
$ working_dir=$GOPATH/src/github.com/goharbor
```

9.4.2.2 Creating a Branch

Code changes should be stored in a new branch of the forked code repository. The name of this branch should be "xxx-description", where "xxx" is the number of the issue. Pull requests should be based on the header of the master branch. Do not mix the code from multiple branches into a single pull request. If the pull request cannot be merged cleanly, please update it with the following command:

```
# goharbor is the upstream original code repository
$ cd $working_dir
$ git fetch goharbor
$ git checkout master
$ git rebase goharbor/master
$ git checkout -b xxx-description master   # create new branch
from the master branch xxx-description
```

9.4.2.3 Develop, Build and Test

The basic structure of the Harbor code repository is as follows, in which some key folders are annotated and explained:

```
├── api      # API document folder
├── contrib  # Contains documentation, scripts and other useful
content provided by the community
├── docs     # documents saved here
├── make     # Build resources and Harbor environment settings
├── src      # Source code folder
├── tests    # API and e2e test use case
└── tools    # Supporting tools
```

The following is the structure of the "harbor/src" source code folder, which is the developer's main working directory:

```
├── chartserver        # Source code that handles the main logic of
Helm Chart
├── cmd           # Contains the source code of the migration script
used to handle the database upgrade
├── common         # The source code of some common components, such
as DAO, etc.
├── controller       # Controller code, which mainly contains API
parameter processing logic
├── core          # The source code of the main business logic,
including REST API and all service information
├── jobservice       # Source code of the JobService component
├── lib          # A public library containing logic such as log
processing and database ORM
├── migration             # Harbor data migration code
├── pkg         # The logic implementation code of each component of
Harbor
├── portal          # Harbor graphical management console (front-
end) code
├── registryctl        # Registry controller code
├── replication        # Source code of synchronous copy function
├── server         # Routing and middleware code logic of HTTP server
├── testing         # Test cases for back-end components
└── vendor          # Go language code dependencies
```

Harbor uses the coding style recommended by the official Go language community. For detailed coding style guidelines, please refer to the official Go language documents.

When there are code changes, contributors need to adjust or add unit test cases to cover the code changes. At present, the unit test framework of the back-end service adopts "go testing" or "stretchr/testify". Running "go test -v ./..." or using IDE integration plug-ins can execute Go language test cases. For newly introduced code, it is recommended to use stretchr/testify framework to develop unit test cases. When you need to mock a specific object, you can use the vektra/mockery tool to automatically generate the mock object into the corresponding package under the "src/testing" directory for future reuse.

If the code change involves the modification of the API or the introduction of a new API, the contributor also needs to adjust or add API test cases to cover the corresponding changes. In Harbor, the API testing is an important means to verify each function of Harbor. After installing and deploying the Harbor environment containing each component, trigger each API test case to complete the functional verification of the designed scenarios. Harbor's API testing is driven by the Robot framework. The Robot framework is a Python-based scalable automated testing framework. Through the Robot framework, functions such as directory switching, inputting information, running scripts with parameters, checking running results and assertions can be easily achieved.

The front-end test framework is based on Jasmine and Karma. For more details, please refer to the Angular testing document, or refer to the existing test cases of the Harbor project. Run the “npm run test” command to execute the test cases of the front-end code.

9.4.2.4 Synchronizing with the Upstream Code Repository

When you find that the code of the local new feature branch is out of sync with the goharbor/master branch, you can use the following commands to update:

```
$ git checkout xxx-description
$ git fetch -a
$ git rebase goharbor/master
```

Note: You need to use “git fetch” and “git rebase” command to synchronize the code instead of the “git pull” command. The “git pull” command causes the code of the master branch to be merged into the feature branch and leave a code commit record. This makes the code submission history confusing. In addition, developers can also consider changing the “.git/config” file through the “git config branch. autoSetupRebase” command so that each code branch can automatically perform the rebase operation.

9.4.2.5 Submitting the Code

Since Harbor has integrated the Developer Certificate of Origin (DCO) checking tool, code contributors need to add Signed-off-by information to the commit to pass the check, that is, adding a "Signed-off-by" line to the commit message to indicate that they comply with the code contribution requirements. The “git” command line provides a “-s” option, which can automatically append Signed-off-by information to the commit message, which can be used when committing code changes, such as:

```
$ git commit -s -m 'This is my commit message'
```

9.4.2.6 Submitting a Pull Request

After completing the code and writing test cases, code contributors can push the local branch to their own forked repository on GitHub:

```
$ git push <--set-upstream> my_harbor <my_branch>
```

After the developer submits the code, the automated test of GitHub Action is automatically triggered. Before submitting the pull request, you need to ensure that all automated tests pass in the code repository under your GitHub account.

9.4.2.7 Automated Check

In order to ensure high-quality code submission and reduce the workload of code reviewers, Harbor enables several automatic checks before the code review process starts. After the contributor submits a pull request to the Harbor master code repository, the below automatic checks will kick in.

1. Contributors of a pull request must provide the DCO, otherwise the check fails and the pull request cannot be merged.
2. Detect the code unit test coverage and provide a report of the coverage changes by using the GitHub integrated application codecov. Considering the error range, the reviewers generally require that the coverage of the test maintains at the existing level, and the decline in coverage should not exceed 0.1%.
3. Scan the submitted code for security vulnerabilities through GitHub's CodeQL scanning tool. If high-risk (error) vulnerabilities are found, the check fails and the code cannot be merged.
4. Evaluate the code quality and generates the results by using the GitHub integrated application Codacy. If the submitted code violates the best coding practices and falls into the "unacceptable" range, the check fails. Codacy automatic evaluation is currently a non-compulsory inspection and is only for reference of the code submitters.
5. Harbor 2.0 has enabled the continuous integration (CI) pipeline driven by GitHub Action. This pipeline includes multiple stages: code format checking (including misspell, gofmt, commentfmt, golint and govet), back-end service unit testing (UTTEST), front-end UI unit testing (UI_UT), API testing using database authentication (APITEST_DB), API test using LDAP authentication (APITEST_LDAP) and project packaging function test (OFFLINE). A failure of any stage results in the overall failure of the pipeline, which prevents the final merging of the code. The specific GitHub page is shown in Fig. 9.1.

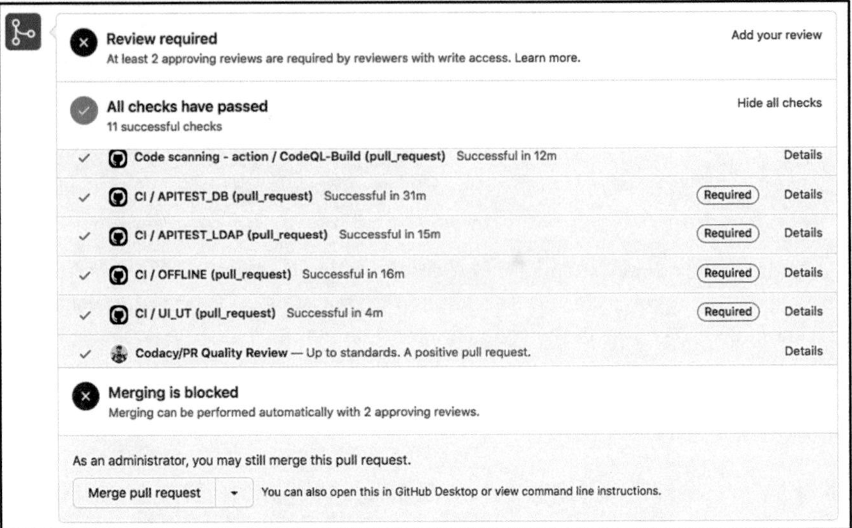

Fig. 9.1 CI checking of a pull request on Github

9.4.2.8 Code Review

After all the automatic checks have passed, each pull request will be assigned to one or more reviewers, who will conduct a comprehensive code review on the correctness, vulnerabilities, improvements, documentation, comments and code style. The comments made during the review will be committed to the fork branch. After the review and approval by at least two maintainers, the contributed code can be merged into the official code repository.

If it fails the review, the maintainers will provide the reasons for the rejection or improvement proposal in the pull request. The contributor can submit the code after some modifications:

```
$ git commit -m "update"
```

Contributors need to perform a rebase operation to ensure that each pull request contains only one commit (merging the corresponding commits through the squash operation may be needed):

```
$ git rebase -i HEAD~2
```

Pushing the changes to the GitHub code repository again triggers the update of the pull request:

```
$ git push my_harbor
```

If you encounter problems while contributing code, you can seek help from other developers through GitHub, Slack or mailing groups.

Printed in the United States
by Baker & Taylor Publisher Services